Becoming Sinners

284b - on spirit possession + matters to social location

L63 - a big men testifying

288 - older ♂ less likely to be possessed -

51 - good as of incongruence; sacrifice pigs to ward off planes but at the same time to establish good "working relationship w/ whites

91 - 2 contradictory ongoing myths - but why not just interpret as incongruence!
— as situationally relevant.

96 - some "people" hold contradictory precepts -

ETHNOGRAPHIC STUDIES IN SUBJECTIVITY

Tanya Luhrmann and Steven Parish, Editors

Becoming Sinners

Christianity and Moral Torment in a Papua New Guinea Society

Joel Robbins

UNIVERSITY OF CALIFORNIA PRESS
Berkeley · Los Angeles · London

Parts of chapter 4 originally appeared in slightly
different form in "Secrecy and the Sense of an Ending:
Narrative, Time, and Everyday Millenarianism in
Papua New Guinea and in Christian Fundamentalism,"
Comparative Studies in Society and History 43 (3):
525–51 (2001). Reprinted with the permission of
Cambridge University Press.

Parts of chapter 4 also originally appeared in slightly
different form in "On Reading 'World News':
Apocalyptic Narrative, Negative Nationalism, and
Transnational Christianity in a Papua New Guinea
Society," *Social Analysis* 42 (2): 103–30 (1998).
Reprinted with permission.

Parts of chapters 5, 6, and 7 appeared in different form
in "Becoming Sinners: Christianity and Desire among
the Urapmin of Papua New Guinea," *Ethnology* 37 (4):
299–316 (1998), and in "Dispossessing the Spirits:
Christian Transformations of Desire and Ecology
among the Urapmin of Papua New Guinea," *Ethnology* 34 (3): 211–24 (1995). Reprinted with permission.

Parts of chapter 8 originally appeared in slightly
different form in "My Wife Can't Break Off Part of Her
Belief and Give It to Me: Apocalyptic Interrogations of
Christian Individualism among the Urapmin of Papua
New Guinea," *Paideuma* 48: 189–206 (2002).
Reprinted with permission.

University of California Press
Berkeley and Los Angeles, California
University of California Press, Ltd.
London, England
© 2004 by the Regents of the University of California

Library of Congress Cataloging-in-Publication Data

Robbins, Joel, 1961–.
 Becoming sinners : Christianity and moral torment in
a Papua New Guinea society / Joel Robbins.
    p.   cm. (Ethnographic studies in subjectivity ; 4)
 Includes bibliographical references and index.
 ISBN 0-520-23799-4 (cloth : alk. paper).—
ISBN 0-520-23800-1 (pbk. : alk. paper)
   1. Christianity—Papua New Guinea—Urapmin.
2. Urapmin (Papua New Guinea)—Religious life and
customs.   I. Title. II Series.
BR1495.N5 R63   2004
306.6'09957'7—dc21   2003006767

Manufactured in the United States of America
12 11 10 09 08 07 06 05 04
10 9 8 7 6 5 4 3 2 1

For Liz and Hannah

Contents

Illustrations

Acknowledgments

This book has been long in the making. Among the great pleasures of reaching the end of its writing is the chance to thank the many people who have contributed in various ways to helping me write it.

This book is based on fieldwork carried out in Urapmin from January 1991 to February 1993. I am grateful to the Wenner-Gren Foundation (grant 5025), the National Science Foundation, and the University of Virginia for funding this research. While in Papua New Guinea, I was affiliated with the Institute of Papua New Guinea Studies and the Department of Anthropology of the University of Papua New Guinea. I am grateful to both of these organizations for affiliating me and for helping me to obtain the permissions necessary to do this work. I am also grateful to the Administration of the Sandaun Province for permitting me to do this research and for their interest in its results. I am similarly thankful to those working at the government offices in Telefomin for their help in coordinating this research. I also thank the staff of the National Archives of Papua New Guinea for the aid they gave me in using their collection.

This book rests on a foundation laid during my education at the University of Virginia. Roy Wagner, my doctoral supervisor, and Fred Damon and Susan McKinnon engaged all of the earlier stages of this work and were decisive in helping it to take shape. I remain grateful for all they have taught me and for their support of this project. Dan Jorgensen has also been with this project almost from its inception, and his work and our many conversations over the years have shaped in important ways my thinking both about the Min and about anthropology. I thank him for all the ways he has helped me in the course of my work.

At Reed College, I thank Gail Kelly and Robert Brightman for creating a stimulating intellectual environment in which I was able to take some of the early steps toward developing the book.

My colleagues and students at the University of California, San Diego (UCSD), have provided crucial intellectual support at every stage of writing this book. Numerous conversations with Don Tuzin and Roy D'Andrade, both of whom have read many of the papers that became parts of this book and then the entirety of the penultimate draft, have helped in many ways to develop the argument and sharpen its presentation. Mel Spiro also read an entire earlier draft and provided helpful comments. The graduate student book group at UCSD was kind enough to read the whole of an earlier draft and provide helpful comments at an important point in the writing process. I thank the members of the group—Christina Augsburger, Jon Bialecki, Eric Hoenes, Nicole Peterson, Karen Radcliff, Jacob Saunders, and Ryan Schram—for taking the time to give me this feedback. Kathy Creely, of the UCSD Melanesian Studies Archive, has helped me to track down many sources and has, along with Don Tuzin and others, contributed to making UCSD one of the best places for doing Melanesian research. I am also grateful to Tom Levy and Guillermo Algaze, respectively the former and current chair of the Department of Anthropology at UCSD, for their general support and for helping me to secure various grants that allowed me time to work on the book. I also want to thank the Faculty Career Development Program for the grant of a quarter-long leave during which I was able write much of the penultimate draft, and the UCSD Committee on Research for providing funds to cover part of the cost of indexing the book.

Tanya Luhrmann and Steve Parish, editors of the series Ethnographic Studies in Subjectivity, read the whole of an earlier draft. Their comments greatly improved the final product. I also want to thank Tanya for numerous conversations that are reflected in various places in the book, and for the work she did above and beyond the call of editorial duty in helping to see the book through to publication.

Several others have read and commented on the whole of earlier drafts of the book or on the dissertation in which I first presented important parts of it. I thank David Akin, Sandra Bamford, Karen Brison, Dan Jorgensen, Bruce Koplin, Tom Maschio, Gloria Robbins, Ronald Robbins, Michael Silverstein, Rupert Stasch, and Mike Wesch for their comments. Others who have given me particularly useful comments on parts of the book or on papers that became parts of the book include Bronwen Douglas, Robert Foster, Gautam Ghosh, Courtney Handman, Holger Jebens, Bruce Knauft, Karen Sykes, Richard Werbner, and Holly Wardlow.

John Barker, Marshall Sahlins, and Bambi Schieffelin have supported this project in various ways throughout its course, and conversations with them very much shaped the argument as it developed. Moreover, each of them read the penultimate draft and provided extensive and constructive comments that helped me to improve the final version. I am grateful for their support and the intellectual work they put into making this a better book.

I have delivered papers that became part of this book at the University of Chicago, the University of Hawaii, New York University, Emory University, the Frobenius Institut, the École des Hautes Études en Sciences Sociales, National Taiwan University, and the University of California, Riverside. I am grateful to those who invited me to give those papers and who commented on them, including Jim Bayman, Stephane Breton, Manuela Carneiro da Cunha, Daniel de Coppet, Jonathan Friedman, Maurice Godelier, André Iteanu, Alan Howard, Holger Jebens, Bruce Knauft, Pei-Yi Guo, Karl-Heinz Kohl, Nancy Munn, Jan Rensel, Marshall Sahlins, Bambi Schieffelin, Bradd Shore, Michael Silverstein, Ivan Strenski, Ho Ts'ui-P'ing, Holly Wardlow, and James Wilkerson.

At the University of California Press I want to thank Stan Holwitz for embracing this project and making the acquisition process such a smooth one. I am also grateful to Jacqueline Volin for overseeing the production of the book so attentively and to Sheila Berg for the thoughtfulness and care with which she copyedited the manuscript.

Passages of this book have appeared in earlier forms as parts of articles that appeared in *Comparative Studies in Society and History; Ethnology; Paideuma;* and *Social Analysis.* I thank the editors of these journals for permission to use revised versions of these passages here.

In Papua New Guinea, Chris Owen, Tony and Maria Friend, and Brian and Jeanette Daysh helped me in innumerable ways. I am grateful also for their companionship. Al Boush shared with me some of his vast knowledge of the Tifal language in several conversations that greatly aided my own linguistic work. Chris and Jane Ganter made me welcome at Duranmin and helped me to understand a bit about the current mission situation. I am also grateful to Diyos Wapnok for the time he took to talk to me about his own past and that of the Min region.

To the Urapmin, more thanks are due than any acknowledgment can provide. It is still a bit of a wonder to me that the community could have been so generous in taking in a stranger and looking after him so well for so long. More than that, of course, they also responded to my persistent questioning and did everything they could to help me understand their lives. It was a lot of work, as I could often tell, and I am very thankful to everyone who undertook it.

Semis, Dani, Amtabuleng, Kaunsil Rom, and David changed their lives in real ways to help me live mine. Their views are well represented here, for I learned more from them than from anyone else. But that does not begin to repay all that they did for me. I am grateful to them for all of their help, and for the lasting friendships that we formed. I also have to thank Wilit for opening my eyes to new vistas during the second half of my time in Urapmin. His early death after I left Urapmin is a tragedy for the Urapmin, for he was a gifted man destined for leadership. The same is true of Seroti, who was the first Urapmin person I met and who began to share his brilliant insights into his culture with me from the first night I came to the community. I remember him here and offer thanks. Yangapnok, one of the oldest people in Urapmin, has also died since I left. Always kind and generous while at the same time fiercely independent, he taught me a lot about a spirit that the Urapmin will have to work hard to maintain in the years to come. To Seligapnok, Babalok, Yami, Antalap, Doti, Igori, Pais, Sapa, Tisoleng, Stendi, Robin, Rosa, Navit, Doris, Boti, Marc, Siniki, Abet, and many others, I give thanks for all of their help with this work. Whenever I have had any reason to imagine that something I have written about a particular person or a quotation I have reproduced might cause some embarrassment in the future I have used pseudonyms in the text. I hope that by thanking people by name here I can go some way toward indicating in a more straightforward way the debt my work owes to these particular individuals.

Some of my friends who are also anthropologists have heard about this project a thousand times over and have contributed a lot to the thinking that gave it shape. Thus I thank David Akin, Sandra Bamford, Holger Jebens, Bruce Koplin, Tanya Luhrmann, Rupert Stasch, and Karen Sykes not only for the specific readings mentioned above but also for sustaining the kinds of ongoing casual conversations in which ideas can be born and find their feet.

I have been extraordinarily lucky in having a family that has supported my work with enthusiasm throughout its long course. Holly Edelman and Melvyn Robbins have always taken a genuine interest in my work, as did my late grandmothers, Rose Robbins and Rae Edelman. My sister, Michele, and her husband, Burt Derman, have likewise been strong sources of support. It is probably impossible to enumerate all the ways my parents, Ronald and Gloria Robbins, have contributed to fostering my interest in anthropology and sustaining my work in the field. Perhaps, then, it is best just to mention how grateful I am for all they have done. I also thank my parents-in-law, Michael and Peggy Waters, for their support both for my own work and that of their daughter, Liz Waters.

And speaking of Liz Waters, she has been with this project every step of the way. I cannot even begin to elaborate the reasons I have for thanking her or the contributions she has made to this book. Nor can I really explain how her passion for her own work sustains me in mine. There is a lot of her and of us in this work. And now there is Hannah too. She had the good sense to come to this project rather late, but her continual good cheer and delight in the world has made the final two years of work on it a joy.

Prologue

A Heavy Christmas and a Pig Law for People

The Christmas season of 1991 was a hard one in Urapmin. The Urapmin community, situated in the remote West Sepik Province of Papua New Guinea, is divided socially and geographically into a top group *(dang kasel)* and a bottom group *(kalang kasel).*[1] This division is not ancient, dating only to the time in historical memory when the Urapmin moved to their present location, and as the Urapmin think about it, it structures very little of their social life. Each group has its own church building, but that is only so no one has to walk far to services. Each also has its own sports team, but that too strikes the Urapmin as natural, since competitive sports require opposing teams. Ideally, the Urapmin say, these two convenient uses of the distinction are about as far as it should go; beyond this, they are fiercely committed to the idea that they are all members of one community.

As important a role as this commitment to unity plays in Urapmin self-perception, however, it was challenged in early 1991, when geologists from the multinational Kennecott corporation made a few visits to Urapmin to prospect for minerals. As it happened, the company was working exclusively on land belonging to members of the top group, as it had in its previous visits in 1989 and 1990. When it came time to fill paying positions for trench diggers and soil-sample collectors, Kennecott operated on the principle of giving preference to landowners, a principle that ensured that members of the top group took the lion's

share of the jobs. Positions at Kennecott were available only sporad-
ically—company representatives came and went without warning and
rarely stayed more than a few days—but it was by far the highest-pay-
ing work that had ever been on offer in Urapmin. Not surprisingly, then,
people from the bottom group were unhappy with the arrangement that
resulted in their being largely excluded from these positions.

The difficult aspects of this situation were never addressed very directly. An early complaint from the bottom group about Kennecott's hiring practices led the company to give positions to a few bottom people
who had significant kinship ties with landowners from the top group.
And members of the top group expressed some unhappiness about the
anger they felt the bottom group was harboring toward them. But the
general issue of unequal distribution of benefits coming to Urapmin
from outside and the strife it was causing never became topics of formal
or even open informal discussion. Instead, people from the top and bottom groups began to express their frustrations with one another by
launching into disputes about other matters whenever the opportunity
presented itself.

At first people talked about these disputes as if they were individual
matters; so and so, who happens to be from the top (or bottom), is mad
at so and so, who happens to be from the bottom (or top), because he
stared hard at him, or because he kicked him in soccer, or because his
sister married down (or up) but no woman has ever come back as a replacement. The prevalence of such individual quarrels was not surprising to anyone. Humans are sinful creatures, people would say, given to
bad feelings and hostility; disputing is just the way of the world. Because
the Urapmin are committed to a kind of Christianity that dwells on human sinfulness, this interpretation of their current troubles came easily
to them.

But as the year wore on and the repeated appearance of conflicts that
pitted people against one another across the top/bottom divide became
impossible to ignore, the Urapmin began to construe their community's
troubles as symptoms of a less precedented kind of problem. Not just individuals but the two groups as a whole seemed to be in open dispute.
By the end of the year, the lines had become so hard that no one could
escape the feeling that a situation marked by an unusual prevalence of
individual disputes had given way to one in which the whole community
was at war with itself.

It was the coming of the Christmas season that finally put the problem the community was having unmistakably on the public agenda.

Christmas is a solemn religious holiday in Urapmin, filled with talk of sin and redemption and organized around rituals aimed at checking the influence of the former and thus ensuring the achievement of the latter. Most years, the top and bottom churches come together to conduct many of the eight or more church services and other rituals that make up the Urapmin celebration of the holiday. In 1990, members of the two churches had worked together to build a large, open-air enclosure in which to celebrate. For many days, they had held services and Holy Spirit possession dances (<u>Spirit disko</u>) in this enclosure, and numerous people had been possessed by the Holy Spirit. Since the Spirit will come to a church only if all of its members have confessed their sins and ceased to entertain evil thoughts and feelings, the success of these rituals left the community feeling extremely spiritually healthy. Indeed, the state of community health the Urapmin achieved during their 1990 Christmas celebrations came to represent a benchmark against which they would measure the decline of their social lives as 1991 wore on. By the end of the year, disputes in full flower, the mood of the community had become so ugly that the church leaders' efforts to set up at least a few combined services for Christmas 1991 seemed doomed to fail. As Christmas neared, they gave up their attempts, officially calling off all combined services and canceling the sports competitions that would also have brought the two groups together during the holiday season.

Their failure to overcome their problems in order to celebrate Christmas in an appropriate way left many Urapmin ashamed *(fitom)*. The answer to shame being withdrawal, quite a few people made plans to celebrate Christmas in other communities, a course of action normally unthinkable at a time of year when the Urapmin spend more time together than at any other and when much of the social work of the community (marriage arrangements, bride-price payments, dispute resolutions) gets done. Those who stayed took to referring to the season as "problem" or "heavy Christmas" (<u>hevi krismas</u>), a term that seemed to be on everyone's lips throughout late December. Since "a heavy" in Urapmin Christian terminology refers to the kinds of problems that push one into sin, and to the fact of a sin itself, the term perfectly captured the sense of moral failure that hung in the air; this was a "sinful Christmas." As Christmas day approached, everyone was sunk deep into chastising themselves for their inability to rise above sin at least enough to properly celebrate one of the two most important holidays of their Christian calendar (the other being Easter).

The collective perception of moral crisis that spread through the community was distressing enough in itself; it was made even more disturbing by the palpable fear of damnation that it brought in its wake. Urapmin Christianity's focus on the need to strive for moral perfection is embedded in an expectation that Jesus' return could come at any moment. Only those morally ready for him when he comes will be saved. The sins that made for the heavy Christmas thus brought with them the threat of failing to secure the perfect heavenly future promised to those who are saved in the last days.

During the twenty-six months I lived in Urapmin (January 1991 to February 1993), people spent a lot of time talking about what bad people they were, how they were lawless and could not get along with one another and live good Christian lives. But only once, during the 1991 Christmas season, did the reality of their lives seem actually to mirror the bleak image of moral collapse that was a staple of their Christian rhetoric. And although people also talked constantly during those same twenty-six months about the imminence of the Second Coming, only once, again during the 1991 Christmas season, did their powerful apocalyptic fears seem not to be leavened by equally strong hopes of salvation. Having had no success at settling their disputes and rebuilding their community, during the heavy Christmas season they found themselves facing a true moral crisis and an impending social collapse as dire as those imaged in their Christian beliefs.

To the extent that it rested anywhere other than in the moral hearts of each Urapmin individual, the Urapmin felt that the responsibility for addressing this crisis belonged to Rom, the Urapmin Kaunsil. Kaunsil is an elected position, and the person who occupies it is charged with, among other things, settling disputes in the community. Disputes he cannot settle he is supposed to take to the District Court in Telefomin. However, all Urapmin agree that sending cases to the District Court is highly undesirable, for once a case is heard there the community has no control over the outcome, and people can end up in jail or paying government fines that send money out of the community. Thus the Kaunsil hears and decides almost all cases in his local court.

Yet by the time everyone had brought the Kaunsil the individual disputes that went into making the heavy Christmas heavy, his docket was laden with more cases than he could possibly settle in a timely manner. Moreover, his diligent effort to settle similar cases throughout the year had accomplished very little. With ill will saturating relations between top and bottom people, disputes between them continued to spring up like mushrooms in the rainforest. Things had reached a point at which it was clear to the Kaunsil that the court system had broken down. Thus the failure of the Christmas season weighed particularly heavily on his shoulders. In his house one night I noticed he had written the phrase "Hevi Krismas" on a little blackboard in the perfect handwriting that was one of the subtler signs of his authority. It was a terribly sad image, a mark of defeat that came from the hand of one of the community's ablest leaders. It also struck me that it made the crisis somehow official; the problem was on the Kaunsil's agenda, set down in writing. But what could he do about it?

In the days after Christmas, the Kaunsil showed remarkable ingenuity in devising a plan to deal with the crisis. Traditionally, and still today, the Urapmin settle disputes between individuals by having them exchange equivalent goods *(tisol dalamin)* with each other in order to "buy the shame" *(fitom sanin)* or "buy the anger" *(aget atul sanin)* of the other party. Once both parties have received goods to buy their shame or anger, the dispute is officially finished and the people involved resume normal relations. The Kaunsil's brilliant plan was to have the top people as a group and the bottom people as a group undertake a tisol dalamin exchange in order to finish all their disputes in one stroke. Everyone would come to the exchange bringing something to give, and each person would find someone from the other group who had brought something equivalent and exchange with them, regardless of whether that person was someone with whom they were actually in dispute. Several of the main disputants, however, would plan in advance to bring equivalent items that they would exchange with one another first, to "open the road" for the remaining exchanges. Once the entire ritual was complete, all the various disputes that made up the crisis would be finished, and the community as a whole could, like the two parties in a traditional tisol dalamin exchange, resume normal relations.

As soon as the Kaunsil began to discuss this plan with important leaders from the top and bottom regions, it became apparent that he had hit on a successful innovation. As news spread, people throughout Urapmin became excited about the exchange. They also spoke enthusiastically about another part of the Kaunsil's plan, this one based less on traditional forms of dispute resolution than on contemporary Christian and postcolonial ideas about the importance of the law. After the exchange, the Kaunsil had announced, a new legal regime would begin. In itself, the idea of a "new law" (nupela lo) was not novel. As the Urapmin see it, the colonial era and Christianity had together brought a new law several decades before. Furthermore, the anticipation of an even newer new law is constantly in the air in Urapmin, because the imminent coming of such a law, to be imposed by an evil world leader, is a staple of the Christian apocalyptic rumors that pepper so much of the community's talk and thinking. But in this case, once they completed the ti-sol dalamin exchange, the Urapmin would give themselves the new law, and while it would not be evil per se, it would be extremely harsh.

This new law had its own slogan: "A pig law for people." As much as the catchphrase "heavy Christmas" had dominated the holiday season, this new one captured the hope of the period immediately following, the one that led up to the exchange. The phrase made reference to a successful legal innovation of the past. During the later part of the colonial era, in the late 1960s or early 1970s, when the position of Kaunsil had only recently been established, the Urapmin had taken advantage of the ability it gave them to exercise governmental-type powers over themselves to institute a new law regarding the treatment of pigs. This law holds that full-grown pigs cannot be in the village. If they come into the village (or into people's gardens), they will immediately be killed. This is a tough law to follow: no one likes to see a pig killed to no ceremonial end, and Urapmin claim the law is the reason that they have many fewer pigs than their Telefomin neighbors. They say, however, that even though it makes them a "rubbish line" (rabis lain) that is perennially short of pigs, it is a law worth having. Pigs that come into villages, rooting up village plazas and leaving their excrement everywhere, and those that find their way into gardens and tear them up routinely cause disputes between people, and these disputes in turn destroy people's "Christian lives" (Kristin laip). In the end, the death of some pigs is a small price to pay for keeping the community from falling into sin.

After the exchange, people claimed, the new law for people would be a tough, single sanction affair along the lines of the pig law. Anyone who broke any law (be it by theft, adultery, or even simple anger)—anyone who in a word failed to be in "agreement" (wanbel) with the Christian standards of their fellows—would be sent to the despised District Court, where the government could have its way with him or her (or, if a case was too minor for the District Court to hear, those involved would be immediately fined by the Kaunsil). As soon as the exchange was over, the Kaunsil promised, he would "file" (fil) the new law at the District Office, where people believe the pig law is also filed (though I could never find it gazetted in the district records). This would give it a sanction higher than that of the Urapmin community, making it very difficult for Urapmin people to evade or repeal. Once in place, people were

Figure 1. People exchanging goods at the dispute resolution ritual. Photo by
Joel Robbins.

confident that the pig law for people would ensure that they never again
found themselves facing another heavy Christmas like the one just past.

The exchange itself, which took place on January 4, 1992, was a
great success. It began with a prayer in which a prominent pastor asked
God to take away the anger from each participant's heart. After the
prayer, people threw themselves into the exchange with the very emotional intensity that was so notably lacking in their Christmas celebrations (see figure 1). Relations between top and bottom people greatly
improved in the wake of the exchange, immediately in fact, and the crisis of Christmas 1991 passed into memory. Urapmin continued to harangue themselves about their lawlessness and inability to live well together; this version of the Christian state of fallenness remained the
primary idiom in which they discussed their lives. But the daily life that
went on around that discussion, that was in many ways produced by it,
became livable once again by virtue of falling short of their worst imaginings. Once again, people began to believe that they might be able control their sinful tendencies enough so that Jesus would take them to
heaven when he returned.

All this happened without the Kaunsil filing the "pig law for people"
that everyone had thought so promising a strategy of social control in
the days before the exchange. It is probably just as well that he held back

from taking this step. One can run a community with very few pigs; it is
harder with very few people. Yet the pig law for people had proven very
good to think with. It engaged the deep Urapmin conviction that lawfulness is the basis of a good Christian life by presenting itself as an innovation that would push the law even farther toward the forefront of
people's minds and thus aid them in their efforts to gain salvation by
subjecting their lawless, willful tendencies to it. It also provided closure
to a dynamic of sin and repentance—with the heavy Christmas and all
that went into it constituting the sin—that the Urapmin nowadays find
familiar. In punishing themselves with this harsh law, they would make
up for the sins of envy, anger, and willfulness that produced the crisis.
Having been thought about in these ways, the pig law for people had already done its work when the Kaunsil quietly let it drop, leaving the formal legal terms of Urapmin life as they had been before.

Looking back on the events of 1991 as an outside observer, it is abundantly clear to me that much of the tension that finally shaped itself up
into the Christmas crisis resulted from the difficulties Urapmin people
had managing Kennecott's presence in the community. Yet this is not
how the Urapmin saw it. To them, the decrepit state of their community
life was the result of their inherent depravity as sinful creatures. That depravity alone, without any assistance from an outside disruption such as
Kennecott's presence, was an adequate explanation of the state in which
they found themselves. One way to look at the argument of this book is
to see it as an attempt to make my perspective as an observer and anthropologist adequate to their experience of their lives. Read this way,
Kennecott becomes a metonym for all the outside forces of change the
Urapmin have experienced in the past four decades, and the despon-
dency of the heavy Christmas stands in for the morally demanding
Christianity that forms so many of the frameworks in which they lead
their lives. How the history of those outside forces coming to bear on the
Urapmin has issued in their lived sense of sinfulness is an important part
of what I aim to explain. With that in mind, let me return briefly to the
problem of heavy Christmas.

　　Beginning from my outsider's point of view, it is not hard to argue that Kennecott's prospecting was the most important cause of the
trouble besetting the community. To be sure, many of the disputes that
fed into the crisis took other topics as their *casus belli*, but Kennecott
had focused people's attention on the line between the two sides and had
started the problems off. Kennecott had accomplished this in part by un-

wittingly delivering a small windfall that was unequally distributed. But that was not the whole of the problem. Everyone, top and bottom alike, fervently hoped that Kennecott would come back and carry out further work and eventually build a mine in Urapmin. People regularly dreamed about this at night, and it was a spur to endless daytime fantasies and conversations. It was this mood of expectation of future riches that made the distribution of the jobs Kennecott offered now such a pressing issue; if things went well with Kennecott, people hoped and feared, today's problems would be just a foretaste of those to come.

It has always been in the nature of Urapmin social life that no one has unique resources to distribute (I may have killed a wild pig today, but you killed one last month, etc.). And in any case no one ever has much to distribute at all, this not being the kind of Highland New Guinea society in which big men occasionally give away enormous amounts of wealth in ceremonial exchanges. Lacking any cultural routines for handling the Kennecott windfall or for thinking about how to handle the even larger one that might come with a mine, the top and bottom groups were involved in a tense, usually indirect series of negotiations over what kinds of distribution routines to put in place in the future. People's inability to think productively about a future mine was evidenced not only in the string of disputes that led to the heavy Christmas but also in the way 1991 passed without a single marriage being made, a troubling occurrence among a group of roughly 396 people that worries constantly over its small numbers. Distress over this matrimonial hiatus became so marked that around the time of the dispute resolution exchange the Kaunsil made a speech exhorting people to marry. "Don't worry if the match is incestuous," he announced, citing an ancestral proverb, "just get married and increase the population." But because the shape of the future was so unclear, and marriage affects land rights, it was not surprising that 1991 had been bereft of new matches. With the future so uncertain, no one knew how to operate in the present.

By complicating Urapmin notions of what might lie ahead, Kennecott's presence disrupted an important aspect of contemporary Urapmin life: the efforts people constantly make to understand their present by imagining its relation to a radically different future, be it one of wealth or, even better, of salvation. It was this collective project of imagining a future, as much as people's current projects, that Kennecott's windfall upset. And because the process of imagining the future is so important to the Urapmin, when Kennecott upset it the ramifications were widespread.

Here we begin to converge on the Urapmin point of view. In thinking about the troubles of 1991 from that point of view, we note that they were profoundly shaped by the Urapmin commitment to a radically different future—a commitment we might see as millenarian in nature. This commitment has been forged in the crucible of forty years of rapid cultural change driven by contact with the West, colonization, Christianization, and finally the coming of independence and its demand that the Urapmin become part of a new nation. In ways I detail later, these cultural changes have made Urapmin life in the present difficult, fraught with half-realized projects and the contradictions between them that keep them half-realized. Destined to remain unfinished in the present, images of these projects in their finished forms are what make the imagined future so full and so important. Like the empty square in those fixed-frame puzzles, the puzzles in which you frequently have to move all the pieces in ways you do not want just to move one the way you do, the Urapmin need the empty space of the potentially perfect future if they are to try to bring satisfactory order to the complex, heterogeneous collection of cultural materials that guides their present.

The Urapmin need to order in a new way the heterogeneous collection of cultural materials with which they live follows from the fact that they are contending with a particular kind of cultural formation. It is one in which two different cultural logics are in play simultaneously. In the Urapmin case the two logics are indigenous and Christian. The Urapmin understand each of these logics in its own terms, and they hold fiercely to both of them. For reasons that will become clear only later, they have not been able to subordinate one to the other, or to make one over completely in the terms of its opposite number. Hence, they live with a kind of double consciousness. Being caught between two systems in this way might be workable were the two systems to mesh neatly, or were it possible to settle on a comfortable division of labor between them. But especially in the area of morality, the Christian and indigenous systems the Urapmin are trying to juggle pointedly contradict one another.

It is through the cracked lens of this contradiction that the Urapmin view their contemporary social life. They experience this contradiction most forcefully in Christian terms, taking the fact that every time they honor the indigenous system they fail its Christian counterpart as evidence of their propensity to sin. Yet despite the sense of sinfulness the contradiction generates, the Urapmin have been unable to address it by jettisoning the indigenous system, as they would have done, for example, had they been able to adopt the strict terms of the pig law for people. Unable to settle the contradiction in the present by letting go of the indigenous moral system, the Urapmin need for a perfect future takes shape as a need for a future in which this cultural contradiction will finally be resolved satisfactorily.

The Urapmin work toward this perfect future most notably in their ritual life and in their efforts at moral self-control. But their dreams of earthly material wealth, the kind they hoped Kennecott would bring, address the contradiction too: for a world in which everyone has as much as they want would be one in which moral decisions, which so often in Urapmin turn on issues of distribution, would be much less pressing, and the contradictions between the systems would less regularly arise. If they were rich, the Urapmin imagine, it would be easier to live what they take to be good Christian lives. When problems with the Kennecott windfall gave a hint that even the realization of their dream of future wealth might not allow them to live lives free of immoral disputes and the sinful feelings of envy and anger that cause them, it exposed weaknesses in one model of that perfect future. In these circumstances, it is not surprising that it set off a major bout of pessimistic moral self-examination.

This discussion, painted in broad strokes, moves us from the coming of Kennecott to the Urapmin experience of heavy Christmas. It also leaves unanswered many of the more interesting questions raised by the Urapmin experience of dramatic cultural change. How did the Urapmin come to construe so much of their lives in Christian moral terms? Why did they, who were never directly missionized, adopt such a moralistic and in many ways harsh brand of Christianity? Why, having adopted it, have they been unable to let go of the indigenous moral system that contradicts its demands? And how, more generally, do people live with two contradictory cultural logics at one time? These are the questions this study tries to answer.

Introduction

Christianity and Cultural Change

Despite the impression the preceding prologue might have left one with, the Urapmin have not been Christian for very long. They are a small group of roughly 390 people living in a remote part of the far western highlands of Papua New Guinea. With their territory situated in the Sandaun Province, the Urapmin are linguistically and culturally part of the Mountain Ok or Min group of cultures, a group that has become well known in anthropological circles for the mythical and ritual complexity of its traditional religions. As recently as the early 1970s, anthropologists who studied traditional religions in the Min region produced some of the most impressive accounts of indigenous religious life in the contemporary anthropological literature (Barth 1975, 1987; Gardner 1981; Jones 1980; Jorgensen 1981b; Poole 1976). These scholars described daily lives dominated by the demands of extraordinarily elaborate men's initiation systems and the secret mythologies and large number of taboos that framed them. Their reports suggested that these religious systems, despite what had been by then several decades of colonization, had remained robust and continued to define the meaningful parameters of life for everyone in the region.

Yet by the early 1990s, the period of my fieldwork, the Urapmin, like many of their neighbors, no longer practiced their traditional religion. By their own account, they had not practiced it since 1977. That was the year that a Christian revival began to sweep through many of the groups in their region. Though the revival had its most proximate origin in movements then flourishing in the Solomon Islands, it brought with it a recognizably Western form of Christianity focused on the revivalist and charismatic themes of the need for a conviction of human sinfulness to accompany conversion, the role of the Holy Spirit in helping converts to address their sinful nature, and the potential imminence of the Second Coming. As the prologue indicates, the Urapmin took the revival's Christian message to heart. They quickly began to see themselves as sinners, and to call out in various rituals to ask the Holy Spirit for help addressing the moral problems their sinfulness caused. They also learned to keep the possible arrival of the millennium always in mind, and to use God's coming judgment as an imaginative vantage from which to evaluate every aspect of their thoughts, feelings, and actions. In short, they almost immediately came to construe their lives in the terms of a recognizably Christian culture.

How did this happen? Two explanations social scientists routinely resort to when confronted by similar cases of rapid Christianization cast little light on the Urapmin story. One argues that intense missionary efforts, backed by the compulsions and seductions of the colonial or Western orders the missionaries represent, are largely responsible for transforming people's lives (e.g., Comaroff and Comaroff 1992, 1997). This argument is a patent nonstarter in the Urapmin case. Although the Urapmin had first encountered Christianity in the late 1950s and, as we will see, by the late 1960s some of them had converted and become active church workers, no Western missionary had ever lived among them. To the limited extent that the Urapmin had contact with the mission before the revival, for the most part it was contact they themselves had to initiate and sustain by going to visit or study with missionaries who had set up shop in other parts of the Min region. Since the Urapmin had to seek out the missionaries and expend considerable effort to remain in contact with them, the missionaries' presence and persuasive power cannot simply be taken for granted. On the contrary, rather than constituting a primary explanation of changing Urapmin motivations and conceptions of the world, the Urapmin engagement with the missionaries itself requires explanation in terms of such changing motivations and conceptions.

The second standard approach to explaining rapid Christianization and similarly dramatic cultural transformations suggests that they occur as a result of radical socioeconomic dislocation. When people enter the market economy in force, or migrate to new locales, this argument goes, their old understandings of the way things are prove unable to help them navigate the new worlds they come to inhabit. In the face of the failure of their old conceptual schemes, they turn to new ones better suited to their current circumstances (e.g., Peel 1968). Yet in Urapmin, the colonial and postcolonial eras have led to very little in the way of socioeconomic change. With the exception of two men who have spent the last ten years working in unskilled positions in Tabubil, a mining town in the Min region, all Urapmin make their way through life as subsistence gardeners. Some have moved to the mining town to work for a year or two, but at any given time no more than three or four men and their families are living away from the community pursuing this option.[1] Hence the "infrastructure" of Urapmin life hardly changed at all during the period that saw their rapid and thorough turn to Christianity. Indeed, if you went to Urapmin and did not listen to what people said but only watched what they did (and if in doing so you ignored the obviously Christian rituals they performed), Urapmin life in the early 1990s would look for all the world like it fit the stereotype of traditional Papua New Guinea village life. This would have been even more the case in the mid-1970s. So, like mission intervention, major socioeconomic dislocation is not a plausible answer to the question of how the Urapmin became so profoundly Christianized in such a short time.

How then to account for the Urapmin situation? In pursuing an answer to this question, I want to break down into two parts the more general question of what happens when people take on a new culture as thoroughly as did the Urapmin. The first part asks how it is even possible for people to take on a new culture so comprehensively. For this is what I am claiming the Urapmin did. They did not adopt Christianity in bits and pieces seized upon as syncretic patches for a traditional cultural fabric worn thin in spots by their attempts to stretch it to fit new situations. Rather, they took it up as a meaningful system in its own right, one capable of guiding many areas of their lives. That is to say, change in Urapmin was not a matter, as so much contemporary anthropology expects, of a traditional culture assimilating a new one and constructing in the process a hybrid entity that is either still largely traditional or else different from both of its starting points. It was, instead, a case in which people seemed to grasp a new culture whole. And because this process involved very little assimilation of the new into the old, it left many aspects of traditional Urapmin culture intact as well. These facts bear importantly on how we conceptualize culture change in the Urapmin case; in the absence of much mixing, the change the Urapmin have undergone requires them to live with two cultural logics, a situation that Barker

(1993: 224) suggests many societies of converts face. To understand the Urapmin case and others like it, then, we need a theory of culture change that can explain both how people are able quickly to grasp the logic of the new without sacrificing the coherence of what came before and how they can live with the two-sided culture that results.

The second part of my modified question asks not *how* it is possible for people to experience the kind of cultural change the Urapmin experienced, but *why* they would be party to such a transformation (Knauft 2002: 48). Although I do not want to confuse individual consciousness with culture here, and I put much emphasis in what follows on the way cultural logics and values can in many respects direct their own working out by drawing people into their logical and evaluative schemes, it is clear that rapid cultural change cannot take place without the participation of those whose lives are shaped by the culture that changes. The Urapmin case raises this question of why people would take part in such change with particular insistence. As a kind of charismatic Christianity very much focused on human sinfulness and the need for constant self-discipline, the new culture the Urapmin have taken on is one that seems to provide them with little comfort. Why would people accept a new culture that teaches them to see themselves in the kind of negative light the Urapmin now turn on themselves? Because they have experienced relatively little social change, one cannot answer this question by resorting to the claim that they now live in such straitened circumstances that coming to see themselves as debased creatures is a small price to pay for gaining access to the Christian fantasy of a better future. Instead, I argue, their willing participation in this rapid change turned on the impact of colonialism in the Min region—but only as that impact was taken up by the Urapmin in the terms of their traditional culture. In general, I argue, the motives for cultural change must originally be given in the terms of the culture that is changing, and this despite the fact that the changes those motives initiate may quickly render the motives themselves obsolete.

Even this rather broadly drawn conceptualization of the Urapmin case illustrates the complexities any explanation of it will have to account for. How does a traditional culture come to motivate change? How can it direct that change without losing its own shape? How can people who start with traditional motivations quickly come to understand a new cultural logic? What kind of culture does this process of cultural doubling produce? And finally, how do people coordinate the two logics that result, and how is the relation between them made livable?

In the next section, I lay the groundwork of a theory of cultural change that can answer these questions. This theory guides my discussion of the Urapmin case in what follows. But it is worth pointing out up front that the relevance of these theoretical considerations extends well beyond the Urapmin case. Indeed, they pertain to issues that are or at least should be at the heart of the anthropology of globalization.

Summing up a good deal of heat and even some light in recent anthropology, it might fairly be said that the discipline has of late been preoccupied with coming to grips with the possibility that the cultures it once thought of as discontinuous in space (and hence discrete) and continuous in time (and hence authentic and enduring) now appear to be becoming continuous in space (and hence interconnected) and discontinuous in time (and hence constantly hybridizing, sycretizing, creolizing, or, more generally, simply changing in one way or another). The recognition that culture may have these features has generated a mass of literature on cultural change that relies extensively on metaphors of mixture. Yet most of this literature does not extend much beyond basic description. As Friedman (1999: 247) points out, "The metaphor of mixture is flat. It juxtaposes rather than exploring the articulation among different elements." Fardon (2000: 149) makes a similar point in his critique of Amselle's (1998) use of such metaphors, arguing that "'mestizo logics' entails no logics at all, it just claims that things were mixed."

There is, as these commentators suggest, a real need to bring some order to the field by exploring the different types of relations cultures can contract with one another and the circumstances that push situations toward one type or another. The viability of such a project of ordering, and hence of an anthropology of globalization more generally, depends on the accomplishment of an even more fundamental task of developing a viable theory of how cultures change; a theory that both accounts for the causes of change and specifies the mechanisms by which it occurs (see LiPuma 2000: 89). In the bulk of this book I work toward the development of such a theory. In the conclusion, I return to the issues of globalization that the Urapmin material raises and ask what progress my account has helped us make toward theorizing them. I mention these issues at the outset, though, lest readers imagine, as people these days sometimes do, that the small size and remote location of communities such as Urapmin somehow iconically renders the study of their cultures and histories of necessity a narrow undertaking and one that is off the beaten track of contemporary anthropological concern.

ON CULTURAL CHANGE

I take culture to be a set of values and categories (or "symbols" or "representations") and the relations between values and values, categories and categories, and values and categories. As will become obvious, this definition does not preclude relationships of contradiction between different values or different categories, or between values and categories, nor does it depend on some firm sense of boundedness (elements are outside a particular culture only when they are both not related to any elements in that culture and when their nonrelation is not itself understood as a significant relational fact within that culture). Given the structuralist bent of this definition, it should come as no surprise that I have drawn liberally on Sahlins's (e.g., 1981, 1985, 1995) influential construction of a structuralist historical anthropology in fashioning my approach to cultural change. As the reference I have already made to values suggests, I also draw on the work of Dumont (e.g., 1980, 1986, 1994). Dumont, like Sahlins, is firmly grounded in the structuralist tradition. But Dumont also fuses that tradition with aspects of the Weberian inheritance in ways that even today remain unique. Drawing on these two influences, he has produced an original account of the relation of values to the elaboration and coordination of cultural logics. As Ortner ([1984] 1994: 381) rightly points out, he should be seen as another major structuralist theorist of cultural change. That is how he is treated here. Properly synthesized, I argue, Sahlins's and Dumont's approaches generate a model that is capable of comprehending situations like that of the Urapmin where the object of analysis is not simply the transformation of a single culture but rather the interplay between two cultures that are operative in the same place at the same time. More generally, it provides a flexible and widely applicable tool for studying cultural changes of many kinds.

As with any theory that has been widely adopted, Sahlins's views have been subject to a good deal of simplification as they have spread (Goodwin 1996). Moreover, in this case the usual forces of simplification have been abetted by the prominence of Sahlins's (1995) debate with Obeyesekere (1992) over the proper way to analyze Captain Cook's death—a debate that has ensured that many people take those aspects of Sahlins's theory that are relevant to the Cook example to be the most important ones. Against this trend, I want to argue that a careful reading of Sahlins's work suggests that he identifies three distinct processes that can be at work in any given instance of cultural change, only one of which is illustrated by the Cook case. These processes are sometimes linked, but there is value in examining each separately before looking at the ways they can be brought together in actual historical cases. Taken as three different processes, they cover a wide variety of kinds of change.

The mechanism that is at the heart of Sahlins's structuralist theory of change is his conception of the way people use cultural orders to shape their construction of and action in the world. When they act, Sahlins claims, people put their cultural constructions into play by using them to refer to the world. In doing so, they establish what he calls a "structure of the conjuncture." In Sahlins's usage, a structure of the conjuncture is "the practical realization of the cultural categories in a specific historical context" (1985: xiv). It is the moment when, in his conceptualization of practice, categories find their purchase on the world. Often, the world to which people refer will conform fairly well to the categories they use to refer to it (indeed, in many cases it will be a world they and others with whom they live have created through the application of those same categories in earlier acts of reference). When this is the case, people's categories undergo little change as a result of their foray into the world. But there are also times when the world does not conform to the categories people use in referring to it (Sahlins 1985: vii). It is when this happens that change is most likely to occur.[2]

When the world does not fit the categories in which people attempt to construe and act upon it, the categories are stretched in ways that change them. In such cases, the structure of the conjuncture becomes a crucible in which "cultural categories acquire new functional values. Burdened with the world, the cultural meanings are . . . altered" (Sahlins 1985: 138).

Cases in which this occurs sometimes look quite dramatic, but at the same time their impact on the organization of a culture can be relatively mild since the relations between categories are left untouched. This is so because even as the categories are forced to change somewhat, their successful application also constitutes a reproduction of traditional cultural understandings in the face of new realities (Sahlins 1985: 125). The incorporation of state currencies in Urapmin and in many other parts of Melanesia initially had this character, as people were able to treat these currencies as versions of traditional currencies and direct their flow in traditional ways (for example, by using them in marriage, death, and other ceremonial payments) (Robbins 1999; Sahlins 1992). The category "valuables" and the uses to which its members were put were not fundamentally altered in their relation to other ideas and practices (as would happen, for example, if money became a category of its own, forging new relationships to the categories "valuables" and "everyday goods" and in doing so reconfiguring the relationship between them as well). These are cases, then, in which a category stretched to encompass a new referent but did not change its relations to other categories.

For many readers, Sahlins's analysis of the Hawaiian understanding of Captain Cook as the god Lono has come to stand as the paradigmatic example of this process by which traditional cultures transform themselves by reproducing their basic shape even as the categories that make them up stretch themselves to take in new elements; it constitutes, that is, the very image of the way the cultural rubber meets the historical road in the structure of the conjuncture. When it serves as a paradigm in this way, its most notable feature is a tight locking of old category and new element that allowed the Hawaiians to construe the new (Cook and his movements) fairly exhaustively in terms of the old (Lono and his rites). So important was this snug interlocking to the Hawaiians that when it threatened to come unstuck by virtue of Cook's failure to conform to their categorical expectations they resorted to procrustean measures to relieve the pressure. But despite the play this model of traditional categories fully encompassing the new has received, it is only one kind of change Sahlins discusses.

If, in the standard redaction of the Cook-Lono account, the emphasis is on the old category encompassing the new with only minor modification, in the bulk of his work Sahlins is more interested in situations in which it is not only a category that changes, but the relations between categories. This he calls "structural transformation," and it is a second kind of change he is at pains to theorize (Sahlins 1985: 143, 138). Sahlins's analysis of changes in the Hawaiian taboo system illustrates this process well (1985: chap. 5). The Hawaiian abrogation of taboo was not simply a matter of a change in their understandings of taboo or of any other single category. Instead, it was the outcome of changes in the *relations* that linked the categories "men," "women," "chiefs," and "commoners" to one another. These cascading changes were brought about by the way Hawaiians employed all of these categories, along with that of taboo, in relating to Cook and his crew. In such cases people manage, as they also do when they use an old category to encompass a new element, to reproduce some aspects of their traditional culture. Most notably, they are able to maintain a sense that their familiar categories are still in play. But on a very fundamental level, their culture has changed by virtue of that fact that the relations between its elements have been reorganized.

The third kind of change Sahlins has discussed is one in which people to at least some extent abandon their efforts to reproduce their traditional culture by continuing to employ its categories in referring to the world and instead make a self-conscious effort to take on a new culture. In the cases Sahlins considers, the new culture in question is the modern Western one. Hence, he calls this process "modernization."[3] Sahlins pays little attention to this kind of change in his most widely read works, where his emphasis has been on the ways people reproduce their traditional cultures even as they subject them to change. Yet in several publications he does take up the issue of how people can leave projects of reproduction behind in favor of efforts at radical cultural transformation (Sahlins 1990, 1992; see also Robbins n.d.). Such efforts, he argues, follow on episodes of "humiliation" in which people come to "hate what they already have, what they have always considered their well being" (Sahlins 1992: 24). This hatred, Sahlins says, cannot be explained simply as an outcome of coercion on the part of the representatives of Western culture, be they explorers, colonists, or postcolonial capitalists or politicians. As he notes, "the question is not simply what forces them to be like us, but why should they want to" (1992: 24). The answer, he suggests, lies very much in the "means of cultural debasement" such as Christianity that convince people in meaningful terms to regard their own traditions as unacceptable (1992: 24). In saying this, he is arguing that the stimulus for this kind of radical cultural change is itself cultural; the humiliations that drive radical change must themselves be made sensible in a particular cultural frame of reference.

As something of a footnote to his major concerns, Sahlins's approach to modernization is suggestive rather than systematic. The notion of humiliation, for example, is something of a placeholder, pointing to a variety of processes of self-assessment that require further investigation. Even more urgent from the point of view of the material analyzed in this book is the question of how people come to construe themselves in terms of a new cultural model of "debasement" in the first place. If the humiliation must be produced from within the new culture, it cannot be the initial cause of people's willingness to take on the new culture, since they would already have to be working with it in order to feel themselves humiliated in its terms. This suggests that the initial humiliation must take place in traditional terms, as I demonstrate was the case in Urapmin.[4]

A second point that is implied but not fully developed in Sahlins's approach to modernization is that it does not assume that as people take on a new culture they must of necessity transform their traditional one. Whereas Sahlins's other two models of change require the traditional culture to change as its categories take in novel content and the relations between them change, his model of modernization argues that people can reach out to take up a new culture in its own terms, without trying, at least in any concerted way, to work it into their traditional categories of understanding. The kind of process this model lays out, one in which people self-consciously work to grasp a new culture on its own terms, is one that can lead to a situation in which people live with two largely distinct and, in important respects, contradictory cultures at the same time. Since the Urapmin live in such a situation, this aspect of Sahlins's model of modernization is important to the argument of this book.

Overall, then, in spite of the need for further specification, Sahlins's model of modernization provides an important complement to the other models of change he presents. Like those models, it explains cultural change in cultural terms, stressing that none of the processes by which cultural change occurs are themselves meaningless or outside of culture. Yet it also covers important cases those models leave unaddressed by opening up the possibility that sometimes cultural change represents a radical turning away from traditional understandings and a coherent grasping of new ones, and by explaining how it is that people who reach out for a new culture in this way can come to live under two cultural systems simultaneously.

To summarize, I have drawn three models of cultural change from Sahlins's work. In the first, people are able to fit new circumstances into old categories. As they do so, they expand the categories of their culture in order to broaden the range of referents to which those categories can be applied, but the relationships between categories do not change. We can call this a model of assimilation. In the second, which can be referred to as one of transformation or transformative reproduction, people's efforts to bring their traditional categories into relation with the world eventuate in a transformation of the relations between those categories. Finally, in the third model, people take on an entirely new culture on its own terms, forgoing any conscious effort to work its elements into the categories of their traditional understandings. Although Sahlins discusses this as a model of modernization, I would argue it can also apply to changes other than modernizing ones (see note 3) and hence requires a different name. One might be tempted to call it a model of replacement, but since the new culture does not necessarily replace the old, I will call it one of adoption; the image here being one that emphasizes the taking on of something new without prejudging what happens to what was there before.

All three of these models of change are related by virtue of their mutual dependence on a more fundamental model of human behavior in which people are held to act in the world in terms of categories that are given their meaning by their systematic relationship to other categories. But each of them depicts a different kind of change that can follow from human action construed in these terms. As I have laid them out here, these models may appear to be related as moments in a developmental sequence moving from less to more extensive cultural change. But although they might appear in this order historically in some cases, it is important to note that they need not always do so. In fact, while we have to draw on the entire suite of models to analyze the changes that have taken place in Urapmin, my account suggests that in the Urapmin case the processes depicted in the model of transformation have never been fully developed and to the extent that they have come into play they have done so only after those of assimilation and adoption were already well under way.

Having taken these structuralist models of change from Sahlins's work, I turn to Dumont to bring the issue of values to bear on the analysis they initiate.[5] I save for chapter 8 a thorough discussion of my reading of Dumont's work. Here I only want to foreshadow that discussion and emphasize how important Dumont's contribution becomes when we move from analyzing the processes of change that bring about adoption to considering how people negotiate the dual cultural situations that result from their operation.

Dumont is best known for his assertion that the elements of a culture (its "value-ideas" in his terms, its categories and values in mine)[6] are ordered in relation to one another by the culture's paramount value. In the context of the approach to change I am developing here, what is crucial in Dumont's work is the way he locates values within culture. In many social scientific discussions, values are considered matters of individual consciousness (Dumont 1986: 249; Munn 1986: 274; see Joas 2000 for a case in point from the hand of a sophisticated sociologist). For Dumont, however, values are a part of culture and a culture's values are expressed in the way that culture is organized. As in linguistic models of markedness, to which Dumont's ideas bear a more than passing resemblance, values are seen as built in to the structure itself (Battistella

1990). Weber's influence on Dumont may well be crucial here, for Weber's treatment of the value-spheres of a culture and their interrelation, considered as something distinct from the value orientations of individuals, foreshadows Dumont's treatment of values as an aspect of cultural structure (Weber 1946: 323 ff.; see Brubaker 1984: 62, 72, for a good summary of Weber's ideas that focuses on the cultural nature of value spheres). The outcome of Dumont's argument for the cultural nature of values is the claim that while there are any number of interesting questions to be asked about how individuals take up, resist, or more generally simply contend with the values embedded in the culture(s) that shapes their lives, it is also analytically possible to consider value on the cultural level alone. What this means for a theory of cultural change is that it has to attend not only to the ways categories are transformed but to the ways values are as well. And given the prominence Dumont gives to paramount values in creating cultural orders, we might argue that from his point of view it is when paramount values change that real cultural change has taken place. In terms of Sahlins's models, it would be when the relations between important values change that one would talk of transformations, and when a new paramount value replaces or comes to exist alongside an old one that one would have the kind of change covered by the model of adoption.

Adopting Dumont's approach in this way, we can also define situations in which people live with two cultures at once as ones in which distinct paramount values are in struggle with one another. In examining such situations, it is useful again to consider how Dumont adopts Weber's discussion of value spheres, this time with an emphasis on the nature of the relationships that hold between the different value spheres within a culture. In both Weber and Dumont, each value sphere competes to make its own demands paramount to such an extent that people will try to honor them even when doing so requires them to shirk the demands of other spheres (for readings of Weber along these lines, see Parsons 1991; Turner 1992). Such struggles between values are carried out by means not only of the demands that values make on practice but also, and of necessity initially, of those they make on thought. For all values require that people work out as fully as possible the logics of the domains to which they apply and that they do so if need be at the expense of working out a consistent version of the logics of lesser-ranked spheres (see Dumont 1980 on the elaboration of ideas of purity as compared to those of power in India, or Robbins 1994 on the elaboration of ideas of liberty as compared to those of equality in the West). Applying this model to situations in which the competing values are those of different cultures, it is clear that accepting the dominance of one value logic and the correlative incoherence of the now lower ranked other would be the price of a stable synthesis of the old and the new in situations of change. It is where such acceptance is not forthcoming that adoption leads to the kind of enduring dual cultural situation found in Urapmin.

In concluding this discussion of Dumont, it is worth noting that one respect in which I do not follow him is in his tendency to suggest that there are only two types of paramount values to be found across the world. One is holism, where value is placed on the cultural whole and the correct hierarchical arrangement of its parts. The other is modern individualism, where value is placed on the individual and its development. While it is true that Dumont tends to treat this pair as if it exhausts the types of paramount values a culture might have, he has also confessed when it comes to Papua New Guinea:

> [W]hat is known about it, and the failure of both substantialist and structuralist theories to this day in that field would seem to indicate that we have not discovered—or that, by comparison with other cases, we have not discovered *at all*—the ideological axes which would provide a relatively coherent and simple formula. . . . In terms of our present interest, these differentiations would lie beyond or outside the opposition individualism/holism, with the result that they would be as badly described from one point of view as from the other. (1986: 215–16; original emphasis)

In light of this statement, I have elsewhere suggested that the societies of Melanesia need to be seen as placing primary value not on the whole or on the individual but rather on the relationship and hence might be called "relationalist" rather than holist or individualist (Robbins 1994). In Dumont's major works on Western culture he is concerned with the processes of cultural change that occur when holist cultures become individualist ones either by processes of internal transformation (1977, 1986) or by encountering individualist ones (1994). My intention here is to bring Sahlins and Dumont together to carry out a similar analysis of the encounter between a relational culture and an individualist one, for it is between cultures promoting these two values that the Urapmin find themselves caught.

My emphasis on the role of values in constructing the struggles that engage those living between two cultures brings up the question of what people consider to be good. This issue in turn introduces a third and final theoretical line of argument that is important to my account of cultural change among the Urapmin. This argument turns on the role of morality in cultural change. For the Urapmin, the recent period of change has been one of moral crisis; it has been a time of constant self-examination and worry over personal and collective wrongdoing understood as sinfulness. Drawing on recent anthropological work on ethical thinking that stresses the point that the moral is a cultural domain in which people are highly conscious of the cultural materials they work with and the contradictions between them, I argue that the Urapmin preoccupation with moral issues is not accidental (Faubion 2001; Laidlaw 2002; Lambek 2000; Parish 1994). Although based in part on an explicit traditional cultural interest in moral issues and fueled also by the legalistic concerns of those responsible for colonizing the Urapmin, the emphasis the Urapmin currently place on morality is also theoretically predictable. This is so because the moral domain—as a domain of conscious choice—is a place where change comes to consciousness. For those caught living between a traditional cultural system and one they have newly adopted, morality is likely to provide the window through which they can see the contradictions with which they have to live. This is why, as I noted in the prologue, the Urapmin conception of their situation so single-mindedly understands and explains it in terms of moral difficulty. In light of the central role morality plays in the Urapmin construal of their own lives, throughout this book ethnographic and theoretical treatments of the moral domain, treatments guided in particular by Foucault's late work, build on one another and culminate in the conclusion in an explicit theoretical argument about the role of morality in processes of cultural change.

My discussion thus far has been oriented to developing a model for the study of rapid cultural change. The models I have drawn from Sahlins and synthesized with some of Dumont's work provide a foundation both for explaining how people can quickly come to adopt a new culture on its own terms and for analyzing the complex cultural situations such adoption produces. The next step in laying out the core argument of this book is to consider why people would be willing to participate in the kind of radical cultural change these models help us to comprehend. The assumption of most anthropologists is that most of the time people attempt to understand new experiences through assimilation and transformative reproduction, thus preserving the relevance of their traditional culture for as long as possible. Hence, their occasional willingness to move toward adoption of the new requires explanation. Sahlins offers such an explanation in his account of the way experiences of humiliation can lead people to embrace modernity in its own terms. To his discussion I added the point that if humiliation is to be the starting mechanism of the move to adopt a new culture, it must be experienced in traditional cultural terms. This means that any account of why a group engages in rapid cultural change needs to begin as a cultural one. In the next section, I lay out a preliminary sketch of those aspects of Urapmin culture that came together to motivate and facilitate their initial efforts to adopt revival Christianity on its own terms.

HUMILIATION AND CHANGE IN URAPMIN

Three aspects of precontact Urapmin culture were particularly important in steering the Urapmin response to contact and colonialism in the direction of adoption rather than incorporation and/or transformative reproduction. First, the Urapmin understood themselves to be important players in a regional ritual system that encompassed all of the groups today known as Min peoples. It was changes to this ritual system leading to a dramatic loss of Urapmin power within it that provided the Urapmin with one of the experiences of traditionally meaningful humiliation that would drive their desire for radical change. Second, precontact Urapmin culture placed great importance on moral deliberation. Intimately related to their social structure, the moral domain was a highly elaborated one in Urapmin culture, and people saw many routine situations as requiring them to make difficult moral choices. In its emphasis on morality, traditional Urapmin culture met its match in the new culture the colonists presented to them. In their dealings with the Urapmin, the colonial powers were as focused on the need for order and lawfulness as the Urapmin were in their own lives, though of course those powers took little positive notice of the moral system the Urapmin had developed to reach these ends. Instead, they regularly conveyed to the Urapmin the judgment that they needed moral improvement and that such improvement would not come until they put aside their traditional culture, learned to follow the colonial law, and began to obey the dictates of Christianity. Already convinced of the difficulty of living moral lives, the Urapmin experienced the legalistic rhetoric of the colonial officers and the moralistic one of the missionaries and evangelists they were first exposed to as severe moral condemnations both of themselves and of their collective way of life. These felt condemnations produced a second experience of traditionally meaningful humiliation that further drove the Urapmin in the direction of adoption.

The two aspects of precontact Urapmin culture that I have so far discussed provided the terms in which they experienced humiliations that motivated them to reach out to adopt a new culture. The third aspect of their traditional culture that requires consideration here operated to allow them to act quickly and effectively on the desire for change fostered by the humiliations they experienced in the regional and moral arenas. We can think of this aspect of Urapmin culture as their social structure.[7] The Urapmin system of descent reckoning is cognatic, and it and the kinship system play relatively little role in determining the structure of their social life. This leaves all adults with a well-developed sense that they have to make choices about how to respond in most situations and that in many cases they can do so in novel ways. Into the organizational breach left by the failures of the descent and kinship systems to provide much in the way of structure step self-made big men who work to guide people's choices and collect them into groups with at least some semblance of stability. Big men's desire to influence people's choices and ultimately to attract followers puts a premium on their willingness to find innovative ways to appeal to people. These social structural tendencies to value innovation on the part of leaders and to allow people to choose new responses in many situations are what enabled the Urapmin to launch their project of adopting Christianity so successfully.

I discuss the Min regional ritual system and Urapmin morality and social structure extensively in other parts of this book. But because they are so important to its argument, a brief introduction to them here will help to orient the analyses that follow. It also allows me to introduce the geography of the Min region and some of the basic elements of the way the Urapmin are organized both socially and in space.

The physical layout of Min country provides the map on which the traditional regional ritual system was laid out (see map 1). In this system, each group possessed its own rituals, sacra, and bodies of sacred knowledge. Every group's rituals, sacra, and bodies of knowledge were necessary to the successful operation of the system. But each group's endowments were also ranked relative to the others, such that the rituals, sacra, and sacred knowledge of some groups were important to the fertility (including both agricultural success and the growth of boys into warriors) of the whole region, and those of other groups were primarily important in ensuring their own fertility. The Telefolmin, near neighbors

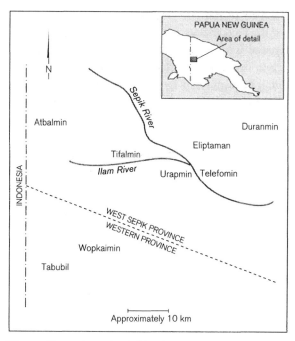

Map 1. Urapmin and neighboring groups

of the Urapmin, are generally agreed to have been at the top of the ritual system by virtue of having possessed the most potent rituals and sacra and the most extensive collection of sacred knowledge. At the far edges of the system were groups such as the Baktaman, who fully recognized Telefol dominance of the system and claimed to perform their rituals in complete ignorance of the sacred knowledge that made sense of their workings (Barth 1975). Along the continuum of ritual primacy that stretched from Telefomin to Baktaman, the Urapmin saw themselves as occupying a lofty place.[8] They ranked themselves either as highly as the Telefolmin or just below. Evidence I present in chapter 2 suggests that at least some other groups also shared this high estimation of the importance of the Urapmin in the regional system.

Colonization and, with it, the coming of Christianity initiated a slow but persistent dismantling of the Min regional ritual system. In doing so, it removed a key context in which the Urapmin defined their own importance. And even as the colonial era saw the decay of the ritual system that made the Urapmin key players in the religious life of their region, it also saw a restructuring of the region along new, modern lines in ways that threatened to render the Urapmin peripheral not only to the religious lives of their neighbors but also to their economic ones. A closer look at the spatial layout of the region makes clear why this should be so.

The Urapmin live in the southwest corner of the Ifitaman valley. The valley is primarily populated by Telefolmin people, among whom the government and the mission opened their first and still most important stations in the northern Min region in the late 1940s (Jorgensen 1981b). The placement of these stations has ensured that the Telefolmin, who had been central to the traditional regional ritual system, maintained their centrality in the changed order that came into being during the colonial era. It also ensured that in spatial terms the Telefomin station would become a central place in the region. The importance of Telefomin in the emerging colonial spatial order rendered the Urapmin peripheral to that order in a way they had never been to the traditional one.

Although they share the Ifitaman valley with the Telefolmin, because the Urapmin lacked (and still lack) an airstrip they quickly became more marginal than many other, more distant groups to what went on at the Telefomin station. Tucked away in their corner of the valley, the Urapmin are segregated from Telefomin by the Sepik River gorge. Although the Urapmin do own some land to the north of this formidable barrier, all of their villages are to the south of it. Hence, while as the crow flies the central villages of Urapmin are only twelve and a half kilometers west of the government's District Office at the Telefomin station, the trip to the station is a far lengthier one than the map would suggest. The fittest Urapmin can walk it in about four hours, but taking it at the more leisurely pace people usually prefer renders it a trip of six hours or more. A round trip takes up at least a whole day and often becomes a two-day affair. For government and mission personnel who were not as acquainted with bushwhacking as the Urapmin, the trip was so difficult that they rarely undertook it, leaving the Urapmin to come to the station and seek out most of the relatively little (compared to other Min groups) contact with the government and the mission they have had.

Throughout the colonial and postcolonial periods the marginalization of the Urapmin continued to deepen. Today, the distance between Urapmin villages and the Telefomin station looms even larger in people's lives not only because the station houses the government offices, the mission headquarters, the closest regularly stocked trade stores, and the health center but also because it offers the closest regularly serviced airstrip. It is from here that Urapmin people sometimes take the short flight to Tabubil, the site of the Ok Tedi mine and the one "modern"

town they visit. Tabubil is now the most central place in the Min region
as a whole, surpassing even Telefomin in its importance to most groups.
It is on the land of the Wopkaimin, traditional trading partners of the
Urapmin. As they did traditionally, the Urapmin sometimes walk to this
area, now usually with the express purpose of reaching Tabubil. As the
crow flies, this walk is more than forty kilometers, and it passes over
the imposing Hindenberg wall that rises up behind the mountains of the
Behrmann range that constitute the southern edge of the Ifitaman valley.
The walk takes two full days and the better part of a third. The Urapmin thus recognize themselves as marginal to this center as well, and
they have watched their former trading partners who live near it advance much further in the modern economic and educational order than
they have been able to do.

Other groups with whom the Urapmin traditionally interacted regularly, and still do today, include the Tifalmin (Wheatcroft 1976) to the
west and the Faiwolmin (Jones 1980) to the southeast. These groups
have not experienced as much contact with Westerners and modern institutions as the Telefolmin and Wopkaimin, but all of them have had
airstrips from early on in the colonial period and have thus been more
fully integrated than the Urapmin into the modern order centered at
Telefomin and Tabubil.

Of course, the Urapmin did not experience marginalization along all
these dimensions at once. Tabubil, for example, did not start to become
a central place until the 1970s, and the town was not built until the early
1980s. But from very early in the colonial period, indeed from when the
station was initially established and the Urapmin were passed by in the
first round of mission airstrip construction, the trend of their marginalization was obvious to them. We can get a glimpse of how this marginalization spurred on Urapmin efforts to change by looking at how they
interacted with another Min group, the Atbalmin, who live to the west
of Tifalmin (Bercovitch 1989). Throughout the colonial period and during much of the postcolonial period, the Atbalmin, whose scattered
settlements made it hard for the government to bring services to the majority of them, have remained even more peripheral to the modern order
than the Urapmin. The Urapmin responded to Atbalmin marginality by
reasserting their own religious importance in relation to them. As soon
as the first few younger Urapmin embraced Christianity (see below),
many of them went to Atbalmin as missionaries. The Urapmin were also
quick to go to other places that had little contact with Christianity and
set themselves up as evangelists and pastors. In this way, they reclaimed

much of the religious authority they were losing with the decline of the regional ritual system at the same time that they also, because the mission paid them to act in these roles, staked a place for themselves in the emerging economic order.

In the Urapmin rush to missionize the Atbalmin and other marginal Min groups, we can see how difficult their loss of ritual priority and growing economic marginalization were for them. We also get an initial indication of the way adopting Christianity allowed them to assuage the humiliations these setbacks caused. It was, then, the experience of humiliation connected with their peripheralization in the Min region—an experience understood very much in terms of the traditional value of being central to the region—that in part drove the Urapmin desire to radically change their culture and led them to begin to pursue the course of adopting Christianity.

I say the humiliations of their regional marginalization "in part" drove the Urapmin in the direction of adopting Christianity because there was also a second source of humiliation that was important during the early years of colonization. Throughout the colonial period, the patrol officers the Urapmin encountered stressed to them their moral backwardness and their need to follow the colonial law if they were to live as ethical people. The officers' emphasis on morality was supported by the moralizing tone of the Baptist Christianity to which the Urapmin were first exposed, which similarly pointed out to them that their traditional way of living was not morally sufficient to gain them salvation.

The twin assault the administration and the first bearers of Christianity (who at the outset were for the most part other Min people who had more experience than the Urapmin with the mission) leveled on the Urapmin sense of themselves as moral people was another source of humiliation. The Urapmin took these discourses of morality and the law seriously in part because the early colonial period was suffused with a sense of disorder, threat, and terror that encouraged them to work hard to determine what was demanded of them. But these discourses were able to humiliate the Urapmin, rather than simply demand obedience from them, primarily because in the terms of their traditional culture they took living ethically to be of great importance. As I noted above, Urapmin social structure afforded everyone a great deal of choice as to how to live. Along with this openness to choice came a strong cultural emphasis on the need to exercise moral judgment in making the many decisions of social import that people had to make. Morally sensitive on traditional grounds, then, the Urapmin responded powerfully to government and Christian claims that they were ethically immature and ignorant. These humiliations led the Urapmin first to an effort to adopt wholeheartedly the colonial law, and, as we will see, patrol officers regularly reported that they were model subjects in this regard. Later, once they became more familiar with Christian doctrine, they were quick to engage its moral system as well. The second half of this book is focused on their encounter with that moral system and their response to the ways it both resembles and contradicts their traditional one. In the present context, however, the important point to recognize is that it was the traditional Urapmin preoccupation with morality that made them susceptible to being humiliated on moral grounds during the early part of the colonial process, and that this moral humiliation joined the humiliation of their declining regional importance in pushing them to reach out to adopt Christianity in the strong sense in which I am claiming they did.

Inasmuch as Urapmin social structure motivated their sensitivity to moral issues, it played a role in providing the terms in which they understood the humiliations of the colonial era. As important to my argument, however, is the way it also made it possible for the Urapmin to respond so quickly and successfully to those humiliations; for it is one thing to want to change and another to succeed in doing so. A brief sketch of Urapmin social structure will make clear the way it facilitated the project of change the Urapmin undertook.

As was the case in describing the Min ritual system, I can best describe Urapmin social structure by starting with an account of the physical landscape to which it gives shape. The 396 Urapmin live in villages *(abiip)* most of which are strung along the top of a ridge that juts out of the foothills of the Behrmann mountains (see figure 2). The Urapmin call the ridge Bimbel from Bim, the spirit that is the cause of earthquakes *(bim)*. Long ago, Bim flattened out the top of the ridge in one of its bodily paroxysms, making a nice, relatively level surface on which to build villages. During the period of my fieldwork, there were five villages laid out along the top of the ridge. Moving roughly south to north, these villages were Danbel (Muli Kona), Salafaltigin, Drum Tem, Atemkit, and Dimidubiip (see map 2). One of these villages moved during the time I was in Urapmin, and another had begun to move as I was leaving, yet they kept their positions relative to one another. In addition to these villages, there were two others that the Urapmin referred to in Tok Pisin as "places at the sides" (saitsait ples). One of these, Makalbel, was perched in the Behrmanns just above and to the east of the main ridge.[9] The other, Ayendubiip, was situated not on the top of Bimbel but on the part

Figure 2. The Bimbel ridge looking north. Danbel village is in the foreground at the right, and the top Urapmin church and Salafaltigin village are in the center foreground. Photo by Joel Robbins.

of it that slopes steeply down toward the junction of the Ilam and Sepik Rivers.

The Bimbel ridge slopes gently downward from south to north. This provides the physical basis of the distinction between top and bottom Urapmin. Drum Tem and the villages that lie to the south of it (including Makalbel) constitute "top" Urapmin; the northerly villages of Atemkit, Dimidubiip, and Ayendubiip compose "bottom" Urapmin.

Urapmin villages are in all cases clearly discrete entities and are understood as such. But almost all of them are within easy walking distance of one another, and the total area they cover is not great. The greatest distance is between the two outlying "side" villages—Makalbel in the south and Ayendubiip in the north—which are separated by a distance of about four and a half kilometers. But Makalbel is only a kilometer from Salafaltigin, and Ayendubiip is similarly close to Dimidubiip. Furthermore, if these two villages are ignored, any two villages of the central core of Urapmin are no more than two and a half kilometers apart. In fact, the villages of top Urapmin are separated by no more than half a kilometer, and the same holds for Atemkit and Dimidubiip in bottom Urapmin.

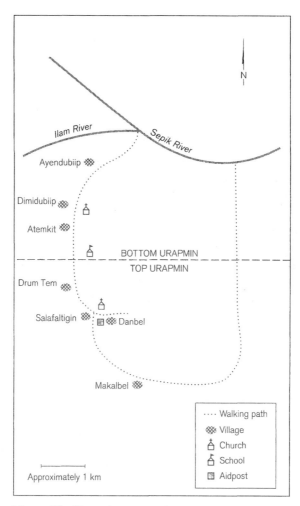

Map 2. The Urapmin community

Urapmin villages are generally U-shaped, and they are striking for the way their packed-dirt plazas, assiduously kept free of grass and weeds, stand out from the greenery of their surroundings and the imposing rainforest that always lies not too far in the background. Yet as impressive as these villages are as evidence of the human capacity to carve distinctly human places out of even the most imposing natural environments, they are only one center of Urapmin life. The other center, one that is in many ways more important than the villages, is the forest *(sep)*.

It is in the forest that the Urapmin make the swidden gardens *(lang)* that provide them with the bulk of their food in the form of taro *(ima)* and sweet potato *(wan)*—the two most important staples—along with pit-pit, sugarcane breadfruit, and a variety of other crops. It is also in the forest that Urapmin men hunt for the birds, marsupials, cassowaries, and wild pigs that provide a small but highly valued supplement to the Urapmin diet. So important are these forest activities to the Urapmin that much of the time they do not live in their village houses *(am)* but in bush houses *(sep am)* that they build near their gardens and hunting grounds. These houses can be almost as elaborate as village houses, and they provide a physical index of how important forest life is to the Urapmin.

From a social structural point of view, what is most striking about how the Urapmin come together in villages and how they cooperate to use the forest is that very little in these regards is determined by kinship links. Two factors combine to render the Urapmin kinship system a poor source of structural rules and idioms. The first is that descent in Urapmin is reckoned cognatically and connects people not only to the kinship categories *(tanum miit*—what for present purposes we might think of as "clans," though the designation is not quite accurate) of their parents but also to those of their grandparents. Because grandparents also have multiple memberships to pass on through their own parents and grandparents, most people in Urapmin can claim membership in most or all of the broader social categories that the kinship system constructs. Social category memberships thus do little to differentiate people or provide a set of fixed positions from which they can relate to one another.

The second factor that renders the Urapmin kinship system structurally ineffective follows from the fact that the Urapmin strongly emphasize and in almost all cases achieve endogamy within the Urapmin community. Since this community is small (consisting in 1992 of only 231 adults who were over seventeen and thus married or of marriageable age)[10] and people must marry beyond the circle of their first cousins, this results in everyone understanding themselves to be related to everyone else, often in fairly direct ways.

The Urapmin combination of cognatic descent reckoning and endogamy within the group does not, of course, lead to a situation in which people claim all of their social category memberships at once, nor does it lead to one in which they actively participate in all of their possible kin relations at the same time. What it does lead to is a situation in which people always have choices about whom to relate to and on what grounds. This is true of residence—for people choose whom to live with and most people will live in several villages of very different social composition during their lifetimes (and some people will even maintain houses in more than one village at the same time). They also choose whom to garden and hunt with, and the social composition of these work groups can change garden by garden and hunting trip by hunting trip. Hence, in Urapmin patterns of social grouping are constantly changing, and even when they appear momentarily stable, everyone knows they remain subject to change at any time.

The description of Urapmin social life I have just laid out is one that stays very close to the Urapmin understanding. People are able to construe whomever they live, garden, or hunt with as kin, but precisely for this reason they do not generally refer to kin links in explaining why they or others decide to affiliate with particular people in particular instances. Instead, they refer to people's wills *(san)*. People do, they say, what they want. It is on the basis of what people will that they make social decisions and that society comes to take the shape it does. The will is thus very much at the center of Urapmin social thinking and provides a way of making sense of a social situation that is in fact highly fluid and always open to change.

One might surmise that such a highly open-ended social system would be impossible to live in, for it would fail to provide even the minimal continuity and predictability that people need to operate successfully in their everyday lives. To the extent that this is true, it should not be surprising that two features of Urapmin social structure do work to contain this open-endedness, or at least to slow down its realization to a manageable pace. One of these features is an elaborate and important set of ideas about the way moral persons should temper the expression of their wills by having some regard for what the Urapmin call the law *(awem)*. Like the will, the law is a core idea of Urapmin social structural thinking. Put most simply, Urapmin ideas of the law hold that once one has chosen to relate to people by living or working with them, one owes them some consideration in at least the near future. Examples of such consideration are that one should stay in a village one has joined until it moves, or continue gardening with people with whom one has started a garden until the garden is harvested out and returned to fallow. There are many more complex ideas of lawful behavior that I discuss later, for the fraught relationship between the law and the will is at the heart of traditional Urapmin moral thinking, but even these few examples are enough to indicate that the notion of the law works to contain the open-endedness of Urapmin social life by tempering people's free exercise of their wills.

The second feature of Urapmin social structure that militates against its open-endedness is the place it leaves open to big men. Big men are self-made leaders who play a key role in stabilizing Urapmin social arrangements. One of the primary ways the Urapmin talk about what big men do is to say that they "arrange" *(daptamin)* people. They do this first and foremost by collecting people into villages. They also arrange work groups for major projects such as roofing houses and constructing pig fences. Finally, they are also involved in organizing hunting and gardening groups, sometimes directly and sometimes by defending two or more people's legal rights to garden or hunt in the same areas. Equally as important as the big men's role in constructing these groups in the first place are the efforts they make to keep people engaged in them once they have joined. When people move to willfully opt out of a group they have joined, it is the big men who first recruited them who most strenuously remind them of their lawful obligation to stay. In this way, the big men work both to form Urapmin sociality into structural shape and to keep it from too rapidly losing that shape as people pursue their willful courses through life.

Thus far I have treated the big men's role in working against the open-endedness of Urapmin social life. But this is only half the story. For big men also thrive on that open-endedess. Because all Urapmin have many choices about whom to live and work with, each big man competes against all the others for followers. In doing so, they exploit people's ability to choose by trying to pry them away from other big men and into their own camps. In looking for ways to enhance their ability to compete for followers, Urapmin big men are always open to trying innovations that make their villages and social groups more appealing than those of others. As the Urapmin place in the Min regional ritual system declined, one such innovation they embraced was Christianity.

Big men themselves did not bring Christianity to Urapmin. This was first accomplished by a group of young men and women who went to Tifalmin to study the new religion with recent Telefol converts who had set up a Bible school there. But it was the big men who allowed these young people to go. And it was the big men who, shortly after they left, allowed a Telefolmin man, himself just recently missionized, to set up a short-lived Bible school in Urapmin that prepared another group of young people to go to Telefomin to study at the mission school. Finally, it was also the big men who allowed these young people to introduce what they had learned into Urapmin life when they returned by building churches and schools of their own. As we will see, the big men had a greater stake than anyone else in traditional Urapmin religion. But the benefits of embracing innovations that would attract followers were too great for them to dig in their heels in defense of the old religious order, especially as the regional prestige hierarchy that was part of that order began to crumble. It was their willingness to support change that allowed the Urapmin to adopt Christianity so quickly and without, as in many places in the world, creating or exacerbating tensions between the young and the old in ways that would split the community between traditionalists and those who embraced the new religion (e.g., Leavitt 1989; Maxwell 1999; Tuzin 1997).

The foregoing discussion of the Min ritual system and Urapmin morality and social structure traces the broad outlines in which the first half of this study discusses why the Urapmin reached out to adopt Christianity and how they were able to be so successful in doing so. But this book is not just about how and why the Urapmin adopted Christianity; it is also about how they have come to live lives defined largely in its terms. In addition to being a book about cultural change, then, this is an ethnography of a Christian culture. As such, it belongs to a still small group of anthropological works that focus on people as Christians. In the next section, I take up some of the reasons why there should be so little in the way of an anthropology of Christianity and situate my discussion as an attempt to help bring one about.

ON STUDYING A CHRISTIAN CULTURE

Until recently anthropologists have not shown a great
deal of interest in Pacific Christianity, regarding it perhaps as a product of Colonialism rather than as authentic local culture.

Ben Burt, *Tradition and Christianity*

[M]ost anthropologists still regard Christianity as foreign intrusion and continue to pursue the fading ves-
tiges of uncontaminated traditional religions. . . . [F]ew
anthropologists incorporate the Christian presence into

studies of village societies. Christianity is the perennial
outside force—threatening, corrupting, or merely dust-
ing the surface of the authentic focus of anthropological concerns. In and of itself, it is of no interest. It can
never become "cultural."

John Barker, "Christianity in Western
Melanesian Ethnography"

The first essential in a modern fieldwork study is to
obtain as full an account as possible of the existing
tribal culture. In this due prominence must be given
to elements taken over from or introduced by the
Europeans. . . . Christianity, in so far as it has been
accepted, must be studied like any other form of cult,
in its organization, doctrines, ritual, manifestations in
tribal life, attitudes towards it of individual natives, and
so on. . . . This is easy enough to say. In practice it is
sometimes difficult to apply, not so much because of
technical obstacles as because of the outlook engen-
dered by the training that most anthropologists receive
before going into the field. If I may refer to my own experience, I found it difficult, when actually in the field,
not to feel disappointed at having to study the religion
of the Kxatla by sitting through an ordinary Dutch Re-
formed Church service, instead of watching a heathen
sacrifice to the ancestral spirits; and I remember vividly
how eagerly I tried to find traces of a worship that was
in fact no longer performed. And it seems so silly to
record the details of a Christian wedding or confirma-
tion ceremony with the same fidelity, let alone enthusiasm, with which one would note down the "doctoring"
of a garden or a new hut.

I. Schapera, "Contact between European
and Native in South Africa (cont.): 2"

Any study that aims to examine the cultural aspects of Christianity in a
particular place has to confront the remarkable dearth of similar works
in the annals of ethnography. Certainly, as Burt and Barker point out in
the epigraphs above, Christianity has never been a focal concern for
Melanesianist anthropologists. In this regard, however, Melanesianists

hardly stand out from anthropologists of other regions; as one might gather from Schapera's comment, Christianity has never been a major topic within the discipline more generally.

Harding (1991) has recently proffered a similar observation about the lack of anthropological studies of Christianity and has suggested that it has come about because from the point of view of anthropology, not all others are created equal. In particular, she argues, Western Christian fundamentalists constitute a "repugnant cultural other" that anthropologists neither want to study nor want to read about. Later, she implies that Christianity itself, rather than its fundamentalist expression alone, seems to be the problem. While anthropologists are eager to use ethnography to get beyond crass stereotypes of "cultural 'others' constituted by discourses of race/sex/class/ethnicity/colonialism," the same is not true for those constituted by discourses of "religion, at least not Christian religion" (Harding 1991: 375; see also Mahmood and Reynolds 1995: iii).

Harding explains this disjunction between good and bad others by suggesting that fundamentalist Christians, and, we may add, many other Christians as well, have rejected the very modernity on which anthropology is based. It is their difference that defines who "we" are (see also Harding 2000: 62). To recuperate them to reasonableness by showing, as anthropologists invariably must, that they make sense in their own terms would be to lose our assurance that we make sense in ours. In the face of this threat, Harding argues, even those who are devoted to bridging cultural gaps are careful to maintain their distance from Christians.

One can imagine other explanations for the anthropological aversion to Christianity besides that offered by Harding. For example, as Taussig (1993: 8) puts it in a related discussion of the anthropological discomfort with colonial mimesis more generally, the original Western provenience of Christianity may well strike some as rendering it a threat to corrode "the alterity by which . . . [anthropological] science is nourished." Or, wherever Christianity shows up outside the West, it may run up against what Thomas (1994) claims is a widespread anthropological tendency to recoil from hybrid cultures; a tendency nourished by the ideas of cultural authenticity to which both Burt and Barker allude and by the biases in anthropological training that Schapera discusses. Yet however we choose to explain the anthropological aversion to Christianity, what is most important in the present context is that we recognize that it exists and consider how it might affect our ability to carry out research among people for whom Christianity has become important.

Barker (1992: 185), who has done more than any other scholar to establish Christianity as a viable topic among Melanesianist anthropologists, points to the most serious obstacle the aversion to Christianity
poses to our ability to understand those who follow it when he says
that it renders us unable to see Christianity as cultural. The results of
this perceptual handicap take several forms. Some anthropologists see
Christianization only in terms of cultural loss (Harkin 1997: 47; see also
Clifford 1986), as if in adopting it, people were not also involved in
grasping a new cultural order in which to live (cf. Geertz 1973: 150).
Others cannot hear the Christian statements people make as sincere or
as possessed of much meaning. Sometimes they are dismissed as clichés
(as if much of what we call culture was not made up of things almost
everyone says and most people say more than once), or as fragments
from a wider set of Christian understandings that are only poorly or
partly understood. Finally, a third group places such thoroughgoing
stress on the continuities between Christian and indigenous ideas that
they produce accounts in which Christianity is represented as syn-
cretized to such an extent that it is in reality nothing more than traditional religion tricked up in new clothes (cf. Burt 1994: 13). Although
there are differences between these ways of framing a study and analyzing ethnographic materials, they are alike in that anthropologists can
use all of them to cordon off Christianity from their real object of study
by declaring it something less than cultural.

These ways of rendering Christianity something less than cultural—
something less, that is, than a system of categories and values with its
own coherence—are all relatively lacking in subtlety, but anthropologists have used all of them numerous times in discussing Melanesia and
other regions of the world. They give on to the kind of generic statements like this one from Naficy—someone with no particular interest in
Christianity, the Arctic, or Papua New Guinea but possessed of a sophisticated grasp of currently popular models of cultural change:

> As a mode of social and cultural homeostasis, syncretism helps those under
> duress to survive, and to preserve important aspects of their original culture
> by adopting the outer forms of the new culture while retaining for a long
> time much of the original inner meanings and value systems. . . . Studies of
> religious syncretism from the Arctic to the Papua New Guinean tribes of
> the Markham valley have shown that often underneath the syncretic prac-
> tices borrowed from Christianity or side by side with them there flourishes
> in psychic life, emotional orientation, and fundamental attitudes the pre-
> Christian native values and beliefs. (1993: 18, 229; the second part of the
> quotation is the text of an endnote placed at the end of the first part)

The metaphoric imagery of inside and outside, underneath and on top that structures this statement is widespread, and its deployment, even without further argument, often seems enough to carry assertions about the relative unimportance of Christianity in any given case. But my point is not that the view embodied in Naficy's claims would be wrong in all such cases, although it surely is in some. The real danger is that if we hold this view, we are likely to seek out situations in which it is correct and thereby relieve ourselves of the burden of discussing Christianity in cultural terms without compromising the validity of our ethnographies.

The Comaroffs' influential studies of the encounter between the Southern Tswana of South Africa and a group of British Nonconformist missionaries (1991, 1992, 1997) are a case in point. Although the Comaroffs tell us in several places that some Tswana women, some marginal men, some of those living far from the mission, and, in the later part of the period they consider, some elites embraced Christianity quite tightly and in fairly "orthodox" terms (1997: 93, 105, 154; 1991: 238–40, 310), these people are not their focus. Instead, their interest is in those for whom "the gospel . . . made little sense" and who thus "ignominiously ignored or rudely rejected" it (Comaroff and Comaroff 1991: 199). The main story that emerges from the history of the particular Tswana they choose to focus on is one of how they resisted Christianity, only to find themselves drawn into the culture of capitalism that the missionaries also conveyed. As several readers have noted, it is not a story in which the cultural aspects of Christianity have much of a role to play (Landau 2000: 503; Meyer 1999: 72–73; Peel 1995: 588–89).

When working with people who have largely succeeded in resisting Christianity, it is appropriate to give the cultural content of Christianity very little play. Yet in focusing on such people, we only perpetuate the absence of an anthropology of Christian cultures. This leaves us with little to draw on in confronting situations, like that of the Urapmin, in which people are indisputably living their lives at least in part in Christian terms. Given the number of people around the globe who would fit this description, the anthropological failure to illuminate their lives has to be reckoned a major one.

In focusing on the Christian culture of the Urapmin, this book joins a small but growing group of works that address this failure by taking the cultural aspects of at least one kind of Christianity seriously. The kind of Christianity in question is the Pentecostal and charismatic branch, focused on the availability of the gifts of the Holy Spirit to the faithful. In the last several years, sensitive, book-length cultural studies of this kind of Christianity have begun to appear from Africa, Jamaica, and Native North America (e.g., Meyer 1999; Austin-Broos 1997; Dombrowski 2001). Taken together, they represent a radical reorientation in anthropological work on Christianity among non-Western groups; a reorientation that aims to leave behind techniques that allow one to explain Christianity away as less than cultural and instead explore how it is that people can live their lives in Christian terms.

Given the historical lack of interest in Christianity among anthropologists, it is fair to ask why Pentecostal and charismatic Christianity has of late attracted their attention. In a study of the growing interest in Pentecostal and charismatic Christianity among anthropologists working in Papua New Guinea, Douglas (2001) offers two explanations for why it, unlike other kinds of Christianity, has succeeded in establishing itself among Melanesianists as a viable object of specifically cultural study. One is that with its emphasis on dramatic, Spirit-filled rituals and, in the Papua New Guinea case, on the imminence of the coming millennium, it appears in many ways similar to the kind of religions anthropologists have long studied in the region: in the terms of the quotation from Schapera above, it does not confront anthropologists with religious practices that seem totally unlike the ones they were trained to study. I think this explanation accounts for some of the attention Pentecostal and charismatic Christianity have received, but I doubt that the newfound interest in Christianity is wholly based on the way this version of it renders an often all too familiar religion exotic. In fact, Douglas's second explanation, one that does not depend on this aspect of Pentecostal and charismatic Christianity, will, I think, prove more important in the long run. This explanation holds that anthropologists have had to engage with Pentecostal and charismatic Christianity in Papua New Guinea because Papua New Guineans themselves have impressed its importance on them. Papua New Guineans have done so, I would argue, because they have generally engaged Pentecostal and charismatic Christianity much more profoundly than they have other kinds of Christianity. In my terms, they have adopted it rather than attempted to assimilate it or put it in the service of a transformative reproduction of their own culture. Once people have adopted any kind of Christianity in this way, one cannot study their culture without studying the cultural aspects of their Christianity. This goes a long way toward accounting for the interest in the cultural aspects of Pentecostal and charismatic Christianity not only in Papua New Guinea but also elsewhere.

The argument that anthropologists are interested in Pentecostal or charismatic Christianity because the people they study are deeply engaged with it raises, of course, the question of why it has proved so appealing in so many parts of the non-Western world. This is a complex question over which much ink has already been spilled by scholars working in several disciplines (e.g., Cox 1995; Martin 1990, 2002; Robbins 2001b). I do not want to rehearse the various debates here but rather will refer to them in appropriate places in the body of the book. I do, however, want to flag one point that has continuities with the core themes I have taken up in this introduction. Recent studies from Africa and Native North America suggest that Pentecostalism is often appealing to people like the Urapmin who are marginal not only on a map of the world that includes the West but also locally (Dombrowski 2001; Maxwell 1999; Meyer 1999). These are people who, as the model of adoption presented here would suggest, have been humiliated or otherwise diminished in traditionally meaningful terms. It is not surprising that Pentecostalism, with its emphasis on the accessibility of the power of the Holy Spirit, proves attractive to people in this situation. By making the Spirit available to everyone, Pentecostalism radically localizes Christian authority, and because it is institutionally very decentralized, it does not cast people into peripheral roles in churches whose headquarters are elsewhere (Robbins 2001b). Finally, by virtue of its otherworldliness and millennialism, it directs attention away from the earthly landscapes in which people like the Urapmin see themselves as occupying the fringes. Thus while experienced marginalization and its attendant humiliations act as a push factor in the adoption process, the cultural content of Pentecostal and charismatic Christianity itself constitutes a pull factor. Given that the cultural content of this form of Christianity is crucial to its spread, there is little room in studying its converts for approaches that explain away that content.

In concluding this discussion, I want to add a final note point about the status of Christianity in anthropology and particularly in the anthropology of Papua New Guinea. This point has to do with the role of the monograph form in establishing anthropological areas of inquiry. Despite Barker's and Burt's reports on the rather dismal state of the Melanesianist study of Christianity in the recent past, as Douglas's (2001) article indicates a small literature has begun to build on this topic in the past few years. Quite a few recent monographs either have a chapter on Christianity or consider Christianity in some detail while pursuing other focal topics (e.g., Douglas 1998; Errington and Gewertz 1995; Eves 1998; Jolly 1994; Knauft 2002; Kulick 1992; Lattas 1998; LiPuma 2000; Smith 1994; Strathern and Stewart 2000). Several collections of articles now exist as well, either on local Christianity in general (Barker 1990a) or on specific topics such as Christian Millennialism (Kocher Schmid 1999; Stewart and Strathern 1997, 2000), Pentecostal and charismatic Christianity (Robbins, Stewart, and Strathern 2001), and Christian transformations of gender relations (Jolly and Macintyre 1989). Further, several thoughtful articles and book chapters that are part of long-term ethnographic projects focused on Melanesian Christianity have also begun to appear (e.g., Barker 1990b, 1993; Jebens 1997, 2000; Schieffelin 1996, 2000). Finally, several important overviews have examined this work and charted its development in relation to Melanesian studies more generally (Barker 1992; Douglas 2001).

Yet despite this recent publishing activity, full-length monographs focused directly on Christianity and culture in Melanesia are rare, and of the four that exist, only one, published in German, deals with Papua New Guinea (Burt 1994; Hayward 1997; Jebens 1995; White 1991).[11] In cultural anthropology, I would argue, this lack of monographic treatment indicates that a topic has not yet arrived. One of the reasons the monograph has always held such an important place in cultural anthropology is that it requires that the author get the weighting of elements right. In articles, one is allowed to shift all the emphasis onto a specific element of a culture even if that element is not particularly important when considered alongside others. In a monograph, such disproportion is fatal. This is a monograph that argues that Christianity has tremendous weight in Urapmin culture—that it has become cultural with a vengeance. As such, it aims to join the other works on Pentecostal and charismatic Christianity cited above in exemplifying the viability of an anthropology focused on Christianity as a cultural phenomenon.

OUTLINE OF THE BOOK

The following outline gathers up the themes of this introduction and indicates how they all hang together in the argument of the book. Chapter 1 is in large part an account of how the Urapmin attempted to take the events of the early contact period and, following them, the terms of an emerging colonial order and work them into the confines of their traditional understandings along the lines suggested by the model of assimilation. The categories that were crucial in this exercise were first that of exchange, which the Urapmin used to comprehend the period of contact and the early years of colonization, and then that of taboo/law. Both of these indigenous categories bore important similarities to the categories with which Westerners approached the Urapmin, and these similarities afforded the Urapmin some success in encompassing Westerners within their own understandings. The colonial notion of law was particularly central to this encounter, for it initially fit well with Urapmin ideas about taboo; both referred to sets of fine-grained rules applying to behavior rather than feeling and regulating people's relations with powerful and sometimes violently punitive others. Since taboo had always been important, the colonialists' emphasis on law and lawlessness resonated with Urapmin concerns, and, prodded by colonial displays of force, the Urapmin were quickly able to imagine themselves living in terms of it.

Chapter 2 takes up in detail the changing place of the Urapmin in the Min region and explores how the humiliation this caused them led big men to encourage young people to take the first steps toward the adoption of Christianity. It begins with a detailed account of the traditional regional religious system, for it was in terms of their loss of centrality in this system that the Urapmin experienced many of the humiliations that led them to desire change.

In chapter 3, I consider the revival movement in which those Urapmin who had not yet converted to Christianity by the mid-1970s—by far the majority of the population—did so. Here the process of adoption came prominently into play, as the Urapmin endeavored to comprehend and then develop ways of living within a wholly new revivalist Christian culture. Having taken on this Christian culture and come to see themselves in its terms as sinful beings, a new cycle of humiliation began in which Christian notions of debasement drove an even more thoroughgoing Urapmin engagement with the religion that both produced this humiliation and promised to rescue them from it. The workings of this dynamic, I argue, were what finally drove the Urapmin, once they had begun to negotiate the logic of Christianity, to develop the elaborate set of Christian institutions and rituals that have made that religion such a central feature of their contemporary life.

The book's first part, then, explains how a new culture very rapidly assumed centrality in Urapmin life. The second part explores how the Urapmin live both with this new culture and with the older one that, I argue, in many respects still also remains in force. Contemporary Urapmin life is largely driven by a struggle between Christian and traditional values and structures of understanding to dominate its unfolding. This struggle does not take place in all cultural domains, for Christianity has succeeded in leading the Urapmin to discard many of their traditional categories of religious understanding and practice. Yet traditional social structural and moral ideas remain in play and continue to structure the living and laboring arrangements by which the Urapmin provision themselves and reproduce their social existence. These ideas come into direct conflict with Christian conceptions of the moral person and his or her relationship to others. The chapters in this part all in one way or another examine these conflicting sets of ideas and the ways each attempts to transform the other.

In chapter 4, I show how Christian millennial notions endeavor to devalue traditional living and laboring arrangements—and thus establish the claims of Christian morality as primary—by reconfiguring Urapmin notions of space and time. Traditional and Christian notions of morality and sociality are the foci of chapters 5 and 6, respectively. In these chapters, I show that both sets of ideas deploy similar categories of lawfulness and willfulness but that they relate them differently to one another and, crucially, attach different values to them. The similarities have provided a fertile soil from which various conjunctural relatings of the two systems can spring up, but the differences are fundamental enough that thus far the two systems have not formed any stable synthesis resulting in a transformative reproduction of the traditional or the Christian system. Instead, traditional Urapmin moral and social thinking proclaims the Christian life impossible to live, while Christianity condemns traditionally morally acceptable routines as sinful. In chapters 7 and 8, I argue that the contradiction between these two evaluations motivates much of Urapmin ritual life and millennialism, both of which provide arenas in which the Urapmin struggle to accommodate the traditional aspects of their lives to the demands of their Christian religion.

The focus of chapter 8, the final ethnographic chapter of the book, on Urapmin millennialism follows from the fact that, as Parsons (1991: 243) notes, borrowing a phrase from Crane Brinton, people work explicitly toward realizing their paramount (or in his terms "ultimate") values during periods of social movement or "active religion." This observation holds true for the Urapmin, for it is during those periods when they are caught up in millennial fervor and living in what anthropologists would recognize as a millenarian movement that the contest between their relational and individualist values is most publicly evident. Chapter 8 thus focuses on Urapmin millenarianism because it lays out in explicit terms the Urapmin experience of the difficulties they find themselves facing in trying to live under two paramount values simultaneously.

In the conclusion, I consider what these ideas about kinds of cultural change and the role of values and morality within them, along with the Urapmin exemplification of certain issues they raise, can add to the debates about globalization that I mentioned briefly above. I suggest that the kind of analysis undertaken here provides some substance to notions like hybridity and allows us to begin to talk about the internal structure of cultural mixtures and the stakes (which I suggest are often moral ones) involved in living within them.

THE LINGUISTIC SITUATION IN URAPMIN

The indigenous language of the Urapmin, also known as Urapmin or Urap *(urap weng)*, is a member of the Mountain Ok subfamily of the Ok language family. Healey (1964: 40), the linguist responsible for defining the Ok language family, has claimed that the Urapmin speak the Tifal language, but subsequent work has shown this to be unlikely (A. Boush, pers. com.). Widespread multilingualism among Urapmin speakers allows many Telefolmin to imagine that the Urapmin actually speak their language among themselves. This too is not the case. While the Urapmin do regard the Tifalmin language as closer to their own than that of the Telefolmin, it is clearly not a dialect of either one. Although the kind of linguistic work that would allow us to speculate about its history has not been done, what is clear is that Urap should be regarded as a separate language contained within Healey's (1964: 38) Division A of the Mountain Ok subfamily along with Telefol, Tifal, Faiwol, and others.

More important for our concerns here, the linguistic situation in Urapmin is currently complex. Urap is everyone's first language. However, Tok Pisin, or what is sometimes known as Neo-Melanesian, is also very widely spoken. Tok Pisin is one of Papua New Guinea's national languages, and it is the most important lingua franca in rural areas of the country. In the early 1990s, Urapmin children were quite fluent in Tok Pisin by the age of twelve or so. They learn the language from older children and in school. Although policy forbids its use in the school, where English is supposed to be the sole language spoken, it is the only language that teachers and students share. Although no one comes out of the school even approaching fluency in English, all students learn Tok Pisin and become literate in it. In the early 1990s, most men younger than forty-five and women under thirty, whether or not they had attended some form of primary school, were fluent in Tok Pisin.

While one often hears Tok Pisin spoken in daily life, and Urap is now studded with loan words borrowed from it, it does not challenge Urap as the primary language of the community. There are, however, contexts in which Tok Pisin is valued and routinely used. As it is elsewhere in the country, in Urapmin Tok Pisin is identified with modernity and with Western institutions (Kulick 1992). Thus the contexts in which it is most often used are modern ones. These include local government meetings, to some extent local courts (at least when officials are speaking), and, crucially for this account, Christian services and discussions of Christian themes.

There are areas in Papua New Guinea where indigenous people have worked exhaustively to translate the vocabulary of Christianity into their native languages (see, e.g., Renck 1990). It sometimes seems as if the Urapmin, by contrast, have actually made conscious efforts to resist such translation. Many key Christian terms do not have Urap equivalents, or if Urap equivalents have been found, they are rarely used. Given that a great part of the appeal of Christianity is its connection with things modern and Western, it makes a certain sense to allow it to remain in the language that is also connected to those things. Furthermore, the refusal to translate fits well with the model of adaptation as the taking on of a new culture in its own terms that I employ in this study. But whatever the cause of this refusal to indigenize the vocabulary of Christianity, its effects are clear: Urapmin Christianity relies a great deal on Tok Pisin. This is not to say that only Tok Pisin is spoken in Christian contexts, but more of it is spoken in those contexts than in most others, and, importantly, the core Christian vocabulary items remain in Tok Pisin regardless of which language is being spoken.

Because this is so, I have taken Tok Pisin seriously and have analyzed some of its terms with the care often reserved only for those from indigenous languages. It is clear that Tok Pisin terms such as *namba, sin,* and *Holy Spirit* that I examine in what follows are semantically rich ones for the Urapmin. Without treating them as such, it would be impossible to provide an adequate account of Urapmin Christianity. As Tok Pisin becomes more and more important even in remote communities in Papua New Guinea, I imagine that anthropologists pursuing a variety of topics will have to begin to accord it the attention that I give it here (e.g., Foster 1995b).

I had studied Tok Pisin before arriving in Urapmin and began my work in that language. From the outset, I studied the Urap language regularly, usually daily, with two Urapmin men. I continued this work throughout my stay, moving on to working with them to transcribe texts after basic language teaching was no longer necessary. Although by the second year of my stay my comprehension of spoken Urapmin was adequate to allow me to follow what was said in many of the contexts I regularly encountered, my spoken production was never what I would have liked it to be. I could convey basic information and ask questions on topics that interested me, but Tok Pisin speakers invariably preferred that I address them in that language. For the reasons discussed above, directed interviews on Christian topics were conducted primarily in Tok Pisin.

Unless noted otherwise, I have translated all biblical passages that appear in the text from the Tok Pisin New Testament most often used by the Urapmin. This is the *Nupela Testamen Ol Sam,* published by the Bible Society of Papua New Guinea. In all cases, I have to the best of my ability translated these texts as the Urapmin read them, giving the Tok Pisin words the meanings they have in the Urapmin community.

I write Tok Pisin words using the Roman alphabet–based orthography standard in Papua New Guinea. The Urap language is similar enough to English phonologically that in its case too I have not had to make use of special orthographic symbols. However, Urap does distinguish between long and short vowels, and I indicate long vowels by doubling the representation of the short vowel (e.g., *aa*). As I have previously mentioned in a note, Urap terms are given in italics, and Tok Pisin terms are underlined. This treatment is employed on their first use in each chapter and their first use in a construction not previously presented.

THE FIELDWORK SITUATION

I carried out fieldwork in Urapmin from the beginning of January 1991 through early February 1993. I lived in top Urapmin, but I spent some time in all of the Urapmin villages and visited bottom Urapmin fairly regularly. Furthermore, one of the language teachers I worked with on a daily basis was from bottom Urapmin. Thus, although my knowledge of the flow of daily life comes primarily from my experience of top Urapmin, my contact with bottom Urapmin was sufficient to convince me that what was going on around me day to day was in general terms representative of what was going on everywhere in Urapmin.

As I discuss in detail in chapter 4, the Urapmin sense of how the world is organized has been radically transformed by the distinction they now make between "white" and "black" people and places. On a very basic level, the most important fact about me for many Urapmin people was that I was white and came from a white place. I have discussed the role this played in my fieldwork in detail elsewhere (Robbins 1997b). I will not review that material again here, but I refer readers who are interested in this topic, or who simply want a fuller picture of the fieldwork setting that produced this book, to that published piece.

Like many male field-workers in Papua New Guinea, my contact with women was never as regular or sustained as it was with the men with whom I was most close. I was, however, trained in anthropology at a time when anthropologists clearly recognized the problems with developing an analysis of a culture based solely on material gathered from men. I tried to counteract these problems in several ways. As I was developing interpretations in the field, I checked them with women as well as men. I also paid careful attention to statements women made in public contexts and made sure to take them into account as my analysis developed. I also included statements by women in my translation work, thus assuring that their voices were represented in the corpus of texts on which I have drawn (see, for example, the woman's confession presented in chapter 5). Finally, my wife, Elizabeth Waters, was in Urapmin for a total of nine months conducting botanical research. She became close to several women, and through her I also gained some sense of women's more private daily concerns. Taken together, I have some confidence that these measures have allowed me to produce an account that puts those aspects of Urapmin Christian culture that men and women share at its center. Wherever I do not think this is the case, I have pointed it out.

There is a second, conceptually quite distinct issue that has to do with the absence of gender categories as a major element in my analysis of Urapmin culture. Previous work focused on traditional Min cultures has stressed the central role notions of gender play in organizing people's understandings of many domains (e.g., Jorgensen 1981b, 1991; Poole 1982). Why is this feature missing from my account of Urapmin culture? It is missing because, as far as I could determine, it is largely absent from contemporary Urapmin thinking. Urapmin gender ideas appeared relatively disorganized in the early 1990s, with people claiming to have very little to say about the differences between men and women and demonstrating in a host of ways that they were not using these differences to think about distinctions in other parts of their lives. In part this surely follows from the way Christianity has introduced some measure of equal participation in a religious domain that was previously almost entirely a male preserve. Probably even more important, I would speculate, is the extent to which the black/white distinction and the allied oppositions between "heathens" and Christians and tradition and modernity have taken on the organizing role gender used to play. For both male and female Urapmin, the most salient facts about their lives in very many contexts are now that they are black and are striving to become good Christian moderns, not the gender differences that divide them. I intend to take up the declining salience of gender as a cultural category more fully elsewhere, but I hope I have said enough to indicate that it occupies the role it does in this study not because I have forgotten it but because my account reflects the extent to which the Urapmin have done so.

PART ONE

The Making of a
Christian Community

CHAPTER I

From Salt to the Law

Contact and the Early Colonial Period

[G]ifts, with all their possibility for both tribute and sub-
terfuge, condescension and deference, serve as a metonym
for cross-cultural transaction, for the complicated meetings
between peoples.

Leigh Eric Schmidt, "Practices of Exchange"

FROM CONTACT TO COLONIALISM
IN MELANESIAN ANTHROPOLOGY

In 1984 a seminar was held in Papua New Guinea that was later published under the title *Papua New Guinea: A Century of Colonial Impact,
1884–1984* (Latukefu 1989). As Latukefu (1989: ix) reports in his introduction to that volume, the seminar was initiated by a committee "set
up to organize activities to commemorate the entry of colonial powers in
1884, into what is now the independent nation of Papua New Guinea."
Here, then, we have the elite of a recently independent nation celebrating the centennial of their colonization. Even before readers have a
chance to reflect on this, the editor himself raises the matter of how odd
it seems, only to attempt to dissipate the sense of strangeness that hangs
over this committee and its work by pointing to the "unique nature of
the colonial experience in the Pacific in general and Papua New Guinea
in particular" (Latukefu 1989: ix). After all, the argument goes, Papua
New Guineans did not have to fight for their independence. And in comparison with "other parts of the world, such as Africa, Asia and the
Americas[,] . . . [i]n the Pacific, with the exception of French Territories,
colonial experience was different, less repressive, more peaceful though
tension and conflicts were never entirely absent" (Latukefu 1989: ix). If
the colonial period was not so bad, he argues, then perhaps it is not so
absurd to celebrate it, even after it has given way to independence.

This idea that the people of what would become Papua New Guinea had, by comparison with other colonized peoples, a relatively easy time of it with colonialism is fairly widespread (e.g., LiPuma 2000: 23; Schieffelin 1995: 556). In the world-historical scheme of things, colonialism did come to Papua New Guinea late in the game. This is especially the case in the Highlands, where colonialism was primarily a mid-twentieth-century project. Possessed of more sophisticated technology that allowed it to bring more benefits to the colonies than in the past, and hemmed in by international opinion fed by the developing global media and expressed through such organs as the United Nations, mid-twentieth-century colonialism was sometimes in intent and of necessity in appearance a kinder and gentler enterprise than its historical forebears. Because this is the case, the image of the exceptionalism of the Melanesian colonial experience that Latukefu uses to dust the air of the uncanny off the Papua New Guinea colonial centennial celebration is not on the face of it inappropriate.

But this received wisdom about the light touch of colonialism in Papua New Guinea can be misleading if it encourages anthropologists to neglect the task of examining how the colonial era has left its mark on contemporary life. This is to a large extent what has happened in the scholarship of the region. In part shaped by an interest in representing the people they study as relatively "untouched" by the Western world, but at least as fundamentally rooted in their sense that the colonial presence was a mild one, Melanesianists have generally been more likely to write of "contact" than of "colonialism." For the most part, their efforts have gone into reconstructing the heroic efforts made (on both sides) in accomplishing early meetings, and into analyzing the cognitive fireworks these meetings set off, than they have into engaging in considerations of the drudgery, dull routines, and undoubted moments of cruelty that came to mark colonial life as exploration gave way to administration.[1]

Only recently, and in keeping with the growing anthropological interest in colonialism elsewhere, have Melanesianists begun regularly to integrate accounts of the colonial era more fully into their ethnographies (e.g., Lattas 1992, 1993, 1998; Clark 2000; Keesing 1992 on the Solomon Islands). As they have done so, they have been led to question what Brown (1995: 11), one of the pioneering ethnographers of the Highlands, calls the "Australian myth of benign colonialism." This recent work raises issues not only of violence, though that is being taken more seriously, but also of the supposed mildness of the colonial impact on the cultures of the region. What anthropologists who examine colonialism are finding is that the colonial era, in both its peaceful and its violent manifestations, has shaped Melanesian societies far more deeply than was suggested by much of the earlier writing on the region.

Despite their growing visibility, current efforts to make the impact of colonialism on the cultures of Melanesia central to regional ethnography face one potential red herring. Many contemporary Papua New Guineans hold whites in very high regard. They also often ridicule the postcolonial order by comparing it invidiously with the colonial one (see Piot 1999 for a comparable African case). These attitudes are particularly prevalent in rural communities, but they also have adherents among the urban elite, as is suggested by the very existence of Latukefu's volume. Taken at face value, these attitudes might reinforce an anthropological tendency to see the colonial past as having had nothing but a benign and anyway fairly slight influence on the present. Yet these attitudes should not be taken this way. Rather, they cry out for explanations both of the situations that produced them and of the nuances that lie behind their apparently straightforward surfaces. Only careful accounts of colonial history can provide such explanations. Any anthropology of colonialism in Melanesia thus has as one of its most pressing tasks discovering how these positive evaluations of the colonial era came to exist and how they have influenced postcolonial social life.

The Urapmin for the most part look back on the colonial order with this sort of fondness, though there are aspects of it about which their feelings are more mixed. When the Urapmin speak positively about the colonial period, they point to it as a time of great lawfulness. It was a time when they learned from the colonialists' law and from their Christian religion how to behave and were sufficiently fearful of these new leaders to obey strictly their dictates. They speak of the colonial period as the time when "the law came and got us" (lo i kam kisim mipela), or alternatively as the time when "we got the law" (mipela kisim lo). As these phrases suggest, "the law" in Urapmin usage often metonymically stands for the whole of the colonial project. This chapter explores how the Urapmin came to single out the law as the core of the colonial enterprise and discusses why they claim to have so welcomed its arrival among them. In answering these questions, it also uncovers some aspects of the colonial period that the Urapmin found far from benign.

In terms of the models of change laid out in the introduction, both the colonial period and the contact period that preceded it were dominated by relatively successful Urapmin efforts to understand the colonial order in terms of their indigenous categories. One of these categories was exchange. The Urapmin had always understood their social world as one in which exchanges created relationships. The colonists shared a similar idea, and the Urapmin were thus able to comprehend many of their early encounters with whites in terms that were comfortable to them. One of the things the colonists most wanted to give the Urapmin as their part of the colonial exchange was the law. In this instance too the Urapmin were able to construe what the colonists had in mind in familiar terms because the colonial legal system, consisting of myriad fine-grained rules for behavior, was one the Urapmin were able to work into their category of taboo. It was the ease with which the Urapmin were able to comprehend the law in their own terms, along with the violence that accompanied its introduction, that made it so central to their understanding of colonialism. Eventually the social relationships built on colonial models of exchange would break down, and the law would come to overflow the indigenous category of taboo in which the Urapmin attempted to contain it. But that is in the future. Looking only at contact and the early colonial period, one can tell the story of these early engagements largely in the framework provided by the model of assimilation.

Before proceeding to the details of Urapmin colonial history, I should introduce one additional process of change that was important during the colonial period and the postcolonial period that followed. This process is one I will call "incorporation." In my usage, incorporation occurs when one group takes over the institutions of another group and makes them their own. The process of incorporation differs from that of adoption by virtue of its focus on the localization of *institutions* and the way such localization allows local people to play the roles that are central to them. Any of the three kinds of cultural change that I have called assimilation, transformation, and adoption can take place as part of incorporation. For example, people may understand an institution they are incorporating by assimilating it in many important respects to a traditional one, or they may adopt an introduced understanding of the institution that accords closely with the way it is understood in the culture from which it comes. Both instances are, however, equally cases of incorporation, and this is why it makes analytic sense to single out incorporation as a specific kind of change.

Throughout the colonial and postcolonial periods, the Urapmin have worked consistently to incorporate modern, white institutions into their own local social life. Errington and Gewertz (1995: 22) have recently argued that what they call "emulation"—the effort to take up the practices of the whites—"might be seen as a particularly Melanesian form of resistance, one by which local groups attempted to maintain or enhance their own worth." For the Urapmin, what I am calling incorporation, founded on practices of emulation, allowed them throughout the colonial era to maintain control of the institutions that shaped their lives, even if those institutions were borrowed from white culture.[2] In their drive to incorporate Western institutions, the Urapmin themselves went to work for the colonial officers and became enforcers of the colonial law. They also became Bible teachers, missionaries, and pastors. And their goal for development was and remains the creation of a regime in which they will be laborers for and owners of businesses in their own area, an end toward which they have become, with very limited success, trade-store owners and cash crop farmers. We will see this dynamic of incorporation at work throughout the chapters in part 1, and it will be nowhere more obvious than in the way the Urapmin have used Christianity to make of the law a local project.

CONTACT

Colonial rule began in the Min region in the late 1940s. Although Westerners found their way to the area several times before this, Urapmin contact with them was minimal. In September 1914, Richard Thurnwald, a German anthropologist, was the first European to make contact with the Telefolmin (Craig 1990: 141). Although he seems to have traversed a good deal of the central Telefomin territory, he did not venture onto Urapmin land. As is clear from the reports of other early patrols, and from Morren's (1981: 44) map showing their routes through the Telefomin area, the same is true of the Karius and Champion patrol of 1928, the Taylor and Black patrol in 1938–39, and the Thurston party of expatriates who, fleeing south from the north coast of what is now Papua New Guinea, passed through the Min area while escaping the Japanese in 1942.

Among these early groups of European visitors to the Telefomin area, the only one to visit Urapmin, and the one the Urapmin credit with first contacting them, is the Williams party. In 1936 and 1937, an American named Ward Williams was working on behalf of American and British mining interests and led a group that explored the headwater areas of the Fly and Sepik Rivers looking for mineral deposits (Campbell 1938: 232). Williams's group included eight Europeans (a ninth was added later as an extra pilot) and twenty-three native carriers recruited from coastal areas. This group spent five months, from October 1936 to February 1937, camped in the Telefomin area (Kienzle and Campell 1938: 463). The group's contact with the Urapmin seems to have been minimal (Robbins 1998a: 52). Although the Urapmin had heard from their neighbors about the earlier patrols to the area and they were well aware of the deadly fighting that went on between the Mianmin and the Taylor-Black patrol (see below), the stories they tell about the Williams party represent for them the real beginning of their account of the coming of the whites.

Some Urapmin living in the early 1990s who were young teenagers at the time remember the coming of the Williams patrol. One story they tell about it recounts the predicament the Urapmin faced in trying to find a name for these new, white beings. Playing the story for laughs by highlighting the absurdity of how little the Urapmin understood about the newcomers, an older man named Babalok pointed out that the Urapmin originally called the members of the Williams patrol the "Wilumin." They had learned this name from the Telefolmin, who according to Babalok simply "made it up." Babalok refers to Wilumin as the *tanum miit* of the newcomers. *Tanum miit,* literally "root" or "origin" of the man, is the word Urapmin use to refer to the social categories into which they divide themselves. Telefolmin were obviously building on the morphology of indigenous tanum miit names, attaching to Williams's name the *min* suffix that often appears at the end of such ethnonyms.[3] But the contemporary Urapmin do not know that "Wilum" originated with the name of the patrol's leader. Instead, they assume that the Telefolmin had no particular reason for giving the visitors this designation. They find it funny that their forebears had to use a completely unmotivated name for the first whites they encountered, and the humorous effect is only intensified by the way the Telefolmin tried to build this new name on the scheme of indigenous ethnonyms.

The second term Babalok remembers the Urapmin having for whites also draws laughs. Because of the way they smelled, the Urapmin abandoned Wilumin and took to calling whites *dalabal,* which refers to the odor of a penis gourd. This one had a clear motivation, though it too was "made up" in the sense that it was not a name that came from the whites themselves. Only later, Babalok claims, did the coastal carriers that accompanied a different patrol teach the Urapmin the "correct" term for whites. This term is *tabalasep,* and it is still in use today as the correct term for whites.[4] This story confirms that the Williams party was likely the first to contact the Urapmin. In addition, its theme of how the Urapmin had to cast around to find something as fundamental as the right name to call its members indicates the confusion of those early contacts and points to how many questions about the whites they left unanswered.

Given the uncertainty that surrounded the coming of the whites, it is not surprising that tales of fear are also prominent in the corpus of stories of early contact. The Urapmin often talk about how they would run helter-skelter to hide in the bush when they saw people in Western clothes coming down the trail. Planes too were frightening, and people assumed they were some sort of nature spirit *(motobil)*. The Urapmin were sure that some of these planes "that made the ground shake" were the physical manifestation of *bim,* the spirit responsible for earthquakes, or were sent by it. As they usually did when spirits made people sick, but this time on a huge scale, the Urapmin responded to the planes by sacrificing pigs in the hope that the spirit would take the offering and leave them to themselves.

Despite their fears, however, the Urapmin also remember that they soon were able to establish reasonable working relationships with the Williams patrol and with other whites they met during the precolonial period. These early visitors demanded little, and they had much to give. Consequently, these relationships were built primarily on trade in material objects. Campbell, one of the members of Williams's party who visited the Urapmin, remarks, "[During the] earlier weeks of our stay there [in the Telefomin area] they would eat salt by the handful, as much as we could give them. This always remained our most valuable article of trade" (Kienzle and Campbell 1938: 472).

Urapmin too mention the importance of salt as mediating their early contacts (and it would remain important well into the colonial period). In Babalok's telling, "We were afraid when we first saw whites, but they enticed [grisim] us with salt. We tasted it and it was good. And then they gave us matches and showed us how to make fires. Then we went and got them food, sweet potato, taro, and bananas and we gave it to them. We exchanged." Such an exchange, of course, indicates the founding of good relations on Urapmin terms—for the Urapmin had always built friendly relationships with outsiders on the basis of exchange, as in the custom by which men have trading partners (*tisol dup,* lit. "wealth friend") in other Min groups.

That the exchange of salt and matches for local foods has come to stand for the relationship that ultimately held between the Urapmin and the first several patrols suggests the generally satisfactory tenor of these

early contacts from the Urapmin point of view. For the most part, contacts during this period were sporadic and made few demands on the
Urapmin other than that they overcome their fear enough to engage in
trade. Overall, the Urapmin do not tell many specific stories from the
precolonial contact period, and most of the ones they mention stress
how quickly they came to desire the salt the whites brought and how
happy they were with the other trade goods that came their way. As
Craig (1990), in an impressively detailed piece, has argued was the case
in Telefomin, in Urapmin the early contact period left people with an
overwhelmingly favorable impression of the whites, an impression that
provided a firm foundation for the colonial efforts to come.

The centrality of exchange in the Urapmin memory of the early contact period also points to how much their indigenous orders of motive
and action continued to govern social life at this time (see Schieffelin
1995). Although their social landscape was beginning to shift, the paths
that people followed through it remained much the same. Indeed, the
name Wilumin suggests that whites were treated at some level as just
another group on that landscape. Precontact Urapmin lived in a society
in which there was a division of esoteric powers between different social
categories (tanum miit). Members of one category controlled the wind,
for example, while others had special powers over rain. Likewise, the
Wilumin possessed some remarkable powers—especially that of flight
and of the violence of the gun. Similarly, each of the tribes in the region
produced goods that were its characteristic contribution to the regional
trade economy, and so too the Wilumin brought their salt and matches.
To be sure, the Urapmin also imagined that the whites might be "super-
naturals," or returning ancestors, but as O'Hanlon (1993: 22) remarks
for the Wahgi, "[T]his interpretation . . . had an experimental, matter-
of-fact quality to it," and it seems that it was rather quickly abandoned.
In any case, supernatural beings had always been inhabitants of the
Urapmin landscape, and *min* had always worked as a suffix for both
"human" and "supernatural" groups. Even if the whites were supernat-
urals, then, that would not preclude the Urapmin from finding them a
reasonably intelligible presence in their world.

In sum, stories from this early period suggest that the Urapmin were
able to interpret the whites into their world in such a way that they
largely fit within given social classifications rather than badly over-
flowing them. Everything unfolded much as the model of assimilation
would predict.

THE EARLY COLONIAL PERIOD

Although the colonial era proper would not begin until 1948, the contact era effectively came to an end in the Telefomin area during World War II. In 1944, the Australians rebuilt and extended the Telefomin airstrip for possible use as an emergency landing strip for planes en route between Australia and the base the Allied Forces in New Guinea had established in Hollandia (Champion 1966: 215). From the time of the airstrip extension until the end of the war, the Australia New Guinea Administration Unit (ANGAU) maintained a post at Telefomin. Champion (1966: 216) thinks that they also did "some patrolling" to "some of the outlying villages." Craig (1990: 145) notes, in writing about this period, that "there is some indication that ANGAU officers were less than delicate in their handling of New Guineans but I could find no specific references to what happened at Telefomin." There are indications in the archival records that they were at least highhanded in their treatment of the Tifalmin (see below). Although it is unclear to what extent the Urapmin were influenced by this early permanent Western settlement at Telefomin, it is clear that for the Telefolmin the settlement marked the dissipation of the benign atmosphere that had surrounded white-local relations during the contact period.

After the war, in June 1948, Ivan Champion, a man who in 1937 had made one of the first patrols into Telefomin, returned to "this remote outpost" to select a site for a government station (Champion 1966: 212). It was Champion's visit that would initiate in earnest the Australian effort to colonize the district. After scouting the area, Champion decided the post should be situated by the Telefomin airstrip, a recommendation he took back to Port Moresby. "[B]efore the end of the year," he reports, "two patrol officers and their force of police opened the first patrol post at Telefomin" (Champion 1966: 216).

From this point until independence in 1975, we have two voices to attend to in sketching colonial developments: we can complement Urapmin oral histories with reports filed by the officers who led patrols to Urapmin. In their reports, many of the officers raise issues that were obviously preoccupying those on the front line of colonization and "consolidation" in newly opened areas of Papua New Guinea. Chief among these issues were those concerning the imposition of the law and the problem of transforming the flagging Urapmin interest in reciprocal exchange into a desire to enter the market economy. The colonists wanted to create a situation in which people would be controlled not by their exchange relationships with specific whites but by their fear of the law and by their desire to obtain Western goods. The concerns that fill the early patrol reports are strikingly similar to those that appear in Urapmin oral historical accounts of the period, suggesting that the Urapmin paid close attention to what the early colonists told them and ultimately gave colonial messages an important role in the new culture they would construct during the colonial and postcolonial periods. Certainly the emphasis on the importance of the law that is such a marked feature of contemporary Urapmin culture emerges from this historical investigation as an Urapmin transformation of something on which the colonial officers laid great emphasis .

On March 3, 1949, Patrol Officer J. R. Rogers and nine native police officers set off on what was likely the first government patrol to the Urapmin area (2 of 48/49).[5] This may well have been only the second overnight patrol out of Telefomin, and one of Rogers's objectives was to train the police detachment in patrol procedures, "the great majority of" them having "had little experience in patrolling" (2). The other goals of the patrol were to put an end to the tribal fighting that was rumored to be occurring between the Urapmin and their traditional Tifalmin enemies to the west and to get some idea of the population of the groups living near the government station (2). The inexperience of the police contingent in this newly opened area should strike one as odd; in general, one would imagine that experienced hands were needed in areas where people were unused to being visited by patrols. This point is worth noting because, as we shall see, during the early years of the station, the Telefomin area was constantly plagued by the mistakes made by the inexperienced staff sent there.

The patrol initially received somewhat of a "cold" reception from the Urapmin, but "the atmosphere became more cordial after the writer had set the broken arm of a young man who had fallen from a tree, that morning" (9). Apparently, the Urapmin had ambushed some of their Tifalmin enemies on March 2, killing thirteen and losing only four. News of this fighting was what had brought Rogers to Urapmin, and as he reports it he was able in fairly short order to enlist the Urapmin in his plans for peacemaking: "The Urapmins [sic] agreed, rather reluctantly, (after first endeavouring to persuade the writer to join forces with them and wipe out the Tifalmins [sic]) to make peace if the Tifalmins were willing to do so. The three most influential men from the Urapmin area then accompanied the patrol as interpreters, guides and peacemakers" (9). Having enlisted the support of the Urapmin, the patrol set out the next day for Tifalmin.

Although the Tifal initially moved to attack the patrol and keep it off their land, Rogers was patient and was eventually allowed to make contact with a Tifal leader and present him with a hatchet and a bush knife. The Tifalmin explained to Rogers that their reason for attacking the patrol was that the first two whites to enter their area, John Black of the Hagen-Sepik Patrol and a "Masta Bob" from the crew that constructed the airstrip, had stolen garden food and a pig from them. Rogers immediately gave compensation to the owner of the pig and distributed salt as a compensation for the food taken from the gardens. This was a canny move on Rogers's part, perhaps more appropriate than even he realized, for among the Min people there is no statute of limitations on making compensation or returning debts. People are quite satisfied to be compensated even well after they have been wronged (see Akin 1999). In this case, Rogers was quickly rewarded for his appropriate behavior, at least as his report tells it. He distributed the compensation and, seemingly immediately, "[p]eace was . . . made between the Tifalmins and the Urapmins." Rogers finished up his visit by "explaining the functions and purposes of the Administration to the influential men" and telling them "that fighting and cannibalism must cease" (10).

As Rogers recounts it in his report, peacemaking comes across as a fairly simple process. The Urapmin remember that they performed with the Tifalmin an "equivalent exchange ceremony" *(tisol dalamin)* of the type discussed in the prologue. Although this form of dispute settlement was traditional among them, they had never before undertaken them with their traditional enemies, with whom there previously had been no way to end wars short of trading homicides until they were balanced. The use of exchange as a form of peacemaking in this case may have been Rogers's idea, for there is evidence that he knew about such techniques for settling disputes, having witnessed them used within a single group in Telefomin (6). Whether or not Rogers himself suggested the exchange, however, it seems to have had the desired effect. As far as I can discern, there was no further fighting between the Tifalmin and the Urapmin after this patrol.[6]

This first patrol of the colonial era established two things for the Urapmin. First, the government was willing to continue to engage in the kinds of exchange relationships that had made the contact period run smoothly. The payment of compensation to the Tifalmin was especially promising in this regard. Second, the government was also going to

demand that the Urapmin change some of their behaviors to an extent
that the early white visitors to the region had not. Fighting wars *(sep
wasi)* with the Tifalmin and the cannibalism that was part of that institution were not contingent practices that the Urapmin undertook only
because the Tifalmin sometimes offended or aggressed against them.
Rather they were practices chartered by sacred myths in which they
were laid down by the creator heroine Afek. Urapmin today are for the
most part glad to be done with war, and they do not complain about the
colonial government's program to stop it. But it remains true that in attacking war, the government from the outset made it clear to the Urapmin that they were interested in setting up and enforcing new behavioral
rules that impinged on important aspects of local life.

On Rogers's next patrol to Urapmin, in early April 1949, he found
them "most friendly and eager to be as co-Operative *[sic]* as possible" (3
of 48/49, p. 5). He came again in June 1949 and took two Urapmin men
back to the station at Telefomin to train as interpreters for the government. These two men, Kweksep and Ambukisep, would become key
players in the Urapmin colonial experience. Well liked by the administration, they played an important role in conveying the law to the Urapmin and in encouraging the Urapmin to work with the government (4 of
48/49, p. 6). Ambukisep was especially well placed to be influential in the
community, for he was the son of Tabasongim, a leading big man and the
man the administration considered the "headman" of the Urapmin (p. 6;
see also 1 of 49/50, p. 7, on Tabsorgim [Tabasongim] as the Urapmin
"headman"). The stories of these two men, and of Ambukisep in particular, run like a leitmotiv through both the patrol reports and the Urapmin oral histories. We will encounter them again later in this chapter.

The next patrol to reach Urapmin was led by Cliffton-Bassett, the acting district officer. This was in October 1949, little more than seven
months after the Urapmin had met their first government patrol. In his
notes on Native Affairs, Cliffton-Basset confirms that the Urapmin have
indeed been pacified: "The Urapmin people have no timidity now and
provided that contact is maintained there should be no more fighting between them and the Tifalmin people" (1 of 49/50, p. 12). The confidence
that the administration now had that the Urapmin had been "consoli-
dated" and were well under control is borne out by the fact that having
visited them four times during these first eight months of colonization,
it would not mount another patrol to Urapmin for ten months after
Cliffton-Bassett's visit of October 1949.

FROM SALT TO THE LAW:
CHANGING CONSTRUCTIONS OF COLONIAL TRADE

As Aragon (1996) and Thomas (1991) have demonstrated, the colonial process is in part carried along by a succession of changing exchange regimes. By the time the administration visited the Urapmin again, in September 1950, the patrol report suggests, it was ready to introduce the Urapmin to some new terms of trade. From this point onward, the patrol officers' rhetoric moves very quickly from one focused on working to make the Urapmin comfortable with the colonial presence and ensuring peace to one that emphasized the considerable obligations the Urapmin would incur as their part of the colonial bargain. The exchange of salt, matches, and bush knives for native foods, so useful in securing Urapmin cooperation and (limited) trust during the contact period and at the beginning of the colonial era, needed, at least as several patrol officers saw it, to give way to a much more demanding exchange in which the administration would give the law, but only in return for Urapmin compliance with the full range of its behavioral dictates. Here is H. W. West, who led the September 1950 patrol:

> The inhabitants of the above areas [Urapmin and Tifalmin] are now accustomed to government patrols and know that, should their rights be transgressed, they may seek redress at the Administration centre. Perhaps the main function of the patrol was to emphasise to the people that in return for the security, freedom from fear and other direct benefits, such as the introduction of steel, seeds and medical attention, which flow from the Administration they have to face certain obligations, mainly to themselves as organised communities, and that they would from now on/be [sic] expected to undertake certain elementary developmental work such as cleaning villages and constructing patrol roads through their tribal lands. The population is of a sufficient density to enable good patrol roads to be constructed and maintained without hardship to the people. (2 of 50/51, p. 11)

The language of "return," "flow," and "obligation" that West uses here places his discussion firmly within the field of exchange. White-native interaction has not ceased to be organized around the model of reciprocity, but the nature of the goods given has changed dramatically. In this way, the theme of the law was smuggled into Urapmin inside the Trojan horse of a form of sociality with which they were extremely comfortable.

West and other patrol officers were not the only ones to conceive of the imposition of the law as a process of gift giving. Indeed, this idea was widespread throughout the colonial community. No less a figure than

Paul Hasluck, the Australian cabinet minister responsible for Papua
New Guinea from 1951 to 1963, was given to using it with some regularity. In 1955, he wrote that the colonial legal system and its model of
justice was "in historical fact, a gift that we have brought them" (cited
in Hasluck 1976: 189). A similar rhetorical framing appears in an address Hasluck made before the House of Representatives: having mentioned that thousands of Australians died in Papua New Guinea during
the two world wars, he goes on to note that "over a period of more than
70 years we have given not only laws, not only money, not only good
government, but the blood of our children to nourish its [Papua New
Guinea's] future" (Hasluck 1960: 4). Here the law appears as the first
and as such perhaps the most obvious of the Australian gifts. The patrol officers who visited the Urapmin thus carried with them a well-
established model of the law as a gift to be given.

During the early period of Min colonization in which West was writing, the "law" the patrol officers aimed to give was largely concerned
with establishing new standards of village cleanliness, the upkeep of
roads, and the building of rest houses for patrols. Given that no such
public works had been on the agenda in precolonial Urapmin, however,
West was asking for significantly new investments of labor in calling on
people to perform these tasks.

But these laws applying to the physical upkeep of "organised communities" are not the only ones West wanted to see enforced in Urapmin. He also thought at this early point that the Urapmin and other
groups visited on this patrol were ready to comply with the laws concerning individual behavior enshrined in the Native Affairs Regulations
(NAR), the legal code applied to indigenes in the colony. Because it so
clearly echoes in contemporary Urapmin concerns with the law and with
issues of individual responsibility, I cite at length from West's discussion
of these issues.

> I consider that the territory discussed above [which includes Urapmin,
> Feramin, Eliptaman Telefomin, and Tifalmin], with the possible exception
> of Tifalmin, should now be regarded as under government control and I in-
> tend to enforce certain provisions of the N.A.R. from now on, especially in
> relation to acts or omissions which are both offences under the N.A.R. and
> repugnant to native social and moral codes. Stealing is common, even wide-
> spread, for such small communities. It has been necessary, too, in all vil-
> lages to warn fathers against the practice of shooting an arrow into the
> thigh of a daughter who refuses to marry a man of the father's choice.[7]
> Two or three cases have been reported where death/has [sic] resulted from

such wounds, usually some time afterwards when portions of the arrow-head, which remain in the wound when the arrow is removed, rot and cause poisoning.

Another section of the N.A.R. which will be applied following warnings given in all villages is that relating to the spreading of false reports. There can be no doubt that such reports, usually relating to some action the Administration is said to be planning, are designed to cause fear and discontent, usually amongst people against whom the instigator, or instigators, of the rumour bear a grudge. Nevertheless, the source of such rumours is frequently difficult to isolate and as the natives gain confidence in the Administration the damage false reports can do will diminish correspondingly.

The notion of individual responsibility for crime is not clearly comprehended by these people who are accustomed to support from the group to which they belong when exercising their rights and to being held jointly responsible for the transgressive acts of any one of their group. Thus, on several occasions, where a native from one village has committed a crime, such as stealing a pig from another village, and it is thought that the matter has been reported to the Administration officer, the whole community has fled and remained away from the village for several weeks. Every opportunity has been seized upon to explain that the Administration imputes all blame to the actual culprit and that under no circumstances will property be confiscated or hostages seized by way of retaliation. In any case our conception of individual responsibility is gradually being accepted and appreciated by the people in the vicinity of the Government station but the problem of recalcitrants absconding to such distant places as FEGOLMIN will place an obstacle in the way of justice for some time to come. (11–12)

West's report demonstrates obvious intelligence and shows that he has put some thought into the plans for the law enforcement program he proposes. But his concluding paragraph, where he takes up the issue of people's lack of understanding of individual responsibility, intimates that his hopes may be a bit premature. Further, the mistake he makes of listing as similar matters both stealing, something the Urapmin themselves condemned precolonially, and shooting an unhappy bride in the leg, which was a fully accepted custom, suggest that he may not have been fully aware of the obstacles he and others would face in implementing his plans. But the main question that arises when we read this report with the benefit of hindsight, recognizing how early in the colonial process West is making this attempt, is why he felt this was the right time to begin enforcing the colonial law.

The existing data make it impossible to give a full answer to this question, but we have several important clues toward a partial answer. Having little familiarity with the rhythm of change in longer colonized areas

that they could have used as a comparative touchstone in their evaluation
of the Telefomin situation, the young and inexperienced patrol officers
who served in Telefomin may simply have been eager to move the colonial process along in an area that, now pacified, seemed to present no major obstacles. There is also a possibility that they simply parroted during
their patrols and in their reports rhetoric about law enforcement that
they had learned as part of their training. In making issuing and enforcing the law the focus of their efforts, the patrol officers certainly were
bringing their work in line with the main thrust of the Australian colonial
effort during this period. Australian colonialism of post–World War II
vintage was most comfortable with itself when it made giving and policing the law its goal. Rowley (1965: 67) gives the matter the blunt phrasing it demands: "In the British tradition, the first emphasis has always
been on law and order, and the suppression of practices 'repugnant to
(our) humanity.'" Along with these factors, West was obviously motivated in part by the problems caused by the spread of false reports,
many of them concerning the government (see note 6). Yet this problem
was clearly subordinated in West's report to a concern with imposing the
law in general. The nuisance such rumors had been causing seems not to
be a primary cause of his determination to launch the larger project.

Picking up on the idiom of exchange that West relied on in the first
passage quoted above, the one he used in writing "in return for the security . . . and other benefits . . . which flow from the Administration
they have to face certain obligations," I want to suggest another reason
that the law suddenly appears out of nowhere to loom so large in West's
report. Recall the happy coincidence that characterized the contact period: both the whites and the Urapmin assumed that the exchange of
goods was an appropriate way to forge relations during first contact.
The exchange of goods also played a major role in the first patrol's approach to the war-ready Tifalmin. Obviously, exchange was crucial to
the formation of relationships throughout the contact and early colonial
periods. Yet in the same report we have been examining, West notes that
the developing intercultural exchange was in danger of breaking down:

> [S]ome economic incentive must be offered if these people are to develop.
> Once a knife and a tomahawk have been obtained the Telefomin Adminis-
> trative Centre has little to offer that the adventurous youth cannot obtain
> or experience in his own tribal community.
>   It seems that the next step in the development of the area should be to
> send labourers to the coast so that *new wants may be developed,* experi-

ence gained, horizons widened and new ideas imparted on their return home. (12; my emphasis)

It is hard not to detect here an unease on West's part that the small goods trade that has up until now kept the colonial wheels greased was starting to lose its appeal. From the Urapmin point of view, one can imagine a growing recognition that all of this trade was not building up the sorts of moral relations between them and the whites that they had hoped exchange would create. Instead, the whites were attempting more to control them than to become their allies (cf. Burridge 1960; Lawrence [1964] 1971). Once the Urapmin realized this, they would have been less excited about the trade.[8] But from the patrol officers' point of view, this lack of excitement would appear not as a comment on the failure of a developing relationship but as a failure of desire, as willingness on the Papua New Guineans' part to back out of the colonial project altogether when what seemed to be their limited needs for Western goods had been met.

That something like this scenario of an exchange system in collapse shaped West's decision to put the law at the center of the colonial exchange is confirmed in a report that L. T. Nolen submitted on a patrol he made in March 1952 to the same areas covered by West's patrol. In a section titled "Future Policy," where he cites West's report, Nolen writes:[9]

> The Natives of the four groups visited [Feramin, Urapmin, Eliptaman, and Telefolmin] have now reached a stage in their economic development when the knife and tomahawk are no longer an incentive to work either on the station or in their gardens to produce extra food for sale to the Administration or mission. . . . The government has, in the eyes of the natives, brought them nothing except knives, tomahawks and few other lesser trade goods. They now have enough of these and therefore the government has exhausted its usefulness. . . . The purchase of food and building materials by trade goods is no longer economical among the inner groups. As an example of this, a large pig could be bought for a small knife when the station was first established, [now] a large bush knife and a superior quality tomahawk will sometimes buy a small pig after a lot of bartering. There is no shortage of pigs in the area. (2 of 51/52, p. 6)

Nolen's solution to this problem of spent desire and the hardships under which it places the colonial relationship is to suggest, with West, that people be sent to work in a "more sophisticated area" where they "would develop new wants" (6). He also proposes to introduce money into the area and to open a trade-store to keep it circulating.

But along with the specific solutions that Nolen proposes, it is crucial to notice that he also follows West in asserting that the time has come "[w]hen the Law [sic] can, and should, be enforced without overdue consideration to their relatively short period of contact" (5). Furthermore, Nolen's interpretation on the next page of an attack on the government station that some people in the region were rumored to have been planning indicates that he, like West, held to the model of colonialism as a kind of trade. Apropos those implicated in the rumor, he writes, "[T]hese people had reached a stage in their development where, having seen what the Government had to offer and the price they were to pay for it, they were undecided whether to accept or refuse" (6). Even more than West's, Nolen's report is haunted by images of trade refused—both for small goods and for the whole colonial package.

West and Nolen relied in their work on a model of the colonial process in which an exchange of the law for compliance to it would come to substitute for one in which the government gave trade goods for returns of food and friendship. The patrol officer's promotion of moral exchange need not in all cases have been cynical either, for many patrol officers saw the laws they promulgated as ultimately protecting the natives' interests by ensuring their health and security (Fitzpatrick 1980: 78), while at the same time the native gift of obedience to the laws allowed the officers successfully to carry out their job of managing the district's affairs. Hence, the eventual replacement of material by moral exchange was for them the ideal trajectory that colonial relations ought to follow (see Aragon 1996 for a comparable account). Faced with the "inner" Telefolmin group's (those nearest the station) rapidly slackening interest in the material goods on offer, West and Nolen figured they should probably move quickly to impress on the Urapmin the new terms of moral traffic.

Nolen in particular comes across as determined to communicate to people that they must obey the law. In his report, he mentions that "the natives have been told that if they fail to come up for census in the future they will charged [sic] under the section of the N.A.R.'s" (2 of 51/51, p. 8). In an area where many were still apprehensive about coming face to face with whites (and where they had good reason to fear coming into contact with patrols; see below) and where, as Nolen (8) recognized, people often live at garden sites scattered around the bush, this was a strong demand that would prove onerous for the people to meet. If nothing else, the hard line he took on this matter shows that Nolen was not shy about laying down the law.

We can understand why such an emphasis on the law might be premature at this point, and at the same time begin to get a sense of what the Urapmin mean when they talk about the law today, by looking at the content of the code that West and Nolen insisted the Urapmin should follow. From the first, of course, the officers stationed at Telefomin had sought to suppress "repugnant" practices: warfare and homicide, cannibalism, platform burial in trees. But the law of the Native Affairs Regulations, the law West and Nolen suggested they were ready to enforce, was far more elaborate and intrusive than those first prohibitions. Aimed at regulating everything from agriculture to hygiene, labor to medical treatment, the regulations were the thin wedge of administration efforts to colonize everyday life (Comaroff and Comaroff 1991). Mair writes about the first Native Regulations of British New Guinea, which the later Australian regulations resembled, in a way designed to indicate the near-absurdity of their presumptive reach:

> The First Native Regulations of British New Guinea . . . soon came to be regarded as the means of effecting such changes in village life as were considered desirable. Should improvements in village sanitation or an extension of cultivation be sought, a regulation was introduced imposing the requisite obligation on every native. Hence the patrol officer had the right to dictate on a wide range of subjects. Natives could be penalized for burying the dead in villages or under houses. A village could be ordered to move from an unhealthy locality. Grass had to be cleared round the villages to a distance of fifty yards from the nearest house. The owner of a house could be ordered to repair or rebuild it or, if it was overcrowded, to increase its size or build an additional one. The destruction of abandoned houses, or houses incapable of repair, could be ordered. . . . A village might be ordered to dig wells, and the village constable was responsible for protecting springs and wells from contamination. He also organized the maintenance of roads and bridges on village land. There was a penalty for failure to use latrines where they existed. Orders might be given for water to be removed from canoes or other possible breeding grounds for mosquitoes, or for diseased dogs or pigs to be killed. Inoculation against infectious diseases might be made compulsory by Order in Council. Village constables could order parents to bring a child for medical examination. Natives could be ordered to submit to examination for venereal diseases, and penalized for failure to notify them or for having sexual relations while suffering from such a disease. (1970: 67)

Mair continues with this list in a second, even more outrageous paragraph covering laws pertaining to gardening, schooling, divorce, and dress.

My point is not that West and Nolen presented all of these laws to the Urapmin during their first lectures on the law, or that they sought at this point strongly to enforce the bulk of them—though some of these laws and many others besides were no doubt announced to the Urapmin at one time or another, and some were enforced. What is important is the very broad sweep of these laws, the innumerable aspects of daily life they sought to regulate. The general message of the patrol officers' imposition of laws such as these was that the law itself was important, that the new order would be one obsessively focused on the need for lawful behavior. For the Urapmin of the early 1950s, many of these laws could not have made much sense. Unaware of the rationales that underlay specific laws, such as those that made them line for the census or those that made them dig latrines, the Urapmin came to understand obedience to the law as an abstract good. Because of this lesson, even today the Urapmin are prone to treat Western-derived rules as simple, brute rules, not putting them in a hierarchy of more and less important ones: obedience itself is what is important, regardless of the content of the law.

Under these new terms of trade, the patrol officer became a lawgiver and law enforcer. While the officer himself may have imagined that he was engaged in a variety of activities, some of them extralegal, such as censusing and encouraging village hygiene, the Urapmin were likely to construe all of his actions under the sign of the law. To refer again to Rowley (1965: 79), it was difficult "for villagers to distinguish between his [the patrol officer's] judicial actions and those taken under his police or general administrative powers." The patrol officer himself thus came to stand for the law, and to model a kind of leadership that used legal-moral rhetoric as one primary tool of its authority.

Given how important the law would become to the Urapmin, we might, despite reasonable doubts about West's and Nolen's decision to introduce these ideas so early in the process of consolidation, want to credit them with making a move that was at least pragmatically effective. Without the benefit of hindsight, their superiors did not see the matter this way. Neither A. T. Timperley, acting district commissioner of the Sepik District, nor his superiors in Port Moresby were happy with the hard-line approach Nolen was taking toward promulgating the law. Timperley, in a covering memo he sent along with Nolen's report to J. H. Jones, director of the Department of District Services and Native Affairs, drew the latter's attention to Nolen's handling of the issue of mandatory attendance at the census. This was an area in which Nolen had announced to the people that he would immediately begin enforcing the law. Timperley wrote: "TELEFOMIN *[sic]* is a new area and the O.I.C. [Officer-in-Charge; i.e., Nolen] has been instructed to exercise patience in dealing with the people. TELEFOMIN has been gazetted a penal district but this does not require the prison to be filled to capacity" (stored with 2 of 1951/52, n.p.). The sarcasm of Timperley's final sentence conveys the critical tenor of his comments. Jones's reply was stronger still, perhaps even outraged. I quote from his letter at some length:

> We are in complete agreement with the opinions expressed in your covering memorandum. Please bring to the attention of Mr. Nolen that this Headquarters does not share his apparent view that a stage has been reached when the law can be enforced without proper consideration to the relatively short period of contact. Four years is definitely not enough, particularly when the quality and the experience of the staff available does not compare with that used to open up other similar areas, and it should take at least 10 years to reach the stage that Mr. Nolon *[sic]* has in mind. Law and order must be maintained but there should be no over-emphasis on the penal code; common-sense is required. The greatest care is to be taken to ensure that the people do not come to regard the Administration purely as a "policeman" and that the Government is not interested in the future development of the natives *[sic]*. If after four years it is the general feeling of these people that they have already reached a dead end, it is clear that the speed with which they have been brought under control has been far too rapid and is the cause of any frustration which may exist. (Stored with 2 of 51/52, n.p.)

Strong words, these. Jones obviously had no sympathy with the legalistic line West and Nolen had been pushing. Indeed, he ended his letter, perhaps in follow-up to his disparaging comment on the inexperience of the staff that had been posted to Telefomin in these early years, with a bald rebuke of Nolen:

> It is noted that Mr. Nolen was appointed a Cadet Patrol Officer in the latter half of 1949 and that he has served in Rabaul and Kokopo only and then proceeded on leave before being posted to Wewak. It would therefore appear that Mr. Nolen has as much to learn about his work as the natives of Telefomin have to learn about Administration.

So the administrative higher-ups would have liked a less precipitous focus on the law. They would have liked a gentler process of moral colonization. But Mr. Jones's call to rein in the legalistic emphasis West and Nolen had been promulgating came too late to significantly change the course of colonization in the area. And it came too late precisely because of Nolen's "inexperience," if that in the end is what we want to call it. For Nolen's highly questionable activities as the officer-in-charge would soon issue in a complete collapse of the colonial effort at Telefomin. And this collapse would invite a government response that left no doubt about the seriousness of its intentions when it came to enforcing the law. Indeed, the government force shown in dealing with the consequences of Nolen's tenure in office would concretize and permanently fix for the Urapmin the legalistic essence of the colonial modernity that Nolen himself, along with West, had been presenting.

"BIG ARMED PATROL ON WAY": VIOLENCE AND LAW IN THE EARLY COLONIAL PERIOD

To this point, this discussion has largely confirmed the received wisdom that colonialism in the Highlands of Papua New Guinea was a relatively gentle affair. To be sure, the Urapmin were often afraid of the whites who visited them, unsure of their nature or their intent, and the colonial officers for their part were busy waging a battle of considerable symbolic violence in an effort to reconstruct the grounds of Min sociality. But physical violence, terror, and abuse have not entered our story as yet. They do not feature in the patrol reports at all, and other parts of the archive that might have mentioned them are lost (see below). From the Urapmin side too this theme is muted. Urapmin are always reluctant to reopen old conflicts that have been settled by expressing any lingering anger over them. It is not only poor form to do so, but it is physically dangerous, since anger is a cause of illness. Thus the oral historical archive is also relatively quiet on these topics. But listened to carefully, it provides some hints that all was not as gentle as it seems in the early colonial period. Taking these hints and following them up through some published work on other parts of the region allows us to significantly complicate the picture of colonial beginnings I have painted thus far in ways that help to explain further why the Urapmin saw the law as the most important part of the colonial package.

Both Craig (1990: 145) and Morren (1981: 43) argue that with the founding of the District Office at Telefomin the relationship between the Min people and whites immediately began to deteriorate from its contact period high. Urapmin stories about the early colonial period support the impression left by Craig's (1990) account: the early colonial period was one marked by regular, violent abuse of authority on the part of both the native police and the patrol officers.

The "inexperienced" patrol officer Nolen, in particular, appears to have badly abused his authority. Simpson (1953: 221), a travel writer who visited Telefomin while Nolen was the officer-in-charge, describes Nolen thus: "Laurie Nolen was twenty-six, good looking and well-built; the beard and the long hair in lieu of a hat suited him. In the Australian Navy during the war he had seen New Guinea, liked its promise of a less fettered life, applied for District Services and, when he was accepted, done his training course." Simpson goes on to describe the three servants Nolen had in Telefomin, perfect complements to a life that was not only less "fettered," but perhaps almost comfortable. What Simpson leaves out of his account was the Eliptaman woman Nolen had taken as his live-in mistress (Craig 1990: 120, 128 n.8). When the woman's husband came to the station to get his wife back, Sergeant Tokoruru, perhaps the most senior police officer on the station, "rejected his demands" and beat him "on the head with a stick, causing blood to flow over his face" (Craig 1990: 128). Tokoruru would have had good reason to demonstrate the harsh treatment that would meet men coming to the station to collect their wives or sisters, for it is clear that many of his own police regularly had sexual relations with local women (Craig 1990: 146–47).

Although Urapmin contact with patrol officers and police was less frequent than that of the Telefolmin who lived near the station, they too were subject to the high-handed sexual exploitation of the police and the brutality that followed in its wake. By late 1953, the police had had sexual relations with at least six women in Urapmin. The Urapmin, who fret constantly over their small population and are strictly endogamous, worried that the police would take the women with them. In the end, the police left the women, but they jailed three men, relatives of some of the women, who had protested the abuses.

The sexual exploitation and summary imprisonments were not the only causes the Urapmin had for complaint about the patrols. The Urapmin also tell of how the patrols burned bush houses, stole food and pigs, and beat people. Furthermore, the patrol officers and police were verbally abusive, telling the Urapmin that they were pigs and dogs, or that they were the children of cassowaries and wild pigs (see also Craig 1990: 129). Urapmin take "bad talk" (weng mafak) extremely seriously and assume that it causes sickness. They thus complain bitterly even today about the humiliating diatribes of the patrol officers and the police. That all of these practices, from sexual exploitation to verbal abuse, were commonplace on patrols, especially during Nolen's tenure as officer-in-charge, is confirmed in Craig's (1990) work on the situation at the station and on the administration's patrols to Eliptaman and Mianmin.

What all of this means is that the Urapmin received the patrol officers' messages about the importance of the law in conditions of considerable terror.[10] Although, as noted, the Urapmin hold it to be dangerous to dwell on bad situations and negative feelings of the past, and despite the fact that Urapmin people today routinely praise white behavior for its lawfulness, they readily admit that these early years of the colonial period were "a hard time."[11] At the same time that the administration's actions angered the Urapmin, however, the terror they inspired also motivated the Urapmin to find a way to comply with demands that they follow the law. The importance of colonial violence in driving home the need for lawfulness is particularly marked in Urapmin recountings of the two most violent episodes they witnessed during the colonial period.

During Nolen's tenure, two Urapmin men, along with three from the Eliptaman group of Telefolmin, were drowned when a raft they were riding while on patrol with Nolen overturned in May 1953 (3 of 52/53). Having long since been compensated for the deaths, the Urapmin do not at present speak of this event with rancor. But they report that at the time it greatly angered the Eliptaman, who had already been severely provoked by Nolen's theft of one of their women and the beatings his police administered to those who tried to take her back.

On November 6, 1953, the Eliptaman, acting in response to these abuses, killed two European patrol officers, one of whom was Nolen's replacement, and two native constables. The attack was premeditated and amounted to a violent rebellion against the colonial order then in place.

Champion (1966: 219) notes that "the Administration was stunned" by the rebellion. There had never been an organized attack against the government on this scale "in the history of either Papua or New Guinea." Not surprisingly, the administration response was quick and very intensive in its efforts to find those who had carried it out. As Jorgensen (1996: 194) reports, "Planeloads of police landed at the airstrip and combed the surrounding countryside" searching for those who participated in the rebellion. Under the headline "Big Armed Patrol on Way to Check on Massacre," the *Sydney Morning Herald* of November 12, 1953, reported that an "armed Government patrol of 123 men has entered the Telefomin Ranges" to investigate. These investigative patrols cast a wide net, seemingly bringing into Telefomin anyone the officers imagined could have been involved in the rebellion. By the middle of April 1954, "184 male natives as well as numerous women and children had been contacted and brought to the station" from the villages involved in just one of the attacks (special report, Telefomin, July 5, 1954, p. 2). In a statement that suggests how many people the government was willing to implicate in its investigation (ironically contradicting West's lessons on individual responsibility!), the district commissioner, Mr. El- liot-Smith, notes that on July 10 "most of" the men of the Elip Valley "are now in Wewak on trial or as crown Witnesses" (Telefomin Patrol Report, Special, June 1954, n.p.). The show of government force—un- precedented in terms of the numbers of agents involved, the obvious ex- tent to which those agents' goals put them in a relation of antagonism toward local people, and the agents' ability to remove huge numbers of locals to the unimaginably distant coastal town of Wewak—left a deep impression on all the people of the region.

While the Urapmin were not directly involved in the killings, they harbored an innocent young Eliptaman man who had turned up for the census at his home village in time to watch his relatives attack a police- man sent ahead to ready the people of the area. Terrified of the possible repercussions of what he had witnessed, he fled to Urapmin. Whether or not the Urapmin were afraid of possible government punishment for harboring this refugee from the scene (who had Urapmin relatives and later married a Urapmin woman), they certainly saw the manhunt and court case that ensued as proof of the seriousness with which the ad- ministration was ready to enforce the law that West and Nolen had been presenting to them.

Indeed, the Urapmin account of what transpired in Wewak shows that at that time they subscribed to a particularly harsh view of the law's op- eration. The Urapmin hold to this day that all of the Eliptaman men charged in the case were made to stand in a huge pit. All around the top of the pit stood police armed with guns ready to slaughter the guilty. Only the last-minute intervention by the British queen saved the Eliptaman from dying in a bloodbath. The swift and overwhelming force the Aus- tralian government sent to enforce the law in the wake of the rebellion, a force chillingly symbolized by the image of the armed soldiers surround- ing the pit, highlighted the law's importance and reinforced the Urapmin conviction that obedience to it was the colonists' primary concern.

As resounding a message about the law as the administration's post- rebellion crackdown sent to the Urapmin, it was not the last dramatic one they would receive. For many Urapmin had one more opportunity to witness at first hand the violence to which the administration was willing to resort in the enforcement of its law.

This opportunity came on an administration patrol to the Tifalmin area on which many Urapmin acted as carriers. The Tifalmin, to whom patrols must have looked liked invasions by their Telefolmin and Urapmin enemies, had never been comfortable with them and often confronted them aggressively. During one such confrontation in March 1956, the patrol responded by killing a Tifalmin leader. Like most of the materials pertaining to the rebellion, the report for this patrol is missing from the National Archives of Papua New Guinea. The only official notice of what transpired on that patrol that I was able to find comes from a later patrol report that mentions that "[i]n March, 1956 an attack by Tifalmins on a patrol resulted in one of their party being killed" (7 of 1955/56, p. 5). However, some Urapmin who were on that patrol are still alive, and its story is widely known in the community.

The patrol had been warned by a leader of the lower Tifalmin group not to proceed to Bafumin in upper Tifalmin, for an attack had been planned. When the patrol proceeded anyway, it was met by a line of Bafumin armed with bows and arrows. As the Bafumin began shooting, the members of the patrol hid behind the metal patrol boxes that held their cargo. Then one of the carriers, a Feramin man, was hit in the arm by a Tifal arrow. He screamed out, "Government, they have shot me." In response, the patrol leader told the police to shoot over the heads of the amassed Tifal and to kill one of them to "give them a mark" and scare them off.

The police carried out these orders. One of the Tifal big men, Sumal, had brought a large number of arrows with him. Before he had begun firing he put some down on the ground (hunters usually hold a few arrows pressed to the front of the bow, but Sumal must have had too many arrows with him to do this comfortably). As he reached down for them, the bullet hit him. Apparently, he had glared at the police (lukluk strong) and they in turn had aimed for him. Once Sumal had been hit, the Tifal scattered and the patrol officer and a policeman went to examine him. He was dead. The bullet had "cooked [him] like soup, and [he] had turned yellow." The patrol officer brought an old man from Bafumin to identify the body, but he was unsure who it was. Then they brought an old woman, who was shaking with fear and wetting herself, and she told them they had killed Sumal, a big man. That was when "the kiaps [knew] they [had] killed a leader." That the government killed a big man would have been particularly significant for the Min people witnessing the scene, for in the warfare traditions of the region killing an enemy leader leaves his people immediately disorganized and demoralized.

As the Urapmin tell it, this is a story about the administration's resolve to enforce its law, which required communities to welcome patrols that came to visit them, and about the power it put in service of this resolve. It is also a story about the fear in which it is appropriate to hold that power. Sumal's body, yellow and cooked like soup, even today stands as an index of local perceptions of the fearfulness of that power.[12] Reinforcing the message of the government's response to the rebellion, its murder of Sumal further inclined the Urapmin to attend carefully to the laws it promulgated.

As notable as these stories of government violence are, they are not the only stories the Urapmin tell about how they came to appreciate the importance of the law during this early part of the colonial era. Many Urapmin also insist that they quickly recognized that the law was legitimate on its own terms, not just an arbitrary code that happened to be backed by the government's overwhelming force. One basis on which the Urapmin recognized the law's legitimacy was their traditional concern with taboos and standards of good behavior. Although there are distinct differences between traditional Urapmin moral codes and the law of colonizers, differences I discuss in detail in a later chapter, the Urapmin were accustomed to relating to powers outside their control (i.e., spirits) by following an elaborate set of behavioral rules. Furthermore, Urapmin culture had always put some emphasis on self-regulation and the need to abide by the community's moral codes. Thus the government's general concern with these matters struck them as familiar on some level (cf. Comaroff and Comaroff 1991: 247; Murphree 1969: 161–62). Another, equally important basis of the law's legitimacy was the consistency with which the Urapmin believed the government applied it. The administration played no favorites in its application of the law to different Min groups, and even, the Urapmin note, to itself. This is one of the primary lessons they took from their understanding of the outcome of the trial that followed the rebellion.

To see how the Urapmin arrived at this conclusion, we can return to their account of the trial. In the Urapmin telling it was the queen who called off the execution of the prisoners. The queen holds a strong fascination for the Urapmin, as well as for many other Melanesians, because the colonial forces represented her as their ultimate leader. This is undoubtedly why she appears in this story, despite the fact that we know from historical records that she did not attend.

In the story of the trial, the queen is represented as a figure who supported the Min people. She did so, the Urapmin claim, because she understood the colonial law that was brought by the early patrols. In the case of the rebellion, she realized that that law was on the side of the Min people.

Imagining what the Eliptaman defendants said in their defense during the trial that followed the rebellion, the Urapmin say they argued that "we are happy to learn white ways" but not to suffer the patrols to lose carriers to drowning, kill pigs, steal food, abuse us physically and verbally and take local women. The dialogue that then transpired between the queen and the defendants, the dialogue that led the queen to spare their lives, focuses on the role of the law in the colonial process. Here we return to the scene in which, in the Urapmin telling, the defendants are gathered in a pit, surrounded by police ready to fire down on them:

> Then the Queen came to hear court, with the police ready to fire. . . . The Queen came and asked[,] "What trouble did the kiaps [government officers] make at your place?" "They taught us the law and started a school but they also killed local men who went on patrol with them, threw them in the water, and they took our young women or wives and committed adultery with them. They took our pigs and showed all kinds of bad behavior to us. That is why we killed them."
>
> Then the Queen said, "They should not have done that, it is their own fault [that they were killed]. You [speaking to the kiaps now] should only give the law."
>
> Then the Queen stopped the police from firing.

This story of the queen's intervention on behalf of the defendants reiterated the message that the law was the most important gift conferred by colonialism at a time when it might have been lost in the noisy lawlessness of the early government officers and the violent Eliptaman response to it. In the story, the queen flatly states that the law is at the center of the colonial process. "You should only give the law," she tells the patrol officers. But the story also demonstrates that the law could sanction the administration, for the law spared the defendants because the kiaps themselves had violated what the colonial code demanded of them. The consistency with which the Urapmin believed that the queen applied the law was important in convincing them of its legitimacy.

As the Urapmin tell the story, the Eliptaman defendants explained to the queen that they were "happy to learn white ways." So too were the Urapmin. These ways are enshrined in the law, and in the aftermath of the violence that marked the early colonial period, and with the growing evidence the Urapmin believed they had of the law's legitimacy, the Urapmin were more convinced than ever that they would have to master these laws if they were to successfully adjust to the new world opening out before them. It is perhaps unsurprising that for the rest of the colonial period, patrol officers would regularly represent the Urapmin as a very well behaved group, quick to adopt the law and free from major crime.

BECOMING LEGAL SUBJECTS

In the period that followed the rebellion, the administration again took the establishment and enforcement of the law to be its primary task. Even as late as 1965, it was still the administration's primary concern. In April of that year, the assistant district commissioner (ADC) gave instructions to Patrol Officer Gill for his upcoming patrol to Urapmin. Since the census had been revised just six months before, the ADC who sent Gill out on patrol felt that there was no need to revise it again before the end of the year. This left Gill in the rather rare position of being able to carry out a patrol that was not oriented to the specific task of updating the census but rather took as its object "routine Administration." What this routine administration was to consist in was as follows: "[T]he opportunity should be taken to discuss with people the provisions of the Native Administration Regulations [sic] relating to law and order generally, disposal of corpses, and general sanitation of villages" (8 of 64/65, letter). Here again we find the administration's concern with law and order at the forefront: given any free time, reemphasize to the natives the importance of the law.

While the administration's focus on the law remained steady throughout the decade that followed the rebellion, the content of the law and the level at which the administration enforced it did undergo some changes; as the 1950s wore on, the administration both more rigorously enforced the law and increased the area of Urapmin life that was covered by it. By the late 1950s, patrol officers began regularly charging those who failed to attend the census or otherwise breached the law in the Court for Native Affairs. In the village book for Urapmin, used to record census information and short comments about what had happened on patrol, we learn from a cryptic note that three Urapmin men were brought to Telefomin in 1960 for "too enthusiastic arm waving." In 1962, three census absentees were each sentenced to one month imprisonment in Telefomin (6 of 61/62, p. 13). Reports from this period also suggest that the administration was starting to become more insistent that people obey hygiene laws and bury the dead. In general, officers seem to have begun demanding obedience not just to the letter of the law but also to its spirit. In a report from 1959, the assistant district officer conducted a patrol in which he first noted that "the Urapmin villages were as usual well cleaned up." But he also noticed that the area around the villages "is not all that could be desired," and this prompted him to issue "instructions . . . to clean the area behind the houses" (5 of 58/9, p. 6). As it stepped up enforcement, the administration seems, at moments like this, to have found the determination to demand not just that native life meet a surface standard of lawfulness but also that it actually be lawful in all of its hidden cracks and crevices.

A particularly important aspect of the administration's effort to infuse the law into all the dark corners of native life at this time was the opening up of the Court for Native Affairs to cases in which Urapmin brought charges against one another. If the whole panoply of laws the government wanted natives to follow was to take root in Urapmin, it would need the Urapmin to develop a legalistic attitude toward themselves and their social life even in the absence of a patrol. This attitude would make a peaceful, ordered social life a local goal and would look to the government as a "dispenser of justice" when individuals prevented the group's attainment of that goal through their unruly behavior. The shift in consciousness required here is a major one that can be partly glossed by describing it as a move from governance by coercion to government by hegemony. Not only would the Urapmin be expected to take over the government's laws as their own, but they would be expected to police themselves by reporting troubles to the Court for Native Affairs that patrol officers set up on their rounds.

Urapmin took to this new demand that they shape bits of local social life into the subject matter of court cases in short order, despite the fact that it represented a profound trick of social conceptualization for people not used to it (Tuzin 1997). The Urapmin embrace of litigation appears abruptly in the patrol reports. In his report from a patrol in April 1960, Assistant District Officer W. T. Brown writes: "In the Past twelve months the URAPMINS have been in the transition phase between 'sabre rattling' and litigation. They now appear to have plumped for litigation and the patrol was greeted with innumerable petty disputes and squabbles" (5 of 59/60, p. 3).

In the next report from the Urapmin-Tifalmin census division, from January 1961, R. A. Calcutt confirms Brown's guess that the Urapmin had chosen the way of the courts over that of the palmwood club. Writing about both the Tifalmin and the Urapmin, Calcutt notes, "The people seem to be becoming interested in settling disputes by litigation, rather than by more traditional methods. One case was heard in the Court for Native Affairs, and several more minor disputes were settled out of court" (4 of 60/61, p. 3). McCarthy, the director of the Department of Native Affairs who had earlier castigated Nolen for being too quick off the mark in his efforts to introduce the law, responded enthusiastically to this report, noting that "it is indeed a great credit to our officers [sic] work which has brought about this increase in confidence in the establishment of law and order." And he is right to see this report as marking a rubicon crossed, for with their acceptance of the Court for Native Affairs as an institution they could put to use in their own social life, the Urapmin had conclusively shown that they had become the kind of legal subjects that the administration wanted to make them.

McCarthy's excitement over the Urapmin embrace of the colonial legal system caps a period in which patrol officers regularly report that the Urapmin are noteworthy for their lawfulness. Throughout the era in which the administration moved to extend the reach of the law in the Telefomin District, the Urapmin emerge as one of their great success stories. The patrol reports also reveal that one of the causes of this success was the Urapmin ability to begin, even at this early date, to incorporate the law. Such incorporation, making the law at least in part a local institution in which the Urapmin had important roles to play, is evident in the way they treated the Court for Native Affairs, but it begins even before that court is introduced and extends beyond its introduction. Their incorporation of the law was crucial to moving the law to the center of Urapmin culture, and thus I examine it in some detail in the final section of this chapter.

INCORPORATING THE LAW

The first firm indication that the Urapmin had fully embraced the law comes in the form of an incident that occurred some years earlier than the introduction of local cases into the Court for Native Affairs. In August 1957, a visiting patrol officer explained to the Urapmin that it was their responsibility to turn in to the government one of their number who had recently escaped from the Telefomin jail. Shortly after receiving this lecture, the Urapmin located the escaped prisoner and returned him to the station at Telefomin (2 of 1957/58, p. 13). As the patrol report containing the information of this shockingly cooperative move on the part of the Urapmin made its way up the bureaucratic hierarchy in which these reports circulated (see Errington and Gewertz 1995), the responses it elicited were almost touching in their eagerness to take this as a sign of great colonial success in an area that, in the shadow cast by the rebellion, had just recently stood as the paradigmatic case of administrative failure. The acting district officer in Wewak began his letter to the assistant district officer in Telefomin with the remark, "[T]he major work of consolidating our position in the area around Telefomin has progressed another step forward. The fact that the Urapmin voluntarily returned an escaped prisoner speaks for itself." McCarthy was at least as enthusiastic. In his letter back to Wewak, he noted as his second point that "[t]he action on the part of the URAPMINS [sic] in returning the escaped prisoner is a remarkably satisfactory action."

The patrol officer who reported the Urapmin return of the prisoner, G. F. Booth, also noted a "general improvement" among the Urapmin, who were becoming "a more settled and orderly group." He gave credit for this improvement to Ambukisep and Kweksep, the two young men who had worked as interpreters at Telefomin. Booth referred to them as "two stalwart supporters of the TELEFOMIN Government" and arranged for them to be given a reward for their help in arranging for the return of the escapee.

This report foregrounds the role Kweksep and Ambukisep played in shaping the Urapmin accommodation to the colonial order. That these two men were able to acquire special roles in the administration during the early stages of colonization gave the Urapmin some stake in the success of the new government. It also suggested that there would be places for the Urapmin in the new world the government was bringing into being. All of which is to say, Ambukisep and Kweksep initiated the process of incorporation that became the primary Urapmin project of the colonial era.

Ambukisep's and Kweksep's behavior during this period launched two trends that would be central to the process of incorporation as it unfolded throughout the colonial and postcolonial periods. First, they began a tradition whereby those Urapmin who were aiming for positions of leadership would ally themselves with the government rather than lead movements of resistance against it. Most of the current Urapmin leaders are from their generation. Like Ambukisep and Kweksep, they encourage their followers to obey the government's laws and to see the administration as creating an order in which they have a stake.

The second trend is that of Urapmin leaders aligning themselves with the law and speaking in the name of its authority. Ambukisep and

Kweksep, according to the patrol report, were responsible for teaching the Urapmin the law, and impressing on them the need to obey it. This theme is implied in other reports as well. One might wonder at the ability of two young men to speak with authority in this largely geronto-cratic society. But Ambukisep and Kweksep of course had the advantage of their privileged relations with the government behind them, and Ambukisep likely benefited from the support of his father, the big man Tabasongim. Big men had always dispensed "advice" *(weng kem)* in the course of moral harangues *(weng kem bakamin),* and their stern lectures are today remembered as the most important parts of the lengthy men's initiation rituals (see chapter 2). Yet in the course of the many changes colonialism was to bring, the role of leaders as moral authorities might well have been lost. What Ambukisep and Kweksep achieved was the appropriation of the administration's moral discourse for the purposes of local leadership (see Lattas 1998: 286). In demonstrating that with the administration's backing Urapmin people could themselves authoritatively speak this discourse of the law, Ambukisep and Kweksep took the first step toward incorporating the law into Urapmin as a local institution.

Making use of the Court for Native Affairs to settle local disputes was another way of incorporating the law. At the same time that the court was becoming an important institution in Urapmin life, the administration gave the incorporation process another significant push by beginning to appoint local representatives of the colonial order from among the Urapmin. On a 1960 patrol, ADC Brown made a note in the Urapmin village book listing the people he had selected to serve as "provisional village officials." By this time, the government had recognized two "main" villages in Urapmin, Dimidubiip and Kemuviip, and so Brown listed two "village chiefs," or Luluai, one from each place. He also appointed three assistants to the chiefs, called Tultul, one each from the main villages and another from one of the four other villages that made up Urapmin at that time. Kweksep had died in 1958, but Ambukisep, not surprisingly, was appointed a Luluai from Kemuviip, and he would continue to be the only Urapmin singled out by name in the patrol reports. Seligapnok, like Ambukisep a younger man, probably not much older than thirty at the time, was appointed Tultul from Kemuviip. Seligapnok had worked on building the Eliptaman airstrip in 1958 and was probably well known to the government. He would go on to become one of the most influential big men in the Urapmin community, a position he held throughout the period of my research. At least one of the men suggested for office, Digengim, was considerably older. He had been listed with other older men as one of the village leaders in an earlier report, and his appointment broke with a general tendency among the Urapmin for younger men to assume middlemen roles with the government. When, after two months, Brown checked on the officials that had been provisionally appointed, he found that they were "fulfilling their duties satisfactorily" (5 of 59/60, p. 3). Thus, by 1960, the village government system was in place in Urapmin.

The Luluais, supported by their Tultuls, were intended to be the government's representatives in their villages. Scaglion (1985: 87) writes that these officials were supposed to "represent the Government, enforce its orders, and report infringements." Patrol reports indicate that they were responsible for seeing that the Native Affairs Regulations were followed and that village hygiene was maintained and for bringing court cases to the government's notice. From 1964 onward, they were also responsible for organizing government work, mostly path clearing and other tasks related to community upkeep, that would take place on Mondays. As the Urapmin saw it, the requirement that people work on these Mondays was also part of the law, and the Tultuls and Luluais were responsible for reporting those who violated it. In carrying out their various duties, village officials were in an important sense charged with bringing the administration's law to the Urapmin and, as part of this effort, bringing those who breached that law to the administration. The law had finally found its first official local representatives.

But the offices of Luluai and Tultul meant more to the process of incorporation than simply providing the law with its first official local anchors. These were the first roles of colonial authority of any kind that the Urapmin themselves could fill. Previously, some Urapmin had occasionally occupied temporary roles as laborers, either performing casual work at Telefomin or hiring themselves out as carriers on patrols, and from time to time Ambukisep and Kweksep had also been able to assume the slightly more exalted role of interpreter, but none of these roles were permanent or carried any official authority. By contrast, the Luluais and Tultuls were government officers with the authority of the administration fully behind them, albeit probably at some distance. Furthermore, they occupied their roles full time, everyday, until such time as the government replaced them with someone else from the community. Here was a colonial order with a permanent place in it for some Urapmin. As Urapmin took over these roles, they began the project of incorporating the government, and in the process they took another step toward making colonialism a local, quotidian phenomenon.

Nothing was more important to this process of incorporation than the notion of the <u>namba</u>. For Urapmin, the primary referent of the Tok Pisin term "namba" as it applies to village officials is the metal badges that the government gave Luluais and Tultuls to mark their status. People talk of these early badges as if they had an almost mystical power to confer authority on their wearers, and the term is now used metaphorically to refer to any formal recognition a person receives from outside Urapmin (Robbins 1997a). That the Urapmin would focus on the badge itself as a metonym for the office it represented was not surprising, inasmuch as men at different stages of initiation and ritual leadership were traditionally differentiated by special wigs and various other aspects of adornment. But what is most interesting is how the notion of namba marked for the Urapmin a new kind of authority, one based on support from the powers of the colonial realm. Although Ambukisep and Kweksep were able to wield the authoritative discourse of the administration law, they did so without the benefit of an official identity that tied them to the colonial order as other than its subjects. The Luluais and Tultuls were the first people who pulled off the feat of localizing the colonial order in their very identities, a feat symbolized by their possession of nambas, and the fact that they did so made the development of their offices important moments in the colonial transformation of Urapmin culture.

In saying all this about the importance of the development of their roles, I do not want to exaggerate the actual power the Luluais and Tultuls held. Despite their novel ability to turn Urapmin individuals into representatives of the colonial order, the weaknesses of the offices of Luluai and Tultul severely limited the impact their incumbents were able to have on daily life. Able to represent the law but not to enforce it, Luluais and Tultuls were always reliant on outside powers in a way that remained obvious to the people they led. To enlist those outside powers in specific efforts, the Luluai and Tultul needed to act as informers. But when they did so, they violated expectations of in-group loyalty that have always been strong in Urapmin. Village officials, then, could only back up their authority by pursuing actions that immediately compromised their standing as fit leaders among the people they led. Given the perils they faced trying to fulfill their leadership roles over terrain made treacherously rough by this contradiction, it is not surprising that con-

temporary Urapmin do not recall these early village officers as particularly powerful. For their part, patrol officers reporting from around the
Telefomin area throughout the 1960s similarly seem rarely to have been
satisfied that the village officers either understood their jobs or carried
them out well (for similar observations from other parts of Papua New
Guinea, see Rowley 1965: 79; Scaglion 1985: 92). But despite their lack
of power, the Urapmin remember the names of all the men who filled
these roles, and they often remark that "they were the first to get the
namba." Furthermore, it would not be long before they were replaced
by another kind of local official whose power was much greater.

In 1965, just a few short years after this system of village leadership
was put in place, some people from the Telefomin area were clamoring
for the introduction of a new type of governmental apparatus to replace
the village officer system. What these people hoped to institute was a local government council (LGC). An institution that was already operating in other parts of Papua New Guinea at that time, the LGC differed
from the village official system most notably by allowing local people to
elect their officers and by allowing these officers to sit in judgment at local court cases. The reasons the Telefol gave for wanting to establish an
LGC reveal that they were interested in this new governmental system
because they were concerned about law and order and about the weakness of the village officials when it came to enforcing it.

In February 1965, the ADO at Telefomin, Mr. J. Wearne, attached a
cover letter to a subordinate's patrol report that he was sending to the
district commissioner in Wewak. Wearne had only arrived in the area in
December 1965, and he took the opportunity of this letter to remark on
his initial observations about the state of affairs in the district. In the letter, he raises the matter of people wanting to start an LGC. He quotes a
man named Sinoksep, who other documents suggest was a member of
the District Advisory Council. I have been able to learn nothing more
about this council or about Sinoksep's role on it. His name, however,
constructed from the Telefol word *sinok* (rat) and the common mascu-
line name suffix *-sep*, indicates that he was a local man. He was probably from Telefomin, and the views he expresses are probably Telefol
views, given that the relatively cosmopolitan Telefolmin were in the best
position at this time to have heard about LGCs or witnessed them in action elsewhere in the territory. In any event, we know that Sinoksep had
not discussed these matters with the Urapmin or the Tifalmin, because
they would complain in a later report that he had never visited them. Yet
wherever he came by them, the concerns Sinoksep expresses in the quo-

tation below about the village officials and the hopes he claimed people held for the LGC look much like those we would expect the Urapmin to have harbored.

Wearne writes:

> I have gathered that quite a few people would like a Local Government Council. I have spoken to Sinoksep, who has previously told me that he would like to see Councils introduced, and asked him what advantages he expects from a Council. He and others expect that Councilors will be able to control villagers and village affairs including housing, sanitation and law and order more ably than do the present village officials. Sinoksep stated that at present village officials are in the main disinterested and ineffectual. (Filed with report 5 of 64/65)

Here the desire for control, for law and order enforced at every level, reaching down to the minutiae of housing and sanitation, a desire the administration itself had been working to foster, is expressed as a native rationale for changing the administration's system of governance. Here too is a recognition of the limited ability village officials possessed to exercise such control successfully. Of course, in saying all of this, Sinoksep might have been simply serving colonialist rhetoric back to his superiors, currying favor or at least trying to make persuasive arguments for introducing the LGC by playing to the administration's concerns. But what we have learned about the Urapmin embrace of the law during this period, and the uncanny resemblance between Sinoksep's tone here and that of contemporary Urapmin discourse on the need for leaders to "control" people, make this interpretation less plausible than it might otherwise be.

The LGC was established in the Telefomin District in 1968. As the Urapmin understood it, its most important feature was the expanded powers it gave to their local official, now called a Kaunsil (Councilor), powers far greater than those possessed by the village officials he replaced. The Urapmin, that is to say, took advantage of the council system and the expanded powers it offered them to work toward completing the task of incorporating the colonial government and its law.

The mechanics of the LGC structure, which are still in place today in Urapmin, are relatively straightforward on the local level. The Urapmin are responsible for electing one Kaunsil to represent their interests in meetings with Kaunsils from other areas at meetings held regularly in Telefomin. The Kaunsil is also responsible for enforcing the law and carrying out public works at home. Along with electing the Kaunsil, the Urapmin are charged with selecting several Committees *(Komiti)* who, as ward aldermen, help the Kaunsil maintain local order and keep in touch with the concerns of his electorate. After an initial period in which elections were held yearly or biannually, Kaunsils are now elected to five-year terms.

Kaunsils had and continue to have far more room for political maneuver than their predecessors, due to their power not just to propound the law but also to enforce it. From a very early date Kaunsils were given a variety of governmental powers that had never been exercised locally before. At least in Urapmin understanding, Kaunsils could, by bringing proposals to the Kaunsil meetings in Telefomin, set laws applicable either throughout the region served by the council or in the locality of the proposing Kaunsil (the pig law discussed in the prologue originated in this way). They were also able to demand both that people carry out road maintenance and other public works projects (now called "Kaunsil work") and that they attend informational "Kaunsil meetings." Furthermore, they were given the power to fine or otherwise punish those who failed to turn up at these activities. Even more strikingly, they were soon charged with hearing "local courts," deciding guilt or innocence, and imposing punishments.[13] This last responsibility gave them control of that part of the colonial apparatus that had the power to define "lawfulness" in its broadest sense.

In responding to their newfound judicial authority, the first Kaunsils no doubt followed Ambukisep and Kweksep, the early government interpreters who were so influential in bringing the law to Urapmin, by forging their styles of moral discourse on the template of what they heard from the lips of the colonial officers. But the Kaunsils could also go beyond the harangue to actually emulate the punitive concomitants of colonial rule. Several of the early Kaunsils are remembered as extremely strict in their enforcement of the law, quick to fine and ready to sentence those guilty of various crimes to hard labor at public works. The tempers that some of them brought to their defense of the law are legendary. What they established, by all accounts, was a local replica of the colonial order focused on its system of law and punishment.

With the advent of the LGC, the law had finally come home to Urapmin as a largely local institution. The Urapmin could make the colonial project of lawful living their own. They could play the roles not only of the compliant colonial subjects but also of the meritorious colonial officers who enforced the law. As we will see in chapter 2, the Urapmin adoption of Christianity followed a similar trajectory of incorporation. Christianity, like colonial legalism and the governmental structure that enforced it, began as a highly valued foreign discourse but was fully embraced only when it became, through the office of the Holy Spirit, an indigenous possession. Furthermore, as we will see, the Urapmin built their understanding of Christianity on the bedrock of their grasp of the colonial imperative of lawfulness.

CHAPTER 2

Christianity and the Colonial Transformation of Regional Relations

From the early 1960s on, Christianity loomed larger and larger in the Urapmin experience of the colonial order. Examining how its role in their lives evolved and expanded, and how it ultimately came to provide them with a privileged idiom for discussing the colonial and postcolonial orders, takes us to the heart of the influence their colonial history has had on contemporary Urapmin culture. This examination also allows us to consider what is in comparative terms the most distinctive aspect of contemporary Urapmin life: their intense commitment to a culturally sophisticated version of the colonists' religion.

The first question outsiders familiar with contemporary Urapmin life are inclined to ask is, why did the Urapmin convert so quickly and thoroughly to Christianity? After all, the Urapmin were colonized only forty years ago, they were never directly missionized by Westerners, and they are still living largely traditional lives in material terms. How, then, did the Urapmin come to embrace the colonial religion so tightly? As straightforward as this question is, the answer is not simple. In large part it is not simple because the literature on conversion from "local" to world religions, while extremely rich ethnographically and historically for certain areas such as Africa, is theoretically unsettled.[1] There is no agreed on standard for what a clear, useful account of conversion should look like.

Scholars who discuss conversion from "local" or "ethnic" to world religions tend to rely on one of two approaches to explain why people would be attracted to the new religion (Laitin 1986: 36–38; Peel 1977; Kipp 1995). One of these approaches is utilitarian in character and focuses on the worldly advantages, in terms of material goods, position, power, prestige, and so forth, that accrue to those who convert. The other emphasizes matters of meaning, and argues that converts are attracted to the new religion because it renders meaningful new situations that defy the sense-making capacities of their traditional ways of understanding the world. Both of these approaches have some merit and, I will argue, can be productively used together. But before laying out a plan for joining them, I need to consider ways to guard against some pitfalls that are inherent in each approach, so that the new synthesis is not made with faulty parts.

The utilitarian approach is most prone to difficulty, often enough becoming something of a caricature of itself. The gravest danger that threatens those who use it is that they will allow some universal notion of what is valuable to supply the motive force driving people's interest in the new religion. Who would not want rice or steel axes if they had none, the analyst imagines. The problems of ethnocentrism and circularity (How do we know they wanted rice? They converted to get it) that haunt this approach are too obvious to require elaboration. The way out of these difficulties is equally obvious. Those who would explain conversion in utilitarian terms have to pay close attention to the kinds of goods, powers, and prestige converts actually seek. Information about the shape of local motivations can only come from a careful analysis of the culture that provides them (Sahlins 1976, 1992). If this procedure is followed, the utilitarian argument comes to rest on the sound point that in their early approaches to a world religion, people are motivated by their own culturally given goals, not by those that the religion itself posits of the subjects it aims to create.

A second problem with the utilitarian approach is that those who use it often assume that the worldly motives that put the conversion process in motion also dominate its outcome. It is this theory that gives us the notion of "rice Christians" and others like it. The claim here is that those who convert from a local to a world religion for pragmatic reasons rarely come to understand that world religion as anything more than a means to locally defined worldly ends. This stance is particularly useful for scholars who want to claim that traditional religion survives very much intact beneath a veneer of Christianity or some other world religion, a common argument among anthropologists. But for those who believe that cultures actually do change and who want to study this process, it is not a very helpful line to take. Several scholars, aiming to open up a side road that would let them jump off the main path of the utilitarian argument before it reaches this dead end, have recently pointed out that the motives that initiate the process of conversion are often transformed as it progresses. Those who came to Christianity for locally defined utilitarian reasons may stay with it for reasons of a wholly different sort (Laitin 1986: 37–38; Kipp 1995). Having made this point, scholars who take this position generally turn from an argument framed in utilitarian terms to one focused on meaning.

"Intellectualism" is the name usually given to the approach to conversion that focuses on issues of meaning. Horton's (1971, 1975a, 1975b) influential articles on African conversion and the controversy they have generated have been important for defining intellectualism as a distinct approach (see also Fisher 1973, 1985; Horton and Peel 1976; Ifeka-Moller 1974; Ikenga-Metuh 1985). For Horton, people turn to world religions because they are looking for new ways to explain, predict, and control the world around them. Phrased in this way, there is a bit of a utilitarian tinge to Horton's account as well, something he perhaps recognizes in a later work, where he suggests that "intellectualist/pragmatist" might have been a better tag for his approach than "intellectualist" alone (1993: 13). Yet his primary focus has always been on the cognitive attractions of conversion, and those who have followed him have for the most part emphasized the importance of meaning in his model. Thus Peel (1977: 122) claims that in an intellectualist analysis "the fundamental question of a religion is whether or not it is true—in the sense of whether it corresponds to the experience of potential adherents." Laitin (1986: 36) similarly argues that the "'intellectualist' theory of conversion claims that the new religions provided an answer to the problem of meaning on an issue in which the former religion was silent." At bottom, then, this approach is built on the argument that conversion allows people to comprehend and live meaningfully in a changed world.[2]

The intellectualist approach is less given to difficulties than the utilitarian one. By urging scholars to pay attention to the details of local culture and the way Christianity articulates with them by covering ground they leave unoccupied, it does not encourage blandly ethnocentric arguments about motive. It is also less given to serving as a prop for those who want to argue that conversion ultimately leaves traditional culture untouched. Yet it has a difficult time accounting for the very early stages of conversion, those in which people first engage the new religion with little sense of what it might provide them by way of intellectual resources. Since Christianity is unlikely to appear as fully coherent on people's first encounters with it, one imagines that motives other than strictly sense-making ones probably sustain those early contacts. Very often these motives are of the kind postulated by a culturally reconstructed utilitarian approach. That is to say, the utilitarian approach tends to do a better job than the intellectualist one when it comes to accounting for people's initial drive to make contact with Christianity.

At this point, we have arrived at an account of how the utilitarian and intellectualist approaches can make room for one another. Good at explaining the initial impetus toward conversion, the utilitarian approach gives way to the intellectualist one when it comes time to explain why in some cases people stay with the new religion and come to engage it deeply. Conversely, the intellectualist approach, weak when explaining people's initial interest in world religions, can leave this job to the utilitarian theory without consigning itself to irrelevance. This détente suggests a two-stage model of conversion, one in which utilitarian concerns eventually give way to intellectualist ones as people come to understand the religion they are converting to. Simple though this model is, it has at least two advantages over those that either ignore one or the other of these approaches or have no principled way of relating them. First, it hypothesizes that what can look like chaotic processes of change actually have a structure. As we will see, this structure is apparent in the Urapmin case. Second, it encourages analysts to offer explicit explanations for why the second stage does or does not occur. Those who argue that the content of Christianity or other world religions has never meant much to those they study need to explain why this is so despite what we might call their first-stage conversion. Similarly, those who argue that the second stage did occur among the people they studied need to explain this as well. The provision of explicit answers to these questions would do a good deal to enrich the literature on conversion.

By virtue of the way it gives both traditional motives and new understandings a role to play in the process of change, this model of conversion also articulates well with the model of change as adoption that I developed in the introduction. In the adoption model, the initial impetus to adopt a new culture is formulated in the terms of a group's existing culture. It is humiliations or other disappointments that make sense in traditional terms that drive people's efforts to change. So too in first-stage conversion it is people's traditionally phrased understandings of what things of value they lack and might be able to attain through con-

version that frame their pragmatic approach to a new religion. By contrast, in second-stage conversion the real work of adoption takes place
as people grasp a new set of cultural understandings in its own terms. In
chapter 3 I look at second-stage conversion in Urapmin and show how
the Urapmin came to engage the culture of revival Christianity. Here, I
take up the first stage of Urapmin conversion. During this stage, Urapmin interest in engaging Christianity was very much tied up with
changes in the regional ritual system in which they participated. It was
a sense of being propelled out of the center of that system that drove
them to seek change. Therefore, I begin my discussion of this stage with
a consideration of that regional system and the ways it began to change
during the early part of the colonial era.

THE STRUCTURE OF REGIONAL RELATIONS
AMONG THE PRECONTACT MIN

Before the coming of the Australians, the Urapmin recognized themselves as standing in an important position with regard to their neighbors. Their social landscape was populated by "foreigners" *(ananang)*,
rarely encountered, and by traditional ally *(dup)* and enemy *(wasi)*
groups made up of other Min people. Unlike foreigners, the other Min
groups were an integral part of the Urapmin world, and their sense of
themselves was formulated in relation to them. The main axis of comparison among Min groups was religious, and groups were defined vis-
à-vis one another by the parts they played in a loosely integrated but culturally highly salient religious division of labor. Images people had of
this division of labor allowed for both egalitarian and hierarchical understandings of the relations between different groups. Drawing on
Gewertz and Errington's (1991) notion of commensurable differences,
those that differentiate people without precluding the possibility of
equality between them, Jorgensen (1996: 193) notes that the "ensemble
of Mountain Ok cultures constituted a regional field of commensurate
differences . . . where the differentia between groups were intelligible in
terms of a common matrix of features." All groups had, for example,
food taboos, and all had initiations divided into various stages. While
the specific taboos and stages varied, all of the groups recognized that
the practices of the other groups were roughly equivalent to their own
and essentially legitimate. In some cases the variation in practices was
seen as part of a division of ritual labor necessary for the survival of the

entire region; in other cases it was at least acceptable. There was no proselytizing aimed at smoothing out the differences.

Yet within this field of roughly equivalent differences, there were also hierarchical distinctions that singled out some groups' religious knowledge, practices, and paraphernalia as more potent or more fundamental to the system as a whole than those belonging to other groups (Jorgensen 1996: 193). Most of what has been published about the region suggests that all groups held the most important ritual site to be the Telefolmin cult house known as the Telefolip, first built by the ancestress Afek and continually rebuilt on the same spot by the Telefolip line of Telefolmin (Jorgensen 1990b). Another house built by Afek at Bultem, a possession of the Wopkaimin, was also widely regarded as an extremely important site. Along with a hierarchy of ritual sites, the Min distinguished between groups in matters of religious knowledge and ritual power. As was the case with ritual sites, so too in the areas of mythological knowledge and ritual priority other Min groups tend to accord the greatest importance to the Telefolmin (Barth 1975; Jones 1980; Poole 1976).

The Urapmin do not dispute the importance of Telefolmin ritual and knowledge in matters of traditional religion, but their attitudes toward their own ritual powers and mythological endowments, which they see as quite central to the system, put in question the accepted Telefol and anthropological understanding of the regional hierarchy of religious importance among the Min. Many of the claims that bear on these matters of regional religious prominence involve secret knowledge. Thus dialogues on these matters are neither public nor straightforward. Making matters yet more complex, Urapmin are not given to "boasting" or to making disparaging comments about other groups. Compared to the Telefolmin, for example, who are quick to assert their religious preeminence, the Urapmin phrase their competitive claims to regional religious importance only in subtle ways. You have to listen for them between the lines of their prideful assertions about the former importance of their powers, or in their seemingly straightforward assertions about the way things were in Urapmin. What both of these types of statements imply but do not state baldly is a comparative denigration of what was known or practiced by other people. Overall, though the Urapmin are little interested in pointing out their superiority over others, they are unwilling to give ground on the issue of their former importance to the region.

When Urapmin assert their unique role in traditional religious mat-

ters, the most widely known aspect of their ritual inheritance to which
they point is a cave known as Wim Tem. This cave sits in the bush just
west of the main areas of Urapmin habitation. It looms large in Urapmin versions of the secret knowledge at the heart of the entire regional
ritual system, Afek's *weng awem,* and some of the old woman's bones
are among the powerful relics that it harbors. The Urapmin formerly
performed rituals in this cave, and in an associated house called the Wim
Am, that had important ramifications for agricultural success throughout the Min region. The possession of a ritually central cave is unique to
the Urapmin among all other Min groups. Other well-known ritual sites
of regionwide importance among the Min are all houses, some more
highly ranked than others but all still "commensurable." As a cave,
however, Wim Tem is singular, and only the Urapmin can perform the
rituals associated with it. Even the Telefolmin, confident that they know
the important ritual and mythological secrets of other Min groups, do
not make this claim when it comes to the Urapmin (Jorgensen pers.
com.), and no other group imagines that they could take the place of the
Urapmin as ritual custodians of Wim Tem. One supposes that an appreciation of the religious irreplaceability of the Urapmin may explain
why the expansionist Telefolmin have always remained staunch allies of
the Urapmin, never taking advantage of their far smaller numbers to
overrun them and take their land.[3] Whether or not that is true, the Urapmin certainly point to their possession of Wim Tem as proof that they
were important players in the regional ritual system of the Min, for the
rituals they performed in Wim Tem and the Wim Am were fundamental
to the agricultural success of all Min people, especially as regards the
growth of sweet potatoes.

Urapmin mythology contains tantalizing hints of an even stronger
claim to importance on the part of the Urapmin, though the existence of
two contradictory versions of the secret story in question makes interpretation particularly difficult here. To begin with, the Urapmin, along
with other Min groups (Brumbaugh 1990: 62), claim that the ancestress
Afek was intending to build the central Telefolip house at Salafaltigin, in
the heart of the Urapmin territory. But after the "old man" (Awalik) surprised and raped her at Salafaltigin, she decided to shift the site of her
most important cult house. After she killed her assailant and brought
him to the area that would become the village of Telefolip, she built her
major cult house there and placed his bones inside. It was from this
point on that Telefomin became the central place in the Min regional
system. This myth has the virtue, from a Urapmin perspective, of as-

serting their original ritual centrality, though it also makes explicit their loss of that privileged place.

This theme of centrality lost to others runs throughout Urapmin mythology and serves as an indication of the intense interest the Urapmin have in explaining to themselves their place in the region (see Robbins 1999 for a detailed discussion). But it is also rivaled by a slightly more submerged theme of centrality retained (cf. Young 1971 on "submerged rank" in Kalauna). In this regard, Urapmin mythology makes some claims about the origin of the Urapmin that are unusual when considered alongside those usually made by other Min groups. Most versions of Min secret mythology hold that the various ethnic groups of the region are descendants either of Afek or of one of her younger sisters (Jorgensen 1996: 193). The Urapmin have a similar mythical tradition of their own descent from Afek in which they claim to have been her firstborn, the Telefolmin having been born last. But the Urapmin also have another myth in which they claim not to be descended from Afek at all. In public contexts, the only clue one gets that this second origin account exists comes in the form of occasional claims made by Urapmin men of varying ages (beginning from about twenty) that "my mother is from here, my origin is not from somewhere else." Since the Urapmin, like other Min people, believe that Afek came from the east (perhaps, they say, from Hagen), this statement is puzzling. Older men (those in their mid-thirties or older) will be more explicit, asserting, "Afek is not our mother, she was just a loose woman" (*leep unang, rot meri*) who slept with men she met on the road and gave birth to the ancestors of other groups.

Beyond these two relatively public and often repeated contradictory statements, one enters the realm of extremely secret myth, known only by older men. Some of these men tell a story of an alternate origin for the Urapmin. In this story a legitimate relationship (as opposed to those between Afek and the men she meets on the road) between a local male spirit *(motobil)* in the shape of one kind of animal and a female spirit in the shape of another led to the birth of the first Urapmin. This account asserts that the Urapmin are unrelated to the Telefolmin. It also makes the Urapmin the true autochthons in a land in which the Telefolmin are strangers. This account goes on to show how many of the other Min groups, though not the Telefolmin, actually have their origin in Wim Tem.[4] With this assertion, the Urapmin completely redraw the mythological map by which many Min people and their anthropologists have known the region.

Not all Urapmin elders believe this radical account of Urapmin origin. Some adhere to a less extreme version in which Afek gives birth to
the first Urapmin man but then turns her baby over in adoption to the
spirit-animal who acts as the mother in the extreme version. This spirit-
animal nurses and otherwise raises the infant along with his father, the
male spirit-animal from the first version. This couple raises the boy inside Wim Tem, and when he grows up he fathers the Urapmin. Although
this account does not take a position on the role of the Urapmin in the
origin of other Min groups (i.e., one can hold this version and still see
Wim Tem as the origin of most Min groups), it flatly contradicts the
claims that the mother of the Urapmin is not Afek and is an autochthon
rather than a migrant.

Both versions of the origin mythology have their adherents in the
community, and the contradictory assertions that separate them do not
look to be resolved soon. Furthermore, there is evidence that the two
versions have existed for some time, as Brumbaugh (1980) reports the
Urapmin claim that "our mother is from here" in a dissertation based on
fieldwork in the late 1970s. At one point during my time in Urapmin, the
clash of the two versions almost received a public airing. The youngest
of the acknowledged community experts in matters of secret mythology,
an extraordinary man named Kendi, holds to the second version, which
we can call the "adoption" rather than the "autochthon" version. In
1992, he attempted to organize a public meeting in which he planned to
gather all of the elders and have them together tell the story of Urapmin
origins to the people. By making this information public, he hoped to
settle a variety of land disputes that had been plaguing the community
and to prevent similar disputes from arising in the future. Given the importance secret knowledge still holds as a basis for the power of big men
(*kamok;* see chapter 5), I did not expect Kendi's plan to stage a public
revelation to be successful. What surprised me was the extent to which
Kendi's faith in his own knowledge was shaken when he discovered that
many of the big men held to the other, autochthon version of the origin
story, a story he claimed never to have heard. The confusion caused by
his discovery of this lack of consensus led him to scuttle his planned
meeting. This put an end to any hope he or I might have had of learning
of some level of secret knowledge at which the two versions achieved reconciliation. I should add that Kendi was, in my experience, unique in
claiming to know only one version of the mythology. All older big men
know both versions, and as far as I could discover the majority of them
hold to the autochthon version. Invariably, big men dismissed the ver-

sion they did not believe as just one of the many misstatements that preserve the secrecy of important mythological knowledge.

Ultimately, I want to argue that the existence of these two contradictory origin accounts provides us with evidence of how the Urapmin view their relations to other Min groups. Indeed, I think that the different accounts reflect a real ambivalence in Urapmin feelings about their relations with their neighbors. This ambivalence in turn becomes important to the way the Urapmin came to adopt Christianity during their first-stage conversion. Before I develop this argument, however, I have to consider one other potential explanation for the existence of the two versions. Whereas my explanation highlights the contradiction between them, this one argues that it is more apparent than real.

The explanation I ultimately want to reject argues that the variations between the origin myths are a product of a breakdown in the mechanics of the elaborate system of secrecy that controlled the distribution of Urapmin mythology. I describe the overall system of religious secrecy later. Here, I want only to sketch briefly the way the corpus of Urapmin secret mythology was shaped by the rules that controlled its distribution and consider the effects a change in those rules might have on its content.

All important Urapmin myths exist in several versions, each appropriate for different audiences. Versions to be told to younger men and women, for example, leave out important information and, crucial to my argument here, may actually include misleading information that will be contradicted by later versions (Robbins 2001c; see also Jorgensen 1990b). One of the primary identities that determined which version of a particular myth a male could hear was his initiation level. The Urapmin stopped performing initiations in 1977, and even in the 1960s some men who had converted to Christianity refused to be initiated into the system's higher grades. As these men grew older, questions would arise as to whether to tell them the myths appropriate to their age group or deny them this information on the basis that they had not attained the appropriate initiation level. Even now, there is no normative way of handling this problem in Urapmin. Older men will tell more secret versions to men with whom they are close while withholding them from others of the same age. Middle-aged men who have not cultivated close relations with big men will know little, whereas eager ones may learn more than they might have at their current age by aggressively courting the big men. The Urapmin say that even when the initiation system was intact, most important revelations took place on the basis of these kinds of private relationships (see Crook 1997). One could only learn so much in initiations, they say. The most important knowledge came from big men who you courted with many gifts of game and labor so that they would pass it on to you. Still, the system of initiations gave the process of revelation a scaffolding, and no one ever suggested that a big man would tell important secrets to a favorite who had not first completed the appropriate step in the initiation series. With the loss of the scaffolding provided by the initiation system, there is at present no structure for the process of revelation and there is no control over which versions of a myth are known by which men.

Given the shapeless, wholly contingent pattern of revelation that holds in Urapmin now that men's private relationships and not their structural identities are the prime factors affecting what they know, there arises the possibility of disputes about the priority of different versions of the specific myths. It can no longer be assumed that an older man will always know a more truthful account than a younger man. The system has always likely bred discrepancies. As Barth (1987) has argued, the practice of "storing" knowledge for a long time in the minds of older men who rarely share it gives those men's imaginations ample time to change details and otherwise innovate on what they know without interference from the conservative forces public debate would bring to bear. But even if public debate never occurred in the past, older men were at least faced with the need to reconcile their versions of key myths when they had to produce cooperative tellings during initiations. Furthermore, the group revelations of the initiations ensured that all men of a certain initiatory level would have at least once heard the same story. Now, even these checks on innovation are gone. With the passing of the initiations, big men need never settle their differences of understanding, and younger men of equal stature may have been exposed to radically different accounts of important mythological episodes. Without the anchor formerly provided by the initiatory organization of revelation, discrepant versions of important mythical episodes presently float freely around the secret side channels of Urapmin understanding, never having to come to port to be either refurbished or discarded as no longer seaworthy.

On the basis of these changes in the processes by which knowledge is transmitted, it would be plausible to argue that the existence of two discordant versions of the Urapmin myth of origin is an outcome of a situation in which the means of ratifying specific mythic details as the "truest" ones have broken down. Perhaps the adoption story was a less secret version of the autochthon story, and initiates would learn the former first, only to have to discard it when they encountered the latter. Or perhaps the adoption story was the final one that initiates learned. Now, without initiation stages to rigidly control the order in which initiates learn the myths, the ranking between these two versions has been lost. And without the exigencies of staging a new initiation to force the elders to decide which is more truthful, it is unlikely, given how closely this se-cret knowledge is guarded, that they will make such a determination.

There is no wholly convincing argument against this explanation for the existence of the two origin myths. However, that there are indica-tions in Brumbaugh's work that both versions were important even in the late 1970s, when the Urapmin had just begun the process of dis-carding their initiations, suggests that perhaps the equifinality of the two versions predates the current disorganization of the system of knowl-edge management. If such were the case, of course, then contemporary changes in practices of revelation could not be used to account for the existence of the two "true" versions of the myth. And even if we could show that before the collapse of the initiation system one of the versions was held to be less true, to be a "trick" *(famul)* version told to younger men, we would still need to explain why the Urapmin would choose to highlight the issue of their relationships with the Telefolmin and other groups in the region by considering it not in one but in two quite differ-ent stories. As Jorgensen (1981b) and others have shown, Min people mystify their mythology not in random ways but around core cultural issues such as the meaning of gender and the problem of order (see also Barth 1975; Poole 1976). The question then becomes, why did the Urapmin think that regional relations were worthy of similarly compli-cated treatment?

Whether or not the eldest, most knowledgeable Urapmin ever held only one version of the origin mythology to be the most true, what I am suggesting is that we are justified in treating the existence of the two ver-sions as evidence that the determination of their place in the Min region was one of the core social issues that Urapmin secret mythology under-took to elaborate on in its characteristically contradictory and deceptive way. Taken together, the adoption version and the autochthon version point to a contradiction in which Urapmin see themselves both as a part of their region and as apart from it, as one of an equivalent series of groups created by Afek and subordinated by her to the Telefolmin in matters of ritual and as the heirs of a unique creation of their own that later led to the origin on their ground of many of the other Min groups. This dual representation of the Urapmin as both enmeshed in their re-gion and disconnected from or independent of it reappears in other parts of their mythology, belief, and practice. In a discussion elsewhere (Robbins 1999) of how Urapmin think about and use *bonang* (shell money)—which they insist originated in Urapmin despite the fact that the social reproduction of the community currently depends on people "pulling" it in from outside—I show that in important ways the two mythical pictures that the Urapmin present of themselves, as independent and as regionally embedded, are both true: they are in many ways self-sufficient in ensuring their own cultural reproduction, but in other ways they are also dependent in their efforts to do so upon the flow of material goods and, previously, ritual power from other groups in their region.

This contradictory experience of being both connected to and independent of their neighbors is relevant to all Urapmin; it is a part of the existential situation of each of them. This fact is the basis of my explanation for the coexistence of the two contradictory versions of the Urapmin origin. It, rather than the breakdown of ritual secrecy, is why there is no predictable distribution of the two versions of the origin myth between different segments of Urapmin society. Jorgensen's (1983) study of the different conception beliefs held by Telefolmin men and women is the one careful study we have of the stable coexistence of discrepant ideas in a Min culture. The case Jorgensen examines, however, is different from that considered here in that the two beliefs are distributed neatly, women holding one belief and men another. The basis for this distribution is the fact that "the world of women differs from the world of men," particularly because women do not have access to the realm of secret cult ritual (Jorgensen 1983: 65). In the present case, what we have to explain is not a skewed distribution but why the same people would continue to hold two contradictory accounts even when they claimed one of them was false. They do so, I am arguing, because the dialectical relation between these two myths works to highlight a real contradiction the Urapmin face. By problematizing the perception of a regional situation that is in fact complex, the two myths together gain a hold on the Urapmin imagination that obviates any need the Urapmin might feel to synthesize them or discard one in favor of the other.

I have undertaken this long discussion of the way Urapmin mythology reflects their views of the place they occupy in the Min region because one of the main challenges the Urapmin faced in the early colonial period was that of adjusting to a rapid restructuring of regional relations brought on by the varied colonial fortunes of the different Min groups. The contradictions between the two origin myths attest to the fact that the Urapmin worry over these issues and are concerned with exactly what kind of claims for importance they can make for themselves within their region. Allied with the militarily and ritually powerful Telefolmin, possessed of religious traditions that represented them as at least equal to if not preeminent among their neighbors, the Urapmin certainly did not see themselves as a marginal group. But their sense of themselves as broadly equal to and secretly more cosmically important than other groups was badly shaken by the events of the early contact period.

THE COLONIAL TRANSFORMATION
OF REGIONAL RELATIONS

The regional dislocations of the colonial period were first evidenced as growing discrepancies between Min groups along what the Urapmin would come to see as three axes: integration into the colonial and post-colonial political structure, possession of Christian knowledge, and access to "economic" development. As the Urapmin would have seen things at the time, this way of parsing the emerging inequities was new. Traditionally, there was no clear separation between the religious, the political, and the economic. Ritual was central to production, and productive success was proof of correct ritual observance. Similarly, big men were both ritual and political leaders, and much of their political power was founded on their possession of secret ritual knowledge. Seeing all of these domains as related, throughout the 1960s the Urapmin attempted to address their growing sense of marginality by working on all three fronts at once, attempting to become part of the modern political order by becoming lawful and pursuing both Christian education and economic development. In all of these endeavors, they were struggling to catch up with neighbors who had surpassed them in sophistication and no longer so obviously depended on them for ritual services.

From the outset of the colonial period, the Telefolmin people were at an advantage in the race to achieve some measure of mastery in the new order by virtue of the presence on their territory of the government station, its airstrip, health center, and school, and the mission. Of course, the Telefolmin faced considerable hardships because of their proximity to the colonial center of the Min area: they felt the brunt of colonialist violence before the rebellion, and demands on their labor were always heavier than those placed on outlying groups (Craig 1990). But the Urapmin were also quick to notice that the Telefolmin had access to schooling, Christian religious training, vegetable marketing, and casual labor on a much larger scale than they themselves enjoyed. From the moment the station was established and the colonial order put in place, the Urapmin began to suffer under the fact of being "rural" or "remote" where once they had been quite central. In the Tok Pisin terms they now use, they were becoming a <u>bus lain</u> (bush line).

As difficult as the ascension of the Telefolmin was for the Urapmin, it at least had a precolonial precedent. They were, after all, represented as the ritually most important Min group in the more public and widely held versions of the regional mythology. Far less easy for the Urapmin to countenance was the rapid rise of other neighboring groups, traditionally far less central, whose participation in the new order accelerated as either the government or the mission built airstrips on their territories. The Tifalmin, traditional enemies living just west of Urapmin, are a case in point. The Baptist mission completed an airstrip on their land, one of the first two they built, in March 1959 (5 of 58/59, p. 4). As soon as the airstrip was finished, the expatriate missionary and mission nurse stationed at Telefomin began making fortnightly visits to Tifalmin. On these visits they would provide some religious instruction, buy vegetables to be freighted back to Telefomin, and run their trade-store. Suddenly, the Tifalmin were having regular contact with whites and were being provided with steady opportunities to learn Christianity, earn money, and purchase store goods. Shortly after the airstrip opened, Tifalmin also became the site of a full-time medical aidpost staffed by a Telefol medical orderly who dispensed medicines and dressed wounds.

There can be little doubt that the Urapmin felt somewhat left behind by the developments going on around them. Certainly the reaction of the patrol officers to their marginalization was rapid and decisive. They responded to the development of the Tifalmin airstrip by downgrading their estimation of Urapmin sophistication. Previously, patrol officers had always remarked positively on the speed with which the Urapmin had grasped the law and on their growing capacity to behave as good colonial subjects. Living close to the station, and pushed along by Ambukisep, the Urapmin had always appeared in the reports as relatively "advanced," though of course lagging far behind the Telefolmin. Barely a year after the airstrip opened at Tifalmin, however, patrol officers, who usually visited Urapmin and Tifalmin on the same patrol, began to write differently about the Urapmin. In a report from April 1960, ADO Brown writes, "[T]he URAPMIN people although closer to TELEFOMIN station have not yet achieved the confidence of the TIFALMINS as they had less contact with Europeans, and strangers" (5 of 59/60, p. 3). On the very next patrol, not undertaken until January 1961, a new ADO, Mr. Calcutt, notes that "the Urapmins [sic] had not advanced as much as the Tifalmins, who had the advantage of regular contact with the Administration aidpost, and the Mission school and fortnightly visits." He went on to see as progress on the Urapmin side the fact that the Urapmin were regularly using the aidpost at Tifalmin, despite the traditional enmity between the groups (4 of 60/61, p. 3).

Did the Urapmin recognize that they had fallen behind the Tifalmin in the estimation of the patrol officers? I would not be surprised if they did, since patrol officers and native police were not beyond using denigration to motivate people they felt were not "progressing." Furthermore, in a well-documented parallel case from what is now Zimbabwe, Maxwell (1999: 114) argues that people in the Katerere region were well aware of hierarchical distinctions colonial officers made between ethnic groups and that members of higher-ranked groups often deployed the colonists' rhetoric in describing those ranked below them. And even in the unlikely case that the Urapmin were not aware of the way they were viewed by the administration, they certainly would have begun to recognize that the pace of change had picked up among their neighbors while remaining agonizingly slow for them.

Moreover, new relations of dependency between the Urapmin and their neighbors were beginning to take shape from the late 1950s on. For the most part, the Urapmin were only able to earn cash by working for the government as casual labors doing maintenance work around the station. Since the government provided no accommodations for casual laborers, Urapmin who wanted to participate in the nascent market economy of the region were obliged to stay with and eat from the hands of Telefolmin friends and relatives. They also had to prevail on their friends and relatives in Telefomin and Tifalmin when they needed to seek medical care. Finally, as we will see, they soon became even more extensively dependent on these two groups when it came to learning about the Christian religion. The overall trend during this period was one in which Urapmin efforts to engage the modern order made them more dependent on their neighbors than they had ever been before. And as this dependency increased, so too did the Urapmin realization that they were a bush line, forcefully marginalized by the colonial classificatory hierarchy of more and less advanced groups.

These complex shifts in regional alignments upset the traditional Urapmin perception of their centrality to and potential autonomy from the regional system around them. In response to the humiliations this dislocation caused, the Urapmin aimed to provide themselves with a place in the new order that maintained something of the regional centrality and independence they had enjoyed in the past. It was this goal that provided the framework in which their first utilitarian approaches to Christianity were carried out.

Yet in the early 1960s, Christianity was not the only project the Urapmin undertook with the aim of restoring their self-sufficiency and sense of mastery of the world as it stood. What they called "development" (<u>defelopmen</u>) also had it attractions. As their current hopes that Kennecott will build them a mine attest, dreams of development continue to be important in contemporary Urapmin life. However, Urapmin engagement with Christianity now far outstrips that with the market, and on the level of meaning the former has profoundly encompassed the latter. Urapmin are now given to reminding themselves that development brings only "the things of this earth" (*towal diim mafak mafak,* <u>samting bilong graun</u>), not those of ultimate importance. This religious encompassment of development has been encouraged by the Christian denigration of earthly things. But during the colonial period, it was also driven by development's failure to succeed on its own terms. Before turning to the rise of Christianity among the Urapmin, then, I want briefly to consider the abrupt rise and precipitous fall of their hopes for development.

THE FAILURE OF DEVELOPMENT

For most rural Papua New Guineans, and the Urapmin are no exception, "development" is, like "law," one of those multivocal modern symbols that is very difficult to gloss in any simple way (Dundon 2002). In Urapmin, "development" refers to everything from a few chickens surrounded by a bush material fence or a tin roof on one's house to the advent of a gold mine on one's land. But what all the things the Urapmin want by way of development have in common is that they would allow them to create the institutions and trappings of the market economy for themselves, in their own villages, and as much as possible under their own direction. That is, development for them would be an incorporation of the market economy similar to the incorporation of the Administration that they achieved by becoming government officials and appropriating the discourse of the law. Successful incorporation in these terms was crucial to the Urapmin project of sustaining self-sufficiency in the face of changing regional relations.

It was during the 1960s that the Urapmin first formulated the hope that they could achieve development. When a 1965 patrol visited them, the Urapmin brought the matter up to the patrol officer. This is the first instance in which development is mentioned so explicitly in the patrol reports, but it is clear from how well articulated Urapmin desires already were at this point that they had been entertaining these ideas for some time. Smalley, the patrol officer, writes that "the people showed interest in starting a business" (8 of 64/65, p. 3) and that one man who had been to the large colonial town of Lae (probably to the hospital) said that this would be "the only way they could acquire money in the area" (4). Another person asked about the possibility of growing coffee (4). Feeling that it was "dangerous" to make promises that would later go unfulfilled, Smalley emphasized in his report that he impressed on the Urapmin that the poverty of their soils and the distance between them and any major commercial center made it unlikely they could ever start a major business locally (pp. 3, 4). This is a disappointing refrain with which the Urapmin would soon become all too familiar.[5]

In fact, it was a refrain that was widely heard throughout the region. Noting Telefomin's distance from any major markets and the high transport costs involved in exporting goods from the area, patrol officers routinely predicted that no real development would take place even at the Telefomin station. Along with problems of location and terrain, these officers also knew that the Administration had little interest in making the kind of effort required to bring development to the Min region. In the wake of the rebellion, the emphasis was firmly on establishing and maintaining respect for the law rather than on fostering development (Jorgensen 1996: 194). Min people recognized this, and like the Telefolmin, the Urapmin sometimes imagine that the government withheld development in retaliation for the rebellion (Jorgensen 1981b: 43–44). As one Urapmin man put it to me, "The Australian government helped us with making roads and wanted to improve village life, but then the Eliptaman killed the patrol officers and the government stopped making roads." Very quickly, then, many Min came to share the patrol officers' understanding that development was not likely to play an important role in their future.

The growing recognition throughout the 1960s that development would not be quick in coming to the area was doubtlessly disappointing to all of the Min groups. But for the Urapmin, who lacked even the airstrip or mission presence that was transforming the lives of their neighbors, the news that little more was likely to happen was particularly discouraging. Even in an area that was undeveloped as a whole, an outpost like Urapmin, separated from the Telefomin airstrip by the Sepik gorge and from the one at Tifalmin by a series of mountains that made road building unrealistic, stood out for its especially dim prospects. During his April 1965 patrol, Smalley explained the Urapmin situation to them in particularly plain terms. "[O]ne can only emphasise to them," he writes, "their great distance from anywhere" (8 of 64/65, p. 3). Surely Smalley's point could only have deepened the growing Urapmin sense of their marginalization in the new order then taking shape.

The Urapmin initially responded to their poor prospects for development at home by sending some young men out to work two-year contacts on coastal and Highland plantations. For a little more than a decade, from 1965 until the late 1970s, the plantation stint was an important sojourn for younger Urapmin men. But as much as some young men enjoyed the chance to leave Urapmin, see other parts of the country, and earn some money, the rest of the community was never better than ambivalent about this form of wage labor. They did not like the way it took young men out of the community without in any way offering the community development in return. Like casual labor at the government station, it was a way to earn money to buy the newfound necessities of modern life—pots and pans, blankets and plates—for one's family, and to put away money for use in ceremonial exchanges. But it did nothing to address the fact that the Urapmin were falling behind their neighbors in the race to connect with the new order and put it to their own uses. Indeed, as a route to forging such a connection development in general was quickly proving a dead end. For the Urapmin, this meant they would have to take the other open road that led in this direction—that laid down by Christianity.

THE ARRIVAL OF CHRISTIANITY

At the same time that development was proving itself a nonstarter in the Min region, Christianity began offering the Urapmin opportunities to regain a sense of regional importance and find roles for themselves within the new order; if they could not be workers or businessmen (bisnis man), they could become students of Christianity and eventually evangelists and pastors in the employ of the mission. The first stage of conversion in Urapmin was thus dominated by the Urapmin aggressively seeking out Christian knowledge and incorporating new roles based on it into their social life.

Contemporary Urapmin like to say of their community, "We have lots of pastors here." At first, I interpreted this as an expression of the Protestant notion of the priesthood of all believers. But the Urapmin were speaking quite literally, referring to the fact that many Urapmin men had served officially as pastors (pasta) to Christian communities or as evangelists (evangelis) to "heathen" ones both in Urapmin and among other Min groups.[6] Of men who were between the ages of thirty-five and fifty in 1992, just over half (roughly twenty-one out of forty-one) had served as pastors or evangelists. If we count those who either had some significant Christian schooling or served as deacons (dikan) in the church, a respected role often taken by illiterates who are very knowledgeable in Christianity and devoted to the church, we can add quite a few more people to the list. Overall, at least three-fourths (more than thirty) of the Urapmin men in this age group have at one time in their lives been largely absorbed in studying Christianity, and many have gone on to devote much of their time to preaching it in an official capacity.

The story of how so many men came to be pastors dominates Urapmin accounts of the first stage of conversion. Although the Urapmin themselves are the primary characters in this story, its telling has to begin with the coming of the missionaries. The Australian Baptist Missionary Society (ABMS) began building its station in Telefomin in 1952, and by the time of the Telefol rebellion in late 1953 there was an expatriate missionary living there full time. Barr (1983b: 109) sorts the missions that have worked in Papua New Guinea into three groups based on whether they are associated with "mainline denominational churches," "conservative evangelical groups and fundamentalist sects," or "Pentecostal groups." Though he makes this classification for other purposes, I borrow it here for what it can tell us about several of the prominent emphases of ABMS's program. The ABMS fits solidly within the "conservative evangelical" category. Unlike many of the mainline churches, such as the Lutherans and the Anglicans, but in keeping with the Pentecostal and Fundamentalist groups, ABMS missionaries had little use for the traditional culture of the Melanesians among whom they worked. They demonized local rituals, claiming they were things of Satan, and pushed for their complete abandonment. But unlike many of the Pentecostal and Fundamentalist groups that have arrived in Melanesia recently, the ABMS shared with the mainline churches a commitment not only to saving souls but also to contributing to the growth of health services and economic opportunities in the areas they served. As we will see later, these two foci of the ABMS—their scorched earth policy in regard to local culture and their involvement in medical and economic development—would greatly influence the Urapmin understanding of Christianity, as would the Protestant nature of their brand of Christianity.

But in 1953 such influence was far in the future. For the first few years that the mission was set up at Telefomin, it is unlikely that the Urapmin had any contact with its representatives. Initially, the Urapmin area was an officially restricted one to which missionaries could not travel. By the mid-1950s, however, missionaries had begun to go afield from Telefomin to deliver their message to the hinterland. In his report of a patrol to Urapmin and Tifalmin in August 1957, Booth noted that "[n]ow that the ELIPTAMIN and FERAMIN areas have been opened to the Baptist Mission the next step will be the opening of the URAPMIN" (2 of 57/58, p. 17). From that point on, Urapmin contact with representatives of the mission, especially indigenous ones, increased quickly. But much of this contact would not take place on Urapmin soil.

FINDING CHRISTIANITY

By the mid-1950s, the ABMS had settled on a plan of educating "selected nationals" and sending them out to more remote communities as evangelists (Draper and Draper 1990: 136). In all of the cases mentioned in the patrol reports, these evangelists, in the first instance usually Telefolmin men, moved quickly to establish schools at their new posts, focusing on teaching Tok Pisin, Tok Pisin literacy, and the Bible and its message. It was as students in such a school that the first Urapmin to do so would learn about Christianity.

By early 1959, the mission had opened an airstrip at Tifalmin and missionaries were flying in every fortnight to preach, run a small tradestore, and attend to prenatal and infant welfare. Then, in 1961, the mission set up a small school near the Tifalmin airstrip (4 of 60/61, p. 3). This school was staffed by two Telefolmin men, some of the first to begin implementing the mission's strategy of using trained indigenes to evangelize groups living beyond the station.

As luck would have it, the airstrip and the school were located in Okbiliviip, the easternmost village of Tifalmin and the one closest to Urapmin. At least twenty years before the coming of the Pax Australiana, an Okbiliviip man had fled to Urapmin. Rather than kill him, as one faction urged, an Urapmin leader took advantage of the opportunity to recruit another follower and gave him land and a wife. The union proved fertile, and by the early 1960s there were several Urapmin families with strong paternal ties to Okbiliviip. Added to this sturdy connection were the links established through the children of Tifalmin women captured in war and married to Urapmin men. Ties between the two groups were strong enough that as early as 1955 a patrol officer mentions that the Urapmin had recently been allied with the lower Tifalmin (including those who would later occupy Okbiliviip) in a feud with the upper Tifalmin "over women" (1 of 55/56, p. 3). The density of existing relationships connecting the Urapmin and the people of Okbiliviip and the fact that the village of Okbiliviip itself was not far from the western edge of Urapmin territory together made the mission school (and the aidpost) by the Tifalmin airstrip the most approachable outpost of the modern world to which the Urapmin had yet had access.

Between 1961 and 1963, no fewer than nine young men attended the mission school at Tifalmin. These men made regular weekend trips home to work in their gardens and collect garden foods, but it seems that they lived much of the three years between 1961 and 1963 in Tifalmin, initiating the disturbing trend in which the Urapmin would become dependent on their neighbors not only for religious instruction but also for material support while they sought to learn about Christianity.

All of the men who attended the Tifalmin school were young, about sixteen years old, and most of them would go on to live singular lives, engaging with the mission and with the white world in ways none before them had and few after them would. The core of the group was made up of two sets of brothers all of whom were from the village of Atemkit: Letap and Inis and Pais, Antalap, and their half brother, Seli. Letap would later become the most powerful Kaunsil in Urapmin history, known both for the harsh punishments he meted out to Urapmin lawbreakers and for the way he put his fiery personality in the service of winning major LGC projects for the Urapmin, including the school that was built at the beginning of the 1980s. Inis, his brother, later served, along with Emos, another of this Tifal group, as the most dedicated Urapmin missionary to the Atbalmin—departing for Atbalmin in the 1970s and only returning in 1991. And it would be Pais and especially his younger brother Antalap whom the Urapmin would credit with being the most powerful early forces in bringing Christianity to them.

According to the Urapmin who attended the Tifalmin school, the teachers focused on instructing students in how to speak, read, and write Tok Pisin and in rudimentary arithmetic. All the accounts of what went on in later years in these bush Bible schools stress the importance of Bible education as well. The mission's plan from the beginning was to

take the students that excelled in these subjects in indigenously staffed
schools like that in Tifalmin and bring them to Telefomin, give them additional training in literacy and arithmetic while also giving them intensive religious instruction, and eventually send them out as evangelists to
start schools of their own. Many Urapmin did well in Tifalmin, and by
about 1965 Antalap, Pais, Emos, and perhaps Seli and Inis were studying in Telefomin and becoming part of this self-perpetuating evangeliz-
ing apparatus.

Even as the Tifalmin school was becoming a popular destination for
some young Urapmin, Christianity also began to establish itself in Urapmin proper. In 1963 or 1964, a Telefolmin man named Lemkiknok
came to Urapmin and started a school. As it happened, his tenure in
Urapmin was relatively short, no more than three years and probably
less, and it ended on a sour note. Sometime after his arrival in Urapmin,
he started up an affair with a young local woman. When she became
pregnant, either the Urapmin themselves or the mission—local accounts
disagree on who took the initiative—removed him from his post. But
the school he created in Urapmin played an important role during the
first stage of Urapmin conversion.

The school was located in the top area of Urapmin, and this is reflected in the fact that a slight majority of Lemkiknok's students (five out
of eight) were from the top group and the others had strong links to top
people. This skewing sharply differentiated his school from the one in
Tifalmin, which was attended only by Urapmin from the bottom group.
The balancing of top and bottom participation in schooling accomplished once Lemkiknok began his school has proven important in
Urapmin history. As I have already noted, Urapmin is now a completely
Christian community. Nowhere in their oral history do the Urapmin
speak of an uneven spread of Christianity among broad social categories. From this early point, when people from top villages started attending Lemkiknok's school, there were Christian students from all
parts of Urapmin. This initial balance laid a solid foundation on which
to build a Christianity that would include all Urapmin.

In terms of curriculum, people remember that Lemkiknok emphasized the word of the Bible and also devoted much of his teaching to Tok
Pisin language and literacy, which squares with the evaluation of the
ADO in a letter he sent to Wewak in 1964 (6 of 63/63, n.p.). The Urapmin list eight men who were committed students of Lemkiknok. While
the lives of these men have not been as spectacularly unique in shape as
those of many from the Tifal group, most of them also served as evan-

gelists elsewhere, and all but two of them have been very important to the development of the Urapmin church up to the present.

The changes Lemkiknok brought to Urapmin were not only those he taught in his school. He also taught his students to play the guitar, and he introduced the competitive sports of soccer, basketball, and volleyball. Along with attending to their lessons, Lemkiknok's students cleared a huge open space near the school that still serves as the Urapmin soccer field today. That Lemkiknok introduced Western sports along with literacy and the Christian message does not seem to the Urapmin to be a matter of contingency. For Lemkiknok also taught the Urapmin, who traditionally participated in no organized competitions, that competition was not simply a matter of the ball field. The classroom itself was similarly set up to produce "winners" who were passed on to the school at Telefomin and "losers" who stayed home. Everyone who talked to me about their education in the early Christian schools in Tifalmin and Urapmin mentioned the importance of the examinations that sorted out those winners who went on to train to become pastors, evangelists, and teachers from the losers whom the mission "let go" (lus). Some of those let go became active deacons, but none achieved the literacy necessary to serve as pastors, evangelists, or teachers. As we will see, the notions of winning and losing would also decisively shape Urapmin conceptions of salvation.

Before Lemkiknok left, six of his students "won" their examinations and moved on to the Telefomin Bible school. Arriving around 1967, they joined the other Urapmin who were already there, having enrolled after completing their studies at Tifalmin. Most of these students would spend two weeks in Telefomin and then work on their gardens at home for four weeks or so. This schedule was a comfortable one for the students and for the Urapmin community. When the students were in Telefomin, they were housed, clothed, and fed by the mission, and they were given "pastor pay." One of them, Antalap, was even given a salaried position as a cook for one of the expatriate missionaries. By giving them salaries and a place to sleep, the mission was becoming the one place in Telefomin where the Urapmin had their own foothold and did not have to rely on the Telefolmin to find their balance. Without knowing it, perhaps, the mission was addressing at one time Urapmin concerns with their growing religious dependency (by training them to be religious leaders themselves), their growing material dependency on the Tifalmin and the Telefolmin, and their difficulties entering the cash economy. Since the first stage of conversion was driven by Urapmin attempts to fashion a place for themselves in the new order that gave them as much importance and autonomy as they had in the old, the mission very quickly began to realize the hopes the Urapmin had invested in it.

EMULATION AND THE LOCALIZATION OF THE PASTORATE

As matters turned out, Lemkiknok's hasty departure once his affair became public did not disrupt as much as it might have the development of Christianity among the Urapmin. Just at the time Lemkiknok was leaving, Antalap had finished his studies in Telefomin and was ready to return to Urapmin to take up the teacher's post. Because he worked as a cook for the mission, Antalap had not needed to spend two weeks of every month at home growing food. His course was thus accelerated, and he was the first Urapmin to complete his studies. By virtue of his several years of close contact with the white missionaries as both a student and a cook, when Antalap returned home he was unique among the Urapmin for the intensity of his engagement with the colonial order. Many older Urapmin like to tell a humorous type of historical story about how once, when following their early colonial habit of running off to the bush when they saw people in Western clothing coming on the path from Telefomin, they unwittingly ran away from an Urapmin person who had somehow acquired the sartorial accouterments of the whites. For many, the first Urapmin misrecognized in this way was Antalap. As these anecdotes suggest, his return home to teach represented a significant moment in the incorporation of Christianity. It was, as were the moments when the first Luluai, Tultul, and Kaunsil received their nambas, a time when the Urapmin could say something akin to "we have met the colonial other and he is us."

On his return, Antalap continued to run the school Lemkiknok had started, taking on a new crop of students, many of whom would in turn go on to study in Telefomin. To the "extracurricular" program of sporting events and guitar playing, he added a trade-store, the community's first. It was also around this time that the government provided the Urapmin with an aidpost. With this addition, Urapmin began to have, minus the airstrip, all of the accouterments of bush modernity that the Tifalmin had. Indeed, all of the pieces were in place for a successful Urapmin emulation of even so grand a modern place as the Telefomin station. And the Christian school was at the center of it all.

When it came to spreading the Christian message in Urapmin, Antalap had several advantages over Lemkiknok. He was, of course, a speaker of the local language, and this gave him a much broader and more attentive audience for his message. Furthermore, as a Urapmin, he had a far greater claim on the community's trust. Even though they were allies, the Urapmin suspected and continue to suspect the Telefolmin of killing them through sorcery *(biis, tamon),* something the Urapmin never do to one another. The Urapmin desire to learn the new religion, part of their larger goal of making a place for themselves in the new order, was strong enough to overtake any concerns they might have had about letting Lemkiknok live among them, or, for that matter, about sending their children to Tifalmin to live with their traditional enemies. But they could trust that Antalap had Urapmin interests in mind in a way they could never trust outsiders. As Rom saw it from his vantage as a teenager when Antalap returned:

> Both parents and young people considered [skelim] Lemkiknok. He said we should learn Tok Pisin and learn how to read and write and then read the Bible and become pastors. Lemkiknok said the white men said this book is the talk of God and some of the things that people do [now] are sins. Some people thought he was lying. "There is no place up above the sky where there is a God," they said. Some young people, Pais [Antalap's brother] and Antalap, understood a little bit. When young men from Urapmin preached and translated what they said then people knew it was true, God exists. Then some, only a few, got baptized.

Rom's words confirm that Antalap's arrival and that of other locals who could act as teachers was important for the spread of Christianity in Urapmin. Today, many older people who never attended school say that it was Antalap who was really the first to bring the Christian message to Urapmin. It was during his tenure as head of the school that the first baptisms took place in Urapmin. Among those who were baptized were the first few people who had never studied outside of Urapmin to take this step. Thus at its initial moment of real incorporation, when it first came under local leadership, Christianity also took its first tentative steps toward becoming a community-wide religion in Urapmin.

TRADITIONAL RELIGION
AND THE SOCIOLOGY OF CONVERSION

Rom's statement quoted above tells us a good deal about the force of Antalap's teaching. But it also tells us that only a few people responded to it by taking baptism. He went on to add that "many were not interested—even the third, fourth, and fifth times" baptisms were held.

Clearly, many Urapmin were not willing to adopt Christianity even as
more and more of their relatives were becoming deeply involved with it.
Following up on this point, it is worth pausing here to look both at the
social characteristics of the early converts and at some explanations for
why this group had the characteristics it did.

Since the mission's baptismal records are missing, I have relied solely
on Urapmin memories to get a picture of who were among the first
Urapmin to be baptized. Not surprisingly, the students who went to
Telefomin from either Urapmin or Tifalmin were the first. All of them,
as noted above, were teenagers when they began their studies. However,
the Urapmin do not single out the baptism of these young men for extensive comment. Rather, in talking about "first converts," Urapmin
emphasize that after Antalap returned some men in their mid- to late
thirties took baptism. In particular, people mention that Seligapnok and
Amtabuleng, two of the three most important big men in Urapmin today, took baptism during this period in the late 1960s. So too did a few
men then in their late twenties or early thirties, none of whom had completed Bible school, though at least two had begun studies and then
dropped out. The significance of Seligapnok's and Amtabuleng's conversions, as marked by their baptisms, follows from the fact that they
were the first men who had been fully initiated into the traditional religion to become Christian.

A consideration of some aspects of traditional Urapmin religion
sheds light on why the Urapmin single out the conversions of Seligapnok and Amtabuleng for comment, rather than the earlier ones of the
young Bible school students. Like other Min peoples, what Urapmin
now call their traditional religion (*alowal imi kukup,* pasin bilong tum-
buna) was centered on a men's cult that controlled the fertility of crops,
promoted success in hunting, and ensured the growth of boys into men.
Most major rituals of this cult were multifunctional in character, serving for example both to increase taro fertility and to initiate those young
men participating in them for the first time. While there were many rituals, referred to as "steps" *(ban),* that had an initiatory component,
there were four major ban that all men were initiated into in a fixed sequence: *dagasel* ban, *mafum* ban (named for a type of headdress woven
into the hair of the initiates), *imalwat* ban (taro/drum), and *tap* ban.
Men would be initiated into different stages from when they were as
young as six years old up through their late teens and into their early
twenties.

As discussed above, ritual leaders parceled out important religious-

cosmological knowledge to initiates in different, fuller, and often contradictory versions as they moved up the steps of the ladder of initiation.
All Urapmin men remember the trickery of ritual leaders. They also to a
man recall the physical brutality of the initiations, which included significant ritual "hazing" (see Jorgensen 1981b for examples of brutality
in the similar initiations of the Telefolmin). Those who missed the initiations express relief at having avoided these beatings, and elders are
happy not to have to administer them anymore (for a comparable case,
see Tuzin 1982, 1997).

These features of the traditional ritual system have to be taken into
account when analyzing the conversions of the young Urapmin men
who had become students at the Christian schools. None of the young
men who studied in Telefomin and went on to become pastors was fully
initiated. Indeed, none of them was ever initiated beyond wat ban, in
which they were "shown the drum" and told of its origin. Crucial to our
inquiry is the fact that because these men were less than fully initiated
and had never embarked on the more private personal study of Urapmin
religious knowledge that postinitiates carried on at the feet of big men,
they cannot in simple terms be said to have converted *from* Urapmin religion *to* Christianity. In important ways, their lack of knowledge meant
that they left behind not a faith or worldview but a religion they only
dimly understood, one they knew to be violent, confusing, and marked
by trickery, for one in which teachers promised to deliver religious truth
to all of them.[7]

Urapmin adults, especially men, also construed their children's engagement with Christianity in ways shaped by the initiatory system. The
boys who went to Tifalmin and those who studied with Lemkiknok did
so with the permission of their fathers and the big men who "looked after" *(tiinmolin)* them. From the point of view of these older men, sending their children to Christian school would have been an experiment of
the type that, as we will see, older men frequently undertook as they
weighed the value of Christianity. From the point of view of the ancestral religion, it was an experiment seemingly without much cost. As
lower-level initiates, these boys were not important in running the initiatory system or carrying out other religious tasks. And even if their
time in school forced them to miss an initiation they might have been included in, they could join in the next time it was performed.

Such, then, is the background of the earliest Urapmin conversions to
Christianity. Children who knew little about their ancestral religion
were sent to school by elders able to carry on traditional religious prac-

tices without their participation. At these schools, the children studied Christianity for several years and then had themselves baptized. With Antalap's baptism of Amtabuleng and Seligapnok, this picture changed drastically.

When they took baptism, Seligapnok and Amtabuleng were not only fully initiated men, they had also served as initiators. Why they took baptism when they did is not clear, except to say, as they do, that they did so because they had realized that God truly exists. Seligapnok had served as a government Tultul for some years, and thus he must have had relatively extensive contact with whites, though it would have been rendered somewhat superficial by his inability to speak Tok Pisin. Amtabuleng had not been a government officer, but like Seligapnok he was a rising leader who traveled often, including to Telefomin. Perhaps their wider experience, which would have brought them into contact with the more sophisticated Christians in Telefomin, led them to pay more attention than others to what their younger relatives who attended school could tell them about Christianity. Such secondhand study, which would have become even more frequent when Antalap began to preach relatively sophisticated sermons in the Urapmin language, must have been a major spur to their developing conviction of the truth of the Christian message.

Seligapnok and Amtabuleng are also extraordinarily intelligent and are canny observers of their fellows. What they would have been observing in the late 1960s was the growing influence of Christianity on younger men. They also would have noticed the slow breakdown of the initiation system and the consequent weakening of the authority of community leaders that it underwrote. They would have seen, that is, that the grounds of Urapmin religion and leadership were beginning to shift.

One of the things that would have brought this message home to them was the way that, as the 1960s wore on, some Urapmin men influenced by Christianity began to refuse to participate in the final stages of initiation. Going against the wishes of their fathers and brothers, they refused to undergo initiation because, they claimed, they were afraid of God's response should they take part. Knamti's story can serve as an example of the kinds of conflicts that surrounded this issue. Cared for by his own much older brother and also a ward of Seligapnok, Knamti had attended Lemkiknok's school. When the time came for his cohort to take part in tap ban, he and several others refused to undergo this final and most important of the major initiations. As he tells the story:

> My [older] brother pushed me to go to tap ban, but I stood up on the side of the mission. He was a heathen and he pushed me, but I said, "I won't hear what you say. I am thinking of straightening my road to heaven. You are my [older] brother, my one blood, but I won't hear what you say." He said, "It is all right." I said, "It is what I believe, I won't go with you."

The language of this quotation is full of phrases that express how seriously Knamti felt himself to be challenging his brother's authority, and they hint at the anger that accompanied their exchange. In using the verb "push" (pusim), Knamti indicates at the outset that his brother has gone beyond the types of persuasion the Urapmin consider legitimate. Pushing other people, or even oneself, can cause illness and serious accidents to occur. Even leaders and authority figures such as older brothers do not have license to force their will on others in the naked sense implied by this word. In reporting that he told his brother "You are my [older] brother, my one blood," Knamti indicates that he recognizes the ground of his brother's authority. He does this by stressing his brother's seniority and their close relationship.[8] Despite that authority, however, Knamti insists, "I won't hear what you say." In Urapmin usage this perhaps better translates as "I won't obey you," for to hear someone's talk (weng senkamin) is to do what they ask or suggest. Thus in this exchange Knamti is in the painful position of acknowledging his brother's authority while at the same time suggesting that he has here overstepped its bounds and in any case will not be obeyed. Challenges like this led to many serious disputes. The importance of these disputes is evidenced by the very fact that Knamti actually described this one to me, going against the usual Urapmin tendency to avoid recalling past strife in order to do so.

As Knamti's story demonstrates, if seniors had once imagined they could send young men out to learn about the religion of the whites only to reinsert them into the initiation system some time later, in the latter part of the 1960s they were learning that they were wrong. That plan quickly ran up against young people's grasp of Christian exclusivism, its refusal to countenance continued engagement in "incommensurably" different practices (see Douglas 1995: 69).

All told, at least fourteen men who belong roughly to Knamti's cohort refused to take part in tap ban, and many men younger than them did not participate in the third initiation, wat ban. Even as fewer and fewer men were willing to undergo the latter stages of initiation, elder men continued into the mid-1970s to initiate into the earlier steps young boys who had little choice. But with disputes like those Knamti had with his brother becoming routine, men such as Seligapnok and Amtabuleng must have begun to realize that the initiation system was headed for severe difficulties.

The advent in the mid-1960s of opportunities for teenage men to sign on for two-year stints as plantation laborers also taxed the initiation system and the authority of the community's elders. Plantation work removed potential initiates from the community for long periods, leaving them unable to attend upper-level initiations with their cohort. Beyond that, it also provided another arena in which some young men could skirt the authority of their elder male relatives. A patrol report from April 1965 states that for the first time some men from Urapmin had recently gone to work on a copra and cocoa plantation on Buka (8 of 64/65, p. 9).[9] Among the seven men who went were two of Amtabuleng's younger brothers, who would have been about sixteen and nineteen at the time. Amtabuleng himself was out hunting when the recruiters came. He returned to discover that his two charges had left for two years without consulting him. He suffered considerable anger and worry over their departure. Moreover, that they had such an opportunity to leave without consulting him must have brought home to him and others the new independence that was becoming available to younger men. This independence, shown both here and in young men's refusal to undergo initiation, spelled difficulties for the old order and the religion that was a part of it.

When Amtabuleng and Seligapnok decided on conversion in the late 1960s, they would have had ample opportunity to take stock of these signs of change. By throwing themselves into the Christian life, these two men, younger members of the fully initiated cohort and aspiring leaders, were making themselves part of the new religious and social order they saw emerging.

The conversions of Amtabuleng and Seligapnok stand out for the Urapmin because these were the first men with a strong stake in the traditional religion to embrace the new one. They were also the first two Urapmin to be brought to the new religion at home and by their own people.

I have considered the social circumstances surrounding their conversions in some detail not because any one of them can be taken to be a final cause of those conversions (which in any case Seligapnok and Amtabuleng credit to God), but because I think they indicate that by the late 1960s the first stage of conversion was beginning to come to an end.

The first stage of conversion gives way to the second when Christian meanings have come to shape people's world to such an extent that those meanings themselves, rather than ones drawn from traditional culture, begin to provide the motive for conversion. With this change, the situation begins to resemble that depicted in the model of adoption, the one in which people have taken on a new cultural system to some extent on its own terms. Knamti and his cohort's refusal to participate in the higher stages of initiation suggest that this shift from first- to second-stage conversion was beginning to occur. Recall that Knamti and others defended their withdrawal from the initiation system in Christian terms: they wanted to straighten their roads to heaven. This is Christianity suddenly acting as a motive force in Urapmin life.[10] Amtabuleng's and Seligapnok's conversions acknowledge, I would argue, that Christianity had become for many of the younger generation a crucial framework for producing Urapmin life, and thus one in which that life increasingly had to be interpreted.

Despite these early intimations of a move to second-stage conversion, however, it would occur in full force only with the advent of the revival in 1977. Before turning to the revival in the next chapter, I need to conclude this account of the first stage of conversion by considering how the early Bible school graduates lived their lives in the years between their graduations and the late 1970s. For these graduates drew on their experiences during this period to guide the revival as it unfolded.

THE RISE OF THE URAPMIN PASTORATE

Antalap only ended up running the Urapmin school for a few years. In 1969 the mission sent him to take a course with the Evangelical Alliance at Laplama in the Highlands, and from there, after a brief sojourn back in Urapmin, he spent several years studying at the interdenominational Christian Leadership Training College at Banz, near Mount Hagen. It would not be until 1990 that Antalap returned to living full time in Urapmin. When Antalap left in 1969, his older brother, Pais, who had been studying in Telefomin, took over the school. With this succession, the Urapmin proved able to provide for themselves spiritually without the help of their neighbors; from this time on, there would be no more Telefolmin evangelists living in Urapmin or student sojourns to Tifalmin. Indeed, the late 1960s was a time of growing Urapmin independence in the modern order, reversing the trend toward dependency that marked the early and mid-1960s. In 1968 the administration put the LGC system in place, significantly localizing many aspects of colonial-style government. As previously mentioned, by this time Urapmin also had its own aidpost, relieving its residents of the need to go to Tifalmin or Telefomin for minor medical treatment. By the end of the 1960s, then, the Urapmin seem to have made great progress in their project of bringing the colonial order to their home ground: they had a locally staffed Christian school and a local government made up of the Kaunsil and his Komitis, and for good measure they had an aidpost. All that continued to elude them was the steady wage work that development would have brought.

In the early 1970s, the Urapmin began to address this last problem by carving out a niche for themselves as indigenous evangelists and pastors. By 1971, the first Tifalmin group and the first class of Antalap's students had passed through the mission school in Telefomin. Some of them returned home to help Pais run the Urapmin school, but the mission sent many of them out to work as evangelists among other Min groups, and some would stay on after these groups were converted, becoming pastors to the churches they had built. These were steady, skill-based, paying jobs, similar in kind to the government positions as teachers or aidpost orderlies that no Urapmin had secured up to that time (or has found since).

Surely other groups around the Telefomin area had trained men ready to do this evangelical work. The Telefol man Lemkiknok, for example, had done this sort of work in Urapmin and other Telefol men had done it in Tifalmin. But the Urapmin were well positioned to take many of these jobs because they were able to communicate with the Atbalmin, the largest target population on the mission's proselytizing agenda. With a population of twenty-four hundred living in tiny home sites widely scattered across 147 square kilometers of territory, the Atbalmin had proven difficult for the Administration to patrol and presented insurmountable obstacles to any mission attempt to set up operations at some central place from which they could reach the bulk of the population (for the figures, see Hyndman and Morren 1990: 17; see also Bercovitch 1989: 4). For these logistical reasons, the Christianization of the Atbalmin was quite obviously a job for indigenous evangelists.

The Telefolmin do not speak the Atbal language, nor do the Atbalmin understand Telefol speech. Although the Urapmin language differs from Atbalmin as well, the difference is not so great, and many Atbal and Urap are bilingual in each other's languages. Tifalmin people too can communicate with Atbalmin people, but I am not sure they ever had a strong presence as evangelists among them. Perhaps, in the early 1970s, as mission outreach to the Atbalmin was beginning, the Tifalmin were preoccupied with mineral prospecting, which was then under way on their territory. In any case, what is clear is that from the early 1970s until the early 1980s many Urapmin men served as evangelists and then as pastors in the mission's ambitious outreach effort to Atbalmin.

So many Urapmin men served in Atbalmin that "pastor to the Atbalmin" is the most significant employment category in Urapmin accounts of their past. But while Atbalmin was over the years the primary place to which the mission posted Urapmin evangelists, there were many opportunities to go elsewhere as well. Some Urapmin went to small, outlying Telefolmin communities, such as Atemkyakmin, that did not have pastors of their own. Others went to areas on the border of Urapmin and Atbalmin (Siktaman), or even to Urapmin villages on the border with Telefomin that had not been participating in the Christian activities going on in the more central Urapmin villages. Before the revival in 1977, at least eleven Urapmin men had served as evangelists and pastors outside of Urapmin, at least four more were trained to do so, and another five were being educated to take up this work. By the mid-1970s, then, Urapmin had become a community that stood out for its pastoral calling.

To convey a sense of how profoundly their Christian labors shaped the lives of these men, I will present a brief life history of one of them, Igori. An early student of Lemkiknok, Igori passed his examinations and spent roughly four years at the Telefomin Bible school, starting in 1967 and continuing through 1971. During that time, as he puts it, "[T]he mission looked after us. The church looked after us and bought us clothes and food and paid us and gave us housing. They taught us and tested us. Some failed the exams and they were let go [ol i lusim ol]. Those who passed went on to become pastors and those who passed before us became teachers [e.g., Antalap]."

After he finished school, the mission sent Igori, along with another Urapmin student named Endori, to Atbalmin, where he stayed for four years. When he left Atbalmin, in about 1974, Igori took up a job as pastor at Kabinbil, a village on the Telefolmin-Urapmin border that lies about thirty minutes walk from his home village, Atemkit. Moving back to Urapmin, but to a village just inside the border, close to Kabinbil, Igori built a church where he remained as pastor until just before the revival in 1977. In 1977, he was living in Telefomin. The mission there had hired him to be "a pastor and look after the mission hostel" for children attending the Telefomin community school. His wife was also

employed washing the children's clothes. Then, in 1979, he returned to
Kabinbil to serve as its pastor for another two years. That brought him
to 1981, when the Ok Tedi mine was preparing to start up and construction jobs were plentiful in Tabubil. In a move that was not uncommon, Igori left the pastorate to seek one of these jobs.

Finally, after the leader of his Urapmin village died in 1986, Igori was
called back by his relatives to serve as their Komiti. He possesses the ex-
quisite combination of a stern and prideful demeanor, an intense concern for others, and a basic generosity that characterizes the most successful Urapmin big men. Since his return, he is one of the very few men
who are clearly, in the eyes of all Urapmin, standing on the verge of becoming such a big man. Even as he has begun to move into a position of
community leadership, Igori has continued to be an avid Christian,
preaching when called on and regularly "supporting" (sapotim) the pastors of his church by repeating or extending their sermons in the discussions that sometimes follow them. But having devoted himself to local
politics, he has not served as a pastor in Urapmin or elsewhere since he
left Kabinbil in 1981. By his own reckoning (which must include his
schooling in Telefomin), he worked as a pastor for fifteen years.

While Igori has lived a life largely given over to Christian work, his
story is not unique or extreme. Two men from the original Tifal class,
Emos and Inis, spent the better parts of two decades in Atbalmin, only
returning to Urapmin in the early 1990s. After his extensive training in
the Highlands, Antalap worked as a mission teacher in Telefomin, a
"national missionary" (as opposed to a mere "evangelist") to the Atbalmin, and a "circuit pastor" directing the work of all of the indigenous pastors in the Telefomin area. He too did not fully settle again in
Urapmin until the early 1990s. His brother Pais, who also spent a year
at the Christian Leadership Training College in Banz, served many years
as pastor in Urapmin, and is now the pastor at one of the squatter settlements in the mining town of Tabubil. By comparison with the lives of
these men, Igori's stands out as average—as taking a course that was the
standard for ambitious men of his generation.[11] It should be clear, then,
that many Urapmin who came of age in the 1960s and 1970s have spent
crucial periods of their life deeply engaged with Christianity.

Their experiences while working as evangelists cemented the faith of
all these young pastors. As they point out, they faced many obstacles to
their evangelical work from hostile members of the groups to which they
were sent; many of those to whom they went to minister "spit" (spetim)
at them, ridiculing them for their beliefs. Given the Baptist mission's

complete lack of toleration for local custom, it is not surprising that the evangelists' radical message drew angry responses. Despite the contempt they often met with, however, all of them stuck out their assignments. Having stood fire, they returned home deeply committed Christians, well practiced in preaching the message of their new religion. When the revival began, they were already skilled in the art of helping people to interpret what was happening to them in Christian terms. By putting this skill to work during the early years of the revival and into the present, these pastors have been very much responsible for the sophistication Urapmin Christianity today displays.

By the mid-1970s, the Urapmin focus on Christian work, rather than on laboring, for example, for the mineral surveying teams that had some years earlier set up shop among their neighbors, began to look like a very shrewd move. As Jorgensen (1996: 196) points out, at this time most mineral prospecting work dried up. The high hopes it had raised among the people of the Min region did not disappear, but mixed with frustration they began to smolder as development once again proved an elusive goal (Jorgensen 1996: 196). During this period of disappointed waiting throughout the region, when even temporary jobs with prospectors were practically nonexistent, the Urapmin could point to many people successfully placed in important positions within the mission as their stake in the emerging modern order. As a community of Christian specialists, they had regained their religious and economic autonomy and had once again fashioned an important place for themselves in the Min region. The first stage of their conversion, driven by the desire to accomplish these traditionally framed goals, had been a success.

By way of finishing up this account of the first stage of Urapmin conversion, it is worth following the story of the rise of the Urapmin pastorate to its conclusion. During the early years of the revival, the niche of paid mission worker would collapse. In part, this followed from the success of the mission's plan to use indigenous evangelists to reach as many people in the region as quickly as they could. As the 1970s wore on, fewer and fewer groups remained heathen, and most soon had people of their own who were qualified to serve them as pastors. With independence in 1975, the mission also began to localize its efforts. Among other things, this meant it slowly phased out the practice of paying evangelists and pastors who served outside of their own groups. Even in Urapmin itself, where there at least remained a call for pastors to lead church services, the scope of the role began to shrink when the government opened a local primary school in 1981 and took over from the village Bible schools the tasks of teaching literacy and Tok Pisin (a language the government school intended to avoid but ended up unintentionally teaching).

For the pastors trained through the early 1970s, these changes did not represent much of a hardship. In the early 1980s, a mad rush to build the township of Tabubil to service the Ok Tedi mine opened up more paying jobs than had ever been available in the region. Possessed of educational certificates, fluent in Tok Pisin, and demonstrably Christian (which even expatriates who are irreligious tend to think is a very desirable quality in a "national"), the Urapmin pastors and evangelists made excellent candidates for these jobs. Between 1982 and 1984, many of them wrapped up their now volunteer mission assignments and headed for Tabubil.

The years of easy employment in Tabubil were destined to be brief. By 1985 or so, the Tabubil construction boom was winding down, and work for local men was not nearly so plentiful as it had been. Hiring preferences weighted toward men from the Min area have ensured that there are always jobs available for a few Urapmin men at any given time, but because they are qualified only for unskilled posts, there have never been places for great numbers of them since the boom. Yet the lack of both pastoral posts and company work that the first generation of Urapmin pastors now faced did not bother them particularly, for by this time they were well into middle age, and, as in Igori's case, they were ready to return to Urapmin to take up their places as part of the core male cohort of the community.

It was young Urapmin men considering their futures in the mid-1980s and later who would most feel the burden of the lost Urapmin pastoral niche. With wage work once again scarce, they continued to put their strongest efforts into becoming knowledgeable Christians. Yet since the collapse of the paid evangelist system there have been few roles in which they can bring this knowledge to bear. Young people from the top group in 1991 succeeded in getting the leaders of their church, all of whom are men who came of age in the era of mission training and paid evangelism, to let them at least preach. Some young men, though, seem positively nostalgic for the era in which Urapmin filled the ranks of mission workers. In 1992, one young man went so far as to start a Bible school for illiterate adults, especially women who had not attended the village Bible schools of the late 1960s and the 1970s. Unfortunately, he insisted on daily morning attendance, and because of this burdensome schedule the school folded shortly after it began. Another young man, after training himself for several years and securing the endorsement of the mission (now run by local Telefolmin people), left in 1991 to serve as a pastor in a small Atbalmin community. His family vigorously protested this plan, since they believed that this Atbalmin group had for years been killing their relatives through sorcery. But he felt he had been called by God and went despite his family's objections, only to die in suspicious circumstances within a year of his departure. He had been a brilliant young man, widely regarded as one of the great hopes for the Urapmin future. With his death, one sensed that the door on evangelical work had finally swung shut. But it speaks to the success the Urapmin had in reaching their first stage goals of incorporating the modern order through Christianity that by the early 1990s the most promising young men had come to a point where they were emulating not the whites but this golden era of the Urapmin past.

CHAPTER 3

Revival, Second-Stage Conversion, and the Localization of the Urapmin Church

The 1970s and early 1980s were a period of intense revival activity throughout many parts of Melanesia. Numerous communities were swept by waves of healing, prophecy, visions, tongue speaking, and other ecstatic phenomena that their members interpreted as outpourings of the gifts of the Holy Spirit. In retrospect, this era might well be seen as something of a Melanesian "great awakening." For although the historic and ethnographic materials are still not sufficient to prove such a claim conclusively, enough has already been written to allow us to state with confidence that this series of revivals made Christianity important in many parts of the region in a way it never had been before (Barr 1983a; Burt 1994; Eyre 1988; Flannery 1983a, 1983b, 1984; Leavitt 1989; Robin 1981, 1982; Tuzin 1989, 1997). In the terms introduced in the preceding chapter, in many cases it moved people from first- to second-stage conversion, leading them to remake their worlds and their own motivations in Christian terms. This chapter examines how one of the revivals of this period brought about such a transformation among the Urapmin.

At the same time that the revival spurred the move to second-stage conversion among the Urapmin, it also brought their project of incorporating and thus localizing the institution of the church and the broader colonial order to a successful culmination.[1] It did this by grounding the authority of Urapmin Christian leaders in the inspiration they received from the Holy Spirit. Previously, the authority of the evangelists and pastors was wholly a product of their connection to the mission and their possession of the Christian knowledge it taught them. But once they could gain knowledge directly from the Spirit through the interpretation of their own and others' dreams, visions, and other ecstatic spiritual experiences, they were able to run the Urapmin church and monitor its progress largely without outside guidance. As the revival grew, then, the mission's importance to the Urapmin faded until it was almost imperceptible.

This move to a locally directed church could not have come at a more opportune time. Papua New Guinea had achieved its independence in 1975, but this was not a happy turn of events for the Urapmin. Instead, it raised anew all of the issues of lawlessness and lost centrality with which the early colonial period had tormented them. The world of lawful autonomy and Christian accomplishment they had been constructing for themselves during the colonial period still seemed to them too young to stand on its own, without the support whites had been providing it (even if only from a distance): they accepted in this respect colonial administrative and mission rhetoric about their need for further civilizing instruction and help. In the absence of that help, they wondered what would prevent them from lapsing into lawless, damnable chaos. Furthermore, they worried that with the Australians in whom they had invested so much gone, they would be politically and economically dominated by more populous and better-educated groups from their region and from elsewhere in Papua New Guinea. The localizing thrust of the revival took the edge off many of these fears. This is why the Urapmin tend to speak of it, much more than the coming of independence, as the decisive break in their postcontact historical experience.

This chapter discusses the taking on of a Christian culture that constitutes second-stage conversion and the localization of the church as part of its account of the revival. It also attempts to explain the success of the revival by showing how these two processes worked in tandem. In his classic discussion of the Aladura churches of the Yoruba, Peel (1968: 288) characterizes what I am calling second-stage conversion as something that happens when Christianity moves from being a "dependent variable," governed by a "social situation" that determines its uses and expression, to an "independent" one, "modifying the behavior of individuals" and creating new social situations of its own. He suggests that the metamorphosis of Christianity into an independent variable tends to occur when local people come to occupy "stable clerical roles" from which they can teach the new religion to their fellows and "protect" it from those who would modify it so as to put it to traditional uses. He argues, that is to say, that the localization of the church (as I call it) drives second-stage conversion. I accept this unidirectional causal argument as far as it goes, but I also want to extend it by suggesting that in revival situations there can exist a kind of amplifying feedback relationship between processes of localization and second-stage conversion such that an increase in either one can drive the further development of the other.

In the Urapmin case, this feedback relationship is built on the crucial role knowledge plays in both processes. I have already noted that the access Urapmin pastors and evangelists gained to knowledge given by the Holy Spirit was at the heart of the process of localization set off by the revival. But knowledge was also important to the process of second-stage conversion. Revival Christianity demanded that its "true" converts understand the world in its terms, but to do this they must have knowledge of those terms. With a traditional religion that turned on the possession of secret information, and having approached Christianity largely through its schools, the Urapmin had little trouble understanding the force of this point. But if everyone in the Urapmin community was to live their lives in Christian terms, then they would need access to knowledge previously available only to those few who had been to school. It was only during the revival, when the Urapmin first understood God and the Holy Spirit to be giving knowledge directly to the schooled and unschooled alike, that the conditions were set for second-stage conversion to make Christianity a general frame of reference within the community.

As people began to gain the Christian knowledge that led them toward second-stage conversion, they also came to respect the authority of the pastors and deacons who helped them to understand the experiences they were having; in this way, second-stage conversion drove the localization of religious authority. For their part, pastors and deacons used their newfound authority to further steer people in the direction of interpreting the traditionally untoward but now frequent ecstatic experiences they were having in Christian terms; as Peel predicts, they promoted and shaped second-stage conversion by making sure that people developed a Christian understanding of what was happening to them. Once this feedback loop between localization and second-stage conversion was established, the two processes fed off each other, producing a synergy that drove the revival forward.

Given that this dynamic was at the heart of the revival, it should not be surprising that Urapmin accounts of it frequently focus on the knowledge it brought. It was during the revival, they say, that they first knew God truly existed and that they finally came to understand the world in which he wanted them to live. Throughout this chapter, I focus on how the Urapmin gained this new knowledge and how they came to find it convincing in spite of a traditional epistemology that inclined them to extreme skepticism. It is against the background of this discussion of the revival as a changing regime of knowledge that my account of second-stage conversion and localization takes shape.

THE ORIGIN OF THE REVIVAL
AND THE ECLIPSE OF THE MISSIONARIES

The origin of the Min revival can be traced in the story of Diyos, the one person who might legitimately claim to have been its leader. I hedge a bit here on the question of leadership because as a type of religious movement, in particular as a type of Melanesian religious movement, the Christian revival is in regard to leadership somewhat anomalous. On the one hand, revivals are, like other movements, very much guided by leaders who help to initiate and shape them with their preaching and other promotional activities (Lambert 1999). On the other hand, these leaders are not, pace Burridge's (1987: 369) claim about the leaders of "revival and renewal" movements in general, prophets in the sense that term has taken on in the literature on Melanesian religious movements (e.g., for Melanesia, Burridge 1960; Lawrence [1964] 1971; Schwartz 1962; Worsley 1968). That is to say, while revival leaders might be prophets in the Old Testament sense of those who criticize the moral and spiritual state of those around them, they are not the kind of prophets whose personality dominates the movements they initiate and whose charismatic authority comes to stand at the center of a new ecclesiastical structure that they and their inner circle of followers create. Instead, revival leaders tend to move more or less into the background of the movements they initiate as participants come to understand what they are experiencing as a revival sent by God that is unfolding within the confines of their own Christian churches. This has been the trajectory of Diyos's leadership of the Min revival.

My account of the development of the revival before it reached Urapmin draws on a variety of historical sources, but it is very much shaped by a several-day-long interview I had with Diyos in 1992, from which all quotations are drawn unless otherwise specified. To the extent that

Urapmin talk about how the revival developed before it reached them, their stories accord well with Diyos's account. In both, there is a tendency to highlight the theme of the growing independence of the Min church. For, as will become evident, Diyos's story is in large part one of how he staked his claim to independence from the mission. In doing so, he established a paradigm of using God's gifts to claim control over one's own life that would be taken up by many Min people during the revival he led.

An extremely intelligent, thoughtful, and deliberate man, Diyos was one of the first people in the Telefomin area to be educated by the mission. When his classmates graduated in 1961 and went to start the Bible school at Tifalmin that the first cohort of Urapmin students attended, Diyos took up a position as pastor in his native Eliptaman. Then, in 1968, he, along with Antalap from Urapmin, went to take a course at Laplama in the Highlands. He subsequently spent four months in Australia as a guest of the mission before moving to the Christian Leadership Training College (CLTC) in Banz (where Antalap was also a student). Altogether, Diyos spent three years at CLTC.

During his stay at CLTC, Diyos often prayed for an answer to the worrisome question of where he and his wife, Mandi, would go when he finished his training. Just at the time he began to pray for guidance in this way, Diyos met some men who had come to CLTC from the Solomon Islands. These men told him about a revival that had recently "broken out" (bruk) in their home area.[2] The effect these conversations had on him was immediate. "As they told me about how a revival worked," he says, "I thought to myself that a revival must arise within the Telefomin church." To his prayers for guidance about his own future, Diyos quickly added a plea for God to send a revival to Telefomin. From that time on, the rise of a revival in the Telefomin area remained one of his most cherished hopes.

Over the next several years, there were no signs of revival in the Min area. But during this time, Diyos did have a series of visions in which God answered his requests for guidance.[3] The most important of these directed him to establish a Bible college (Baibel koles) in Duranmin, a Min community far removed from the mission station at Telefomin. Diyos went on to build the school, but local oral histories and scholarly accounts differ somewhat in their explanations of how this came about. Jorgensen (1996: 197–98, 206; 1981a: 76) reports that the founding of the school and the appointment of Diyos as its director were mission initiatives undertaken to realize "post-independence policies stressing the localization of positions previously held by expatriates" (1996: 197). But, as Jorgensen (1996) also notes, local people, including the Urapmin, firmly believe that the plan for the school originated with Diyos and followed from the divine directive he received in his vision. They remember it, that is, as a declaration of Min religious independence, an assertion that the Min were ready to claim some Christian religious authority for themselves. The siting of the school in Duranmin, too far from the Telefomin station for expatriates to exercise any effective control or supervision, and a location the missionaries were in fact initially reluctant about (Jorgensen 1996: 206), expressed this assertion in concrete form.

From the vantage of the present, it is difficult to determine with precision the extent to which the founding of the school was primarily a mission project or one that Diyos undertook without their support, at least initially. Regardless of how that question is answered, however, the most important point for our purposes is that the Urapmin and other Min people saw it as a local Christian initiative. In describing the founding of the college as an outcome of Diyos's determination to follow the instructions God had given him, Min accounts highlight a process of the dispersal of Christian authority that has commonly taken place in conservative evangelical and mainline churches touched by movements in which people experience divine revelation. In these churches, established ecclesiastical authority can do little to defend itself against the proclamations of inspired congregants without alienating those of its members who believe that God has begun to communicate directly with some or all of them. Churches long used to established patriarchal structures of authority, for example, find they must give space to women called by the Spirit to speak (Cox 1995: 123 ff.). Similarly, in the United States, white Christians who remain true to their religious doctrines are compelled to recognize that those of all races are equal, at least when they are being used by the Spirit. In colonial and postcolonial situations, where mainline missions led primarily by outsiders have long dominated the Christian scene, local people often find in the agency or idiom of God or the Holy Spirit a basis on which to assume control of their own churches (Bays 1993). Diyos's call to establish his college in Duranmin was the first move in this independent direction that the Urapmin remember.

And as such a move, it was successful. By 1976, the Duranmin Bible College was up and running, with several Urapmin students in attendance.[4] Then, in early 1977, shortly after it opened, Diyos had the last in a long series of visions in which God had regularly promised to give

him "something important" (bikpela samting) in the future. For years,
he had interpreted this phrase as referring to the revival for which he
had been praying. With his school in place and a group of loyal Christian gathered around him, he had high hopes that the time had finally
come when God would deliver it. Accordingly, he reported the vision to
his students and together they settled in to wait to see if the revival
would come.

Three weeks into this period of waiting, a student from Mianmin had
a vision that led him to stand up at the morning devotion and announce,
"You students and teachers, all of you people, the Spirit of God is not
with you. It is only with one teacher from Mianmin and his wife, with
Diyos, and with me. It is only with four of us. The rest of you, no, you
don't have it." His diagnosis was immediately seconded by Josi Bungsep,
a woman from Telefomin who was teaching at the school. She proclaimed that the student spoke the truth. "We don't come to church
every afternoon and morning, and it is because we do not have the Spirit
of God that we do not come." Everyone heard this, said Diyos, and the
service ended. Diyos's wife, Mandi, apparently moved by what Josi had
said, went to stay with her, leaving Diyos by himself to ponder what had
occurred.

Diyos puts particular emphasis on this moment in his story of the revival, and this despite the fact that it is the only episode in which his own
role is not especially important. Yet it is not difficult to understand why
he sees it as a crucial event. In order for a revival to begin within a congregation, members of it must cultivate a sense of "decline . . . out of
which the faithful are called to new heights of spiritual ardor and commitment" (Blumhofer and Balmer 1993: xii; see also Harding 2000:
131). The Mianmin student's proclamation fostered precisely this sense
of spiritual failure, providing the fertile soil from which the first shoots
of the Min revival would spring.

Three days after the student's vision, Diyos spoke to everyone at the
college, "the teachers, the women, and the students," and told them that
he thought God was ready to do something with them that night. He
called them to come gather and pray that evening and "see what God
does with us" (wanem samting Gat i mekim long yumi). At 7:30, Diyos
went to the church and began to sing. One by one the people came, but
they were not happy, not smiling. They just sat sadly in the church. It
seems that what the student had identified as a demoralized state had
only settled in more snugly since he diagnosed it in his vision.

But on that night Diyos would not have it. He told his congregation,

"You can't just sit there like sick people. You [must] praise God in song and in prayer." Following this directive, he again bared his sense of expectation by asking, "And what will God do with us tonight?" And then he began to preach. He chose to base his sermon on the story of Nicodemus's visit to Jesus (John 3 : 1–21), a story that emphasizes the need for followers of Jesus to be born again and to move from a literal to a metaphorical, spiritual understanding of their faith.[5] As is routine in Min services, at the end of his sermon Diyos asked his congregation to pray.

> I said, "Okay, you close your eyes and pray." When I prayed, this prayer was better [winim] than prayers from before, than all other prayers. The prayer came with something like a FIRE [Diyos gave this word great emphasis during the interview]. This prayer wanted to take me, break out of the church and fly outside. But at the pulpit there was a big post we cut and I was standing there to preach. I held this post tightly now, I prayed for it, I prayed and then I finished and I said "*afan*" ["it is true"—Telefolmin and Urapmin use this as English speakers use "amen"]. The Holy Spirit appeared. The fire came right to my shoulder, it came here and it went there, like a grass knife [sarep] it cut across [the church]. All the people sitting down there [in the church] it kicked [kikim] them around. They fell down, they cried, and they called out. . . . The revival went like a light. It was March 10th.

As Diyos reports it, this was followed by people leaving the church and running around like pigs, not bothering to go to their houses to get food or sleep. They cried over their conviction of their own sinfulness and shook as the Holy Spirit entered their bodies. This lasted until morning and just kept "going and going." Rom, the Urapmin Kaunsil, was a student in Duranmin at the time (though he was not possessed by the Spirit there), and he remembers this ecstatic behavior continuing for three weeks, day and night—"[I]t was not gentle [isi]. . . . [W]e went three weeks without sleep." It was, Diyos concludes in a broken sentence, "a different kind of, an important thing."

The first morning after the revival broke out, Diyos radioed Lindsay Smith, an expatriate missionary at Telefomin, to tell him what was happening. Smith immediately sent several planeloads of people to see this "important thing." One of those who came was the secretary of the Australian Baptist Missionary Society, who according to Diyos said to him, "Diyos, God is with you. Look at this important thing of yours." Smith also spoke approvingly, conceding that God's power was now with Diyos, his student, more than it was with him; he said to Diyos, "I am your father, but now you have surpassed [winim] me because I need to get this power, my people in Australia have not converted." This recounted scene represents an explicit moment in the passage of religious authority into local hands. And the mission backed it up, taking no efforts to block Diyos's attempts to spread the revival (Bennett and Smith 1983; Draper and Draper 1990: 137). In fact, Diyos reports, as Lindsay Smith was leaving to return to the mission station he asked when Diyos would be coming to Telefomin, implying that he should come and spread the word about revival. As if to make it perfectly clear from whom he was now taking direction, Diyos answered, "I will come when God tells me to."

Within a relatively short period God did in fact inform Diyos that the moment had arrived for him to send "two teams" to Telefomin and another teacher from the school to the Telefolmin people at Wabia. Diyos and Mandi went to the church in Telefomin. Many people came to hear their report, and as they listened the revival "broke out" there too. Then, according to Diyos, he sent people to Eliptaman and Urapmin, where the revival similarly broke out. God told him to go to Oksapmin as well, at the far eastern edge of the Min area, and once again revival broke out. "Revival broke out," Diyos went on, "in every part of the land of the Min people: Tumobil, Munbil, Yapsi, Mianmin, Olsobiip, and Tabubil." [6] In all of these cases, it was Min people, trained at the locally founded and run Duranmin Bible College, who brought the revival. At this point the missionaries were no longer even a minor part of the story, which was now dominated by local people who took direction only from the Holy Spirit. To see what this meant for the relationship between the people of the region and the Christian religion, we turn to a consideration of how the revival unfolded in Urapmin.

REVIVAL COMES TO URAPMIN

The path the revival took from Duranmin to Urapmin was rather direct. Igori, whose life history I recounted in the preceding chapter, was working at the mission's student hostel when Diyos and his two teams came to Telefomin. He attended the very service during which the revival began in Telefomin. His brother Rom, who was then a student at the college, was among Diyos's traveling party, along with his then wife, Sakena. Together the three of them and a few other Urapmin who had come to Telefomin to see what was happening went back to Urapmin and brought news of the revival. According to Rom, he stayed in Urapmin for only three days, but during that time, many people were possessed by the Holy Spirit [kisim Spirit]. This was how the revival began in Urapmin.

The phenomenon that epitomizes the early days of the revival for most Urapmin is possession by the Holy Spirit. Spirit possession was a new practice for the Urapmin in 1977, for they had no indigenous tradition of it. They spoke of possession as being "kicked" by the Spirit (Spirit i kikim mi), a violent turn of phrase that succeeds in capturing the experience to which it referred. Urapmin remember feelings of enormous sadness brought on by deep conviction of sinfulness. Their bodies became extremely hot, and they cried in anguish as they recognized the enormity of their need for correction. They furthermore found themselves immediately convinced that Jesus' return was imminent and that it would usher in the day of God's final judgment.

Many Urapmin say that it was only after having this kind of powerful experience that they finally truly converted to Christianity. For those who did not have these experiences directly, merely witnessing others having them had a similarly powerful effect. As one person put it, echoing a point made by many others, "[A]t this time the strong heathens [who were not possessed] saw this [people being possessed] and they were afraid. They came back to the pastors and said, 'It is true, God exists. I must get a Christian name and be baptized.'" By April 1978, when the missionaries at Telefomin prepared a "statistical summary" of the movement's effects, they listed Urapmin as having only twelve "heathen folk remaining" (Bennett and Smith 1983: 136). Shortly after that, by the end of 1978 at the latest, all of Urapmin would be Christian.

The conviction of sinfulness, impending judgment, and the need for repentance that came upon people in the early days of the revival picked up and transformed the concern with lawlessness that the colonial administration's legalistic rhetoric had already bequeathed to them. This Christian transformation of the rhetoric of the law is one of the most potent legacies the revival has left to contemporary Urapmin culture. It forms one of the primary subjects of the second part of this book. In the next two sections of this chapter, however, I want to focus on the way the Urapmin say that the revival brought them new knowledge about the existence of the Christian God, the world he had created, and the demands he makes on people. This knowledge came not only through possession but also through all of the gifts that the Holy Spirit gave in such great quantities during the early part of the revival: healings, prophetic dreams and visions, fits of tongue speaking, and other "mira-

cles" (<u>mirikal</u>). For the Urapmin, it was the Christian knowledge these
gifts conveyed that was, as they understood it, the primary cause of their
conversion.

KNOWING THE CHRISTIAN WORLD

According to the classical statements of the intellectualist position that I
drew on in formulating my approach to conversion, second-stage conversion is spurred on by people's encounters with new situations that
their traditional religion cannot explain. Most proximately for the
Urapmin, these inscrutable experiences were the ones of revival itself. As
the revival unfolded, the possessions, visions, healings, and other miracles proved resistant to traditional Urapmin explanations. At the same
time, drawing on Peel's point that second-stage conversion comes about
when a local clergy is in place to provide and police a Christian interpretation of the world, it is important to remember that by the time the
revival came to Urapmin the community already had a large number of
men with extensive Christian training and pastoral experience. These
men guided people's efforts to understand what was happening to themselves and to those around them; they helped them, it might be more accurate to say, to turn ecstatic experience into Christian knowledge. In
this section, I examine several of the ecstatic avenues to knowledge that
opened up during the revival.

One new kind of knowledge the pastors could draw on to formulate
and authorize their interpretations of revival was that which they gained
from reading the Bible and textbooks about the Holy Spirit they had
used at school. What was new to them was not reading itself but the
ability to apply what they read so readily to community life. Also new
was the transformation of reading into something of an ecstatic experience itself as people began to pray that the Spirit would guide their interpretations of the texts they read. The force of this ecstatic aspect of
reading is attested by people's use of the term "to have a vision" *(tiin
bagelmin)* for reading. Like visions and other ecstatic experiences, reading gave one information about things that were usually hidden.

Kati's experience gives a good indication of the way the ability to read
was understood during the revival, and of the role it played in charter-
ing the authority of the Christian leaders. When the revival began, Kati
had been serving as a deacon. He had converted a few years earlier after spending two and a half years studying under Antalap and others at
the Urapmin Bible school. He converted, he explains, "because some-

thing changed in my heart. It was like when you want to make a garden
or build a house, you think a lot about it." But despite his schooling and
Christian conviction, Kati still could not read very well. "I tried hard,
but I had no father," he told me, indicating that he felt a lack of guidance in his literacy studies. He and others at his level "pretended to read
and write" (giaman ridrit), but something was missing.

In 1977, Kati went to Telefomin to see the first revival services and
returned with Rom, Sakena, and Igori to announce the revival in Urapmin. As revival began in Urapmin, Kati said, "God's Spirit came and
gave me strength [strongim] and opened my eyes." Suddenly, Kati could
read and understand what he read. "The Bible was in the open [ples
klia]. I could read and write." Flush with the possibilities his new skills
opened up to him, Kati "became an evangelist" and started to preach at
night around a fire in the middle of Dimidubiip village. As he preached,
"people fell down" in the possession trances that marked the Spirit's arrival. By Kati's own account, at this point he "became a leader," and, as
we shall see, he went on to perform some of the most influential individual actions of the early revival period.

I have heard Kati recount this story, which he tells as a testimony (testimoni), several times, always conveying a genuine sense of awe at what
God had done for him. We might perhaps interpret God's intervention
in his life as a construction Kati has placed on the kind of gestalt shift
that occurs when one moves from sounding out words syllable by syllable to actually reading and taking meaning from what one reads. Several Urapmin are fascinated by this shift that occurs during the process
of acquiring literacy (Robbins 1998a: 248). But Kati's story also makes
a point about the new meaningfulness reading took on during revival.
For he describes how reading suddenly provided him with knowledge he
could put to use in his life; the Bible and Urapmin life suddenly made
sense together, rather than as two mutually exclusive frames of meaning. And his ability to bring them together made him a leader.

Looking at the matter more broadly, one can argue that the revival
was the first event that Urapmin as a whole interpreted on the basis of
what they read in the Bible. For they understood it on the model of
the Pentecost reported in Book 2 of the Acts of the Apostles. They also
turned to 1 Corinthians (12:1 ff.) and its account of the various gifts the
Spirit gives to help them understand the diversity and uneven distribution of the gifts they received (why some do not get possessed while others do not have prophetic dreams, etc.). Further, pastors relied on the
ethical pronouncements strewn throughout the Bible to offer people

ways of understanding their newfound sense of sinfulness. And finally, pastors constantly consulted the Bible for what it could tell them about the coming apocalypse that was now of such concern to the members of their congregation. By using their literacy in this way, Urapmin Christian leaders were able to bolster their religious authority. At the same time, they wrapped Urapmin experience in the words of the Bible to an extent they had never been able to before, thus encouraging their followers to see their own lives in the Christian terms of second-stage conversion.

Among new avenues to knowledge that became important during the revival, reading was unique in being open only to the Christian leaders (who were by definition those who had been educated). All of the others could be and were traveled by all Urapmin. While the pastors helped to shape people's interpretations of the knowledge they gained from them, the experience of gaining this knowledge and the conviction that comes with such experience belonged to everyone. This wide diffusion of the experience of learning Christian knowledge at firsthand was crucial to the spread of second-stage conversion. In the remainder of this section, I want to examine several of the ways in which it occurred.

Dreams (*lumti,* <u>driman</u>) and visions (tiin bagelmin) were among the most important of these new sources of knowledge. Once the Spirit began to communicate with the Urapmin, all of their dreams and visions became at least potentially messages from God about the state of the present or the future. While Urapmin had previously considered some dreams as at least potential omens, they usually considered them important only for giving information about hunting or impending misfortune (Robbins forthcoming; Lohmann 2000). After the advent of the revival, however, dreams assumed a much broader prophetic role, often interpreted for what they said about the moral state of the church or the timing of Jesus' return. Visions took on a similar prophetic function. During the early days of the revival, many people had dreams and visions in which they saw the sins of others. For the Urapmin, who generally believe that the thoughts and feelings of others are completely hidden, this ability was quite awe-inspiring. More to the point, dreams and visions of sin, redemption, and salvation encouraged those who had them to use the Christian moral calculus as a metric for construing daily life.

An equally important avenue to knowledge that God opened up at the beginning of the revival was that traveled by the newly created category of people known as "Spirit women" (*Sinik unang*, <u>Spirit meri</u>). Spirit women are women who are able to "work the Spirit" (<u>wokim Spirit</u>) by going into trance. While the Spirit shakes them in a characteristic up-and-down motion, it shows them "pictures" (<u>piksa</u>, <u>vidio</u>) relating to the future or to the causes of current illnesses in the community. As she sees these pictures, a Spirit woman also usually speaks in tongues. Her glossolalic utterances are left uninterpreted, but once the trance has ended she explains to her audience what she has seen and the course of action her vision suggests is necessary.[7] Urapmin believe that the pronouncements of the Spirit women come directly from the Spirit, and they often carry great authority. As people say whenever they are inclined to doubt a Spirit woman's declaration, "You should not talk behind the back of the Holy Spirit" (<u>yu no ken tok baksides long Holy Spirit</u>). Thus, along with being able to receive the same kinds of dreams and visions as men, very early in the revival some women also gained exclusive access to a an authoritative way of producing knowledge.

Their new knowledge-producing abilities quickly moved the Spirit women toward the center of Urapmin social life. People consulted them before embarking on long trips to discover if any serious dangers awaited them. They also went to them when they needed help finding lost or stolen objects, or for any number of other reasons, some of which I will give examples of later. But by far the most frequent reason for consulting a Spirit woman was for help in diagnosing the cause of a serious illness or one that had lingered longer than it should. Urapmin believe many of these illnesses are caused by *motobil*, autochthonous nature spirits who people, in the course of their daily lives, often unintentionally offend (Robbins 1995). Motobil are invisible to almost everyone, however, and people usually only "see" them in the negative effects they have on the people they make sick. Spirit women in trance, however, can see them, in fact are "shown" them by the Spirit. They can thus diagnose exactly which motobil has caused an illness and why.[8] After a Spirit woman determines the identity of an offending motobil, she prays, usually in part in tongues and sometimes while still in trance, asking God to "throw off" (<u>rausim</u>) the motobil and banish it to hell.

Spirit women also sometimes see that an illness is caused not by a motobil but rather by the presence of bad feelings, especially anger, in the community. Anger, like all thought and emotion, is usually kept hidden in the hearts of those who bear it, and so in seeing such feelings, the Spirit meri is uncovering a realm as invisible as is that of the motobil. If she diagnoses ill feelings *(aget mafak)* as the cause of an illness, the Spirit woman will insist that all of those involved settle their difficulties and come together to pray that God will remove their anger.

The rise of the Spirit women had two important impacts on the process of second-stage conversion. First, it created a role for women within Christianity. Revivals, and Holy Spirit–centered Christianity more generally, have altered the situation of women in many parts of the world (e.g., Austin-Broos 1997; Brusco 1995; Cox 1995; Tuzin 1997), and this was certainly the case in Urapmin. Before the revival, women seem to have had almost no place in Christianity. Although archival sources suggest that some Urapmin women attended the Christian schools (Robbins 1998a), Urapmin do not remember this. Certainly, none of the women became pastors or evangelists, nor do any make the lists of first remembered converts. It seems likely that patriarchal Urapmin assumptions about religion combined with the general patriarchal bias of the colonial order rendered women little more than spectators during the first stage of Urapmin conversion. Given this, it is not surprising that the Spirit woman role was created outside of Urapmin. Mandi, Diyos's wife, is widely held to have been the first Spirit woman. Other Spirit women, including those in Urapmin, followed her example. By the time of the revival, Mandi had spent many years living outside of the Telefomin area while her husband attended various Christian schools. Thus she had access to patterns of Christian life that gave women a somewhat larger place than they had in the Min area. Through her innovation of the role of Spirit woman, she made such a place available to other Min women as well. This was crucial for Christianity's development into the dominant interpretive scheme for the community as a whole.

The second impact of the rise of the Spirit women relates more directly to the way it provided a new apparatus for the production of authoritative knowledge. Spirit women enabled Christianity to become important in diagnosing and treating disease. They also made it relevant to other daily concerns, such as recovering lost or stolen items or planning for future travels. In doing so, they made Christianity speak to people's quotidian, pragmatic concerns. While ecstatic experiences of conviction led people to recognize that Christianity bore on the moral evaluation of their lives, it was the Spirit women who brought it to bear on many other matters that were of daily concern.

The success of the revival as a movement of second-stage conversion depended on its ability to offer the Urapmin new ways of obtaining knowledge such as those I have outlined. Moreover, these new sources of knowledge had to deliver information the Urapmin found trustworthy. That they succeeded in this task is noteworthy, for to do so they had to meet the stringent and somewhat unusual criteria of epistemological evaluation that the Urapmin and other Min people apply to all important information. I turn now to a consideration of these criteria and the way Christian knowledge was able to meet them.

THE TRUTH OF CHRISTIAN KNOWLEDGE: REVIVAL AND URAPMIN EPISTEMOLOGY

Since Barth (1975) published his widely read book on the Baktaman, a Min group living to the southeast of the Urapmin, the Min people have been renowned among anthropologists for their unusual epistemological conceptions.[9] In his account, Barth argues that the Baktaman work with an "epistemology of secrecy." The characteristic features of this epistemology follow from the way Min people handle sacred knowledge, with ritual adepts not only doling it out to initiates in successive versions each of which reveals its predecessors to have been purposefully misleading but also routinely misleading women and noninitiate boys about its content. Such treatment of important knowledge, Barth (1975: 217) contends, produces an epistemology in which "the value of information seemed to be regarded as inversely proportional to how many share it."

Min epistemology, in Barth's reckoning, is also marked by an important corollary to this belief that the importance of knowledge varies inversely with its distribution. Because important knowledge is kept secret, no one can ever be sure that they have been told what Urapmin like to call "the full story" (weng alic, pul stori) about a given matter. As the Urapmin told me, so too the Baktaman told Barth that in regard to sacred mythology and important items of ritual detail they knew only "what our fathers told us before they died" (cf. Barth 1975: 220; see also Jorgensen 1981b). No one doubts that the ritual leaders of the past, protecting their valued knowledge to the last, took some crucial information to the grave with them. For Barth (1975: 221), the outcome of this loss of secret information among the Baktaman is a pessimistic view of the possibility of ever gaining absolute knowledge and a general skepticism about the value of the knowledge they do have.

Urapmin epistemology accords well with Barth's account as presented thus far, though it is important to add that in the Urapmin case at least it is not only how many people hold a piece of knowledge but also who those holders are that affects people's evaluation of it. Only knowledge held solely by older men and women was likely to inspire widespread confidence.

Both of these criteria at the heart of Urapmin epistemology—the one relating truth to distribution, the other to social status—would seem to put Christianity at a great disadvantage. As the Urapmin often put it, in Christianity everything is "out in the open" (kem diim, ples klia; see Kati's comment about reading above). After all, the "Good News" (gut nius) exists to be broadcast. Christian missionaries and native evangelists were charged with spreading the word of God as widely as possible, and they opened their church services to everyone. Furthermore, those who were so openly offering Christian knowledge to all comers were, at least initially, young men not traditionally renowned for their great knowledge. Epistemologically suspect by virtue of their youth, these proselytizers brought an additional taint to the knowledge they had already rendered suspect by the very act of giving it out so freely. In a community that turns a witheringly skeptical eye on most knowledge claims, these epistemological difficulties might well have proved fatal for the new religion. It is thus important to ask why this did not occur.

The answer to this question turns on aspects of the epistemology of secrecy, at least in its Urapmin version, that Barth and other anthropologists who have worked in the region have not elaborated on, though Jorgensen (1990a: 55) has noted their importance among the Telefolmin. These aspects consist in the epistemological role the Urapmin give to the senses of sight and hearing and the way they evaluate three oppositions related to them: the seen and the heard, the hidden and the open, and speech and action. It was this less well known side of the epistemology of secrecy that provided the door through which Christianity was able to enter Urapmin culture as a source of authoritative knowledge.

We can begin our discussion of the role of the senses in Urapmin epistemology with the opposition between things that are "hidden" (bantap) and those that are in the "clear" (kem). This opposition is pervasive in Urapmin culture, which tends to ascribe the greatest significance to things that are hidden (cf. Bercovitch 1994). The religious secrets (awem) of the men's cult are by no means the only important matters in Urapmin life that are usually hidden. Rather, they are only part of a much larger class of things, many of them in no sense sacred (another meaning of awem), that are not normally widely known either because they too are kept secret or because the Urapmin do not have access to knowledge of them. Root crops growing in the ground, marsupials tucked away in trees or caves (where Afek purposefully hid them), people's wealth stashed previously in walled-off corners of their houses and now in suitcases or cardboard boxes—all of these things and many others normally exist in a state of concealment. Indeed, Urapmin surveying the physical and social landscape see as many outer shells (*ipnal*, lit. "skin") that obscure hidden "insides" *(ibak tem)* as they see things that are readily open to inspection.

In everyday contexts, by far the most important hidden things are the thoughts *(aget fukunin)*, feelings *(aget tem)*, and desires *(san)* of other people. Like many other hidden things, these are concealed in an inside place. In this case, that place is inside the human heart (also *aget tem*), where thoughts, feelings, and desires are understood to arise. Urapmin take it as obvious that one cannot see into another person's heart. They constantly demonstrate this in the way they speak, for they are careful only to make claims to know things that they are sure they do know. Since they cannot have conclusive knowledge of what is in another's heart, they will never venture a guess as to what others may be thinking, feeling, or planning. Urapmin discussions of human actions are thus notable for their lack of any analysis of the motives or intentions that might have produced them. This habit renders the Urapmin social world one as much marked by hiddenness as are the natural and sacred ones; for the Urapmin, hiddenness is a general condition of important things.

The Urapmin preoccupation with hiddenness grounds their evaluation of the senses of sight and hearing. For the Urapmin hold the eyes *(tiin)* to be the quintessential organs of revelation, the primary means of unveiling the hidden, and thus they value sight over hearing as a means to obtaining knowledge.

It is impossible to overemphasize how strong the Urapmin concern for vision is. It shows up in mythology, ritual, language, and daily practice (Robbins 1998a: 267 ff.). Here I will only make reference to a few of the ways it evidences itself, for a full analysis would occupy a chapter of its own. Once, while standing around a village clearing with several Urapmin and watching a dog with its nose pressed to the ground go through its sniffing routine, I said playfully that dogs are "controlled" or "led" (bosim) by their noses. The big man Amtabuleng immediately picked up on this, pointing out that pigs too are controlled by their noses. But people, he proclaimed, are led by their eyes. All Urapmin share Amtabuleng's evaluation of the eyes as the most important human sense organ. They show a tense concern over possible danger to their own or other's eyes that they do not over other parts of the body, calling out "tiin tiin" when they think someone is in danger of sustaining an eye injury. The Urapmin worry so much over eye injuries because they believe that without the ability to see it is impossible to live as a Urapmin person. While there were several deaf or near-deaf people living productive lives in Urapmin during the period of my fieldwork, the one completely blind person (*tiin dinim*—eyeless), a boy about nine years old, was extremely wild in his behavior, and little attempt was being made to train him in even the simplest tasks or manners of Urapmin life. His family and indeed all the Urapmin treated him as if he was unlikely ever to function as anything other than a child.

Vision is so important to the Urapmin because, for them, to live in a particular kind of world is to see it. Thus to say that something has "open eyes" is one way of saying that it is alive rather than dead. Furthermore, when they talk about sorcerers, they sometimes refer to them as *tiin alep*, "those with two eyes." This construction draws on the idea that sorcerers live not only in the world normal people can see but also in one where they can change their form, become animals, travel invisibly, and otherwise defy the constraining regularities that dominate most people's lives. To have a second eye means to be able to live in a second world. Among the senses, only the eyes have this ability to disclose whole realms of life.

There is a story from the corpus of Urapmin secret mythology that illustrates well the Urapmin conviction that much is hidden and that special powers of vision can open different worlds to those who possess them. At one point, long after she had created the humans and many of the animals that populate the Min area, the ancestress Afek decided to hide all of the game animals from people and from dogs (who are closely identified with humans in many contexts). She told all the people and dogs to cover their eyes with their hands *(sigil),* and then she dispersed the game animals into the caves, trees, and other places where they now hide. But dogs had then, as they do now, "bad hands" *(sigil mafak)* that did not allow them to close their fingers, and so they were still able to see even after they held their hands over their eyes. Thus they saw where the game ran to hide. This is why people find it impossible to locate the mostly nocturnal marsupials during the day and very difficult at night, whereas dogs can find them at any time. Dogs live in a world where marsupials are visible; humans do not.

This myth emphasizes the way the eyes can open up a world. It is also worth noting another way in which it foregrounds the importance of vision. As Amtabuleng's response to my remark about dogs being controlled by their noses indicates, the Urapmin are well aware that dogs rely more on smell than on sight in finding marsupials. Yet such is the centrality of vision in Urapmin epistemology that this myth has to render the dogs' ability to find game as something that follows from special visual capacities they possess. This displacement from the olfactory to the visual in a myth that is specifically about differential abilities to gain knowledge of the hidden confirms that for the Urapmin vision is the primary knowledge-producing sense.

This story also makes a point to its Urapmin listeners about how the heavy epistemological weight they place on vision is derived from the way they oppose seeing *(tamamin)* to hearing *(weng senkamin)*. Urapmin prefer to hunt with dogs because when people are left to their own devices they have to rely on their ears as much as their eyes to find game. And while I was always impressed with people's ability to detect the rustle of an animal in motion against the background din of the bush soundscape, they would much rather be able to see their prey clearly, as the story claims dogs are able to do. Earlier, we encountered the Urapmin using *weng senkamin* with a positive connotation to mean "to obey." But where the issue is not obedience but rather gaining knowledge, they insist that hearing is vastly inferior to seeing as a channel of perception.

This judgment shows up not just in regard to hunting; it is everywhere in Urapmin culture. In general, the Urapmin conceptualize processes of gaining useful knowledge in terms not of hearing things but of "seeing" or "being shown" them. The latter phrase is the primary description of what went on in initiations, for example, and each initiatory stage as a whole could be described metonymically by the main things the novices were "shown" during it. Furthermore, those who truly "know" what ground they own claim to do so on the basis that their father "showed" it to them. Teaching and learning are thus understood as made up of acts of showing and seeing, not of telling and hearing. It is not surprising, then, that the verb *-tamamin* can mean not only "to see" but also "to know." In Urapmin, knowledge is in important respects equated with sight.

By contrast to the value they place on sight, the Urapmin generally distrust hearing as a way of gaining dependable knowledge. This distrust is based on their consistently negative epistemological evaluation of "speech" *(weng)*. Human speech is the paradigmatic thing one "hears" in Urapmin (hence, in my experience, the verb *senkamin* never appears without some form of *weng* preceding it), and the Urapmin construe the cries of animals and many other sounds found in nature as analogous forms of "speech." With human speech the prototype of sound, a legendary treachery that marks that form of communication in Urapmin points up the difficulties of relying on aural information in general. Speech, the Urapmin say, is often misleading or empty. This can sometimes be the fault of the speaker, who utters groundless speech known as "mere talk" *(weng katagup)*, or uninformed "nothing speech" *(diisa bakamin)*. But even when people have real knowledge of the topic on which they are speaking, too many things can happen on the way from the heart to the mouth, the Urapmin say, for talk to be trustworthy. It is not so much a matter of people deliberately lying in a Western sense (lexically "to lie" and "to be wrong" are equivalent; both are expressed by the verb *weng famul bakamin*) as it is of speech's seemingly constitutional inability to convey truth (Robbins 2001a). Even if people want to reveal something (e.g., knowledge, feelings, thoughts) hidden inside them by talking about it, the nature of speech makes it impossible for them to succeed.

Since Urapmin do not trust people's speech to reveal things about themselves, including whatever knowledge they might hold, they turn to observing them visually to learn what can be known about them. This leads us to a final key epistemological opposition—that between speech and action. For the Urapmin, it is actions seen, not speech heard, that reliably informs people about their fellows. This belief leads to an almost behaviorist outlook that dominates the Urapmin approach to the world. Consider, as a single example, the way they determine if a young couple is married. Urapmin marriage begins verbally. After a young woman declares whom she would like to marry, her relatives approach the relatives of the boy she has named. If the boy and his relatives say they are amenable, the woman's family brings her to her new husband's house and she begins to live with him. There is at this point no ceremony or ritual to mark the marriage. All that has happened is that the parties involved have declared their willingness to have the marriage occur. Even though the woman is living at the man's house, at this point Urapmin will claim not to know if they are married. Although they have verbally declared themselves wed, no one is willing to accept this as evidence that they actually have entered into a marital relationship. Epistemological scrupulousness demands more evidence than that provided by the speech of the couple involved and the ambiguous act of the woman's residence at the man's house.

The woman's change of residence is an ambiguous sign of marriage because Urapmin dwellings are crowded and provide little room for intimacy; in them, a young woman can much more easily act as a visitor than as a new wife. What Urapmin look for in determining whether a marriage has actually occurred are regular instances in which the couple *act* publicly in the manner of a married couple. Does the woman follow closely behind the man when he heads off to the bush to garden? Because it indicates both that the young couple are engaged together in the primary productive task of the Urapmin subsistence economy and that they may be looking for opportunities to engage in sexual intercourse (which usually takes place in the privacy of the bush), Urapmin consider this scene of a young couple heading off to the bush together the most reliable sign that they are married or at least becoming so. Alternatively, should the woman regularly fail to follow her husband to the bush, choosing to stay home or go to the gardens of her natal family, or should she follow many yards behind her husband, people assume that they are not really married. Other actions too can index a marital state—cooking for one another, for example, or performing duties for one's new in-laws—but none is as prominent in Urapmin thinking as the close single file trip to the bush. What all of these indices share, however, is that they are actions rather than words (*kemin*, doings, as opposed to *bakamin*, sayings); as such they can serve as reliable visual metonyms of the married state as a whole.

The final step in the marriage process is the payment of bride-price *(unang kun)*. This often occurs several years after the woman and man begin to live together, although negotiations over it usually begin as soon as the woman comes to the man's house. The man's family pays the bride-price by draping it over the woman, from whom her family gathers it up. Later, her family returns a payment of food. Payment of the bride-price is an explicitly public act, and once it is complete, the marriage is no longer spoken of as uncertain; it has finally, by virtue of being widely seen, become a known fact (Robbins 2001a discusses this point in greater detail and in relation to ritual theory).

At this point, I have complicated Barth's original presentation of the epistemology of secrecy by examining the distinctions the Urapmin make between things that are hidden or in the open, heard or seen, and embodied in speech or action. While Barth's original point that the knowledge most valued is also that which is the least shared holds in general, it is also true that knowledge of usually hidden things that can be seen to be embodied in action is the most profound and reliable kind of knowledge the Urapmin can imagine. Its original hiddenness guarantees its import, and its acted, visible quality renders it certain. It is such knowledge, that which scores so highly on the epistemological scales of original hiddenness, visibility, and active embodiment, that can withstand the devaluation that might follow from its being widely distributed. During the revival, the Holy Spirit gave people precisely this kind of knowledge of Christianity.

One of the most common ways the Urapmin refer to the beginning of the revival is as the time "when the Holy Spirit came down" (*talak,* kamdaun), "when the talk of God came down," or "when the Bible came down." Using such phrases makes sense to the Urapmin because what united all of their experiences at that time was the fact that through all the diverse ecstatic forms he visited on them, all the gift's his Spirit gave them, the one consistent thing God did was leave his heavenly hiding place and make his power visible.

At that time, and in the present as well, the Urapmin believed that God's existence is for the most part hidden. They often say, in fact, that God is "just talk" (weng katagup). He cannot normally be seen but only encountered through the Bible. This claim puzzled me for a long time. Something that is just talk is, in Urapmin terms, something that is useless and unimportant. Why would devout Christians apply such condemnatory terms to God? In part, the Urapmin said this in order to stress the importance of the Bible; God's word is all we have, so we must attend seriously to that word. But in another sense the Urapmin used this phrase to point to God's hidden nature, to the way reliable evidence of his existence is not easy to come by (see also Robbins 2001a). In terms of the epistemology of secrecy, this hiddenness only increases his value.

Hidden though he usually is, however, God sometimes reveals himself in action, as he did almost constantly during the early period of the revival. When the Urapmin see their own bodies or those of their friends flail in possession, they *see* proof of God's existence. When Jesus appears to them in visions and dreams, they *see* that he exists. When the Holy Spirit *shows* Spirit meris the doings of the indigenous spirits, they *see* God's ability to reveal not only himself but also worlds that are usually hidden. The same holds true for those whom God gives dreams and "shows" visions. In its innovation of all these ways to see God and his power, the revival provided a wealth of visual knowledge so epistemologically sound that its wide distribution could do little to compromise its importance.

Yet despite the soundness of this visual knowledge, the skepticism that characterizes the epistemology of secrecy did not immediately fall by the wayside during the revival. While women and younger men were busy becoming possessed and having visions and dreams, older men watched carefully to see if Christianity would visibly deliver on its promises. They watched to see if the Spirit women really did cure people and if boys ministered to by prayer and possession really did grow as strong as had those who were put through initiations in the past. They watched to see if the people who had begun wantonly to disregard ancestral food taboos suffered the illnesses such breaches were supposed to call forth. They even designed tests in which they planted two gardens and treated one with prayer and the other with traditional ritual and magic. The proof of the stronger religion would be made visible by the garden that grew best. Oral history has it that in all these areas of visual observation Christianity prevailed, showing the older men evidence that God truly existed and was stronger than the spirits of the traditional pantheon. It was such evidence, along with the striking images of enthusiasm that surrounded them everyday, that finally resigned these older men, those with the most invested in the traditional cult and the epistemology of secrecy it fostered, to convert to Christianity.

Urapmin has always been a community that takes knowledge to be central to religion. What this section has shown is that this emphasis on knowledge very much shaped their conversion to Christianity. Conversion was, for the Urapmin, to an important extent a matter of learning how to gain reliable knowledge of God. The knowledge they gained would eventually change their lives in many ways. But it is important to recognize that for all its enthusiasm, the process of conversion was, as the Urapmin see it, one that, like much of their traditional religion, unfolded around the acquisition of knowledge. Having found themselves in the midst of a commotion in which the divine sights finally outnumbered the divine sounds, the Urapmin were finally able to say of God *afanko*, "He is true."

CHRISTIANIZING THE URAPMIN LANDSCAPE

For someone coming to Urapmin in the early 1990s, the most obvious changes wrought by the onset of the revival were those that had to do with matters of belief and practice; one would hear them speaking in the terms of their revival Christianity and see them performing recognizably Christian rituals. But beyond these changes that stand out today, the Urapmin made several changes to their built environment that were also an important part of their second-stage conversion. These changes both evidenced and pushed forward the Urapmin determination to shape their lives around the demands of their new Christian knowledge. I explore two of them here to round out this chapter's account of the revival.

The first involves the material side of traditional Urapmin religion. Its most prominent features were the sacred men's houses and the sacred string bags *(men awem)* they contained. Each village had at least a main men's house, an *ybolam,* and some had other, smaller men's houses as well. In every village, the ybolam housed the bones (usually skulls and bones from the forearm) of important ancestors. These hung on the ybolam walls in sacred string bags rendered sooty and black from the smoke of sacrifices offered to them. For each ancestor controlled a particular part of the natural world such as wind or rain, and they could be entreated to bring about conditions favorable to Urapmin plans. The set of houses as a whole established a ritual division of labor between villages, as most of them had only one major sacred string bag and were thus identified with the work their ancestor undertook.

At the apex of this system of sacred houses was the main Urapmin ybolam. Just before the colonial era, this ybolam had been moved for defensive purposes from top Urapmin to Dimidubiip, the main village of bottom Urapmin. It housed the bones of the earliest and most important Urapmin ancestors. These ancestors controlled garden fertility and the growth of boys, and the main initiations were always organized around the house in which they resided.

Before the revival, men not only performed sacrifices and initiations in these houses, they also slept in them or in men's houses built next to them when they were living in the villages. Around these houses were built a semicircle of women's houses *(unang am)* in which women and uninitiated boys slept. Taboos on various kinds of contact between men and women and fears of the effects of feminine bodily fluids on men enforced this residential segregation. But just as the men's houses were both sacred temples and places of residence, so too were women's houses both places of residence and in some sense temples. Many families hung sacred string bags containing the bones of their deceased male relatives in their women's houses. Men would sacrifice or pray to these ancestors for help in hunting and gardening. Some also kept the bones of deceased female relatives who had distinguished themselves as great pig tenders. These ancestresses would be entreated to help the women of the household in their pig-rearing efforts. Rather than look at the distinction between the men's and women's houses as one between the sacred and the profane, then, it is more accurate to see the Urapmin landscape as one that was crowded with sacred houses and the powerful relics they contained.

If the Urapmin were to abandon their old religion, they had to dismantle this system of sacred houses. During the revival, this is in fact what they did. While some men undoubtedly removed the ancestral relics from their women's houses by themselves, most people were much too frightened of the wrath of these ancestors to carry this out, much less dispose of the bones of the more powerful ancestors who resided in the ybolams. Thus the job of leading these efforts fell to two relatively young men: Pita, an early student at the Telefol mission school and already by 1977 an experienced pastor; and Kati, the man who learned to read during the revival, who was one of the church's deacons. In 1977, Pita would have been about thirty-two years old and Kati only in his mid-twenties. Yet together with several older deacons, men themselves only in their late thirties and by no means important community leaders at the time, they took on themselves the task of removing the physical basis of traditional Urapmin religion from the men's and women's houses.

In spite of the powerful impact the revival was having, this move was not uncontroversial. Kati reports that many people spoke about him and the others behind their backs and predicted that the ancestors would make them sick and perhaps kill them. But even as the move to remove the sacra was controversial, it was undertaken, Pita stresses, only with the blessings of the big men of the community. Though many remember Pita as the one who most often spoke out about the need to remove the bones, he is careful to point out that he was told to undertake the actual work of doing so by the older men who led the community. Those big men were the ones who "looked after" *(tiinmolin)* the bones, who cared for them and sacrificed to them. It was they who had to decide that the time had come to remove them. "I was not," Pita says now, "capable of putting this plan [in place], they would have been furious with me." Nor does Pita credit himself with first suggesting that the bones be removed. Rather, he says, the Holy Spirit had already spoken to a few older men and told them, "You throw these things out." In dispatching him to undertake this task, the big men, on Pita's account, were reacting to a growing, Spirit-led consensus on the need to get the ancestral bones out of the village houses.

The role of the big men in authorizing the removal of the sacra reminds us again of the important role their openness to innovation played in all stages of the conversion of the Urapmin. Just as they early on allowed young people to leave to study the new religion, and just as the rising big men Seligapnok and Amtabuleng were the first fully initiated men to convert, so too in the case of the dismantling of the traditional religion do we see big men fostering the process of change. As Pita indicates, in doing so they were acceding to the wishes of their followers who were caught up in the enthusiasm of the revival. Initially, we know, they had been moving carefully, subjecting the new and old religions to various tests. But their ability to gauge when the depth of Christian conviction among their followers had reached a point from which there was likely no turning back, as well as their willingness to act quickly to put themselves in line with those convictions once they recognized them, did much to ensure the smooth course the Urapmin revival took. In refusing in this case to set their traditional religious authority against the new-found Christian authority of the pastors and other younger, educated Christians, the big men enabled the process of second-stage conversion to proceed. As we will see in chapter 5, this was a canny move on the part of the big men, for they managed to retain much of their overall authority even as they appeared to do away with one of its primary bases. In the present context, however, what is most important is that the big men's ingrained habit of seizing on innovation in the effort to attract and keep followers created an important part of the context in which second-stage conversion was able to take place.

Even with the support of the big men, the removal of the sacra was fraught with tension. This was so because Urapmin did not for a moment doubt that their ancestors still had power. But following a strand common both to the Baptist mission's theology and to that of the revival, they had come to see them as "devils" (<u>debil</u>, *sinik mafak;* lit., "bad spirit"), a category that remains stubbornly plural to this day in Urapmin (cf. Meyer 1999). These ancestors, along with the motobil, are the devils with whom God struggles. The choice the Urapmin faced was whether to continue to ally with these devils or abandon them and seek God's protection. The Urapmin were, as they saw and still see it, wagering that God was strong enough to protect them from the anger they were sure to inspire in these devils by turning away from them.

It was because these ancestors remained powerful that so few Urapmin were willing to take part in disposing of their bones. As Pita describes the process he and others used to remove them, he sounds almost as if he is describing a modern toxic waste cleanup effort. Afraid to touch the string bags directly, Pita and his crew got long poles and, from a distance, hooked them under the handles of the bags and lifted them off the hooks on which they hung. Still carrying the bags at the end of the poles, the crew held them well out in front of themselves until they reached the places outside of the villages in which they deposited them.

As Pita tells it, they went from village to village working in this way until they had disposed of all the sacred string bags.

Today, people talk about this process in aggressively disrespectful terms, as "throwing away" (troimwe) and "getting rid of" or "clearing away" (rausim) the ancestors. Their use of these terms expresses the extremely negative attitude the Urapmin currently take toward their ancestral religion. Yet when people are thinking carefully about the past, they tell the story of abandoning that religion slightly differently. For his part, Pita does say that he dumped the bones of minor ancestors in the holes of old latrines. But when it came to the bones of the ancestors housed in the main ybolam, he acted more respectfully. These he took down to some caves that lay below the village and deposited them there, out of the weather. Others remember that most of the bones were put in caves or laid at the base of great trees in the forest, protected environments in which people themselves sometimes sleep.

Pita and the others took such care with the disposal of important bones because they and others imagined that they might want them back. In fact, the same experimental attitude that marked the process of conversion also governed this move to be done with the sacra of the old religion. As Pita says,

> [W]hen I had finished putting them [the bones] there [in the cave] I put a single statement in place. "All right . . . these bones, the spirits of these bones, these men, we have thrown them away. We can leave them in this cave and we can watch to see about the taro. Or, we can plant taro. If it carries no fruit, then this line of men looked after it. And if we plant this taro and it bears fruit, we can watch [it grow] until we realize that this devil of ours was a lie."

Were the tests to have failed, Pita and the others would have had to retrieve the bones. God would have been tested and found wanting. This was the deal the big men made, the experiment they put in place. As it happened, the tests were, or are remembered to have been, a success. Pita notes that he put the talk of the test in place and waited. Then, as time went on, people observed, "Oh! we do have pigs, we do have gardens, we have [so much] taro that it is rotting because we can't eat [all] of it. Oh! We were just wrong [in the past]." The bones were left where they had been put. The major part of the dismantling of the old religion had been a success.

All that now remained in the villages of pre-Christian sacra were the various magical implements *(serap)* that individuals owned. While not directly connected with ancestors, these items (often kinds of nuts, or special varieties of ginger) aided in hunting, attracting the opposite sex, and other endeavors. It was now felt that people should pray to God for such help and that casting away these objects was part of demonstrating one's faith in him. Many of these objects were, I believe, burned in collective bonfires organized by important members of the church such as Pita and Kati. Others were cast out in the bush in individual acts by which many ordinary people without the extravagant Christian courage of Pita or Kati could prove their faith to God and to themselves. With these magic objects abandoned, even the small, private daily observances of Urapmin religion were gone, replaced by prayers to God for his help in matters great and small.

As the Urapmin see it, once they abandoned for several years the bones of the ancestors they had put in the caves and the bush, there was no turning back from Christianity. I once asked someone if he thought the Urapmin might ever go back to their old religion. Having long thought this question outlandish, I decided to ask it only after learning that some people thought, on the basis of their readings of the Book of Revelation, that tribal warfare would begin again in the last days. If the Urapmin could imagine returning to tribal warfare, I thought, surely they ought to be able to imagine picking up their traditional religion again. But the answer to my question was clear and firm: after how we treated those ancestors, there is no way they would have us back. With the revival in full swing, then, the dismantling of the material embodiments of the traditional religion marked a rubicon crossed.

There is one subtle point the Urapmin leave out when they tell this standard account of how they rearranged their spiritual landscape by clearing out the ancestors. The majority of cult houses throughout the Min region are now gone, having been divested of relics and left to decay in the wake of the revival. The two most prominent exceptions are the Telefolip and the major Wopkaimin cult house at Bultem (Hyndman 1994; Jorgensen 1996). These two houses were built by Afek herself and are of regionwide importance. Even the Urapmin sometimes claim that the people who look after these houses were right to remain heathen, for they are custodians of something that belongs to all the Min people (though at other times they imagine that if secret objects still kept hidden in the Telefolip were made public, the much awaited last days would commence forthwith).

But the Urapmin never had to face the prospect of divesting such an important men's house, for they never owned one. The one site of regionwide significance that they looked after was not a house but the sacred cave Wim Tem. This cave is not in or near any village but is rather in a stretch of forest so taboo that people must look straight ahead when they walk through it. Since important bones were removed to caves or into the forest, it seems that the Urapmin felt no need to tamper with the relics in Wim Tem, for they already occupied such a home. Hence, while the Urapmin no longer practice rituals there, they have not disturbed the cave (their one attempt to desecrate it ended in an outbreak of sickness; since then they have left it alone). The forest near it, which as far as the Urapmin are concerned has never been cut, is unlike any other forest I have visited in Urapmin; having never had its canopy removed, the ground is soft and free of vines, and the upward sight lines are sweeping. Its physical singularity is appropriate to its spiritual one as the last undisturbed space of the ancestral order. In light of this, there is a certain loophole quality to the Urapmin treatment of Wim Tem. They seized on its underground, bush qualities to spare themselves the task of desacralizing it once it became clear that this would not be easy to complete. Although speculation on this score seems dangerous and out of keeping with the spirit of contemporary Urapmin culture, as an outsider it is difficult not to notice that it stands ready should the Urapmin ever wish to revive their traditional religion. Although it is not a preoccupation for people in everyday life, one senses that it represents one of the revival's few pieces of unfinished business regarding the world of the past.

We turn now to the second material change that occurred during the early period of the revival. With the system of sacred houses gone, the challenge the revivalists faced was how to give Christianity a material presence suitable to its new importance in the community. Pita and Kati had cooperated on removing the ancestral bones from the spaces of Urapmin habitation, but they were at odds over how to accomplish this new task. Lemkiknok had built his school at top Urapmin, and this was also the site of the first Urapmin church. By 1977, the church had been moved to a central area between top and bottom Urapmin. For people who went to church only irregularly, this central location was convenient. Although not close to many villages, neither was it particularly far from any of them. Once the revival began, however, people started praying "day and night." At night, in the dark and the rain, people found the trip home from church hard. Kati in particular worried that his group of bottom Christians, especially the elderly among them, needed to have their own church near where they lived. He repeatedly asked Pita, then the main pastor in Urapmin, to "break" (bruk) the church so that he

Figure 3. The splitting of the church moved Christian worship into proximity
with village life. Semis, the congregation's senior pastor, stands in front of
the top Urapmin church. Salafaltigin village is just to the left. Photo by Joel
Robbins.

could build one in the middle of the bottom territory and Pita could
build one on top. Pita, however, was against the idea.

In 1978, Kati took his case to Antalap, now the mission's circuit pastor in charge of local churches. Antalap had Kati count the number of
members he expected to have in his church. When Kati reported that he
had seventy-two members ready to form his church, Antalap told him
to go ahead and build it.

For our understanding of the development of Urapmin Christianity,
the most important effect of this splitting of the churches was that it allowed church work and church attendance to become a part of daily life
for all Urapmin. On the side of church work, both the top and bottom
congregations now required a full complement of church officials, opening these roles up to twice as many people. On that of attendance, all
Urapmin were now able to attend church easily and regularly. In fact, all
but two villages are in earshot of one of the churches; even those who
did not attend a service were liable to hear its singing and catch snatches
of its sermon. With churches close to everyone's homes, Christianity
could continue to weave its way into the fabric of everyday life in Urapmin (see figure 3).

REVIVAL, LOCALIZATION, AND
THE EXPLANATION OF SECOND-STAGE CONVERSION

I have argued that one of the advantages of the two-stage model of conversion I proposed was that it encouraged analysts to be explicit about
why the shift to the second stage did or did not occur in specific cases.
Since the revival inaugurated the second stage in Urapmin, such an explanation would in that case involve explaining why the revival was
such a success once it was introduced. I have explained that success here
by focusing on the knowledge the revival brought and the way the Urapmin acquisition of that knowledge set up an amplifying feedback loop
between the processes of localization and second-stage conversion. In
this conclusion, I want to briefly link this argument to those of the previous two chapters about the nature of the colonial period in Urapmin.

As chapters 1 and 2 argued, the localization of the colonial order
through emulation and incorporation had from early on been an important Urapmin project. Determined to become lawful and to address
their increasing marginalization within the Min region, the Urapmin eagerly seized any opportunity to borrow the authority of the colonial
powers and put it to use in policing themselves and fashioning an independent place within the changing spiritual and political landscape of
their region. At first their efforts in this direction involved taking on governmental roles such as Luluai and Tultul, but very quickly they discovered that the mission provided them with their main chance to realize
these goals. Having pursued this chance with great resolve, by the time
the revival arose the Urapmin were a community with a full complement
of well-trained pastors, evangelists, and deacons. As the ecstasies of the
revival broke out in Urapmin, these educated and officially sanctioned
Christian officials were able to establish its interpretation as a Christian
event and to "protect" that interpretation from those who would transform it into one that relied more heavily on traditional ways of thinking
(Peel 1968: 288). They were also able to set in motion the feedback loop
whereby their own Christian authority grew as people came to interpret
the revival in the Christian terms they suggested. Without a sophisticated local clergy already in place, the revival might never have been as
successful as it was. Its success was thus prepared long before it took
place, during the colonial era when the Urapmin, for indigenous reasons, sent so many young men out to receive a Christian education.

Although I have focused much of my attention on these Christian
leaders, we should not forget that the big men were also crucial to the

success of the revival as second-stage conversion. This was clear in the way they chartered Pita and Kati's desacralization of the cult houses, but it should also be remembered that the Christian leaders who steered people's interpretation of the revival originally acquired their expertise in the new religion with the blessings and support of the big men. With keen eyes trained on the ways that the new religion might help them to attract and keep followers in an era when the traditional religious system was in decline, the big men ultimately did little to stop the revival and much to push it along.

Looked at in hindsight, it seems appropriate that the Urapmin speak of the revival as the decisive break that culminated their colonial experience. It gathered up the issues of emulation and autonomy that so troubled that experience and provided the Urapmin with productive ways of settling them. It also, though I have left detailed discussion of this for later, picked up the theme of lawfulness the early colonial period had so foregrounded. In one stroke, it reinforced the Urapmin belief that lawfulness was of profound significance and also promised them that they had the resources (many of them ritual resources, discussed in later chapters) to realize it on their own, without the help of the missionaries or the colonial government.

To look backward from the revival toward the colonial era it brought to an end tells us only half the story, however. For the revival also established the pattern of the "Christian lives" the Urapmin lived during the period of my fieldwork in the early 1990s. These were lives dominated by people's conviction of sin, their determination to remove it ritually in order to assure themselves of salvation, and their apocalyptic fear that the day of judgment when God would decide if they merited such salvation was near at hand. I have spoken of revival as a "movement" and as an "event" here because such terms are so naturalized in our discussions of these religious phenomena that to describe it without them would have taken more space than I had and demanded more of the reader than I was prepared to ask. But inasmuch as "movement" and "event" imply endings, they describe the Urapmin revival only poorly (Robbins 2001d). Rom once told me that the revival began in 1977 and "the Spirit continues to go until now." Pita, even more incisively, once responded to my query about when the revival had ended by pointing out that it never had. Rather, he said, "revival is our church." It is to the study of that church that the second part of this book is dedicated.

PART TWO

Living in Sin

CHAPTER 4

Contemporary Urapmin in Millennial Time and Space

All cultures situate people in time and space. The point is elementary, but in Melanesia the study of this aspect of culture only really came into its own with Munn's (1986, 1990) work on the spatiotemporal world of the Gawa. In that work, she demonstrates that Gawan projects of value creation not only presuppose a spatiotemporal order but also make positioning oneself favorably in that order part of their very definition of success. The spatiotemporal order also plays a substantial role in the projects of Christian Urapmin. Through their religious ideas and practices, they work to resituate themselves within the new spatiotemporal world that contact, colonialism, and independence have put in place, and they also work to ready themselves for God's final transformation of that order during the apocalypse. But while the spatiotemporal order is important in both Gawa and Urapmin, its construction is achieved very differently in the two places. In Gawa, it is exchange that extends space and binds time. In Christian Urapmin, it is narrative that does so. And one narrative in particular is important in this regard—the millennial narrative of the coming Christian apocalypse. Drawing on recent work on the narrative construction of time and space, in this chapter I want to show how this narrative formulates the most important spatiotemporal parameters in which contemporary, post-second-stage conversion Urapmin life unfolds.[1]

Once, so early on in my fieldwork that I had not yet begun attending church, I was walking with my wife on a deserted stretch of the path that

connects the villages of Urapmin to one another. Seemingly out of nowhere, a teenage boy caught up with us and asked what was happening
with the Gulf War. The war had started the day we arrived in Urapmin.
For reasons that had so far escaped me, the Urapmin were keenly interested in its progress, especially the possibility of its escalation. I had, in
fact, already heard the boy's question numerous times, and I gave him
what had become my usual bland answer: the war was going on much
as before. His response took me aback. It also gave me my first sense of
why the Urapmin cared so much about this distant conflict. The Urapmin, the boy told me, were praying that the war would not get bigger.

> All Baptists pray for this, but the Catholics pray that the war will get big-
> ger. Someone will be putting the triple six on people and taking over the
> world. The Book of Revelation says that in 1993 [it was January 1991] two
> thousand Catholics from Australia will come to Papua New Guinea and
> ask if you are a Christian. If you say no, they will give you the triple six. If
> you say yes, you will die instantly. They give you the triple six by stapling it
> on you. You will want to get it off, you will try, but you won't be able to.

I would hear more about the Catholics, and about this "someone," who
often enough turned out to be the pope,[2] who would lead an army and
put the triple six on people. I would also hear more about a coming massacre of Christians, and about the rise of a "One World Government"
(wan wol gavaman) or a "new world order" (niu wol oda) that would
take control of the world and institute a new law and a new monetary
system. And for those who already recognize here not only the imagery
of the Book of Revelation but also the hallmarks of Western Dispensational premillennialist speculation, it will come as no surprise that I also
heard over and over about Jesus' imminent return and about the "rapture" (repsa) it will trigger. The rapture is that moment when Jesus' believers will meet him in the sky on their way to heaven while unbeliev-
ers, marked with the triple six, will find themselves left behind and
consigned to the torments of hell. It, in particular, was a recurrent focus
of Urapmin dreams, visions, and general discussion.

      This end-time story of the rise of a new, evil government and Jesus'
rescue of his believers from its clutches is one the Urapmin tell constantly. It is nothing short of the dominant narrative of their contemporary life. This dominance emerges with particular clarity when we recognize that Urapmin Christianity can be analyzed as a thing of two
primary parts, both of which are grounded in its imagery and logic. One
of these parts is a firm belief that the millennium is near at hand, a
belief whose content is drawn directly from the narrative. The other

is an overwhelming concern with personal and communal moral self-regulation, a concern that is motivated by people's expectation of the coming judgment the story describes.[3] Intimately bound up with these two faces of Urapmin Christianity, this story insinuates itself into every corner of Urapmin life.

In this chapter, I set the apocalyptic narrative's moral thematic aside in order to consider the way it gives shape to Urapmin millennialism and, through this, to their conceptions of space and time. While there are other, perhaps more "mundane" temporal and especially spatial descriptions one might give of the Urapmin world, it is a central contention here that the Christian apocalyptic spatiotemporal scheme is the one that dominates Urapmin conceptions of the world in which they live. As I explain in the final section, this dominance follows from the way the Christian apocalyptic constructions of time and space have encompassed other such constructions that are present in Urapmin culture.

MILLENNIAL TIME IN URAPMIN

The Urapmin are unceasingly concerned that the return of Jesus may be imminent. Daily conversation is filled with reports of signs that indicate that the last days are about to begin. Urapmin call these reports "world news" (wol nius), and they filter in to Urapmin with visitors from neighboring communities or in the shape of rumors or tattered tracts that Urapmin themselves bring back from Telefomin or Tabubil. A steady stream of world news reports keeps the river of Urapmin millennial expectation constantly flowing. On occasion, however, the river overflows its banks and the Urapmin become caught up in what looks like a classical millenarian movement. People begin to attend church services twice a day. Expectation builds as each service stretches out toward the three-hour mark; during them, it seems at times as if every adult in the community comes forward with a dream or vision of eschatological import to share. Confession services and Spirit possession dances (Spirit disko; which cleanse the body of sin) are arranged, and in conversations outside of church people are preoccupied with their own sinfulness and with questions about who Jesus will take to heaven when he arrives.

Such periods of millennial intensity are, we might imagine, the price people have to pay for spicing their daily life with the bits and pieces of millennial prophecy that make up world news. On the basis of them, it is tempting to divide Urapmin life into a thing of two types or phases: the millennial and the "normal" or "everyday." But while, as I argue most fully in chapter 8, it is valuable to distinguish periods of what I call heightened and everyday *millennialism*, it is important to recognize that at all times millennial concerns are important in Urapmin thinking.[4] In fact, the Urapmin do not much differentiate between periods of millennial intensity and those of other kinds. They do not shift into movementlike periods under the aegis of a prophet or by virtue of some community decision to begin addressing collectively the coming of Jesus, nor do they slip out of them with a sense of disappointment at Jesus' failure to come. Sometimes, as they say, their church is "hot" *(mamin,* hat), driven by the Spirit's presence and charged with Christian fervor. At other times, it is "cold" *(dil,* kol). But at all times, the expectation of Jesus' imminent coming is with them. As they see it, what is crucial is that they constantly bring a millennial sensibility, one they call "looking out carefully" (lukluk gut), to bear on everything they think about or do.

Urapmin millenarianism is a constant feature of people's lives in this way, and it supplies their primary model of time. Although, as I have discussed elsewhere (Robbins 2001c), this model of time is not radically different from the one the Urapmin operated with traditionally, in its current manifestation it is thoroughly Christian and deeply rooted in their Dispensationalist version of the Christian apocalyptic narrative. I thus turn at this point to examining the temporal assumptions of this narrative and of the Western theology that originally produced it.

LIVING IN PARENTHESES: NARRATIVE ABANDONMENT AND CHRISTIAN TEMPORALITY

Even the brief snippets of the content of world news that I offered at the beginning of this chapter would be enough for those familiar with Dispensational premillennialism to recognize that this Western discourse is the source of much of its imagery and narrative style. The story of the rise of the pope and of his One World Government is in fact one strand from a larger fabric of millennial speculation that in North America is associated most famously with Hal Lindsey, whose *The Late Great Planet Earth* (1970) is widely reported to have been the best-selling nonfiction book of the 1970s in the United States (Boyer 1992: 5). Barry Smith, author of such works as *Warning, Second Warning, Final Notice,* and *Postscript,* is a New Zealand–based evangelist who has been particularly influential in promoting similar ideas in Papua New Guinea, where his revival meetings in major cities fill soccer stadiums and his books, cassettes, and videotapes circulate widely (see Smith 1980, 1985, n.d.a, n.d.b). Lindsey, Smith, and others influenced by Dispensational premillennialism promulgate the kind of theology that finds the Antichrist lurking behind the universal product code and the spread of ATM machines and that worries over the strong possibility that the formation of the European Economic Community may be a sign of the beginning of the end times. Many Dispensational premillennialists also took the advent of the Gulf War as a sign that Christ's return was imminent (Boyer 1992: 6, 326 ff.). It was their speculation on this score that lay behind the Urapmin concern over the Gulf War that was so evident during my first few weeks in the community.

The theology of Dispensational premillennialism is rooted in the work of the Englishman John Nelson Darby. Darby developed his doctrine in the late nineteenth century, but it owed its distribution primarily to the efforts of C. I. Scofield. Scofield's Dispensationalist annotation of the King James Version was published by Oxford University Press in 1909 as the *Scofield Reference Bible* and was revised and republished in 1967 as the *New Scofield Reference Bible*. By 1990, the two editions had sold between 7.5 million and 12.5 million copies (one of which I bought in Goroka, the capital of the Eastern Highlands Province of Papua New Guinea) (Boyer 1992: 97–98). The global influence of this theology has been enormous; the "prophecy" sections of Christian bookstores the world over, including, for example, the well-advertised Kaikai Bilong Tingting (Food for Thought) store in Port Moresby (the capital of Papua New Guinea), are filled with books based on its style of biblical analysis. I discuss the ways Dispensational discourse finds its way into Urapmin more fully below, but for the moment I want to focus on how it constructs time.

Darby and Scofield's theological system is called "Dispensationalism" because it divides the past and the future into a series of dispensations, periods during each of which God deals differently with humankind.[5] Most dispensations, such as those that transpired under the "Abrahamic" and "Davidic" covenants, and the one set to take place after the Second Coming, are described in the Bible. However, by means of interpretations of the prophetic portions of the Book of Daniel too complex to consider here (see Weber 1987: 19), the Dispensationalists claim to have demonstrated that the present era, what they call the "church age," is the one period that has been completely left out of the biblical narrative. This means that none of the Bible's prophecies refers to the time between Christ's crucifixion and his Second Coming. Hence the present age falls outside the main line of development of the Bible's story. Charles Larkin, in his classic 1920 (originally published in 1918) text titled "Dispensational Truth, or God's Plan and Purpose in the Ages" visually represents the situation of the church as one of existing in a valley between "the mountain peaks of prophecy." The prophets see the future as a series of ever-higher mountain peaks glimpsed one behind the other until finally "the new earth" comes into view, represented as a planetlike ball floating in the sky. What the gaze of the prophets misses is "the valley of the Church," which is tucked between the peaks of the Pentecost and the Antichrist.[6] Making the same point in verbal terms, Dispensationalists say that the church age exists in "the great parenthesis" (Boyer 1992: 88; Weber 1987: 20). This is, as Weber (1987: 43) nicely phrases it, a period of "suspended prophetic time."

What all of these verbal and visual tropes express is the way Dispensationalists see themselves as living in a gap between the narratives that make up sacred history and those that have already been foretold as structuring the future. What is difficult from the point of view of the present is to know if one has finally landed on the opposite shore where the parenthesis closes and the narrative of the future finally picks up. For the Dispensationalists, who believe that none of the prophecies of the last days has yet been fulfilled (Weber 1987: 11), it is the job of the faithful to be constantly scanning the horizon for signs that the Antichrist is consolidating his power and preparing to reign over the world as prophesied in the Book of Revelation. Once the Antichrist has arisen, Dispensationalists will know that the biblical narrative has resumed. Because the Dispensationalists are always looking for signs that the Antichrist has appeared in this way, they very often view changes in the political order as portending that the players are aligning themselves to enact the drama of the end-time scripted in the book of Revelation.

This Dispensationalist sense of being momentarily abandoned by narrative, of being caught in a middle where things may make sense but they do not make ultimate sense, decisively shapes their understanding of time. Because the Urapmin have adopted the Dispensationalist version of the apocalyptic narrative, it shapes theirs as well.

There are several related features of this Dispensationalist-Urapmin conception of time that I want to draw attention to here. First, because it contends that the present is the one era of history not narrated in the biblical text, it treats the present as radically undetermined. On the one hand, this renders the importance of what happens in the present indecisive; the ultimate meanings of things are not those they have now but those they will have in the future, when Jesus returns. The future is inestimably more important than the present (or the past) in determining the meaning of things. On the other hand, the very openness of the present renders it an important temporal arena in which people can work to ready themselves for the future by leading good Christian lives. The indecisiveness of the present thus insulates the Urapmin and others who follow Dispensationalist lines of thinking against fatalism, providing them with a sense of possibility that fuels their ongoing project of moral improvement.

A second aspect of this view of time, closely tied to the first, is the idea that the future will at some time become radically disconnected from the causal thrust of the present. Nothing happening in the present can force Jesus' arrival, nor can anyone accurately predict when it will occur. The Urapmin frequently quote the heading the Tok Pisin Bible gives in boldface just before Mark 13:2—"There is not a single man who knows the day or the hour" of Jesus' return. Even Jesus himself, they add, does not know the time of his own coming. Another favorite passage is 1 Thessalonians 5:2—"God's Day will arrive like a thief in the night." This passage, even more than the first, insists that the Second Coming will break in on the present completely unannounced. This insistence on discontinuity grounds the Urapmin conviction that one must constantly be ready to face God's judgment, since one has no way of knowing when it will come. This in turn gives further impetus to their determination to ceaselessly use the open present as a time for moral improvement.

The Dispensationalist habit of looking at current events for indications that the last days have begun, a habit the Urapmin have embraced with enthusiasm, does not in any way contradict the conception of the future and the present as radically disconnected. They attend carefully to current events to determine not if the end is *about* to begin but rather that it has *already begun*. The Urapmin treat world news as a potential source of information of precisely this kind. It promises to tell them, at least potentially, that the future has begun; that the Book of Revelation, the one they pore over more than any other, has suddenly become a reliable guide to what is happening now.

The third and last aspect of the Dispensational view of time I want to consider here is its episodic nature.[7] Time for Dispensationalists is divided into discrete eras. This is readily apparent in the way their theology divides all of time, that past and that to come, into distinct dispensations. It is also attested by their style of telling the apocalyptic narrative, for, as we have seen, that style radically distinguishes the future from the present. The Urapmin have picked up this episodic view. In addition to shaping their way of thinking about the present and the future, it very much influences their way of looking at the past. The Urapmin routinely deploy a cliché in talking about their non-Christian past and its relation to the present. "Now," they say, is "God's time" (<u>taim bilong God</u>). To this assertion, they regularly add, "Now is now, and before is before" (<u>nau em i nau</u>, <u>na bipo em i bipo</u>).[8] The present is a discrete era, unambiguously differentiated from the past. Given this orientation to time, they are not inclined to see continuities between the present and the past. Such an episodic handling of time, of the past in particular, is probably as much indebted to the model of Christian conversion the Urapmin inherited from the mission as it is a product of their understanding of the theology that lies behind Dispensational "world news." Its most important feature in the present context is not its origin, however, but the way it complements the other aspects of their view of time already discussed: the openness of the present, the overwhelming importance of the future, and the lack of necessary connection between those two periods (episodes) of time.

Taken together, these features of the Urapmin view of time create a sloping temporal order in which people are forever pitched forward, placing their best attention on the future and their best energy on their efforts to be ready for that future. With the past a discrete period to be decisively left behind and the present a way station of indeterminate importance, there is little in this conception to counterbalance a preoccupation with the end-time to come. Thus it is that the Urapmin find themselves living in a constant state of millennial attentiveness, where almost every action is produced with one eye toward its bearing on the actor's project of salvation.

To give a sense of how this everyday millennial temporality expresses itself in the life of the Urapmin, the transcript quoted below reproduces several nearly consecutive moments from a Sunday morning church service in Urapmin during April 1992. The primary focus of this stretch of the transcript is a report of world news offered by Stan, one of the leading men in the thirty- to forty-year-old age group. This is a rather vague and unimpressive piece of world news, not of the kind that tends to push Urapmin millennialism into high gear. But that is precisely why I have chosen it. It is the kind of report that shows up in Urapmin on a weekly or even more frequent basis. The two turns of talk that follow Stan's illustrate how such mundane reports are taken up in Urapmin discourse and made a part of their Christian lives.

Stan had just returned from the mining town of Tabubil. In his report he is referring to what he saw there. Jimi is a young man who is leading this service. Jani is another young male member of the congregation. The church is crowded, as it usually is on Sunday morning. But this service has already gone on for several hours, most of them filled with a discussion of Church politics in which many congregants have lost interest. People's minds are wandering. As Stan begins to speak, however, everyone becomes attentive. Talk of world news always finds an eager audience in Urapmin. (Ellipses in the transcript represent pauses. I have edited out some repetitions and false starts, which are marked by ellipses in brackets. Material in brackets is my explanatory interpolation.)

Stan: So, I saw a piece of world news down [in Tabubil]. I saw it! The world news that's around, I got it from a [poster]. It said that in May [. . .] starting on the 23rd and going on from there, a sign will appear. And so . . . And so from tomorrow, this month from the 16th to the 19th, four whites will come [to Tabubil] and talk and they will talk honestly about this thing that is going to happen [. . .]. This news, it seems like this kind of thing will happen. That's what it says and they came and said this and I heard it and so in April, May [inaudible] there is one kind of sign that will come up. A sign will appear . . . a sign will appear. That's what it said and this information was all over on notices, they put them all around on doors, in the villages. They put it up and I saw it, I saw it before I came back here. Many of the white people are talking all over the place. They have become afraid. They are very badly afraid of this, they are afraid. They are afraid. In May something will happen and so family, all of us must be afraid about this. What will happen?

That's all, a little announcement . . . and so . . . ah . . . during May it will appear. It is true. It is honest talk: the whites said "we will come up." They said that and left and it is an announcement I heard before I came home. And so, they will come and say all kinds of things about it and we can hear about it. They can talk about it and we can hear about it. They will talk honestly. I heard an announcement about this, that during this month, from the 16th on . . . four whites will come back, during that time they will come up to Tabubil. At that time they will speak. Then the next month, during that month, they say from the 23rd to the 28th, on these days, at this time, it will, a Government will appear. Something will appear. That's what they said. We don't know what will happen. Family, we wait— what kind of thing, what kind of thing will appear? And so, that's all . . . That's the only thing I have to say and so I have spoken and all of us have heard it.

Jani: [Telling a dream:] Last year at Wangbin [a squatter village in Tabubil] I had a dream like that. A man came and spoke. A man came and said, "People, all of you will be running and then you will come up to a log. You will come to a log and then you will jump over to the other side . . . By doing this you will test your belief. If up at the log you are not able to jump over, if you fall back, then you fail. That means you fail." We were running and we couldn't jump over. We bounced off it and at the same time one man got up and as he jumped over the log I saw him start to fly. He started to fly and we were watching him. We were watching him and he went way up between two clouds. That's what he did, and he went up between the clouds and we looked up and we were looking at his legs and then the clouds came together and covered him. He was covered and . . . they were saying, "Hey people it's Jesus." They usually say he will come and take us and go. Now he came and took that man so forget it . . . all of us usually worship him. Now many are not taken, like high school [which accepts very few of the graduates of the Urapmin primary school]. Some of us just go to church and imitate the real believers. All of us have just been imitating his way of worshiping. He kept saying that, he kept saying that and the boys said, "You! Its morning so you get up and go to work," and they were waking me up and I got up and I realized it was a dream . . . that is how it was.

Jimi: [Leading the service] That's how we will do it. We will continue on until the last day, then, when the last days or the rapture take place . . . Family, we will continue on and then that is what we will do . . . only one of us, only a few will go up and the rest of us will go up and fall back down like that. We will be down on the ground. And so [. . .] now we have heard our friend's dream. Stan said that in May a sign, some sort of sign will appear. It [the poster] said that and Stan told us and we have heard it. We know it, it is the last day and so it is time for this. Before is before, now it is the time when God's son is ready to come. He is ready to come. It is coming closer and closer. We don't know. So, family, we have to be watching out for it . . . and so, ah . . . that's enough announcements, lots of people have gone to the villages . . . That's enough.

This small stretch of talk, five minutes or so from a routine Sunday service, illustrates well both the openness to a discontinuous future and the commitment to moral improvement in the present that dominate the Urapmin view of time. Many of the ideas contained in Stan's report are common to most tellings of world news. That the news comes from Tabubil, that the signs of the Second Coming will appear first to whites, that the most important sign will be the rise of a new government— these are all staples of the world news genre that I deal with in the next section. In terms of the current argument, what stands out about Stan's report is the very strong sense of foreboding, the notion that something is about to happen. Given the lack of detail about what might happen, Stan's speech amounts in many respects to little more than a naked statement of the hypertrophied orientation to the future that marks the Urapmin millennial approach to time. Fittingly, when he does try to characterize what it is that will happen, for the most part all he can say is that some kind of sign will appear that points yet farther into the future. This neat compounding only emphasizes the idea that it is the final coming of the discontinuous future that is most important, not the concrete signs in which the coming may be embodied.

Jani, who until recently had been living and working in Tabubil, then tells of a dream he has had about the last days. Urapmin dream or have visions about the last days very regularly. Most of these involve, as does this one, images of many people being left behind when Jesus takes his believers into the sky. In the context in which Jani presents his dream, it does not have the force of Stan's world news. It is, after all, a dream he had some time ago and it makes no precise statement about the timing of the Second Coming. Instead, what Jani's dream does is serve to attach a concrete image to Stan's fragmented apocalyptic reportage. With its description of the rather strange log jumping contest (not a type of contest Urapmin ever described to me at any other time), it points out just how greatly the future will differ from the present. And with its theme of failure, it reconnects their millennial sense of the future with the other main theme of their Christianity: the need for moral watchfulness and reform.

Jimi's closing remarks tie the world news and the dream together. His summaries of them are notably bland, and he does not suggest that either is of any special import. Instead, he stresses the often-repeated points that Jesus is ready to come, that the end is coming "closer and closer," and that now is the time. To this bit of boilerplate, he adds that he and the rest of the Urapmin do not know how the future will unfold and that everyone thus has to be "watching out" for Jesus' coming. This, of course, is another of those bald statements of the attitude that is at the heart of the Urapmin millennial approach to time. Having domesticated both the dream and the world news, thinned them out until they blend in with the most generic of Urapmin millennial thinking, Jimi sends everyone home. Church has already gone on too long; there is no time to discuss these latest revelations.

On other days, Stan's and Jani's announcements might have sparked a move to hold more church services, to have everyone go to confession and then hold a soul-cleansing Spirit possession dance (Spirit disko). But on this day, as on most others, people will talk about what these reports mean primarily in private, taking from them little more than the kind of slight charge that keeps their millennial orientation rolling along. For the most part, that is, they will think about these things while they also go on with the rest of their lives, allowing their millennial preoccupation to exist alongside and color, but not overwhelm, their quotidian plans involving gardening, hunting, marriage, house building, and so on.

As this point makes clear, their millennial sense of time does not demand that the Urapmin give up on daily life. But it does mean that they have to remain ever attentive to the possibility that the Antichrist may rise and put in motion the well-structured, continuous narrative of the end times. Such attentiveness displays itself, as we have seen, in their perpetual scanning of the horizon for signs that he has arrived. These signs almost always come from elsewhere, from Tabubil, for example, and they always point to events that are happening even farther away, in the Middle East or in the United States. Because this is so, the Christian millennial narrative not only constructs time among the Urapmin, it also projects a geography far broader than any they had known before contact. It is to an exploration of the contours of this geography that I now turn.

OWNERSHIP, IDENTITY, AND THE
SOCIALIZED LANDSCAPE OF URAPMIN GEOGRAPHY

The Urapmin geographic imagination is social at its core; within it, every piece of land is owned by some being or category of beings. In some cases these beings are human, in others they are spirits *(motobil)*, but in all cases to know a piece of land well is to know which being or beings own it. Because the Urapmin foreground the theme of possession when looking at the landscape, they tend to perceive it as broken up into discrete units with clear identities that are tied to those of its owners. Using the names of the social categories I discuss in more detail later, they talk of one place as being Awalik's land and another as being Awem Tem's. Or they say that this land belongs to Stan and that to Jimi. In other contexts, they might exhort that this is Urapmin land, whereas that belongs to Telefolmin people. And when people get sick or when taboo ground is in question, suddenly it is the land of this or that motobil (nature spirit) that they talk about. In all of these cases, it is social diacritics that break up the land and give the resulting spaces their contours.

The postcolonial, Christian world is much larger than any the Urapmin had to negotiate before contact. But in construing it, they continue to work with the assumption that all places belong to specific beings. In fact, having met some of the people who inhabit this larger world without having seen the places from which they hail, the Urapmin have become even more dependent on the social aspects of their geographic thinking than they were in the past; they have been forced to construct their map of previously unknown territories solely on the basis of what they know about the people who own them. An inversion of those European maps from the age of discovery that kept assuming places without owners *(terra nullius),* this one specifies a good deal about the people who own the land but very little about the land itself.

In this map, the universe is reckoned as made up of the domains of the three kinds of beings. God is of course the leading light among these new proprietors, and he alone holds the position of rightful spiritual owner of all the earth. But God also has his own dwelling place. This is heaven, or, as the Urapmin refer to it in their language, *abiil tigin,* "the place in the sky." There is also a new kind of human being in the world: the whiteskin *(tabalasep,* waitskin, waitpela man). By representing a new kind of humanity, the whiteskin also reconfigures the existence of the Urapmin and others like them, who are now classified as "blackskins" (blakskin, blakpela man) These racially defined kinds of people have, as the Urapmin now understand it, spatial domains proper to themselves that are called countries (kantri). With this racial distinction and the allied notion of country as their tools, the Urapmin have been able to map the entirety of the new, enlarged landscape that now confronts them.

In drawing this new map, they use the distinction between black and white to divide the world beyond their borders into spaces of two types. There is on the one hand the nation of Papua New Guinea, which is owned by blacks. On the other hand, there is the much larger set of white countries that together make up the Christian world. The Urapmin can and in some contexts do work with sociogeographic classifications that are more fine grained, distinguishing between different groups of Papua New Guineans and making rather confused room for such groups as African Americans and "black Africans" (as schoolchildren call them) about whom they have heard reports. But in general, despite their awareness of these and other complications that beset their two-race/two-kinds of place cartography, the Urapmin consistently orient to the landscape created by this scheme when they think about or act within the expanded world they now inhabit.

In many respects, the Urapmin two-race, two-place notion presents a very simple image of the world's geography. But despite its clean outlines, Urapmin efforts to inhabit that geography are rendered complex by the role Christianity plays within it. For Christianity spans both sides of the neat binary on which that map is based. It is a white religion to which blacks belong. As blacks and Papua New Guineans, the Urapmin know where they belong. They are less certain, however, about exactly where they live as Christians. The Christian apocalyptic narrative addresses this uncertainty by working out the relations among racial, national, and Christian constructions of space and identity. To understand how it accomplishes this, it is necessary to fill in in some detail the nature of the racial, national, and transnational identities by means of which the Urapmin connect themselves to the various places on their map of the modern world.

NATIONALISM AND RACE IN URAPMIN

The Urapmin relate to the space of Papua New Guinea primarily on the basis of their national identity. Pace much of the literature on the weakness of nationalism in Papua New Guinea,[9] this national identity is a strong one. It is based, as the Urapmin see it, on their firm belief that the modern world is properly a world of nations (kantri); one in which everyone must belong to a nation, be it Australia, Amelika, or Papua Niugini. Within that world of nations, the Urapmin recognize themselves as inescapably citizens of Papua New Guinea.

It is difficult to trace the process by which the Urapmin came to accept the inevitability of modernity's national order of things (Malkki 1995). Certainly, their sense of an owned world in which all ground is connected with specific beings encourages them to see the landscape as carved up into an order of this type. This way of looking at the world was also reflected in the traditional regional ritual system, discussed in chapter 2, in which each group that was part of the system was a well-defined entity, each put in its own place by the creator woman Afek. Yet another important part of the background to nationalism in Urapmin has been their reading of the Book of Romans, second only to the Book of Revelation in its importance to the Urapmin. The statements in Romans that pertain to the divine legitimacy of the state have become key texts in Urapmin attempts to think about their current situation. Romans 13:1, "God put the Governments of the world in place," and the book's more general point that everyone lives "under" (i stap ananit) a government, are ones they often draw on when discussing their political situation. Traditional and Christian ideas have thus come together to help the Urapmin construct a model of the world in which the existence of separate nations is completely naturalized.

But to say that the Urapmin understand themselves to be inescapably Papua New Guinean, to say that they are securely within the fold of the nation, is not the same as saying that they are proud of or even content with their national identity. Far from it. The Urapmin see their national identity as a source of much that they dislike and wish to reject in themselves. Their nationalism, as I have argued at length elsewhere (Robbins 1998c), is a "negative" one; they profoundly dislike the nation of which they are a part and feel that their participation in it sullies them.

While a persistent feeling that they are underserved by a weak government contributes in some measure to Urapmin nationalist discontent, they express their negative feelings about Papua New Guinea most often not in the language of political failure but rather in that of race. With the exception of the pioneering if not uncontroversial work of Lattas (e.g., 1992) and more recent work by Bashkow (1999), issues of "race" have received remarkably little attention in studies of Papua New Guinea over the past several decades.[10] Yet, as Kulick (1992: ix–x) has written of the Gapun of Papua New Guinea, so too in Urapmin "skin color [has] acquired a fundamental metaphysical significance." Understanding the differences that follow from being black versus being white is for the Urapmin one of their most crucial contemporary projects, as it is for the Gapun. In these two and no doubt in other Melanesian societies the opposition of black and white skin is now as important in organizing thought as are those other classically Melanesian dichotomies, male/female, kin/affine, and friend/enemy.

Among the Urapmin, the most fundamental fact about black and white skins is that those with black skins are overwhelmingly inferior. Trompf's (1994: 272) point that Melanesians evidence a response that borders on "self-hate in the face of black-white disparities" holds well for the Urapmin.[11] When the Urapmin make a comparison between blacks and whites, it is almost always to the detriment of the blacks. And almost any setting can provide the occasion for such comparisons. When Urapmin quarrel with or steal from each other, commit adultery, or purposely kick each other during soccer games, people inevitably point out that whites show better self-control. When the Urapmin cannot agree to a cooperative work schedule or bemoan their lack of development, people assert that whites are better at getting things done (see Smith

1994). Furthermore, people often add, blacks' lack of knowledge and their inability to discipline themselves precludes the possibility that they could remake their world along white lines.

These sorts of comparisons often arise in public meetings, and undoubtedly serve rhetorical purposes in addition to expressing core Urapmin beliefs about the racial order. More revealing of the profound extent to which racial beliefs organize Urapmin representations of themselves and of the world were the comments people routinely made to me in private or in small groups. Many of these echoed those made publicly, but others concerned the very intimate, sometimes bodily ways in which Urapmin found blacks inferior to whites. Blacks gluttonously eat too much food at one time, cannot control their feelings of lust, anger, and jealousy, have ugly skin, hair, and other bodily features, and give birth to weak children who do not grow as well those of whites and often die in infancy (for comparable observations from another part of Papua New Guinea, see Lattas 1992). Many of the various negative features of black people noted in this list come together in the paradigmatic figure of black deficiency, the sorcerer *(biit)*, a person who personifies black gluttony and lack of self-control; one who kills those of his own race in a malicious fashion supposedly unknown among whites. While my white skin undoubtedly provided the immediate context for some of the observations made to me, their constancy (despite my persistent attempts to discredit them, I heard many hundreds of such remarks during my fieldwork) and the very wide range of people who made them indicated beyond a doubt that the nature of black/white differences was a Urapmin preoccupation not solely related to my presence.

Just as the existence of nations is a fact about the world that Urapmin accept, so too is this racial order in which black people are inferior to whites. Furthermore, the national and racial orders intersect. When making invidious comparisons between blacks and whites, the Urapmin often substitute the phrase "us Papua New Guineans" (mipela Papua Niugini, mipela man bilong Papua Niugini) for "blacks." In using this collective noun to make self-derogatory comments, they express their assumption that they share their perceived deficiencies with all the other citizens of Papua New Guinea. As all of them are black, this makes good sense in terms of the racial model Urapmin use in constructing their own dim view of themselves. As a nation of black citizens, Papua New Guinea is a nation made up of relatively impotent, uncontrollable beings like themselves. This negative impression is one the Urapmin began forming early on in the colonial era when men from other Papua New Guinea societies accompanied the colonial patrols as native policeman and both abducted local women and threatened or beat local men who attempted to stop them. It has been confirmed by things the Urapmin hear about problems that beset other parts of the country, including resurgent tribal fighting in the Highlands, the depredations of criminal raskal gangs in urban areas, and increasing corruption in the national government. Reports of such developments regularly serve to reinforce the Urapmin sense that Papua New Guinea is a nation of black people who are inevitably also "bad people" *(unangtanum mafak)* lacking self-control.

Given these racial ideas, when the Urapmin version of nationalism envisions a homogeneity that "overrides difference" (Handler 1988: 6) among its population, it pictures a homogeneity of black people displaying all the deficiencies such people possess. This is the imagined community as anomic community. In the Urapmin racial binary, where negative qualities are overwhelmingly gathered on the black side, a black nation is destined to elicit little positive affect. This is the basis for Urapmin negative nationalism.

Except in their relatively rare moments of high developmentalist fantasizing, the Urapmin do not imagine that they will ever enjoy better times as Papua New Guineans, nor do they believe that their nation can ever close the gap between blacks and whites. They are confident, however, that things will change radically in the future and that they may well change for the better. They base this confidence on their Christian belief. But Christianity does more than offer hope that the current national-racial regime will be transcended in the future. It also allows the Urapmin to claim in the present a Christian identity that connects them with a white transnational community far more powerful than the nation of Papua New Guinea.

CHRISTIANITY AND TRANSNATIONAL IDENTITY

In relation to Urapmin national and racial thinking, their Christianity is in many ways a counterdiscourse. Against a nationalism that argues that people's most important identities are those they share with their fellow citizens, Christianity offers the Urapmin an identity that links them to a larger community that exists beyond Papua New Guinea's borders. And against the binarism of Urapmin racial thinking, their Christianity suggests ways in which the differences between blacks and whites need not preclude either relationships between them or the possibility of black moral improvement. Just as ideas about race and nationalism combine to create Urapmin negative nationalism, so too are both sets of ideas transformed by the Christian thinking that allows the Urapmin to imagine the transcendence of their racially coded national identity.

The Urapmin believe that their Christian identity links them to a distant community that they imagine is far more successful both morally and materially than their national one. One of the prominent features of this community, and the one most responsible for its overwhelmingly positive character, is the fact that the vast majority of its members are white. Christianity creates this largely white community because it is in several respects a "white religion" (see also Robbins 1997b). First, as Urapmin are quick to point out, Christianity was originally practiced only by white people. It was white people who brought it to Papua New Guinea, and their missions are all housed in white countries. Second, its central figure, Jesus, is white. This is true in a mundane sense; as I was told many times and in many ways, Jesus is white like me. This much, they say, is obvious from the pictures they have seen, ones they take to be actual photographs of Jesus. Further proof follows from the fact that Jesus was born in a white country. As one man explained when I asked about the color of Jesus' skin, "He is not from here, is he? "—the implication being that Jesus was born in a white country and was thus white. Another person put it more plainly, telling me that Jesus "was born in Bethlehem, that is a white place." With Jesus figured as white, Christianity becomes white not only in its primary following but also in its cosmological makeup.

The import of Christianity for the Urapmin is not exhausted by the fact that it is a white religion, however, for of equal importance is the way in which Christianity offers to connect them to the white community from which it comes. In considering this aspect of Urapmin Christianity, we enter a realm of elaborate communal imaginings that lend purpose to and gain meaning from a wide array of concrete practices that bind together distant places on the Urapmin map of the world to create a transnational Christian community. The construction of this transnational Christian community begins with the whiteness of Jesus. Although Jesus is white in a mundane sense, he is also different from other whites with whom the Urapmin have had contact in that they are able to have a significant relationship with him.[12] Unlike other whites who dwell on the deficiencies of the Urapmin and other blacks and on the basis of those deficiencies refuse to relate meaningfully to them, Jesus "came for the sinners" like the Urapmin. He is willing to accept their friendship in a way that other whites are not.[13] Through that friendship, the Urapmin form the one close bond they have to any white being. Given the racial reading the Urapmin give to nationalism and the negative reading they give to the fact of their own race, any transnational bond worth having has to be this sort of transracial one as well. Their bond with Jesus constitutes the most important of these; it is the one around which a larger transnational community has grown.

The larger transnational community is one in which the Urapmin have ties with many white fellow Christians. In the round of daily life, however, the ties that bind this community are vague, and the inequalities that persist between its white and black members are rarely far from Urapmin consciousness. Even as an imagined community, this is one whose future promise is greater than its current achievement. But on specific "ceremonial" occasions the lines of connection that bind the community are drawn taut and the community itself comes to life most vividly in the minds of the Urapmin. The most frequent such occasion is the Sunday morning church service. When the Urapmin attend church on Sunday morning they assume they are part of a worldwide, largely white community of people doing the same thing (cf. Anderson [1983] 1991). This conception of a unified community of members simultaneously working toward the same goal was given voice in a prayer one Urapmin man offered at a Sunday service. "God," he began, "people everywhere are praying to you." On Sunday morning, the transnational community takes on a substantial quality it often lacks at other times.

The fact that world news about the coming apocalypse reaches the Urapmin at all is, as they reckon it, further proof of their membership in a transnational, transracial community. I pointed out above that Urapmin millennialism is largely fueled by bits and pieces of the Western discourse of Dispensationalism. These bits and pieces come to Urapmin via several paths. Urapmin and members of neighboring groups who visit the mining town of Tabubil or the District Office at Telefomin often bring them back when they return. But the Urapmin are quick to point out that this news does not originate in these regional centers. On the contrary, it comes from the wider, white Christian world. It is, the Urapmin say, formulated by highly trained "Bible doctors" (Baibal dokta) living in countries other than Papua New Guinea. The very designation "world news" highlights this foreign quality while also indicating that it pertains to goings-on closer to the center of the global Christian transnational community.

As world news, these rumors address the Urapmin as Christians rather than as Papua New Guineans. They understand their receipt of world news as the final point of an exchange in which white Christians reach out to them with a gift. This is most obvious when, as sometimes happens, world news reaches Urapmin or one of their neighbors in the form of a tattered tract or a photocopy of a tract. These tracts are always greeted with serious interest, and they are more likely than mere verbal rumors to push Urapmin millennialism to a movementlike pitch (Robbins 1997b). The Urapmin understand the tracts as items sent specifically to the Christians of their region by members of the transnational Christian community. Indeed, they often call the tracts "letters" (pas), a usage that highlights the idea that their authors have specific addressees in mind. One rumor was thus traced to a letter that "English and Australian Baptists" sent to the District Office in Telefomin "because they knew we were Baptist." Another tract, this one detailing how "a man has risen up, changed his face, changed the law, and assembled an army that is ready to fight," was supposedly found between the two rows of cans in a carton of tin fish sent to a trade-store among a neighboring group. The appearance of this message in the carton was explained as follows: "A friend, a Christian man, made the fish and put the booklet [buklet] in so that whatever church opened it would know that now the time [for the last days] has come." The paradigmatic "letter" has here become a "booklet," and so too in this case has the addressee become broader, no longer addressed simply to Baptists. All Christians are now the recipients of this message. But in both cases the emphasis is on the fact that members of the larger Christian community are in direct communication with the Urapmin, sending them important information because of the bonds that link the two groups. Because the Urapmin see world news this way, their possession of it becomes a potent index of their participation in the transnational Christian community.

But world news is important not only for the way its arrival indexes Urapmin participation in the Christian transnation. In its content, which always in one way or another bears on the Dispensationalist version of the Christian apocalyptic narrative, it also represents that transnation's greatest promise. For there is tension at the heart of Urapmin Christian social geography that this narrative does much to assuage. Thus we must turn at this point to considering explicitly the way the apocalyptic narrative constructs space.

The tension the apocalyptic narrative addresses can be understood most readily in the form it takes during Sunday morning church services, where it announces itself as a contradiction between the nature of the service as a kind of action and the content of what is said as it unfolds.

As noted above, as a transnationally shared form of action, the Sunday morning service allows the Urapmin to take their place in the wider Christian community. At the same time, however, the content of their prayers and sermons often draws attention to their failure to make themselves worthy to participate in this community, a failure they see as particularly linked to their race and hence their nationality. Church services are regularly dominated by lengthy harangues about people's lack of self-control and their failure to heed God's will by avoiding sin. Not surprisingly, these harangues develop all of the ideas about black gluttony and willfulness that dominate Urapmin racial thinking. Self-control is, in fact, the single most important thing whites possess and blacks lack.[14] With these harangues, Urapmin point to what divides them from whites in the midst of the very ritual that most fully integrates the two groups. Most evident on Sunday morning, this disjunction between the formal spiritual equality of black and white coreligionists, who share a liturgy and set of beliefs, and the Urapmin perception of a de facto spiritual hierarchy, in which whites are better able to fullfil the demands of this religion, haunts all of Urapmin Christianity.

Much of the importance of Urapmin Christian millennialism resides in the way it addresses the tensions this disjunction creates. Despite its emphasis on Urapmin sinfulness and lack of self-control, this millennialism does not simply mirror their construction of racial difference. Rather, it decisively parts company with that racism by suggesting that with God's help and their own proper effort the Urapmin can improve themselves and eventually become the equal of whites. Unlike their racial nationalism, which asserts that the Urapmin are condemned forever to remain citizens of an inferior nation, Urapmin millennialism foregrounds their capacity to change and to thereby become full members of the Christian transnational community. The ultimate expression of this idea of black perfectibility is the Urapmin conception of heaven, a place where those Urapmin who have improved themselves will live in the style of whites and in community with them. Indeed, in heaven, the Christian transnation will take on a substantial form that at present it only imperfectly approaches. It will be able to take on that form because the Urapmin will finally have mastered themselves. In heaven, the tension between shared practice and unequal moral worth will be finally resolved. It is noteworthy that this will occur at a time when the world will be made up of a single place, where the divisions that carve up the current landscape will cease to exist.

As the Urapmin understand it, the millennial narrative not only resolves the tensions between racial equality and hierarchy, on the one hand, and those between proximity and distance, on the other, that wash over their Christian geography, it also speaks directly to their disaffection from their nation. The rumors of world news that constantly renew the millennial narrative are full of the imagery of violent and rapacious state-making projects. New legal and monetary systems introduced almost without warning (something the Urapmin have of course experienced several times in the recent past with the coming of the colonial and postcolonial governments), the evil leader and his determination to force participation in his plans by killing those who dissent, and other staples of this discourse all reckon the coming nation-state as a hellish prelude to the real hell. In this way, the narrative makes sense of their lived national geography as well as of the narrower one in which they struggle for self-improvement and the wider one to which they constantly work to connect.

In discussing the geographic resolution of the tensions within Urapmin Christianity and nationalism, it is useful to return to the idea of the owned landscape that I used to characterize the traditional Urapmin view of the world. Looking at the map of the contemporary world that the Urapmin have created, we can say that the ideas embedded in the notion of the owned landscape have been important primarily for the way in which they break up the space of the world by connecting different beings to different parts of it. The idea that there are white nations and black nations fits this scheme well and requires no revision of its formal postulates. The idea that there could be a single owner of the entire earth or universe, by contrast, is entirely new. When the Urapmin say that God owns everything on the earth, they set up the possibility of an earth that is not broken up into separate domains. True, at present God seems to allow different groups of people (not to mention the spirits with whom the Urapmin still wrestle) some claim on land he more fundamentally owns. But when, during the apocalypse, he finally takes full control of his domain, the earth will have a single identity as God's place. This single place is the model for heaven, a place where a landscape without division supports no social differentiation. With only one owner, the logic of space breaks down, and in the tremors that breakdown unleashes, the entire edifice of race and nation will crumble.

Starting from the premise of the owned landscape, then, the Urapmin version of the Dispensational premillennial apocalyptic narrative both explains the contemporary national order of things and resolves the problems that order poses for the Urapmin. Space, like time, is an arena of a future change for which the Urapmin live their lives in preparation. This focus on future change in both domains has a profound effect on how Urapmin live in the spatiotemporal world they most proximately, physically inhabit.

THE CHRISTIAN ENCOMPASSMENT
OF THE LOCAL AND THE PRESENT

The millennial models of time and space to which the Urapmin subscribe very much devalue the present and the local. They encompass them, in Dumont's terms, determining their meanings and limiting the contexts in which their own demands can appear as paramount (Dumont 1980; Robbins 1994). People approach present concerns and local spaces with a careful eye turned toward how their decisions about them will influence their future salvation. Sometimes, as will become clear, this attentiveness to the future even leads the Urapmin to give up on local space and time entirely, leaving their gardens and daily routines behind for periods of heightened millennial enthusiasm. And even when millennial practice is not in such full swing, the temptation to turn one's back on the here and now is never completely absent; at any given time, some people in the community will be vociferously promoting the idea that people should be spending more time in church and less time devoted to what they call "the things of this ground" (*towal diim mafak-mafak*, samting bilong graun). The demands of the here and now are thus always at best secondary concerns.

The devaluation of the spatiotemporal present is based not only on the belief that it is less important than the potentially heavenly one of the future. It also draws on the conviction that this close-in world throws up impediments to salvation. It is full of the snares that draw people into sin. Its ground produces the crops people are tempted to steal or covet, and its temporally present social world generates the anger, jealousy, and sexual desire that push them into the actions that spoil their Christian life. I will have much more to say about the present social world later. Here, I want to emphasize the hazardous nature of the Urapmin relationship to their land *(bokon)*. Beyond the obvious ways in which the land produces crops that awaken sinful desires, the constant disputes that surround its ownership are one of the primary causes of sinfully aggressive behavior. Indeed, the very disposition of the land encodes previous moral failures, for the Urapmin construe present patterns of land tenure as the result of disputes in the past; the kind of sinful disputes, they say, "we black people have all the time." Furthermore, the land is populated by nature spirits (motobil) who constantly try to draw people into exchange by making them sick and then demanding, through the Spirit women, pig sacrifices *(kang anfukelang)* as the price of releasing their victims. The Urapmin are often tempted to give in to these coercive demands, and occasionally they do turn to sacrifice, but they regard it as extremely sinful to do so; to be a good Christian is to regard Jesus as the last sacrifice and to cease to have positive interaction with the spirits. The spirit-filled nature of the local landscape thus adds to its status as an obstacle to Urapmin moral improvement. On several scores, then, that landscape is the source of as much trouble as good.

Taken together, the various moral hazards that beset their contemporary social and material life lead the Urapmin to conceive of the spatio-temporal present as something to be transcended. Their efforts in this direction lean precipitously toward world rejection and it is by encouraging those efforts that their Christian outlook dominates the way the Urapmin evaluate the world that is near to hand. From the vantage of that Christian outlook, local spaces and times are important not on their own terms but only inasmuch as they provide the setting for people's efforts to perfect themselves.

It is worth noting that the other important introduced spatiotemporal scheme has its own (local) world-rejecting inclinations. In the landscape that development configures, the Urapmin have come to recognize themselves as a "bush line" (bus lain), a group identified with their deep jungle territory as opposed to the more cultured spaces of white and black towns (taun). The state of underdevelopment is here represented as a spatial as much as an economic one (cf. Pigg 1992). As the Urapmin see it, the only way they will be able to move themselves to a more desirable spot on the developmental map is to have Kennecott or some other company take their land to build a mine, in the process physically moving them to another location, one where they will have sawn timber houses and other urban amenities. It was with this goal in mind that they publicly asked Kennecott, at a government-sponsored meeting held to renew the company's mining lease, to "destroy our ground" (destroim graun bilong mipela). Clearly, the rhetoric of development does not provide an effective counterweight to Christianity in terms of keeping the Urapmin anchored in the here and now.

But despite being similar to Christianity in leading the Urapmin to reject their local landscape, in the last analysis development too, like indigenous ideas about the spatiotemporal present, is finally encompassed by the Christian millennial scheme of the world. For as much as the Urapmin crave development, they also recognize that it is only "a thing of this ground." Therefore, it does not speak to their ultimate concerns, and the spatiotemporal world of town and bush that it constructs remains a subordinated one in the Urapmin imagination. The ultimate destruction of the bush will come as the result of God's power, not the company's bulldozer.

The apocalyptic narrative faces little resistance to its dominance of the spatiotemporal structure of contemporary Urapmin culture, and that culture provides no basis on which to value the here and now as of primary importance. But the spatiotemporal present is not completely left out of the apocalyptic narrative, for it is the place in which the narrative situates its moral demands. It is through these demands that the theme of lawfulness that figured so prominently in the colonial history of the Urapmin finds its purchase on their postcolonial lives. Indeed, the story constructs time and space primarily as a backdrop to its most important message: one must live a lawful Christian life in the present in order to benefit from the coming changes that will transform the meanings of time, space, and existence itself. As the narrative requires, Urapmin life in the present is almost completely taken up with the effort to live morally in Christian terms. The next several chapters describe how the Urapmin understand this moral project and how they contend with the obstacles that render its realization difficult.

CHAPTER 5

Willfulness, Lawfulness, and Urapmin Morality

Tolai social order—and this is the core of Tolai law—defines a framework for individual action; it gives choice by limiting its range, but it does [not] prescribe what is good or prohibit what is bad; it does not tell people to do only the right thing; it does not want to bring about a state of affairs where reality matches an ideal; it does not presume to be an ideal order. It is an actual order which permits people to live as human beings—which, as far as Melanesians are concerned, is all that mankind can possibly hope to achieve.

Peter Sack, "'Bobotoi' and 'Pulu': Melanesian Law:
Normative Order or Way of Life?"

Within the millennial space-time they inhabit, the Urapmin struggle for moral perfection and the salvation they hope it will bring. Despite the energy they put into accomplishing their moral goals, however, they find them hard to reach. No doubt this is true on some level for everyone we might want to call Christian, but for different groups of Christians it is true in different ways. In the Urapmin case, their moral difficulties are rooted both in their changing conceptions of morality and in the way these changing conceptions relate to what we might call their indigenous conceptions of "social interaction" or, in a sense I define later, of "social structure." It is on these matters of morality and the conceptualization of social action and structure that Urapmin indigenous and Christian ideas are in greatest conflict—this is where, to use the terms I set out in the introduction, we are clearly on the ground mapped out by the model of adoption, where two cultural systems are operating at once. It is the contradictions and confusions that follow from this unsettled state of dual cultural play that lead the Urapmin to fall constantly short of their moral goals and that produce the conviction of sinfulness that motivates so much of their Christianity.

Because indigenous moral ideas are still in play in complex ways in contemporary Urapmin life, it is necessary in discussing morality in general to follow a procedure I have eschewed elsewhere in this book—laying out an indigenous system of ideas first and only then going on to examine the cognate system Christianity has introduced. Observing this order, this chapter focuses on the indigenous moral system; the next takes up the Christian one and the problems that follow from its relation to indigenous ideas that are still in force.

THE SPECTRUM OF MORALITY IN URAPMIN CULTURE

I borrow the phrase "the spectrum of morality" from Valeri's (2000) discussion of taboo among the Huaulu of Indonesia. It captures quite elegantly the sense in which morality, both for the Huaulu and for the Urapmin, is a single domain composed of ideas and values that are at once related and distinct. In Urapmin culture, the unity of this spectrum is attested by the fact that everything that falls along it is referred to by a single word: *awem*. We have already encountered this word as an adjective referring to that which is "sacred" and "secret." To this list, we have to add its additional adjectival use to modify those things that are "taboo" (as in *nuk awem*, a taboo marsupial species) and its nominal use to refer to specific realms of "law" (as in *alowal imi awem*, the law of the ancestors). The unity of awem as a domain consists in the overlap between these various senses; it refers to *prohibitions* (on speaking that which is secret, using that which is taboo, or acting in ways that are unlawful) that are grounded in kinds of authority that are *sacred* in the sense that they transcend those produced simply by the actions and agreements of human beings.

A further aspect of the unity of the moral domain in Urapmin follows from the fact that despite the sacred authority that backs moral prohibitions of all types, they all seek to guide activities about which human beings have some choice. Behaviors the Urapmin take to be innate, such as, say, breathing or a baby's crying, are not covered. Neither are people enjoined to avoid the inevitable: there is no prohibition against dying when one has been sorcerized, for example. Rather than aim to regulate the innate or inevitable, moral rules seek to govern domains in which human beings are understood to have some freedom. We may well be

touching on what is common to the moral domain cross-culturally here
(Wagner 1981; Faubion 2001; Laidlaw 2002), a point that I take up
again in the conclusion. For present purposes, however, what is important is that this broad translation of *awem* as sacredly grounded prohibitions aimed at shaping the realms of human freedom neatly expresses
the Urapmin definition of morality.

But as much as the polysemy of *awem* ultimately gives way to a fundamental unity of sense that marks off the domain of the moral, the distinctions it generates also provide that domain with its spectrumlike
quality. For as Urapmin culture treats them, law is clearly something
other than taboo, and taboo itself can be broken down into two sub-
categories. These distinctions between law and two kinds of taboo, although not evident at the level of vocabulary (where all are *awem*),
emerge clearly when we examine how these moral systems differently
formulate prohibitions, punish their breach, and orient people in their
thinking about their lives. In the remainder of this chapter, I explore
these three points on the Urapmin moral spectrum and examine how the
Urapmin traditionally worked with them to produce their sense of themselves as moral persons, what they call "good men" *(tanum tangbal)* and
"good women" *(unang tangbal)*.

THE LAW

The law, an area of awem the Urapmin now gloss with the Tok Pisin
term lo (as opposed to tambu, "taboo"), consists of a set of prohibitions
that apply to everyone. One should not kill other Urapmin, nor should
one steal, fight, argue, adulter, utter "bad talk" *(weng mafak)* about
people, or "push" *(nenin)* others to do things they do not want to do.
All of these actions are 'bad' *(mafak)*. Only those who avoid them earn
the appellation "good man" or "good woman." The consequences for
breaching these rules, besides the general one of being known as a "bad
person" *(fenmin tanum/unang, tanum/unang mafak),* include experiencing shame *(fitom)*, suffering possible physical retaliation from those
you injure, becoming susceptible to various kinds of sicknesses caused
by the anger others feel toward you, and having to contend with the
stunted garden growth and poor hunting that are thought to follow
from human disputes. Furthermore, the lawbreaker also risks death by
sorcery. This last sanction is uncommon, for the Urapmin themselves
are unable to practice sorcery (it is a capacity Afek did not give to them).
But if sufficiently provoked, individual Urapmin can take out sorcery

contracts *(biil)* in which they arrange with a sorcerer from another group to kill someone who has injured them by breaking the law. This set of laws and the sanctions that enforce them are fundamental to Urapmin moral thinking. All Urapmin learn them very young, and men say that during initiations, ritual leaders *(tanum awem,* "law-sacred men") put more emphasis on indoctrinating novices in their importance than on revealing secret knowledge.

Stated baldly, as I have presented them here, the prohibitions of Urapmin law are so universal as to appear banal. Foucault (1990: 32) suggests that this is true of moral codes everywhere: they tend toward sameness in their fundamental interdictions. At the same time, however, from the inside of any culture, these rules are charged with import and appear as properly central among the demands society makes on its members. In the Urapmin case they are inflected by an elaborately developed set of ideas concerning the way people's "inner" emotional and intellectual lives can subvert their efforts to live as good men and women. This connection between the inner life and moral behavior provides Urapmin legal thinking with a complexity well beyond that evidenced by a simple list of the behaviors it outlaws.

The notion of an inner life is not foreign to the Urapmin. The heart *(aget),* as I mentioned earlier, is the seat of all thought and emotion. It is understood to be inside the chest *(ibak tem).* Within the heart, "thinking" and "feeling" are distinguished. "To think" is a verb that takes the thinking person's heart as its subject (possessive + *aget fukunin);* as such, it is a process that the person controls.[1] "Feelings" are generically referred to by the term "inside the heart" *(aget tem).* But in contrast to thoughts, feelings are generally spoken of as things that "arise" *(tabemin)* in a person's heart; linguistically and experientially, they are agents that affect the heart rather than operations that the heart carries out, and thus people have less control of them than they do of thoughts. A final aspect of the person, also perhaps lodged in the heart, though this is not clear, is "will" *(san).* Although like thoughts and unlike feelings, the will is definitely part of the person and is, on the linguistic level, obligatorily possessed, it is less like thoughts and more like feelings in that it seems to have a force of its own and can make the thinking part of people a passive onlooker as it "pushes" them in directions their hearts might not be inclined to take them.

The basis of "moral behavior" *(kukup tangbal)* as it is constructed in this psychological discourse is "good thinking" *(aget fukunin tangbal).* Those who base their decisions on good thinking will never breach the code of law laid out above. Those who breach the law by stealing, fighting, arguing, and so on, do so on the basis not of good thinking but at the urging of the will and various emotional states that are tied to it. The primary emotional culprits in this scheme are anger *(aget atul)*, covetousness *(tiin lawut inin)*, and jealousy *(titinin)*. It is not much of a leap to see that all these emotions are expressions of a frustrated will; one that cannot get what it wants or keep what it has. Thus the Urapmin tend to see all lawless behavior as an expression of the will, untempered by the counsel of good thinking and often informed by the urgings of emotion. It is the will let loose as naked desire (in covetousness and adulterous longings) or in a frustrated form (in anger and jealousy) that lies at the root of lawless behavior. Conversely, the ideal moral life as they imagine it in the terms of this scheme is one dominated by good thinking rather than by a willful disregard for the law.

As a moral ideal, this is all well and good. But one imagines that if matters were really as simple as it suggests, the domain of moral thinking would not be so well developed in Urapmin culture. And in fact, matters are not this simple. Urapmin culture not only offers this scheme of the inner workings of the moral person, it also suggests that in many situations the expression of the will, even in ways that do not fully accord with the law, is valuable even if morally risky. This equivocation when it comes to morally evaluating the will is lexically marked in the Urap language, where the term that refers to "lawlessness" *(fenmin)* is distinct from the one that refers to "willfulness" *(futembemin)*. Futebemin behavior is often condemned, but it is also sometimes celebrated. This dual evaluation of the will greatly complicates Urapmin moral thinking. To understand why such complications are necessary, we have to consider how moral ideas are connected with the Urapmin conception of the way their society comes to take the shape it does.

WILL AND URAPMIN MODELS OF SOCIAL STRUCTURE

In writing about Urapmin notions of willfulness and lawfulness, one finds that one is writing not only about morality but also about an indigenous model of social structure. In saying this, I take cultural models of social structure to be sets of cultural representations about persons, groups, and relationships, how they come into being, how they are arranged, and how they can be perpetuated or broken. As I noted in the introduction, Urapmin cultural representations construe social structure as a product of people acting in both lawful and willful ways. These representations stand out particularly starkly in local discussions of social life because the Urapmin have no other models of social structure, for example, as a set of specific rules tied to kinship statuses or as an ideal structure that they must reproduce, on which they can draw when considering these matters. This point is easier to grasp if set against the background of the recent history of social structural studies in Papua New Guinea. Many of these have arrived at the counterfactual claim I have just made for the Urapmin—that in planning social action people do not orient to an image of an ideal social structure or to a set of conscious rules concerning how people in specific ascribed statuses should interact. Indeed, this claim has recently become commonplace in Melanesian ethnography, particularly through the work of Marilyn Strathern (1988; see also the epigraph to this chapter). A brief look at the developments that brought Melanesian-ists to this conclusion should make its import clear.

The dominant problematic in the study of Melanesian social struc-tures had from the beginning of work in the Highlands been based on the segmentary lineage model developed in Africa. This model was based on what Sahlins (1985: 12) describes as "the standard average Radcliffe-Brownian social structure of corporate descent groups, as-cribed statuses, and prescriptive marriage rules." Crucial to this model was not only the existence of these enduring groups, statuses, and mar-riage rules but also a consciousness of them on the part of the "natives" who lived with them. The claim was not that people had to recognize the structure in its entirety but that they had to possess some model of it to which they could orient in planning their actions. As Pitt-Rivers puts it:

> Reading about Africa, one has the impression that its people have a re-markable capacity for stating their customs and beliefs. Norms, it appears, are in everyone's mind and are constantly referred to as guides to conduct. The ethnographer of Africa has never waited for an answer about the cor-rect thing to do. He is among a race of lawyers, it seems, ready to argue every point and quote precedent. (1971: xvii–xviii)

With this model in mind, early ethnographers of the Highlands set out to look for people thinking and acting in terms of corporate groups, as-cribed (kinship and lineage) statuses, and consciously held rules for put-ting these groups and statuses into action.

As is well known by now, the efforts of these early Highlands ethnog-raphers ended in failure. As reports of Melanesians bringing all sorts of consanguines, affines, and even strangers into their "unilineal lineages" and treating them as lineage-mates began to proliferate, the peoples of the region developed a reputation for not being able to color inside the social structural lines very well. It was Barnes, in a classic 1962 article, who finally pointed out how messy the picture had become. What became known as the "loose structure" debate then ensued.

The literature that makes up the debate is now tedious to go through in any great detail. We can move past it quickly by making the very important point that any impression of looseness was our perception, an effect of our expectations and our failure to understand what Melanesians understood themselves to be up to. Yet it is worth pausing to note that the debate developed in such a way as to make Melanesian anthropology the locus of much important cultural analysis from the late 1960s on. For the effort to search out ways to talk productively about what was going on social structurally in Melanesia eventually led Melanesianists to attend systematically to the ways indigenous people understood matters of relationship and social organization; it forced, that is, a turn to the study of culture. The turn to culture in the study of Melanesian social structure in its simplest form involved recognizing that in many societies agnatic "descent dogmas" are used to understand social arrangements regardless of how members of groups are actually recruited (A. Strathern 1973: 42). More complex models followed from Wagner's (1967) pioneering investigations into the ways the Daribi create relationships between people through the sharing and exchange of various substances. What these studies offered were accounts of the "content of kinship" and clanship in Melanesian societies. In them, the study of how people are recruited to groups gave way to that of how people make relationships.

In discussing the cultural basis of kinship and clanship in Melanesia, many scholars focused on the role of indigenous ideas about substances and their exchange in providing a framework that people used to understand the creation of relationships. It turned out that having the proper blood *or* eating the proper food could make one an "agnate" (A. Strathern 1977), just as sharing or exchanging the appropriate objects could make people kin. Studies began to take up the matter of how people direct the flow of substances such as blood, semen, and meat in order to create the relationships that make up their social field (e.g., Wagner 1967, 1977; Clay 1977; A. Strathern 1972; M. Strathern 1988; LiPuma 1988). The focus on substances and their exchange slowly came to replace that on enduring groups and the relations between them. By the time M. Strathern took stock of where things stood in 1988, she was comfortable arguing (in terms to a large extent borrowed from Wagner) that Melanesians do not even have a notion of society as an ideal structure, much less orient to one in planning action. Instead, they have ideas (often concerning substances) about how social action creates "sociality," a flow of relationships that constitutes the ever-changing context of social life.

I think it is a mistake to imagine, as Carrier and Carrier (1991: 8–25) seem to, that the loose structure debate was essentially one produced by a failure to maintain a distinction between approaches that study society on the level of "structure" (ideal, timeless patterns) and those that do so on the level of "practice" (the actions of self-interested individuals undertaken in specific social contexts). From this point of view, Melanesians only came to appear loosely structured because data on practice were brought to bear on the analysis of structure. If these kinds of data are kept distinct, the argument implies, we can have perfectly satisfactory (in traditional terms) accounts of structure in Melanesia and equally adequate ones of practice. What this approach misses is that the distinction between structure and practice is itself a cultural one, and it is one that many Melanesians do not employ in the same way that Western social scientists do (cf. Wagner [1975] 1981: 40). They have not formulated models of structure from which they recognize that practice often deviates. Instead, they imagine that everything we would want to study at the structural level is constantly made and remade through practice. The point of these makings and remakings is not their effects on the "structure" in place just prior to them but rather their ability to further the flow of sociality.

Sahlins's (1985: xi) distinction between prescriptive and performative structures can help to clarify this point. As he notes, both types of structures are defined by the relationship they posit between "social forms" and "appropriate acts." In the prescriptive structures, of which the African models are a classic example, the social forms generate the appropriate acts. In performative structures, typical of Melanesia, the situation is reversed: appropriate kinds of actions create social forms. Prescriptive structures, as befits their emphasis on an already given order, tend to objectify themselves in mythopoetic representations of that order. Performative structures, as we have seen, do not do so, leaving those who live with them without explicit models of society (Sahlins 1985: 53–54). But, and this move is crucial, Sahlins is determined to argue that societies that are constructed performatively are in fact structured. What lends them structure is not a model of society that actors work to replicate but codes of action inscribed in the *habitus* (in a term Sahlins borrows from Bourdieu 1977) of each person who operates within them (Sahlins 1985: 53). In performative societies like our own, or like traditional Hawaiian society, those codes of action involve ideas such as "love" (Sahlins 1985: xii), "will," and "conscience." In Melanesian societies, they often involve ideas about substances and how their exchange creates relationships. Since these ideas are at the core of performative structures, it is not surprising that they are very well developed in cultures that feature such structures. Indeed, I would postulate that societies that have a performative structure will generally also possess very complex ideas about action: what motivates it, how it is carried out, and so on. Since these ideas take the place of mythopoetic representations of timeless structure in prescriptive systems, they are likely to be marked by the very kinds of detailed grandeur anthropologists have learned to associate with those representations.

As I have noted, in many areas of Papua New Guinea, ideas about how people behave in relation to various substances constitute this indigenous theory of action. Readings of any of the Melanesian monographs cited above will confirm this point. The situation in Urapmin is somewhat different, however. Urapmin conception theory, in keeping with their cognatic mode of descent reckoning, sees the woman's contribution of menstrual blood *(suwenam)* and the man's contribution of "penis water" *(wal ok)* as equivalent in their production of the child. While they say that whichever substance is "stronger" in a given case will determine the sex of the child, they do not believe that either substance alone creates any specific features of the body (cf. Jorgensen 1983; Poole 1985). Instead, the two substances mix thoroughly, "like making cement," as one person told me, and together create the child. Children are made up of the blood of both parents and those parents' parents and upward for as far as anyone cares to remember. This conception theory is not complex, and it is not surprising that it does not do much to determine the way the Urapmin think about the different relationships that make up their social life.

How, then, do the Urapmin think about social action and the creation of relationships? They do so in terms of their ideas about willfulness and lawfulness. In Urapmin understanding, social life is created by people acting out their willful desires while taking into account the way these desires are constrained by the lawful expectations that inhere in already accomplished social relations. This formulation is the foundation of their social thinking. It takes the place of the notions of kinship and clanship in what anthropologists usually represent as people's conceptions of their own social structures.

As a principle, it gives a prominent place to the will, and this returns us to our consideration of the contradictory ways the Urapmin morally evaluate this aspect of the person. The importance of willful action in the creation of social relationships follows from the fact that in Urapmin no relationships or social groupings are given by prescriptive social structural rules; they must be created by individual action. This is true for all of the relations and groupings—marriages, families, trade partnerships, gardening and hunting groups, villages, and sports teams—that make up the Urapmin social landscape. In creating these, people have recourse to idioms of kinship and something like "clanship," but these idioms only have force when they are put to persuasive use in willful individual projects of relationship building. On their own, they do not determine any aspects of Urapmin social life.

The structural impotence of these idioms can be seen most clearly in the case of the system of "clanship." The Urapmin divide the social universe into a set of social categories they call *tanum miit* (lit., "man base" or "man origin"). Spoken of in the abstract, the tanum miit appear to be almost a system of fixed clans. There are currently five robust tanum miit in Urapmin: Awem Tem Kasel, Awalik, Atemkitmin, Amtanmin, and Kobrenmin. There is also one named Fetkiyakmin that is largely moribund. Others existed in the past but have died out. In the past, these social categories are seen to have been connected with specific ritual prerogatives and secret mythologies. They are also often spoken of as the largest units that own land. Furthermore, Urapmin tend to see most villages as being primarily the creation of one of them, almost as if each was constructed around a dominant clan.

All of this looks very much like the kind of explicit model of social structure I have been at pains to argue the Urapmin do not have. Yet the true test of this resemblance comes when we look at how these social categories are connected to action. If they did constitute a standard average Radcliffe-Brownian social structure, we would expect them to furnish people with fixed statuses and we would expect people to keep them in mind in planning their actions. When put to this test, however, the tanum miit fail miserably.

People inherit their tanum miit memberships from both their mothers and their fathers. In this, as in all matters of inheritance, Urapmin society is cognatic. But because a person's parents also inherited from both of their parents, people often belong to four tanum miit even before they do any extensive kinship calculations. Because tanum miit do not regulate marriage, this wide fan of memberships through parents is not guaranteed to each person (i.e., some people have parents or grandparents who share tanum miit identities). But this is of little import. As Jorgensen (1981b) has shown is the case among the Telefolmin, most Urapmin can claim to belong to all of the tanum miit that exist at a given time. As members of a community of 390 people who practice strict endogamy and figure inheritance cognatically, people with social ambitions can actually spell out for you how it is they claim membership in all of the tanum miit. Less ambitious people dispense with the actual calculations, but this does not prevent them from confidently asserting their membership in most of the active tanum miit in the community. Therefore, an identity as a member of a given tanum miit can serve as a basis for a particular action, but people are never forced to act in a specific way on the basis of such membership, since they can always claim that they are really members of a different category.

Because tanum miit membership is so fluid, most people most of the time are inclined to disregard it in constructing their social lives. The primary force that prevents them from doing so is the willful action of big men, who, for reasons that are examined below, frequently attempt to compel people to treat these memberships as at least somewhat exclusive and fixed. The tanum miit structure as a whole thus finds its greatest application in the willful projects of big men. In this respect, it is, in Wagner's (1974) terminology, primarily a system of "names" that big men use to organize the action of others. Because it is given its shape by such efforts on the part of big men, the tanum miit system attests less to an articulate Urapmin imagination of an ideal social structure and more to the way willful action provides the impetus that drives the flow of their social life.

The making of marriages provides another striking example of the role Urapmin accord to the will in the creation of social relationships. As in the case of the tanum miit, it is not difficult to construct an account in which social structural rules seem to be behind the construction of Urapmin marriages. In fact, almost all marriages are understood to be instances of delayed, restricted exchange (classificatory Father's Sister's Daughter marriage) in which a woman marries a man from her mother's group. However, this understanding always takes shape after a marriage has been completed, and it frequently has an extremely ad hoc quality, with people radically adjusting the size of the relevant "groups" (which can be two families, two villages, or even, quite often, top and bottom Urapmin) to make the marriage fit the pattern. This conceptual gerrymandering is required because marriages are not made on the basis of a rule of delayed exchange at all. Instead, Urapmin say, they are made on the basis of the wills of women.

All Urapmin say that a woman chooses whom she will marry.[2] She announces her choice in a ritual known as "calling the name" *(win bakamin)* of a man. In the past, and sometimes still, it is expected that once a woman has settled on a prospective husband she will call out his name when, in the presence of some of her relatives, she trips on one of the almost always slippery trails that crisscross the Urapmin territory. Having heard that she has called out a boy's name as she fell, one of her older male relatives (usually a mother's or father's brother) will come to ask her to state her will in the matter of marriage.

In theory, a girl's father or mother can ask her whom she wants to marry. But there is an almost uncanny force to the pointedly asked for and nakedly spoken will in a culture that assumes an extreme degree of psychic privacy. As noted earlier, the Urapmin do not usually speculate on what is in the hearts of other people. Nor are they inclined to ask people about such matters. Thus making a baldly invasive inquiry about a girl's will induces shame in the questioner. People generally feel that a girl's father or mother would be too ashamed to ask for and then hear their own daughter's answer. Even for her uncles, asking a girl's will is considered "hard work," and only big men and aspiring big men really jump at the chance to involve themselves in this process.

Indeed, that the girl gives the first hint she has made up her mind while falling down seems symbolically to mute the force of such an open display of will by revealing it only at a moment of great vulnerability. The uncle's question, too, is robbed of its potential intensity by being phrased in indirect, metaphorical terms. He does not ask "Whom do you want to marry?" but "What water do you want to drink?" The girl answers by naming the stream from which the residents of the boy's village get water.

Once a girl has spoken her will, assuming that she has taken into account the culture's prohibition on marrying first cousins, her family takes her to the village of the boy whose name she has called. After she arrives, the boy and his family have an opportunity to accept or reject her proposal. Should he and his family agree to the marriage, bride-price discussions will start between his senior relatives and her own, but these will likely go on for many months. The couple will start to garden together, to go to the bush together to work and presumably to have sexual relations. There is no public marriage ritual. As discussed in chapter 3, people frequently claim not even to know if a young couple is married during their early months together. Until bride-price is paid and children are born (often not unrelated occurrences), all that is clear is that a woman has expressed her will and that a couple has at least tentatively formed on that basis; as the Urapmin see it, a single person's will has initiated a completely new social relationship.

Urapmin insist that a woman's choice of whom to marry should be made on the basis of her will alone; no one else has any legitimate right to influence her choice. This is not to say, of course, that people do not try to exert influence. Age-mates, suitors, and parents themselves may try to steer a woman in various directions (Robbins 1998a: 450 ff.). But none of their efforts are publicly acceptable, and they risk having the marriage they worked for called off if their meddling is discovered. If a woman's relatives suspect that she has been pushed toward her choice by someone else—say, by a man who secretly courts her or by a sister who tries to convince her that they should both marry to the same village—they will cast doubt on the legitimacy of the resulting marriage and demand an exorbitant bride-price to assuage ("buy") their anger over the wrong that has been done to their relative.

Someone in Urapmin once suggested to me that the practice of a woman calling the name of a man is the prototype of willful action. Given the prominent role this custom plays in Urapmin discussions, I am inclined to assume that this opinion is shared. One reason it can serve to epitomize the creative force of the will is related to people's insistence that it be an entirely uncoerced action. In this case, prior relationships a woman might have cannot place any legitimate constraints on her will. Closed off from the demands of others, her act of will cannot be judged immoral because no one has a legitimate right to expect her to choose someone other than the man she chooses. She writes her choice on a clean social slate. A woman making her choice thus displays a will that is, as the Urapmin see it, completely unfettered. In this respect, as we will see, a woman's deployment of her will in calling a man's name, prototype though it may be, is also unique as an example of a kind of social creativity that is not fraught with moral risk.

THE DIALECTIC OF LAW AND WILL
AND THE PARADOX OF LAWFULNESS

At this point, I have laid out two Urapmin stances toward the will. On the one hand, its expression is understood as the cause of all immoral behavior. On the other hand, its exercise, regardless of the moral dangers it raises, is held to be necessary for the proper functioning of Urapmin social life. These two propositions do not sit comfortably together. But the Urapmin do have an ideal model of how they can be made to accommodate each other in the life of each person. This model is founded on the assumption that if the law and the will are brought into a mutually conditioning dialectic with each other in people's hearts, then their interconnection can be productive.

Within this dialectic, the law's basic demand is that all realized relationships, those of coresidence, affinity, or active kinship set up expectations of "lawful" behavior that ideally constrain or shape the will. In such established relationships, the general lawful expectation of good behavior—generosity, reciprocity, helpfulness—is always understood to apply. Those with whom one has established relationships can, for example, expect one to think of them when sharing food, to answer their calls to work together, and to honor the state of give-and-take in these relationships. Having chosen to live in a particular village, it would be immorally willful of me to disregard attempts to coordinate action among village members. When families go to live in the bush for several days, it is willful of them to leave on these excursions without informing their fellow villagers of their plans. It is similarly an act of willfulness for me secretly to kill a pig and not share its meat with those with whom I usually share (Bercovitch 1994). In sum, all established relationships make some lawful claims on those who participate in them. To flaunt these claims is one of the most common but nonetheless quite serious forms of immoral willfulness. But, and this is a key point, as long as these obligations to preexisting relationships are met, the will is—in this ideal model—free to exercise itself, even in morally questionable ways such as "pushing" and expressing anger, in the production of new relationships.

From the point of the view of the will, the law is sterile with regard to producing new relationships. To completely forgo the exercise of the will is to be a nonperson, one without any relationships, what the Urapmin call in Tok Pisin a rabis man ("rubbish man") and in their own language, in even more morally pointed terms, a "bad man" (tanum mafak). A certain measure of socially creative willfulness is required of everyone if society is to exist. However, even from the perspective of the will, this model recognizes that some respect for the law is necessary in order to maintain those relationships that are already in existence. Without a sense of lawfulness, older relationships would be broken as quickly as new ones could be made.

Hence we arrive at the formulation that ideally governs Urapmin sociality: willful behavior is necessary to establish the relationships in which the law applies; lawful behavior is necessary if those relationships are to continue. Ideally, the impulses of willfulness and lawfulness exist within each person in a dialectical balance that, by respecting the terms of this formulation, allows for both the creation of relations and their maintenance.

This model and the formulation on which it is based are, however, only ideals. They do not determine reality. In reality, the Urapmin feel that people constantly fall short of achieving the balance between opposing tendencies that they demand. In general, the Urapmin feel that everyone is far too willful and shows too little respect for the law. They feel this way because of what we can call the paradox of lawfulness. Urapmin is a small community where every turning toward someone to make a new relationship, or strengthen or transform an older one, simultaneously registers as a turning away from someone else. What is lawful from the point of view of those in one relationship is bound to be perceived from the point of view of those in others as an act of willfulness against themselves (for similar accounts of Min cultures, see Bercovitch 1994; Whitehead 2000; for examples from elsewhere in Papua New Guinea, see Biersack 1980; LeRoy 1979; Munn 1986). A piece of meat shared with one's sister is a piece taken from one's wife. A man who chooses to live with his affines, thus honoring to the fullest his lawful obligations to them, is seen by his own family as willful. A woman helps her brother to make a garden, and her affines see her as willfully ignoring her obligations to them. These scenarios are all products of the paradox of lawfulness—a paradox that haunts Urapmin sociality and causes it to fall constantly short of the ideals that guide it.

Yet regardless of the moral danger to which the creation of social relationships exposes them by virtue of the operation of the paradox of lawfulness, all Urapmin must engage in such activity. Hence all Urapmin struggle with the need to balance willful assertion in the pursuit of new relationships[3] and social contexts with the need to engage in the lawful preservation of older ones. Many Melanesian cultures recognize a tension between lawfulness and willfulness or some cognate notions. But Urapmin culture appears to be unique in expecting everyone to negotiate the relationship between them. In other cultures, each gender is expected to exemplify one of these orientations to action (Brison 1995; Harrison 1985; Kulick 1992), or only big men are expected to balance both impulses while everyone else is expected to focus only on observing the law (Read 1959; White 1980; see Robbins 1998b for further discussion). By means of such differentiated expectations, these cultures shield all or most of their members from the moral difficulties that Urapmin culture requires all of its members to face. I consider below the effects of the universal nature of this problematic in Urapmin society. Here, I want to point out that the Urapmin big men, though not unique in being forced to contend with these difficulties, are those who resolve them most satisfactorily. Exploring how they do so can provide us with a better sense of how these difficulties express themselves in the course of daily life.

BIG MEN AND THE CREATION
OF THE CONTEXTS OF URAPMIN SOCIALITY

One of the first patrol officers to visit Urapmin noted that the community's leaders seemed more prominent than those of its neighbors. This claim has been borne out by later ethnography. Urapmin leaders are more influential than those discussed in ethnographies of other Min groups (e.g., Jorgensen 1981b; Wheatcroft 1976; Barth 1975). From the moment of my arrival, people clamored to tell me about the big men who "looked after" *(tiinmolin)* their community. And throughout my stay, people continued to speak constantly of them. Yet the important role big men play in the minds of their consociates seems almost inexplicable in sociological terms. Big men do not distribute huge amounts of wealth, organize spectacular exchanges, or arrange marriages, and for years they have not even done the stereotypical great man chores of shamanic curing or exercising leadership in war and ritual (cf. Godelier 1986).[4] What big men do manage to do, however, is create the contexts of Urapmin sociality by successfully exercising their wills, and it is in this capacity that they are sociologically central.

Urapmin big men are able to achieve their social prominence because they are masters of the art of deploying the will in ways that are socially productive. The productivity of their acts of will stems from their ability to perform them while at the same time minimally recognizing the constraints that lawfulness places on the will by virtue of already created relationships; most of the time they give the law just enough recognition to avoid serious censure even while being constantly dogged by a shifting chorus of milder complaints. In doing so, they have mastered the dialectic of willfulness and lawfulness and can thus work within it to produce the contexts of Urapmin social life. It is a mark of how difficult this mastery is to achieve that there are at present only four big men in Urapmin, and only two people who seem to be on the verge of joining their ranks in the near future. It is thus illuminating to consider how they do their social work.

The word I am translating as "big man" is the noun *kamok*. *Kamok* does not seem to have any other significant meanings, nor is it made up of smaller morphemes that combine to create its meaning. Its Tok Pisin cognates are <u>bikman</u> and the less frequently used <u>lo man</u> (law man).

There is an informal consensus among Urapmin about what qualities all *kamokim* (pl.) possess that allow them to fill their role. I examine three of the qualities here—great knowledge, the ability to speak forcefully, and the capacity for anger—looking in particular at how kamokim use them in exercising their wills.

Urapmin universally agree that their big men know more than others about the secret traditions of their culture and the history of their society (see Lindstrom 1984 for comparable cases). They are the only people expected to know the sacred stories *(weng awem)* that not only explain the origin of many existing social categories and worldly objects but also contain powerful spells and songs for use in magic and ritual. Even when people who are not kamokim know parts of these traditions, they are not authorized to tell them (Lindstrom 1990), and everyone regularly defers to big men when matters touching on these traditions are in question. Big men are also the most respected historians and genealogists in the community. Urapmin assume that their mentors taught them authoritative versions of this "historical" knowledge just as they taught them the details of the secret tradition. This knowledge makes big men the most important players in disputes over landownership and social affiliation.

In order for big men to bring their knowledge to bear on social life, they must at times communicate at least parts of it. Thus it is not surprising that people regard them as strong talkers. This is the second quality they all share. Kamokim talk all of the time. At church, in village plazas, and at every sort of public meeting kamokim can be heard holding forth. And this talk is not "empty talk" *(weng deesa)* with little social effect. People expect their big men to be able to accomplish a great many things with the power of their speech. Through their ability to deploy social knowledge in spoken argument, for example, big men maintain the land claims of their followers and help them to keep children attached to their households. Their ability to speak persuasively *(oget degamin)* can also gain them new followers and gain their old followers new coresidents as well as help them in various ways to keep social life moving smoothly. In other contexts, their ability effectively to harangue people in a local speech genre known as "strong talk" *(weng titil)* or "clear talk" *(weng kem)* keeps their followers in line and the villages they live in up to the standards of peaceful lawfulness that residents demand. Finally, their willingness to speak strongly and decisively to leaders of groups outside Urapmin and to government officers and company representatives holds the key, many Urapmin feel, to all developments that have so far come to Urapmin (such as the school and the aidpost) and to any they might receive in the future.

In all of these cases, big men use their knowledge and powers of speech to impose their wills on others. By deploying their knowledge and powers of persuasion, they aim to bring about compliance without making others feel unlawfully "pushed." Often enough, however, their efforts to steer people in particular directions—for example, to have them move to a new village, or kill a pig for a particular occasion, or change their work plans so they can participate in one of the big man's projects—lead to anger on the part of their followers and heated disputes with them. Sometimes, too, a big man's willingness to express his own anger plays an important part in his persuasive technique. In fact, the capacity to express their own anger productively and tolerate the anger of others is the third quality all big men share.

As I have noted in several places, the Urapmin fear anger. It is, they believe, a cause of human sickness and can ruin gardens and compromise hunting success. Whereas in the past it seems that it was anger directed at a person that could injure him or her in these ways, Urapmin now believe that one can also injure oneself with one's own anger.[5] But just as the Urapmin are ambivalent about the will, so too do they both demonize anger and recognize its importance in the construction of their social world. The term for anger is *aget atul*. As we have seen, *aget* means "heart." *Atul* is a term that in other contexts can mean "sharp" or what one might want to gloss as "efficacy" or even "active ingredient." Thus, atul is the sharpness of a knife. It is also that which is effective in medicines of all sorts. Taken together, these usages suggest that one core meaning of the term has to do with its ability to accomplish things. Its use in the construction of anger suggests that anger, like sharp knives and effective medicines, is also seen to accomplish things. What it most often accomplishes is the preservation of existing social relations against the willful encroachments of others, or the production of new ones in spite of others' efforts to preserve old ones.

A man who is often angry is called an *aget atul tanum*. At one time
or another, I heard all of the Urapmin big men referred to in this way.
Generally, it is a term of abuse, suggesting that one cannot control oneself and is thus a danger to oneself and others. But when the phrase is
used of big men, its evaluative force is ambivalent. When people feel the
force of a big man's anger directed at them, they are quick to condemn
his angry ways. In other situations, however, they hold that anger in
high regard and will tell you they have confidence in a particular big
man because he is a man of anger. Amtabuleng, one of the Urapmin big
men, once introduced me to a big man visiting from another group as
an "angry man." He clearly meant this as an expression of respect for
the man's accomplishments, though he laughed as he said it, marking
the polysemy of his usage. In general, people cannot fully condemn the
anger of big men because they expect big men to be angry. As followers,
they often depend on their big men to express their own (the followers')
anger in socially productive ways. Disputes regularly take place between
two or more big men who are fighting on behalf of their followers but
stand to gain little themselves from the outcome. This is so because
people protect themselves morally by remaining calm while letting big
men engage in the dangerous tasks of feeling and expressing anger. It is
almost as if the big men live the more emotionally and morally extreme
aspects of their followers' inner lives for them. Given that they perform
this service on behalf of others, those others sometimes feel constrained
not to condemn them.

The notion of the effective anger of the big man brings us to the matter of what it is that big men do and how in doing it they help to create
the contexts of Urapmin sociality. They have great knowledge, excep-
tional speaking abilities, and an unusual capacity to feel and express
anger. It remains to examine how they use these to put their wills in play
productively.

It is important at the outset to understand that every person has one
and only one big man (*nimi kamok*, "my big man").[6] It is difficult for
anyone to deviate from this norm because big men use their persuasive
charms and their capacity for anger to enforce loyalty in their followers.
Anyone who is seen to be drifting between two big men immediately becomes the focus of pressure from each one to follow him exclusively. The
acid test of affiliation tends to turn on the issue of where a person lives.
To live in a big man's village, or in a village that is closer to his than it is
to those of other big men, is to commit to him. By the same token,

people often indicate that they are beginning to move away from following a particular big man by speculating about the possibility of changing residence.

As this might suggest, the most important thing big men do is create villages *(abiip)*. As the Urapmin say, big men "arrange" *(daptemin)* people into villages. Urapmin residence patterns are underdetermined by kinship relations or tanum miit membership. There are, in fact, no rules based on these sorts of social structural categories that indicate where people should live. As a result, Urapmin residence patterns are "chaotic." Most people will live in many villages of radically different social composition throughout their lives. For example, a man may be born in his father's village, move to his mother's village when his father dies, then move to his stepfather's village when she remarries. Later, he may move back to his father's village as an adolescent in the hope of gaining rights to land there. On marriage, however, he may move to his wife's village, particularly if there is a strong big man there who "pulls" (pulim) or "persuades" (oget degamin) him to move with promises of extensive help in cooperative work and rights to land. Later, with children of his own, he may tire of his wife's village; perhaps too much disputing takes place there for his taste. In response, he may move to wherever his stepfather's people are now living. But then, finding that his own growing children are the cause of many disputes in this new village, he may choose simply to take his family and live alone, away from any village (as a few Urapmin families were in the early 1990s). Once his children are grown, he may then move back to one of the villages he lived in before. I have made this list up from the common kinds of moves people told me about in their life histories. It is a complicated itinerary but not a special one in that regard. There is also no reason for it to end where I have ended it; many life histories involve more moves than this hypothetical one. In a woman's case, the trajectory would mutatis mutandis be much the same.

The variety of links our hypothetical man has to the villages into which he moves demonstrates that the residence system is marked by a great deal of choice. Big men attempt to exploit this room for choice by prying people loose from their current residences and moving them to their own villages. At the same time, they are at pains to keep those who have already chosen to live with them from changing their minds. Their goal in all this is to bring together villages of as many people as possible. Urapmin generally feel that the social life in larger villages is richer, with more possibilities for shared eating, pig hunting, and collective labor. Hence, big men aim to build big villages because such villages themselves become part of what they have to offer potential recruits.

The process of recruitment is one in which big men must use their wills and encourage people to behave unlawfully with regard to relationships they already have with others. They "push" or "grease" men who have married young women from the village to live matrilocally despite a general tendency toward patrilocality. At the same time, they encourage the young men of the village to stay at home after they marry, despite the pressure other big men may put on them to live with their wives' families. If young women who grew up in his village become divorced, a big man fights to bring them and their children back. Should such a young woman die, a big man will assert against her husband's people that he or those in his village should be able to keep her children. When the situation is reversed and the wives of men of their village divorce or die, big men struggle to keep these children as well.

Big men not only work to bring young local women and their children into their villages and to retain younger men, they also need to have older men and women living there. Fairly often, but by no means always, the core of this group of older people will be the families of the big man's brothers *(fikning kasel)* or of the children of his father's brother's *(tanum kiyak)*. Villages that have such agnatic units at their core give the appearance of being the products of social structural rules or at least regularities. But life histories demonstrate that at least in the early 1990s many of these brothers and cousins had spent significant time living apart. In most cases, it was only the willful action of a big man that brought them back from other villages to form their own. Thus even the most "predictable" residence units are made, not found. And in all cases, villages built around such cores also include a variety of nonagnatically related adults whom a big man has pulled into the village.

Big men are aided in their efforts to pull people to their villages by the fact that whole villages tend to move every ten years or so. Often a move is undertaken after several adult deaths have occurred in the village. In particular, when one or two senior men of a village die, people begin to feel that it is spiritually threatened and clamor to move. But even in the absence of deaths, few villages stay in one place for more than ten years. At the end of that interval, the basic physical elements of a house, the posts that make up its frame and the slats on which the bark floor is laid, begin to decay to the point where they can no longer be repaired. When the majority of houses in a village reach this point, the big man usually decides that it is time to move. When a village readies itself to move, its members face the decision of whether to remain with the group. Since they are going to be undertaking the difficult task of building a new house in any case, this is an ideal time for them to switch residences. Big men recognize that people about to move are in this situation, and their efforts to persuade or bully people to move to their villages are most intense at this time. Although in most moves a majority of members stay with a village, there is a sense in which every move shuffles the population deck and gives big men a chance to draw a new hand.

When trying to pull people into a village, a big man will use several strategies to bring his will to bear on them. He will try to entice them by promising all the benefits that a big village provides. But he will also try more forceful methods. For example, big men are by far the most practiced wielders of the kinship and clanship idioms in all of Urapmin. Drawing on their superior historical knowledge, big men are quick to remind people of their relational links to him. Since this is not generally an important idiom for their followers, however, they will embellish this line of argument with accounts of all they have done for a person, or for that person's close relatives. Perhaps a big man helped to pay your bride-price, or your father's. Or perhaps he gave your father land and together they made gardens. In general, he will use the kinship idiom and its allied idiom of help given in the past to point out the lawful expectations attached to the relationships people already have with him. And if people remain resistant to his claims, he is always ready to charge them with willfully violating the law in relation to him. Through such rhetorical techniques, he often succeeds in wrapping his own will in the cloak of the law.

Despite their deployment of the rhetoric of the law, however, big men's efforts to woo people to their villages very often involve them in public argument and heated debate. When they are successful in convincing people to switch their place of residence, there is sure to be anger on the part of the big man left behind. Furthermore, big men often have to express themselves forcefully to those they are trying to recruit, sometimes angrily accusing them of ignoring their lawful responsibilities. Hence, the big men's capacities for anger serve them well in their efforts to build villages. Without the ability to use their anger, they would not be able to enforce their will.

The work of a big man's will is not over once he has succeeded in building a village or bringing a new family into it. For just as people have a good deal of choice about which village to live in, they also have decisions to make about how much time to spend in a village in which they have built a house. People sometimes build houses in more than one village,[7] and all people have houses in the bush near their gardens *(sep am)*. For a village actually to function as a social unit, a big man must convince people with houses there to spend time living in them. Although it is expected that people will spend a good deal of time in their bush houses or in a house they have in another village, it is also recognized that there is a fine line that can be crossed from the other side of which people no longer regard the village as their primary residence. Big men work hard to prevent people from crossing this line. A big man tries to get people in the village to make gardens together, to return frequently to the village to cook and eat pandanus *(kyep;* a kind of palm fruit that is usually prepared and eaten by groups larger than a single household), and to contribute to each other's house- and pig fence–building projects. Encouraging people to behave in this way is a task that again calls for him to use his oratorical abilities to cajole and push people, reminding them that once they have chosen to live in a village, they have lawful obligations to the others who live there.

I have devoted a good deal of space to the issue of village construction because villages are a key site of Urapmin social life. "Arranging" them and ensuring that they truly function as villages are the greatest accomplishments of a big man's will. Given that people can always live alone, or can retire almost permanently to their garden houses, the Urapmin are quite aware of the work that big men do to ensure that most people do in fact live in villages and contribute to the collective sociality that they foster. Many lawful relations between people are founded on coresidence, for living together fosters the kind of regular interaction that leads people to regard each other as kin and to develop dense histories of reciprocal giving and communal sharing. In bringing villages together, then, big men use their wills to create one of the key contexts in which the law finds its application.

But while building villages is their most widely ramifying accomplishment, big men also exercise their wills in several other ways that are crucial to the production of Urapmin sociality. Young men and their families, for example, rely on big men to help them procure the shell money *(bonang)* they need to include in their bride-price payments (Robbins 1999). Hence big men place themselves at the foundation of the relationship of marriage. Furthermore, it is big men who coordinate labor for the few projects, such as house roofing and pig fence construction, that families cannot complete on their own (Robbins forthcoming). They thus have a key role to play in the construction of the

Figure 4. Big men taking part in a village court. The Kaunsil, in the center, is flanked by Amtabuleng (standing on the left) and Werisep (sitting on the right), two of the four Urapmin big men. Photo by Joel Robbins.

physical space of the household and in providing the means for people to raise the pigs they use in many of their most important social exchanges. Finally, as I have already had passing occasion to mention in this chapter, big men play important roles in the conduct of land disputes (see figure 4). It is important to note that by defending the land rights of their followers, big men place themselves at the foundation of gardening activities. The garden *(lang),* at least as much if not more than the village, is the primary source of identification for most Urapmin; it is where they do their most significant productive work, and their success in that work is a key proof of their character. People like to assert that they own their own ground and can by themselves hold it against the encroachments of others by reciting the history of their family's use of it. But in fact, most people depend on their big men to argue their cases in local land disputes, both because the big men have greater knowledge of the histories that establish claims and because the big men are not afraid to argue strenuously. Hence, even in the garden, the Urapmin conduct their everyday, lawful social life against the background of a claim to ownership that was in many cases created or at least sustained by the action of a big man who drew on his knowledge and capacity for anger to willfully defend their claims.

This section has focused on the ways the big men use their wills to create many of the contexts of Urapmin social life. We have considered the production of several of those contexts: village life, cooperative labor, marriage, and landownership. In all these cases, social structural rules do not exist that would create these contexts as a matter of course; there are no rules about whom one should live with, work with, or marry. Hence they require willful action if they are to come about. But to be effective, that willful action must be admixed with an appreciation for the law. It is because big men succeed in making this mixture that people not only call them willful and angry, they also sometimes refer to them as "law men," marking the extent to which they both embody and defend the law. It is their ability to bring willfulness and lawfulness together productively that puts big men at the center of Urapmin culture.

BIG MEN, OTHERS, AND
THE HUMAN MORAL CONDITION IN URAPMIN

I have argued that big men are central to Urapmin culture because they are able to use their wills to give shape to the social life in which that culture finds its expression. Yet for the Urapmin, big men are not only good to live with, they are also good to think. As Burridge (1975: 87) writes in his brilliant meditation on the nature of big manship, which has been an inspiration to the analysis presented here, big men reveal "to others the kinds of moral conflicts in which they are involved." They are "characters" in MacIntyre's (1984: 28) sense: they are "the moral representatives of their culture . . . because of the way in which moral and metaphysical ideas and theories assume through them an embodied existence in the social world." The ideas that find embodiment in the life of the big man are those that assert that the will must be used to create new relations but only in ways that do not make a mockery of the lawful expectations that already existing relations put in place.

Big men play at the edge of lawlessness, but they are careful not to cross over into it with any regularity. Successful big men take pains to speak in the name of the law, to point to lawful rationales for what it is that they will (e.g., when they pull people to live in their village by stressing their prior relationships with them), and to use persuasion to allow their followers to see their actions as motivated not only by the will of the big man but also by their own. In this way, they manage to work along the entirety of the arc inscribed by the dialectic of willfulness and lawfulness without ever putting a full stop to its movement.

The verb most often used for what big men do illustrates strikingly well the Urapmin conceptualization of the synthesis of willfulness and lawfulness that they achieve. This verb is *tiinmolin*. Tiinmolin conjoins two ideas that Westerners think of as, if not opposed, at least too divergent to inhabit the same term: willful imposition and lawful care. On the one hand, *tiinmolin* means to "look after." In Tok Pisin this is lukautim. Urapmin emphasize this meaning etymologically, pointing out that *tiin* means "eye," so that *tiin tiinmolin* means "the eyes look after [it]." The sense of looking after is a nurturant and protective one, like "to look after" in English. To look after someone (or something) is to keep them from trouble while "supporting" *(dangdagalin)* their efforts to flourish, to protect them as they go about their projects. It includes a respect for the lawful demands for support and care that the other makes of one. On the other hand, *tiinmolin* also encompasses the idea of controlling something, of being master of it. This is captured in the Tok Pisin bosim. The bossing side of tiinmolin comes out in the way big men push people to do their will.

What we have in the conjunction of these two ideas, looking after and controlling, is a sort of dominating nurture, an imposing benevolence. As much as these phrases may ring as oxymorons in our ears, we have to understand that they encapsulate the Urapmin conception of the activity of leadership. Indeed, the Urapmin do not separate the two senses of *tiinmolin;* they understand lukautim and bosim to be synonyms when used in reference to human relationships, and they use them interchangeably when speaking Tok Pisin.[8] For the Urapmin, the well-balanced combination of lawful nurture and willful control expressed by *tiinmolin* captures what they take to be the most productive synthesis of willfulness and lawfulness.

All Urapmin are capable of appreciating the moral triumph that is the big man's establishment of a successful tiinmolin relationship because all of them face the same moral dilemmas that he does; all of them must navigate the narrow course that flows between willfulness and lawfulness. Urapmin households most often consist of a husband and wife, their unmarried daughters and sons, and their married sons along with their wives and children. But this household configuration does not come about as a matter of course: married sons can establish their own households or can move in with their wives' families. Men, who tiinmolin their families, must thus struggle to keep their sons at home and to build households the same way big men build villages. They must also struggle to coordinate the smaller, shifting work groups that often garden or hunt

together, as well as to willfully extract gifts from their exchange partners. Women, who also tiinmolin their families, must work willfully to
keep their children and their daughters-in-law engaged in their projects.
Young women exercise their wills in initiating marriages, and young men
do so in the construction of sports teams and various "youth groups"
that they tiinmolin. All of these cases and many others that I have not
discussed here are ones in which people use their wills to create social relations. Yet just like big men, these people must balance their willful efforts with a respect for the lawful demands relationships make.

In attempting to balance lawfulness and willfulness, big men and others run the risk of failure. Indeed, there is a sense in which all Urapmin
are doomed to fail at this task. The inescapability of failure follows from
what I previously called the paradox of lawfulness: an action, no matter
how lawfully it meets the demands of any one relationship, cannot help
but look willful from the point of view of another. Because this is so, the
Urapmin imagine that most of the time they fail to balance lawfulness
and willfulness in a fully satisfactory manner. As proof, they offer that
they are an extremely fractious community given to constant dispute.
Histories of almost any sort—residential, marital, political, or territo-
rial—tend to turn on episodes in which one party felt that another willfully withdrew from them and went elsewhere. The very same social relations that the will creates, then, it also tends to take apart, and in doing
so, it leaves at least one of the parties to the relationship in a condition
of moral defeat. For this reason, in Urapmin a healthy sense of social
possibility coexists alongside a mournful awareness of the inevitability
of moral failure.

Nowhere is the sense of the inevitability of moral failure more evident
than in Urapmin beliefs about death. All adults die from sorcery practiced by outsiders. But these outsiders are not complete strangers.
Rather, they are people who hail from neighboring groups and whom
the Urapmin know and have injured in some unlawful way. Everyone
dies because they have some moral "debt" *(yum)* to the person who
killed them. Without a moral breach to provide an opening, sorcerers
cannot kill. Sometimes these debts are unrepaid gifts, but very often they
are other kinds of willful displays, such as outbursts of anger, insulting
laughter at an outsider's expense, or a refusal to share. These breaches,
identified either by the dying person or by mourners in discussions after
a death, often seem very small in proportion to the ultimate sanction
they elicit. But this mismatch does not bother the Urapmin. The point
this belief makes is too experientially obvious for this incoherence to rob

it of credibility. It is that all people are morally culpable, and none of them can expect to escape forever the consequences of their guilt.

To sum up: there is a contradiction at the heart of the legal system of traditional Urapmin morality. Under this system, one is enjoined to use the will to create new social relations and at the same time respect the lawful expectations that hold in those relations that already exist. Yet even when one is not making a wholly new relationship, every act of lawfulness toward one relation appears from the point of view of others as willful disregard for their own demands. This contradiction is never fully resolved; at best it is merely lived with. Because of it, in this part of their moral system the Urapmin find themselves routinely at risk of becoming bad people. This is the cost of what in the introduction I called the marked openness of Urapmin social structure and reflects the way this openness leaves people without any structural alibis for the things they do. To be sure, it is sometimes possible to succeed in balancing lawfulness and willfulness, and big men take on many of the harder tasks in this regard, but it is a trick to get these matters right and everyone fails at it sometimes, finding themselves drawn into disputes about food not shared, gifts not given, gardening work not contributed to, villages not joined, and so on. And though big men provide a gloss on what success in the moral system of law and will looks like, even their success is not complete. Like others, they are often held accountable for their moral failures, and like everyone, in the end they too die guilty deaths.

Central though it is to the construction of Urapmin social life, the moral system founded on the distinction between lawfulness and willfulness is not the only one in play in Urapmin culture. Two distinct systems of taboo join it in filling out the moral spectrum. Both of these are in important respects in dialogue with the system of law. One system, the set of taboos connected to the nature spirits, adopts the legal system's primary emphases and offers the Urapmin further evidence of the dangers of willful behavior. The other, a set of taboos given by Afek, serves to recuperate somewhat the conviction of moral failure produced by the other two systems. More than them, it offers the Urapmin the opportunity to construct themselves as indisputably moral people. I consider these two systems of taboo in the remainder of this chapter.

WILLFULNESS AND THE REALM OF THE NATURE SPIRITS

The Urapmin are constantly aware, even today, that they occupy a landscape in which they are surrounded by nature spirits *(motobil)* who are the original "owners" of almost all the resources they use (Robbins 1995). As the Urapmin experience them, their relations with these spirits serve as an accurate mirror of the moral difficulties that beset relations among human beings (see Gardner 1987: 166 for a comparable Min case). In this mirror, problems of balancing lawfulness and willfulness loom just as large as they do in human society.

The reflective nature of human-spirit relations is exemplified in the case of the "marsupial women" *(nuk wanang)*. These spirit women are the guardians of many of the marsupials that humans hunt and eat. Sometimes one of them takes a fancy to a human man who hunts frequently and begins to have sexual relations with him. Eventually she marries him and gives him dreams telling him where to find game. With this knowledge in hand, he becomes a spectacularly successful hunter. But there is a downside to this arrangement, for eventually the marsupial spirit wife becomes envious of the attention the hunter pays his human wife and begins to feel that she is giving up too many of her wards (the marsupials) in return for too little from the hunter. In a classic example of the paradox of lawfulness, the hunter's lawful behavior toward his human wife begins to appear willful to his marsupial spirit wife. At this point, his marsupial spirit wife begins to send notice of her dissatisfaction to him, causing him to have accidents as he hunts or making him sick. If he does not leave his human wife, she eventually kills him.

Given the dangers associated with marriages to nuk wanang, most men I know say they do not want to marry one. Only one man is currently so married, and he is widely regarded as one of the two most willful, lawless men in the community. For others who have the opportunity (for marsupial women, like human women, choose their potential mates), refusal of marriage to a spirit woman, which involves a temporary withdrawal from hunting, is an important moral act, one in which they demonstrate their commitment to the entire moral scheme in which willfulness must be tempered by a respect for the demands of the law.

Relations with other spirits also raise moral issues. These are phrased in the terms of a discourse of taboo (awem) that serves as an analog of the discourse of law that frames issues of morality on the human level. In discussing the healing work of Spirit women in chapter 3, I noted that spirits sometimes make people sick if they encroach on the territories or use the resources that the spirits own. In response to the danger of such sickness, the Urapmin previously observed a set of taboos designed to prevent them from encroaching on particularly dangerous spirits. On this basis, certain areas were taboo to gardening, hunting, or any sort of loud, incautious behavior. Some game animals, too, have particularly possessive owners and thus could not be eaten by children, pregnant women, or others thought to be too weak to survive the retribution these owners exacted. The sicknesses the spirits caused could be severe, and for the most part people observed these taboos rather strictly.

Despite their best efforts, however, whenever people experienced ill-nesses that did not run their normal courses or suffered accidents resulting in serious injuries, they assumed that spirits were punishing them for breaches of these taboos, albeit often unwitting ones.[9] As in the human world, so too in relation to spirits people who are too willful, whose willfulness leads them to breach the spirits' taboos, find themselves confronted with the fruits of their mistakes. But just as one must exercise one's will in making a social world for oneself, so too must one risk offending the nature spirits, for every act of hunting or gardening carries some risk; even the spirit owners of nontaboo ground or species can, if they feel insulted because someone has "bothered" them, punish that person for a failure to observe their version of the law.

Because the experiences of untoward sickness and accidental injury are universal among Urapmin and because everyone has to encroach on the spirits in the process of procuring their basic subsistence needs, all Urapmin know the experience of recognizing that they have violated spirit-related taboos in the course of living out their daily lives. Thus, like the system of law, the system of spirit-related taboos is of only inconsistent help in their efforts to construct themselves as moral people. The same cannot be said, however, for the other system of taboos the Urapmin formerly observed, those given by Afek.

MORAL SUCCESS AND AFEK'S TABOOS

Many of the taboos the Urapmin formerly followed were based not on the spiritual possession of resources but on the dictates of Afek, the Urapmin creator. These taboos were of several kinds. Many interdicted various types of contact between men and women; for example, they had to use separate paths in some parts of Urapmin territory and eat and sleep separately when living in the village. Others prevented people who occupied specific social statuses based on gender and, for men, on levels of initiation, from eating certain food items, both meat and vegetable. A final set of taboos prohibited all Urapmin from eating certain animals, such as the dog *(kyam)*, the echidna *(yigil)*, and certain species of snakes. The system as a whole was complex, and it left everyone laboring under the burden of at least some taboos all the time. The sanctions for violating these taboos ranged from stunted growth or crop failure (when the violators were initiates) to the more widely experienced arthritic swelling of the joints the Urapmin call *fum*. These punishments were seemingly "automatic"; neither Afek herself nor any other spirit was responsible for enforcing them.

Looked at in comparison with the other two moral codes we have considered, that of Afek's taboos stands out by virtue of the fact that it makes no demands that contradict the requirements of everyday living. It does not condemn the will that the Urapmin are forced to exercise, nor does it penalize people for carrying out activities, such as gardening, that are fundamental to their survival. Instead, the law that Afek laid down was one that all people could successfully follow without jeopardizing their chances of leading lives that were fulfilling in Urapmin terms. It is not that the taboos were not experienced as onerous; they clearly were. Indeed, the Urapmin claim their taboo system was the most demanding of all the Min groups. Mothers are usually most strict with their firstborn children, they say, and as Afek gave birth to them first (as one of the origin myths has it), she saddled them with the most taboos. But as cumbersome as this system of taboos was to live with, it only asked people to forgo things they could do without. No one starved for lack of the foods that were taboo to them, which never for anyone included the main vegetable staples, taro and sweet potato. Similarly, the interdictions of cross-sex contact were not so burdensome as to prevent the development of cross-sex social relations. In Afek's taboos, then, the Urapmin possessed a moral system in which they were able to realize their efforts to live as good people.

It is possible to argue further that the system of Afek's taboos also served to provide people with a technique for managing the paradox of lawfulness that so complicates their relation to the law. For Afek's taboos took the choice out of many situations of distribution, unburdening people of the responsibility of considering all of their relations in making every gift. If you catch a species of marsupial that can only be eaten by women and children, then I as one of your male relatives cannot condemn as willful your gift of it to your female relatives rather than to me. Similarly, my wife cannot condemn my failure to share with her meat that it is taboo for her to eat. Furthermore, by tabooing certain game species to men of hunting age, Afek's taboos often prevent hunters from succumbing to the temptation to eat their catch by themselves in the bush, a degree-zero kind of distribution that the Urapmin call *feginin* and that they strongly condemn as the height of willfulness. Whitehead (2000), in an impressively detailed study of the food taboo system of another Min group, has argued that it is in large part designed expressly to handle problems of distribution such as these. In Urapmin, its success at doing so constituted a second way in which it allowed people to constitute themselves as moral persons.

Finally, Afek's taboos, in their emphasis on controlling cross-sex contact, may also have served to regulate, at least to some extent, the sexual willfulness that expresses itself in adultery. The Urapmin certainly assume that copresence fosters sexual attraction. The relative lack of it in the past may thus have had some role in helping the Urapmin to realize the sexual regulations of their legal code. This would be a third sense in which Afek's taboos constructed a realm in which moral achievement was possible.

In sum, then, Afek's taboos laid out a set of moral standards all Urapmin could reach. It presented them with a fine structure of small, relatively easily followed rules, the observance of which allowed them to constitute themselves as moral people (Lambek 1992). At the same time, it took some of the bite out of the paradox of lawfulness by defining some people as ineligible to receive some kinds of attention, and it structured sociality in a way that made it possible to resist the temptations of breaching the law against adultery. In broad terms, it was through their observance of Afek's taboos that the Urapmin were most able to live lives they could define as morally upright.

Urapmin morality, as I have presented it here, is marked both by an internal complexity that comes from bringing three distinct systems of rules together under a single rubric (awem) and by the way some of its dictates are in enduring conflict with Urapmin assumptions about the kinds of social action people must undertake if their society is to assume a recognizable shape.

The system that I have called the law is the most broadly applicable of the three sets of rules that make up this morality, bearing as it does on all human interactions. Not surprisingly, it engages ideas about how people come to take action that are fundamental to Urapmin social thinking. That it for the most part condemns the very willfulness this social thinking finds necessary presents the Urapmin with a contradiction that lends their life something of a tragic cast, one that is elaborated explicitly in their ideas about intercourse with the spirit realm and the taboos it puts in place and in the notion that everyone dies a guilty death.

But the contradiction is also to some extent attenuated by the existence of accepted standards for creatively exercising the will in concert with respect for the law. To make reference to a distinction I take up again in chapter 6, the Urapmin legal system constituted what Weber (1946: 120 ff.) would call an "ethic of responsibility." This is one in which, while general ethical standards, such as the Urapmin one that the will should not be exercised without regard for the law, are still in play, the results of an action also figure into the calculation of its moral worthiness (see also Schluchter 1996: 88). In this spirit, the Urapmin tolerated actions that successfully created contexts of sociality, even when they were willful. Big men were masters in the operation of this ethic of responsibility, but to a greater or lesser extent everyone had to operate by it in constructing their social lives.

The complications that beset the legal system are also evident in the system of spirit-related taboos that mirrored it. Over against these two systems, that of Afek's taboos stands out for the simplicity of its operation. It was much more an "ethic of conviction." For Weber, an ethic of conviction is one in which people aim to realize the demands of their moral code without regard for the worldly consequences of their doing so. In such systems, one's primary goal is not to affect the world in a particular way but to act on one's commitment to the letter of the law. The Urapmin treated the system of Afek's taboos in this manner, generally struggling to realize its demands as fully as they could in all cases.[10] They were able to approach it in this way because the system of Afek's taboos, unlike the other two systems, confronted them with no demands that contradicted those issuing from other parts of their culture. Through this system of taboos, then, Urapmin could sometimes achieve the untroubled sense of moral success that so often accompanies a life lived within the dictates of a firmly held ethic of conviction.

The Christianity the Urapmin have adopted has significantly challenged all aspects of their moral system. Some it has done away with altogether; others it has transformed and put in its service. It has not succeeded, however, in completely eliminating traditional Urapmin moral thinking. The tensions that have marked its interaction with that which it would replace now dominate how the Urapmin conceptualize themselves and their lives together. These tensions make the Christian notion of sinfulness compelling to the Urapmin. How they do so is the subject of the next chapter.

CHAPTER 6

Desire and Its Discontents

Free Time and Christian Morality

Issues of Christian morality—what it demands, the difficulty of meeting those demands, and the consequences of failing to do so—are consuming topics of conversation in contemporary Urapmin. People are preoccupied with their own sinfulness, and they take it up not only in church but also in private conversations, in village meetings, and in quiet personal reflections on their lives. What I want to consider here is how the Urapmin came to experience themselves as sinners. What, as they see it, is the nature of their sinfulness, and how have they become convinced that they possess it as a quality? I am not asking where the idea of human sinfulness comes from; in the Urapmin case, its provenience is clearly Christian. Instead, I want to know what makes that idea compelling. I argue that for the Urapmin a felt sense of sin derives from the way Christian morality engages their traditional moral conventions while at the same time presenting an alternative set of conventions that, although seemingly remarkably similar, are actually different in ways that make them impossible for the Urapmin to follow successfully. The fact of engagement is important, for it allows Christian morality an entrée into Urapmin thinking, but it is the differences that ultimately produce people's conviction of their own sinfulness.

On the side of engagement, the Urapmin are quick to point out the respects in which Christian morality, as they understand it, is similar to their own. It proffers a similar moral code focused on issues such as anger, fighting, and adultery. And, crucially, it too turns on a distinction between law and will. The way the Urapmin have seized on these similarities has set in train a process that might appear to be what in the introduction I called transformative reproduction. If this were the case, the Urapmin would be assimilating Christian moral ideas into their traditional ones, and the differences between the two sets of ideas would force a transformation of their traditional understandings. Yet even if the Urapmin initially made some moves in this direction, today the mesh of traditional and Christian ideas is so unstable that their relationship is better captured by the model of adoption and its image of two cultural systems operating side by side. Indeed, as much as the Urapmin are aware of the similarities between the two systems, it is the differences that have the greatest impact on their lives, and it is this impact that I focus on in this chapter.

To explore the way the two systems interrelate, I have to describe Urapmin Christian morality in some detail. Given that I have already described traditional morality, my discussion of its Christian counterpart unavoidably takes up comparative considerations from the outset. In the next section I draw on Foucault's late work to put in place a conceptual framework that can guide this comparison. Foucault's framework is especially useful in that it analyzes moral systems into various parts, allowing for a comparison that locates precisely those parts that are similar and those that are different. Furthermore, since he developed it in relation to his own planned discussion of the development of Christian morality, it is also designed in such a way that it highlights certain important aspects of the Christian moral scheme.

FOUCAULT AND THE COMPARISON OF MORALITIES

In Foucault's (1990: 29) accounting, all moralities are composed of two elements: codes of behavior and "forms of subjectivation." As Foucault construes them, moral codes are straightforward in nature: they are simply lists of prescribed and prohibited behaviors. The forms of subjectivation are more complex. Elsewhere Foucault refers to what he intends by this term as "ethics" or, most revealingly, as one's "relation to oneself" (Foucault 1997: 266; see also Davidson 1986: 229). The domain of ethics, taken in this sense, has to do with how "one ought to form oneself as an ethical subject" in relation to the moral code under which one lives (Foucault 1990: 26). It is not the rules of the code that are central to ethics but rather the spirit in which they are observed and the kinds of efforts one has to undertake to make oneself an observant kind of person.

The system that guides ethical self-fashioning is itself made up of four components. The first is a definition of the "ethical substance," that part of the person that is relevant to his or her moral conduct (Foucault 1990: 26). In some systems it is people's intentions that are morally relevant; in others it is their desires, or their feelings, or even their behaviors alone. The second component of the ethical system is "the mode of subjection." This refers to the way people are led to recognize their moral obligations—on the basis of divine law, for example, or on that of the dictates of reason (Foucault 1997: 264; 1990: 27). The third component defines the kind of "ethical work" one must do not just to realize a particular moral dictate but also to make oneself a proper subject of morality tout court (Foucault 1990: 27). Such "self-forming activity" can involve anything from the renunciation of the self to the employment of reason, and it is performed through the use of what Foucault (1977: 265, 223 ff.) calls "technologies of the self." Finally, the fourth component of an ethical system is its "telos," the kind of being one aims to become by acting in a moral way. Like the other three aspects, in this one too variation is possible; in some systems people aim for purity, in others for immortality, upstandingness, and so on (Foucault 1990: 27–28; 1997: 265). Taken together, these four components make up an ethical system. When such a system is combined with a moral code, they together constitute what we can call a moral system.

Two points Foucault makes about his conception of moral systems are of particular interest for my comparative enterprise. First, he notes that because the code and the form of subjectivation are separate components of the moral system, "they may develop in relative independence from one another" (Foucault 1990: 29). Put otherwise, changes in ethics need not depend on or cause changes in moral codes and vice versa. Foucault's (1990: 266) account of the move from Greek to Christian morality turns on this point, for he argues that in this shift the moral code remained largely the same while the ethical system changed. A second aspect of Foucault's use of his scheme that is relevant to our concerns is his claim that moralities can differ in their emphasis on the elaboration of one or another of the elements that make them up (Foucault 1990: 29). Some moralities, those that are "code-oriented," place their "main emphasis" on the code, "its systematicity, its richness, its capacity to adjust to every possible case and to embrace every area of behavior" (Foucault 1990: 29–30). In other, "ethics-oriented" moral systems, it is the form of subjectivation that is foremost, with the greatest elaboration taking place in that part of the moral system that defines the subject's relationship to himself or herself (Foucault 1990: 30). Between these two types of moralities, Foucault (1990: 30) argues, there have historically been "juxtapositions, rivalries and conflicts, and compromises." His own work consists to a great extent in tracing these kinds of engagements.

In considering how Foucault's scheme can illuminate the Urapmin case, I begin by looking at the issue of changing codes. As I mentioned in passing in the previous chapter, as Foucault (1990: 32) sees it codes are everywhere largely similar in their basic principles. On one level, that of what I have called the traditional legal code, the Urapmin case bears him out. The Urapmin themselves point to a basic continuity between this code and the Christian one. But on another level, this point does not hold for the Urapmin case. For along with its legal code, traditional Urapmin morality also consisted of the two taboo codes, one made up of interdictions given by Afek and one made up of those connected with spirits. As the Urapmin understand Christianity, it demands that they throw these other codes aside. Their abrogation of these taboo systems constitutes one of the fundamental changes Christianity has wrought in their lives, and, as we will see, it plays an important part in constituting them as sinners.

There are also significant differences between traditional and Christian moralities in their forms of subjectivation, the most important of which are evident in the confrontation between Christian ethics and those of the traditional legal system. In terms of ethical substance, the two systems have some similarities. In both, the inside of the person is an important target of moral evaluation. Christianity did not need to invent the subject in Urapmin; the traditional ethical system's worry over willfulness, concern with good thinking, and condemnation of even unexpressed anger rendered it similar to the Christian one in the ethical emphasis it placed on the inside of the person (cf. Strathern and Stewart 1998). In terms of the mode of subjection, there is a shift from traditional to divine law, but this too has not constituted a particularly sharp break in the Urapmin conceptualization of ethics. This leaves self-formation and telos as the only two aspects of the form of subjectivation in which substantial ethical differences might be found.

Taking telos first, here we find a significant difference. Traditional Urapmin morality called on the subject to constitute himself or herself as a "good person." However, though it was desirable to attain this status, failure to do so did not lead a person to incur any well-defined penalties beyond those that followed from the individual instances of lawbreaking perpetrated en route to that failure. The Christian telos, by contrast, is not only the conduct of a "good Christian life" but also salvation, the fact of being "taken back" (kisim bek) by God and allowed to dwell in heaven. Hence, unlike the traditional telos, the Christian one promises more than the sum of the outcomes of the individual moral acts that go into reaching it. It decisively links the entire Christian moral system to their expectation of the arrival of the millennium. This is a topic to which I return in chapter 8.

As important as this difference in telos is, it is not the most significant. At best, it must share that designation with the changes in kinds of self-formation demanded by the two systems. In the traditional system, the goal of self-formation was the achievement of a balance of lawfulness and willfulness that enabled one to succeed in being a creative social actor without flaunting any more than necessary the lawful demands made by one's existing relationships. In this scheme, the will was dangerous and controlling it was an important part of how the self related to itself, but it was not completely condemned. In the case of Urapmin Christianity, by contrast, the will is unequivocally condemned. There are no situations in which its exercise is legitimate. Hence the primary goal of Christian self-formation is the renunciation of the will. In making this its aim, Urapmin Christian morality condemns as immoral the dialectal relationship between law and will that is at the heart of traditional Urapmin ethics. This conflict between the Christian and the traditional view of ethical self-formation is, alongside the loss of taboo, the second important ground of people's experience of themselves as sinners.

I make several related comparative points in the conclusion to this chapter, but enough has already been said to orient my description of Urapmin Christian morality and its conflicts with its traditional counterpart.

ON THE END OF TABOO
AND THE MORAL PERILS OF FREE TIME

When talking about the Christian present, the Urapmin routinely remark that one thing that makes it so different from the "heathen" past is now they do not have to follow taboos regulating what they can eat, whom they can eat with, where they can garden, and so on. This change has come about, they say, because Christianity demands that they give up both Afek's taboos and those that follow from the spirit ownership of specific resources. The rationale for this demand rests on the principle

that God created the world and everything in it for humans to use.[1] He
had no intention, as the Urapmin understand matters, of interdicting the
human use of any natural resources or of preventing most forms of contact between men and women.

The two Urapmin taboo systems only came into existence, people
now say, because Afek and the other Urapmin ancestors, who lived
sometime after the era of "Adam and Eve, Cain and Abel, Noah and
Abraham," lied to their descendants, claiming that they had created
everything and setting up both systems of interdictions. With the coming of Christianity, the Urapmin have been able to see that these taboos
were "false laws" (giaman lo). Now that they know the taboos are
"false" and require actions that are contrary to God's will, for people to
continue to uphold them out of fear of the consequences of their breach
would be to go against God's wishes and display a lack of trust in his
power to protect people from spiritual retribution. Having defined taboo
observance as a form of faithlessness in this way, Christianity has rendered it a sin. Hence people are strongly enjoined to jettison the taboo
systems that formerly governed many aspects of their lives.

The Urapmin do not claim that this requirement is difficult to meet.
On the contrary, they profess to finding the abrogation of the traditional
taboos tremendously liberating, and they revel in many of the opportunities it has opened up. Now, they regularly announce with great satisfaction, is "free time" (fri taim), a time when everything is "open" (op)
to them. This notion of free time is very important to the way the Urapmin frame their present situation. That Christianity brought it about is,
in their reckoning, probably its single most welcome intervention in
their lives to date (the only other contender for this honor would be the
gifts of healing that the Holy Spirit has given them). Yet along with this
celebratory response, one can also detect ambivalences in their approach to free time and the taboo abrogation that produces it, and these
ambivalences in turn point to one of the sources of the Urapmin sense of
their own sinfulness.

People's ambivalence about free time takes different forms in relation
to each of the two systems of taboo. When people energetically extol the
virtues of free time, they are most often celebrating the escape it has provided from the dictates of Afek's taboos. People endeavored in the past
to follow quite strictly these taboos on eating certain foods and on contact between the sexes. It is precisely because of their strenuous efforts
to follow these taboos that their overthrow of them at the beginning of
the era of free time has been so meaningful. But it is also true that this

system of taboos was the one segment of their moral spectrum that consistently allowed the Urapmin successfully to construct themselves as moral people. It was a system of rules they could succeed in following without turning their backs on the demands of other parts of their culture. It also took the choice out of many situations of distribution and prevented the development of many situations in which illicit sexual attractions could form. In all of these ways, it provided a very workable framework for regulating the will. The loss of these intricately constructed guidelines for self-regulation has left the Urapmin with the sense that their wills now lack control; they find themselves wanting everything and filled with envy, jealousy, and the ominous conviction that their community is full of potential thieves and adulterers. As they often put it, now "we are too willful, we obey no one but ourselves" (mipela save bikhet, mipela save bihinim laik bilong mipela yet tasol). This cliché pointedly reverses the positive valuation embedded in the notion of free time.

The extent to which the loss of Afek's taboos feeds the Urapmin sense that they presently lack all self-control was brought home to me one day in church when Kiki, an emerging leader and graduate of the Duranmin Bible College, paused in the midst of a typical moral harangue and admonished himself and his listeners, "We must control ourselves, we cannot act like the *katobilin*." The katobilin were men who did not participate in certain traditional and now abandoned men's initiation rites so that they could look after the women and children. Whereas the men who participated in the ritual took on special versions of Afek's taboos connected with its performance, the katobilin were free of extra burdens. In the terms of his analogy, Kiki was asserting that if people want to avoid sin, they must live like those who previously followed an especially strenuous regime of Afek's taboos. In my experience, traditional Urapmin religion is rarely mentioned in church, and almost never in such a positive light. Yet in this case Kiki refers to it because the image of someone following a stringent version of its taboos is the most compelling model he can find for a life of moral rectitude. His statement exemplifies the lingering Urapmin sense that the loss of Afek's taboos has led people to have difficulties constructing themselves as moral subjects. Forcing people to forgo the ethical comforts these taboos once provided is thus one of the primary ways Christianity has led them to see themselves as sinners.

As notable as is people's ambivalence over the loss of Afek's taboos, it is equally pronounced in their attitudes toward the taboos that prevent them from encroaching on the ownership rights of the spirits. To a great extent, the Urapmin have given up these taboos. They now garden and hunt on formerly taboo ground, and many women and children eat marsupials they once avoided on account of their dangerous spirit owners. Yet despite their willingness to give up these taboos, they remain afraid of the consequences of doing so. The stakes involved are evident in the prayers many people address to God asking for special protection before breaching them. As these prayers suggest, the Urapmin believe that the spirits remain in place, watching over their resources. By violating the taboos they are in effect declaring war on the spirits, albeit one in which they can claim God as a formidable ally.

Despite God's support, however, there are some widely known cases in which people have had to beat a retreat after failed engagements with particularly strong spirits. For example, spurred on by the enthusiasm that the revival produced at its height, some Urapmin men went hunting for sacred game in Wim Tem and shared their taboo catch with the community. After many people became ill over the next several days, the big men quickly declared Wim Tem and the hunting ground associated with it once again taboo. In this and similar cases, people feel that in spite of the Christian backing they had for their actions, their willful disregard for the spirits had gone too far.[2]

The debates that currently surround the use of sacrifice to mollify offended spirits turn on similar dilemmas over finding appropriate ways to interact with spirits in the era of free time. The willful behavior the Urapmin now "show" the spirits often results in people coming to suffer the illnesses the spirits send in response. Such illnesses have long stood as an index of out of control willfulness and disregard for (spiritual) others. The traditional treatment for them was the sacrifice of a pig whose "smell" *(tang)* and sometimes blood was given to the spirit in exchange for its release of the sick person. Now, however, such sacrifices are understood as sinful. Instead of relying on them, people try to heal illness through prayers that ask God to send the offending spirits far away and bind their hands and legs so they can no longer make people sick. Sometimes, however, when an illness has lingered, or when it is a child who is ill and may die, people still resort to sacrifice. They do so only after consulting Spirit women who, having been possessed by the Holy Spirit, order such treatment. The role of the Holy Spirit in this process gives contemporary sacrifices something of a Christian imprimatur, as do the Christian prayers that now accompany them (see figure 5). Nonetheless, many people remain convinced that sacrifice is sinful, and

Figure 5. A Spirit woman working in the Spirit at a pig sacrifice she has ordered for a sick girl, who is being held by her mother. Photo by Joel Robbins.

they have trouble believing that the Spirit would order it. They wonder if Spirit women who order sacrifices have actually been possessed by an evil spirit masquerading as the Holy Spirit. As I was leaving the field, debates on this topic had become public and heated. The contention that surrounds this topic, and the agonizing choices people sometimes make to go ahead with offering sacrifices (and, on rare occasions, with honoring taboos), attest to the difficulties raised by the liberation of the will that constitutes free time. In relation to the spirits, just as in the case of the jettisoning of Afek's taboos, the Urapmin no longer have an acceptable way to construct themselves as moral people.

In Foucault's terms, what has been lost in the abandonment of the two systems of taboo is not only their two moral codes but also the forms of subjectivation that were connected with them. While both of these systems were code-oriented, their primary elaboration taking the form of a plethora of specific rules, they also contained techniques of self-formation (observance, sacrifice) that allowed those who employed them to achieve the telos of living as "good people" whose wills were under appropriate control. Christianity, in proclaiming their codes false, also condemns their techniques of self-formation. In doing so, it leaves the Urapmin without any way to constitute themselves as ethical subjects in their relations with the spirits or the things of this world. They are left, instead, with a Christian ethical system that counsels them to look to their inner lives as the only target of their ethical efforts and that offers a set of technologies that are directed toward this end.

The transformation Christianity has wrought in Urapmin morality is arguably similar to the one it brought about for some of those Jews who were the first to take it up. Kristeva (1982: 113 ff.) has argued that in doing away with the dietary taboos of the Old Testament, Christianity moved the source of abjection, or what we can call moral danger, from the outside to the inside of the person. It was no longer the things of the world that were dangerous but rather the human soul; the "ethical substance," in Foucault's terms, was now exclusively the inner reaches of the person.

In contemporary Urapmin, without the two taboo systems, the world is no longer divided into those things that are acceptable objects of desire and consumption and those that are not. Instead, the sole ethical goal has become the control of the inner life, and all of the things of the world are unacceptable objects of desire and consumption because as such they comprise so many temptations to relax that control (see chapter 5). Of course, traditional Urapmin morality also considered the inner life one part of the ethical substance of a person, and it provided techniques of self-formation (such as anger removal rituals) that helped people to put their inner lives in proper order. In the present, however, the construction of an ethical inner self stands alone as the sole consideration of Urapmin moral life. From a combined emphasis on the observation of elaborate moral codes (in the form of taboo) and the need for ethical self-formation, Urapmin morality has become, through the influence of Christianity, wholly ethics-oriented.

Having completely rejected taboo, this Christian ethics orientation defines itself only in relation to the Urapmin code of law. As it does so, it comes into conflict with the conception of ethical formation that traditionally governed the Urapmin relation to that code. It is to that conflict that I now turn.

CHRISTIAN CONFRONTATIONS WITH THE LAW

As I have already pointed out, when the Urapmin consider "God's law" (*God ami weng awem,* lo bilong Bikpela) as a code, it looks little different from their own legal code. What differs is the ethical conceptions by which it defines what one must do to abide by that code and the telos toward which it urges one to undertake such efforts. Most important, Christian ethics enjoins people to establish a new kind of relationship with their wills. Unlike traditional ethical notions, Christian ones leave no room for ambivalence about the will: they condemn it completely and declare its ethical expression impossible. In the Christian scheme, ethical behavior is motivated by the Holy Spirit and expresses God's will, not that of the individual. Personal willfulness and its emotional correlates—envy, jealousy, and anger—have no place in a properly ordered human heart. Thus the core ethical activity of the Christian is the "renunciation" (daunim) of one's own will (*san,* laik) in order to allow oneself to be guided by God's alone. If a person does this, he or she will have a "peaceful heart" (bel isi) and be free from sinful emotions and willful restlessness. Having achieved this inner state, a person will be able to "follow the law" (bihinim lo) and progress on the "road" (rot) toward salvation.

As this last point indicates, the idea of lawfulness remains important for Christian Urapmin. But it has been transformed in two ways. First, is has been internalized, such that obedience to it is first and foremost a matter of "straightening" (straitim) the "heart"; "good behavior" is merely a correlate of this inner work and is ethically worthless without it (cf. Murphy 1997). Second, with the will wholly condemned, the law has become the sole standard by which the Urapmin judge themselves. It no longer has to accommodate the demands of any other principle.

The differences between the Christian and the traditional formulation of the proper inner life may appear small, but they have been of great moment for the Urapmin. It is because both systems are grounded in conceptions of the will and the law and their interrelation that they have been able to come into relationship with one another (cf. Strathern and Stewart 1998: 45). But, at the same time, the significant differences in the way these conceptions are formulated in the two systems have rendered this relationship one scarred by contradiction. In particular, the Urapmin now construct themselves as ethical subjects under a Christian moral system that condemns the will while at the same time they continue to live in a world that demands they create their social life through willful action. This contradiction is, alongside the loss of taboo, another important source of their conception of themselves as sinners.

To fully grasp the effects of this contradiction on Urapmin life, it is necessary to leave off simply describing abstract cultural logics and consider how people use them to conceptualize and talk about their ongoing lives. I do this in the next two sections by examining two texts, a sermon and a confession, that display in some detail the ways the Urapmin undertake the moral regulation of their inner lives.

A SERMON ON THE PEACEFUL HEART

The sermon is an important part of the Urapmin church service (see chapter 7). People look to sermons to remind them of their ethical obligations and to "strengthen their belief" (strongim bilip) by setting those obligations in the context of the coming apocalyptic judgment. The sermon I discuss here was presented on Sunday morning, April 5, 1992, by a young man named Tomi. At that time, Tomi had only recently been appointed assistant pastor ("number two pastor") of the top Urapmin church, and his style lacks the oratorical artistry sometimes displayed by older men with more pastoral experience. But the rather straightforward nature of his sermon is part of the point here, for in its very plainness it reveals some of the basic themes of Urapmin Christianity—the themes that novices cling to when they dare not stray from what they call, following the title of a popular booklet used in preparing sermons, "the core of the message" (bun bilong tok). Tomi's sermon is, in a sense, a recounting of one of the take-away points of most Urapmin sermonizing, given back by someone who is just learning to deliver rather than receive them.

In this sermon, Tomi preached on Galatians 5:22. By the time he began to preach, the service had already been going on for several hours, most of them taken up by a heated discussion of the situation of the church, which had been beset by problems with attendance and by allegations of poor behavior on the part of its pastors. People were tired, hungry, and frustrated, and Tomi was under a good deal of pressure to keep his sermon short. He had also been a bit rattled by the preceding critical discussions. Hence his sermon is rushed and a bit artless. But hurried as it is, it illustrates well the inward emphasis of Urapmin morality.

GALATIANS 5:22

Tasol Holi Spirit i save kamapim gutpela pasin olsem: Pasin bilong sori, na amamas, na bel isi, na pasin bilong larim ol i rongim yumi, na pasin bilong helpim ol man na mekim gutpela pasin long ol, na wokabaut stret oltaim, [verse ends midsentence].

But the Holy Spirit bears the following good ways: The way of concern for others, and happiness, and peacefulness [calmness], and the way of leaving those who wrong us alone, and the way of helping men and treating them well, and always walking straight on the path, [verse ends midsentence].[3]

TOMI'S SERMON

1. Ephesians Chapter 5, line 22 . . . Ephesians Chapter 5, line 22, yes, that's right [he actually preaches from Galatians 5:22]. . . . All right, I will go ahead with God's talk. All right, I will start now. [Reads Galatians 5:22.] All right. This is the way of the Holy Spirit. . . . The Holy Spirit's way is to bear good ways, that is how it is. The Holy Spirit's road, the road the Holy Spirit travels, is like that. That is what the Bible says.[4]

2. So the Holy Spirit creates good ways, like when you are at peace [calm], or in the habit (<u>pasin</u>) of being concerned with others (<u>sori</u>). What is the habit of being concerned with others? [A respondent translates <u>sori</u> into the Urapmin language.] That's it. You are concerned for your brothers and sisters, that is following the Holy Spirit. The Holy Spirit is with you and you give your heart to your brothers and sisters and you are concerned for them. Concerned for them. Do that.

3. All right, another way of being concerned is to be concerned for your friend.

4. All right. Number two is happiness. . . . What is happiness? [Someone translates.] Yes, you have to be happy and you must give your heart to your friend.

5. You are concerned, you are happy and you give your heart to your brother, that's it! That is the good way, that is the good way.

6. All right, number three, peacefulness. What is peacefulness? [Someone answers, "Thinking slowly [calmly]," *agool kup aget fukunin.*] That's it. You think peacefully. . . . You think peacefully and you give your heart to your friend. Being concerned for him, happy for him, that's it, that's the good way.

7. All right, number four is the way of leaving those who wrong (<u>rongim</u>) us alone. What is this way of leaving those who wrong us alone? [No one answers.] If your brother does something bad to you, you stay peaceful [continue to think carefully] and he can do bad things to you. . . . That's it! The Bible is saying it is good to do it that way.

8. I will say the fourth way again, it is the way of letting those who wrong us alone. All right, I will tell you about this. Suppose that you are there, you are there and your friend [or] other people come and treat you badly . . . then turn your back [and say,] "Friend, you can hit me." You say that and you turn your back to him and he can hit you, he can do bad things to you and you don't pay him back, that is the good way! If any of you hold to this kind of way then you are good. This kind of way is good. That is what it is saying. But if he comes to you and then you too, you too treat him badly . . . This is not good behavior. This is what it is saying.

9. All right, number five . . . the way of helping men and treating them right. . . . What is the way of helping people. I want to ask this. [Someone translates "helping your friends" into Urapmin] Yes, you help your friends. If he is hitting you, you help him. When your friend is coming with a very heavy bundle of firewood [you say,] "My friend!" . . . "you are carrying one on top of the other, please my friend, give me some and I will carry it." This is how you do it. When your friend is coming with a string bag of food, you help him, or you see that a friend has a problem (hevi) you go help him, pray for [with] him. When he does wrong, you go help him, pray for [with] him. It says that this is the good way. That's the one. That's the one. That's the one. You must help your friends.

10. You should help anyone [lit., "elder and younger brothers"]. You are peaceful and happy and you go help him, brothers and sisters. This kind of behavior, this is the kind God likes. It says that it is good if you do that.

11. All right, this is the last thing I have to say. I will do the same thing with this last part of the Bible. Don't think I will talk for a long time, I won't be doing that. All right, this is the last talk.

12. The way of always walking straight on the path (wokabaut stret). You must always walk straight on the path. Don't do all kinds of bad things. You must always walk straight on the path and love [give your heart to] your brothers and sisters. Do not weave from side to side [lit., "go over there, come over here," a euphemism for "making trouble"]. If you are going along a road, you must only go well. You have to think about that and walk straight on the path. You must walk straight on the path. [Unintelligible.]

13. All right. I will say it again. I will say it again. [Reading] "But the Holy Spirit bears good ways" [end reading]. If anyone has the Holy Spirit . . . you do good things. If that is what you are doing, then you are a good woman, a good man. . . . And if you do not have the Holy Spirit, then you will go to bad behaviors. You are bad women, you are bad men. Like that, you do not have the Holy Spirit.

14. All right, the way of concern, you are concerned for your brothers and sisters. That is the first one. All right. Happy. You are happy and you remain happy and give your heart to your other brothers and sisters. You are happy. All right, the way of leaving those who wrong us alone. All right,

you see whoever it is come and talk behind your back or [say] bad things about you, you stay peaceful and he/she can come hit you or treat you badly. This is the kind of behavior that is good in the eye of God. All right, the behavior of helping people. . . . Helping others is treating them well. All right. Helping your friends. . . . It is good to help other brothers and sisters. That is what they are saying.

15. All right, the last talk. Walk and always walk straight on the path. Do not weave from side to side. You must be peaceful and always walk straight on the path. You must be [go] nothing but good when you go about on the road. You must be nothing but good when you go about on the road. You must always be nothing but good in your goings about. You must keep being nothing but good when you go about on the road.

16. That is what it said and I will not say anything more. There it is and that is all. That is the talk from the Bible and that is a sufficient amount of God's talk. Thank you.

This is an example of a common type of Urapmin sermon. Galatians 5:22–23 is a "list of virtues," one of many "ethical lists" that appear in the Old and New Testaments (Verhey 1993: 202). Urapmin are very fond of preaching from such lists. In fact, very little of their preaching is based on stories from the Bible. Because all adults (literate and illiterate alike) know these stories well and tell them in other contexts, pastors and others who preach assume their audience can draw on them as needed for interpretive purposes. This frees them to preach from brief passages that either list virtues or vices, as in Tomi's case, or promise impending apocalypse and judgment (the other most popular verses on which to build sermons). They are eager to do this, for they see sermons constructed in this way as helping them to reach their goal of reminding their listeners of what is good and what is bad and of motivating them to live ethically.

At first glance, Tomi's sermon may look like little more than a simple repetition of the list given in the biblical verse. Read carefully, however, it becomes clear that Tomi has introduced some causal links between items in the list that are not there in the text itself. The causal argument he presents sets out one of the core notions of Urapmin Christian ethical thinking.

The list of virtues Tomi is drawing from continues in verse 23 (which he does not address) with the addition of "gentleness" (pasin bilong isi isi) and "suppressing the desires of the pre-Christian heart" (daunim laik bilong olpela bel; the New English Bible [NEB] has this as "self-control"). Western interpreters of the whole list often break it up into three groups of three virtues each: concern for others (NEB "love"), happiness ("joy"), and peacefulness ("peace") are grouped as "Christian habits of mind more generally"; leaving those who wrong us alone ("patience"),[5] helping men ("kindness"), and treating people well ("goodness") belong together as "special qualities affecting a man's relations with his neighbor"; and finally, always walking straight on the path (NEB "fidelity"), gentleness, and self-control form a set of "general principles of Christian conduct" (Fung 1988: 271). I have seen other commentaries describe the three divisions with more pith as sets of virtues that are aimed, respectively, "inward, manward, and Godward." What Tomi has done, in terms of this tripartition, is argue that the inward qualities, especially peacefulness, are the cause of all others.

He first introduces the need for peacefulness in paragraph 6, where it naturally appears as he takes the list in order. In that paragraph, he also links peacefulness with being concerned for others: "you think peacefully and you give your heart to your friend." Note that this is not simply a repetition of those elements of the list already introduced, for the order is reversed. The conjunction here implies causation: it is because you think peacefully that you are concerned about your friend. As his sermon continues, Tomi repeatedly makes the inner state of peacefulness the cause of the other virtues that he lists. In paragraph 7, he says that turning the other cheek requires that "you stay peaceful." In paragraph 10, he announces that you are helpful because "you are peaceful and happy and you go help." In paragraph 15, he similarly puts peacefulness at the base of ethical conduct in general: "You must be peaceful and always walk straight on the path." In this way, the sermon as a whole makes an argument that fostering a particular inner state in oneself—that of peacefulness—is the key to leading a good Christian life.

As Tomi's sermon suggests, the idea of peacefulness is important in Urapmin Christian ethical thought. This is why Tomi highlights it at the expense of the other two inner states, "concern" (or "sympathy") and "happiness," that the verse also mentions.[6] The Tok Pisin term both he and the New Testament use to refer to peacefulness is <u>bel isi</u>. Inasmuch as "anger" (<u>bel hat</u>) is the term with which it is most commonly in opposition, "peacefulness" is the preferred gloss, though "calmness" is also appropriate in some contexts and accords nicely with the way Urapmin translate it into their language as "thinking slowly." Regardless of how we choose to translate the term, however, it is important to note that in both Tok Pisin (<u>bel</u> isi) and Urap (agool kup *aget* fukunin) it is a state of the heart. For Christian Urapmin, it is the ideal moral state of the heart because it is defined by the absence of the negative emotions of anger, jealousy, and envy, and as calmness it also implies a quiescence of the will. Thus Tomi accurately lays out in his sermon the crucial task for those who would render themselves ethical subjects: they must cultivate peaceful hearts.

Along with this message, Tomi takes up a related aspect of Urapmin ethical thought in this sermon. At the outset, he makes much of his chosen verse's proclamation that the Holy Spirit is the ultimate source of goodness in people's hearts and actions (a theme he also returns to near the end, in paragraph 13). The idea that people can only succeed in being ethically upright if they have the Spirit's help is a key tenet of Urapmin ethical thought, and it is explicit in their understanding of peacefulness. People often feel the Spirit is with them and has guided them to take particular actions. They say in such cases that the Spirit "speaks" to them. When they say this, they do not mean that they receive this speech aurally but that they experience the Spirit's guidance as a heart filled with clear thoughts about which they feel no "ambivalence" *(aget arep,* lit., "two hearts"). In this way, the Holy Spirit is experienced as the presence of a peaceful, calm inner state. It stands to reason, then, that without the Spirit's help, this inner state would be impossible to achieve. The key to living a peaceful life is allowing the Spirit to guide one's heart.

With this point, Tomi returns us, at least implicitly, to the topic of the renunciation of the will, for it is only by setting one's own will aside and allowing God's will to direct one's life that one makes a place in one's heart for the Spirit. The Spirit refuses to visit those who are given over to their own wills and the bad thoughts and emotions they foster. At bottom, then, the task of ethical self-formation depends on the control of the will. By touching on the role of the Spirit in the formation of an ethical inner life, Tomi's sermon, rushed as it is, is able to cover almost all of the fundamental postulates of Urapmin Christian ethical thinking. The only one he leaves out in his haste is that which ties the need to live ethically to the coming apocalypse. It is a major theme, and I return to it in chapter 8. In the next section, however, I want to explore how people attempt to fulfill the ethical requirement that they cultivate a peaceful inner life.

SIN, CONFESSION, AND
THE CULTIVATION OF THE ETHICAL SELF

Tomi's sermon exemplifies the extent to which the fundamental subject matter of Urapmin ethics, its "ethical substance" in Foucault's terms, is the inner life and in particular the vicissitudes of the will. Here, I move from exploring that ethical substance to considering some of the ways people work on it, the "technologies of the self" they use to transform that substance in positive ways by renouncing the will and cultivating a peaceful heart.

The two technologies of the self I discuss are moral self-reflection and confession. For Foucault, these constitute the historical core of Christian ethical life (Foucault 1997: 178). They are also, as he notes, tied together; one reflects in order to confess. By examining these two technologies, we can get a good sense of how the Urapmin relate to themselves as ethical subjects. I should note, however, that they do not exhaust the catalog of technologies of the self that the Urapmin employ in constructing themselves as ethical subjects. Because all Urapmin Christian practice is aimed at creating or restoring the ethical self, all of the Christian rituals the Urapmin perform are also in essence technologies of the self. I consider many of them in the next chapter, where I also consider the performative and symbolic aspects of confession. My focus here is on the more cognitive aspects of Urapmin ethical work—the technologies of self they use to think about and recognize their sins.

All Urapmin beyond the age of twelve or so reflect on their feelings and actions in order to identify their sins. If you were to ask anyone at any time what sins they had committed since their last confession, they would be able to provide you with a list. Some among those who are literate keep written lists of them, and everyone, literate or not, aspires to keep a very accurate record. By its very nature, such self-reflection is difficult to report on ethnographically except as people speak about it, and in Christian terms speaking about it constitutes confession. Thus the evidence I provide of its nature takes the form of a transcript of a confession. It is important to realize, though, that the self-reflection that is attested in discrete acts of confession goes on in Urapmin hearts all of the time and constitutes in itself an important part of the way people relate to themselves.

Turning to confession proper, I should explain that during the later part of my fieldwork I arranged to tape record some confessions (Robbins 1998a: 407–12). People confess privately to pastors or deacons. I had already worked closely with two of the pastors, and they were comfortable operating the tape recorder. They asked each person who came to confess if he or she would be willing to be recorded and no one objected. As I discuss in some detail in chapter 7, for the Urapmin, confession is the beginning of a ritual process designed to remove sin from the body. Sins, people said in an imagery they did not consider metaphorical, are not things that one collects for oneself. They were trying to get rid of theirs. If I wanted them on tape, I was welcome to have them. The only concern was that I obeyed the same rules of confidentiality as the pastors who originally heard them. In making this decision, people likely also took into account their understanding (discussed below) of how banal the sins they actually confessed would be.

For many months before I asked about making these recordings, I wondered about the moral issues I myself faced in making them. Despite my qualms, I asked to record confessions out of a conviction that there were important aspects of Urapmin moral life I could not learn about without making such recordings. Although I was greatly cheered by how little worry my request caused among people and by the extent to which the rationale they gave for their lack of concern accorded with other facets of their way of thinking about sin and confession, my sense of unease about this aspect of my research has never fully left me. As it happens, however, in listening to their confessions on tape, I did learn things I never could have learned otherwise about how Urapmin think about their lives in ethical terms. I report these findings here while making every effort to protect the anonymity of the people whose confessions I recorded.

The content of these confessions is mundane (which does not mean, of course, that it is ethically unimportant). No one confesses major moral breaches, such as adultery, to their pastor or other confessors until those breaches have become widely known in the community. In fact, there was a debate one day in church over whether people did or should confess adultery or other socially consequential offenses to confessors, and it was agreed that people did not and should not, in part for fear that confessors would not be able to maintain confidentiality where such socially consequential matters were involved.

Another reason for holding back on confessing major delicts is that once a particular sin has been "given" to God, the trouble that follows from it cannot then be settled in the village court or in higher government courts. In effect, confessing a crime takes it out of the realm of human jurisdiction. We might expect that the guilty could find in this an out; they could confess their crimes so that they would not have to stand trial for them. But in practice this does not occur. Even those who commit serious breaches of the moral code know that they will be living out their lives within the Urapmin community. It is thus in their interest to reach an acceptable earthly settlement of problems with their kin and neighbors. Only after such a settlement has been reached and, in passing, the crime has been well publicized, will the guilty person confess his or her sin to a confessor.

I present below the entire text of a single confession given in the Urap language by a woman in mid-1992. By reproducing one confession in its entirety, I hope to provide a sense of the range of things Urapmin attend to in their efforts to monitor and shape their inner lives. This confession also brings up many of the themes that are commonly expressed in others. As with the sermon, each paragraph is numbered. I have not used any real names in this text. The person confessing often referred to others by using kinship terms, but where she used proper names I have simply substituted common English names. I have also left out some details that might allow identification of people involved and have removed all place-names. In no cases, however, have I changed the import of what was said. I use brackets for explanatory interpolations and parentheses to record important words or phrases from the original texts. I have not transcribed any confessions verbatim. I went over the tapes while in Urapmin with the help of the pastor with whom I worked most often. This translation is thus a bit looser than that of the sermon. Because this confession, like many of them, is quite long, I interrupt it at certain points to introduce my own analyses.

The confession was made by a woman in her forties, "Jenny," who has a recently married son in his twenties named Bob and a daughter named Sheri who is about ten years old. During parts of 1991 and 1992, there was paid work available to Urapmin men building a small hydro-electric system in Telefomin. Men who worked on this project slept in Telefomin during the week. They returned home late Friday night and left again on Sunday after church. They were paid on "fortnight" twice a month. On fortnight Friday, many Urapmin who were not working would go to Telefomin in the hope that their working relatives would share some of their earnings with them. Jenny's husband, Jack, worked at the hydro project, and she begins her confession by discussing her anger over the distribution of some of the money he had been paid on recent fortnights. Although money does not figure as importantly in the confessions of those who do not have relatives working on the project, the sins that Jenny confesses to involving money are tokens of a very common type having to do with anger over the distribution of resources.

JENNY'S CONFESSION

1. Dana went to Telefomin and I sent Sheri with her. Sheri came back and said that Jack gave five kina each to all the other [Urapmin] there but not to us. "I have come with nothing," she said. [I thought to myself] when he finishes work and comes back who will have looked after his gardens? Do those people who got his money look after his gardens? I look after a taro garden and a sweet potato garden. I clean them. Its true that he works and gets paid for it, but when he comes back who will look after his food? This line who got his money can look after him. I said that and I was very angry. This is a sin I committed *(kabukle sin kesi)*.

2. Here is another one. Bob and Sheri went to Telefomin and I stayed here. Jack bought a chicken and gave it along with forty kina to Sheri [it is not uncommon for adults to give rather large gifts to young children, expecting them to share them in the manner of adults]. Her older brother [Bob] put the gifts in his string bag and brought them back. [When they returned to Urapmin] they put these things in the house and then the younger sister [Sheri] said, "He bought a chicken for me and gave me forty kina but my brother brought them back." She told me that and I said [to Bob,] "You give the money to us and we will hold it." He said, "No, I will be holding the money." He said that and then after a while Sheri and I went to the bush and we heard that Bob had sent his wife, Jean, to Telefomin. Jean came back with a bag of rice, a chicken, dripping [canned grease] and all kinds of food she had bought. When Jean and Bob arrived at the bush house I asked her, "Where did you get the money? You took Bob's father's money and you ate it [an idiom for consumption that does no social work]. You just take Jack's money and eat it. Do you make gardens for him too? When he comes will you say, 'We eat your money and we make garden's for you'? Will you say that? Will you say that? No. The food you have bought, leave it until we remake the roof of our house and [then people who help us] can eat it as the payment for the roof making *(am kon diip)*." [Jack has been working in part to save money to buy food with which to compensate those who will rebuild the roof of his house; this is the productive use from which Jean's "eating" is diverting his salary.] Then Bob said, "No, your money is still there. And we put away much of the food, we only ate some of it. We only ate the food we took to Jean's father's bush house and what we have eaten here." They only used part of the food for the roofing payment. The rest they ate and I said, "They ate the little sister's money so the two of them must pay her back." I said this over and over and this is a sin I committed.

3. And also, Bob and Jean brought twenty kina they were holding and carrying around. I said, "This twenty kina must come to my hand and Sheri and I can buy food and then Dana can help us expand the taro garden." But Bob said, "No, I won't give this money to you. I will hold it until I go to Telefomin. Then I will buy food and I will eat and I will help you cut the bush and you can plant taro." So after a few days Sheri and I went to the

village until the afternoon, but they did not come. So we slept for two nights. During that time Bob and Jean used Sheri's money to buy bark rope for making string bags from Jean's father. When they returned to the village I asked Jean, "Where have you been?" She said, "We have been on the mountain hunting and finding bark rope for making string bags." She did not tell me she had bought the rope. Then, when some other people from the village were going to Telefomin, I told Bob to give us Sheri's money and we will go buy sheep tongues and eat. But Bob said, "No, Jean used Sheri's money to buy bark rope." I said to him, "Hey, Bob, lots of times Jean eats money. Do you work and give money to her? Who gives her money? Her father? It's my husband [who works] and he sent it to me and Sheri but the two of you fouled it up. She [Jean] ate it. Now you must stop going to get his pay. She must pay back twenty kina. You didn't eat forty kina, you ate eighty. It's Jack's money, he sent it to Sheri and I, but you two ate our money. If it was another man who did this he would have to go to court, but it is my own child." I said this over and over. "The wife's rope, she bought it for ten kina and another ten kina, this price is too high so we have to discuss this and they have to pay back the money. Bob and his wife behaved very badly *(kukup mafak)* toward me." I said this over and over and I committed a sin. But my money, that his father gave me, they took eighty-one kina and they ate it. "It is good if you deal out half of father's money for us and half for yourselves. But no, you alone have been holding it and eating it up until now it is finished. Now this is the last [money] you eat. I suppose it will have to be, since the hydro project is almost finished [and then there will be no more wage work]. You two took money and ate rice but now the hydro is nearly finished." I told them this over and over. I was very angry about this and I committed a sin. Now I leave it to God.

The first three sins that Jenny confesses all turn on her anger over fairly typical kinds of household problems. For the most part, these have their origin in the paradox of lawfulness that I discussed in the previous chapter, though the ones Jenny reports are also shaped by the fact that the relationship between mothers and in-marrying daughters-in-law is a tense one in Urapmin, as it often is in patrilocal situations. At the time of this confession, Bob had only recently married and Jenny and Jean had not yet established a working relationship. The young couple was also under pressure from Jean's natal family to demonstrate that they would not fail to help them with labor and material gifts. This perhaps accounts for Bob and Jean's purchase of string bag rope from Jean's father at inflated prices, their sharing of store-bought food with her family, and their failure to show up as promised to help Jenny and Sheri make their garden. The newlywed situation is in most cases rife with tensions stemming from just these sorts of causes.

What is crucial for my concerns here is the way Jenny understands her anger over Bob and Jean's behavior, particularly over their "theft" and expenditure of Jack's money, as her own sin. Throughout these first three confessions, Jenny does not for a moment suggest that Bob and Jean are innocent. Indeed, she states clearly in paragraph 3 that they "behaved very badly" toward her. Yet her anger at them, anger that we might take to be justified, disrupts her own relationship with God. We get our first glimpse here of how intently the Urapmin Christian ethical system remains focused on the inner life and how completely Urapmin Christian morality bans anger. A further aspect of these confessions that is very important in Urapmin ethical understanding is the way Jenny's judgment on her anger makes the difficulties she is having with Bob and Jean solely her own problem. She might take some comfort in the fact that they too have sinned, but ultimately she recognizes that it is her responsibility to control her responses to their behavior. The guilt of other parties is immaterial in calculating the evilness of one's own anger. This way of assigning culpability for anger frequently leads people who want to avoid sin to shy away from pressing justified claims for fear of the heated arguments such a course of action might entail. It is better to ignore the problem and remain peaceful than it is to engage it and risk anger. This is so because Urapmin morality quite simply offers no scope for justified anger.

> 4. Here is another one. Joel [the anthropologist] gave one piece of children's clothes to Billy [Jenny's sister's son; a boy of about thirteen] and his parents put it away. Billy has two, no three pieces of clothing. Then we went to get roofing leaves and when we put them on the house he [Billy] gave one of his pieces of clothing to his "little sister" [mother's sister's daughter] Sheri. He said to her, "That's yours and this is mine." They wore the clothes and went to sleep and then Billy's older sister Anne [who is about twenty years old] came and asked Sheri, "Who gave you these clothes?" Sheri said, "No, Billy gave them to me." Anne said, "It's not yours. Billy goes to school and these clothes are for him for school, why are you wearing them." Anne yelled at her and Sheri started crying and came to me. Jeez, Billy gave it to her, he wore it and it was too tight for him. She didn't steal it. I told Anne, "OK, you hurry up and take it," and I took it off Sheri and we went to sleep. In the morning Anne came in the house and I told her, "You are not from a different bloodline, a single bloodline gave birth to you and Billy and Sheri. So its good if all of you wear it. Little sister uses it, older brother uses it, little brother uses it. But you come and lie about Sheri and scold her. When I was young I looked after you, bought you clothes and rice, and you are angry (kros) with me. Now you are grown up so you have to look after my child like I looked after you. She is not someone else [from

another family line]." I said this to Anne and she went to her father and said, "My mother's sister has been angry with Billy and me." They went and told their father this and the next day he told me that I had been angry with them. But I wasn't angry with them. Their father was angry with me. In the morning he accused me and asked me why I was angry with his children. But I was not angry with them, I just spoke to them. "You are angry at me, but I was not angry," [I said to him]. If I had been heavy [angry] I would have sinned, but I only spoke to them and told them this. I told them this and I came back. In this matter, they sinned. And then again, we talked back and forth. About this I have sinned. About this, I am sorry I have ruined God's house [by being upset in my heart]. I have spoken my sin.

This sin as well is rooted in problems over the distribution of resources among close relatives. What is new here is the bit of casuistry Jenny engages in near the end. As she sees the matter, she was never angry at Anne, even though she tore the shirt off of her daughter and handed it to Anne after Anne had scolded Sheri over it. Jenny was not yelling at Anne, she claims, but simply reminding her of all she, Jenny, had done to help raise her. In traditional Urapmin terms, she was simply reminding Anne of the lawful obligations to Jenny and her family that this help had established. To this reminder she added a small lecture on the right way for families to live. Even after Anne brings her father into the matter, Jenny was still not angry. In what sense, then, does she have a sin to confess? It seems that Jenny's sin lies in the simple matter of her "talking back and forth" with Anne's father. Perhaps there was some anger here, or at least there was discomfort. As will become clear below, people are liable to register any situation that makes them feel emotionally uncomfortable (usually understood broadly as *fitom* [shame]) as one in which they have sinned. If the other party to an interaction is angry, even if one keeps control of one's own temper, one's proximity to the other's anger and the discomfort such proximity causes is enough to disturb one's peacefulness and thus make one guilty of sin. Jenny's sin here, then, is her participation in a discussion in which at least one participant was angry.

> 5. And also, George's [one of her older village mates] breadfruit was ripe. Some of the fruit was falling to the ground, some of it flying foxes were eating. I asked, "Who will cut George's breadfruit so we can eat it?" My husband, Jack, went ahead and he cut it and we came and met him and cooked it. But my mouth was not good [perhaps from tooth problems] and I did not eat. I did cook it, it's true, and I heaped it up and they ate it. Then we came back to the village and George and his sons had found out that the breadfruit fruit had been cut down and they said they would charge who-

ever did it. We said, "No, it wasn't anyone else, just us," and we discussed it. This is a sin I committed. I did not eat much, only two. I confess my sin.

In this part of her confession, Jenny eventually confesses to a straight theft. But first she tries out some complex casuistic reasoning, much as she did in the last confession when she argued that she was not angry over the clothes. She points out that the breadfruit was rotting; it needed to be eaten quickly or it would go to waste. Then she insists that she only cooked the food, leaving the actual consumption to her family because of her sore mouth. But in the end she admits to eating two of the fruits, and she confesses this as her sin. I point out the complexity of her ethical reasoning because it conveys to us a sense of how much work people put into monitoring their own responses to situations and into determining when exactly they have sinned. Jenny is not unique in this regard. All Urapmin make these kinds of careful distinctions as they endeavor to conduct themselves ethically in the course of their daily lives.

> 6. The candidates [running for office in the upcoming national election] are always campaigning, night and day, and I am bored and my heart is heavy. I think to myself that you [politicians] don't talk about God's talk, you don't always campaign for God. This is not straight in God's eyes, what you are doing. God's talk goes first, and the campaign of the ground must come behind it. The other way around is not good. Talking about [promoting] the names of people of the ground is coming first and it is not good. I often think this and sometimes I say it. I have been doing that and this is a sin I commit [because I was angry]. I leave it to God.

The frustration over election campaigning that Jenny gives voice to here was commonly expressed at this time, most often in self-satisfied, holier than thou tones. Yet despite the fact that her sentiments were widely shared, Jenny considers her anger over this matter a sin. Hence not only personal anger but also anger that is quite in keeping with the general mood of the community is sinful in the terms of Urapmin Christian morality.

> 7. Yesterday I was at Tim's [her father's brother's daughter's husband, next to whom she lives] garden. His family and my family share one big garden plot. I went past my plot and into Tim's and his wife's plot to get some sticks. I saw some bark peeling off a tree and I pulled it down and on the ground I saw that their cucumbers were very nice [she laughs]. We people of the ground, there is not a good woman or a good man among us. We want things, we look, look hard and longingly at them. Then in my heart it said: "Wait! no, you can't do that kind of thing." Then I stopped thinking about the cucumbers and I went back to my garden. I said, "I saw lots of

cucumbers," and then Sheri went and got one and I was angry with her. I said, "You have made a sin now. I'm very sorry, you have sinned now. I did not tell you to go cut one of the cucumbers, you did it yourself. This isn't ours. It belongs to your older sister [Tim's wife—Sheri's mother's father's brother's daughter] and your in-law's line." I yelled at her and I was angry at my child. I went and saw the cucumbers but I didn't take one. But my child went and took one and it is over this that I have sinned. My heart became heavy over the second thing [Sheri's theft] and so I sinned and now I give it to God.

This confession is complex. It contains two major parts. In the first, Jenny discusses her own strong desire for the cucumbers and in the course of doing so introduces a general reflection on the desirous and hence sinful nature of human beings. It is common for Urapmin to insert such commentaries on the human condition into their confessions (see Robbins 1998a: 406–7 for another example). Covetous desire for things that belong to others, such as Jenny felt for the cucumber, is itself a sin, though in this case Jenny presents her strong desire for the cucumber as the first part of a story about how she successfully overcame its urgings. Narratives of desire aroused and then controlled are also common in Urapmin confession, and they provide another window onto the kinds of ethical dialogues the Urapmin regularly carry on within themselves. Here is another example of this kind of triumphal narrative, taken from a confession of a man in his thirties: "I went to the bush and I was going to knock down Emily's [his sister] pandanus. But I thought again and I did not cut it. This is a sin I committed. I coveted it. I cut a stick [to knock it down]." Although he successfully avoided carrying out a theft, for this man the desire to take the pandanus, the intention to do so, counted as a sin. For Jenny, her success in controlling her desire for the cucumber seems to have saved her from sin. Yet she feels compelled to include the episode in her confession, so it seems likely that she felt some guilt over her initial desire.

In its second part, Jenny's confession dissolves into another report of anger. Without engaging in too much psychological speculation, it seems clear that in this case Jenny identifies with her young daughter (with whom she is unusually close, for reasons I cannot go into here) and that she simply goads her into carrying out a theft that her ethical scruples prevent her from undertaking herself. Her anger, which she describes as extreme, seems to be fueled in part by her guilt over her earlier desire and her displacement of this onto her daughter. The whole episode suggests that people may have ways of pushing their sins from categories they find more troublesome into ones that they are more comfortable with: Jenny might prefer anger to strong desire. In recognizing this possibility, we should not forget that the language of sin is not simply a blunt tool of self-castigation; it is also a vocabulary that allows people to construct the situations of their lives in a variety of different ways.

> 8. And also, I have a cut on my leg. I got this cut down there on the road. This is another bad road. Tim's family made a bridge on this bad road. I walked on the bad road and got some taro cuttings and left the bundle in the middle of the road by the bridge. I planned to pick it up when I came back [she was tired and wanted to leave the bundle for a while]. When I came back to get the taro, the rope on the bridge was rotten and broken. It started to break as I walked on it and I was afraid. I fell into a gap in the bridge and I got this cut when a stick scraped me. In my heart I had a very big pain [i.e., she was very angry] and I said, "He didn't make a good bridge. He made a rough bridge and I fell and it hurts a lot." I didn't call out Tim's name, I called out his [infant] son's name "Max." "Max you ugly nose," I said in my thoughts, "if only you made a good bridge, but its a bad one and it hurts me, you ugly nose." I say that and in my heart I have a big pain. I think that I fell and nearly died. My heart was bad. This is a sin I committed.

This confession adds speaking badly about someone to the list of sins that follow from anger (a list that also includes fighting physically, arguing verbally, and yelling at people). Urapmin believe that abusive speech, like anger itself, can cause illness. It is one of the more common and more roundly condemned sins in their Christian moral code. It is not clear to me why Jenny directed her anger at Tim's infant son rather than at Tim himself, though it fits well with the Urapmin pattern of using smaller things to stand for larger ones in their oratory (e.g., "a small amount of greens" can substitute for "a pig"). Equally interesting is that Jenny's anger is directed at people who have not intended to wrong her specifically. The Urapmin live in a world constructed by their fellows; just as the landscape is owned, so too are the improvements to it connected with specific individuals who must take responsibility for what they have done. There is, as it were, a thin film of responsibility that lies over the landscape. For this reason, many accidents are liable to lead to sinful anger directed toward the person or persons who are responsible for the area in which they occurred.

> 9. Also, Tim's father left a pandanus fruit for us. He told us it was growing by the road and that when we [walked by and] saw that it was ripe we should knock it down, cook it, and eat it. We often do see it on the road.

It is a return for the pandanus we cooked for him. When we saw that it was ripe we wondered, should we cut it or leave it a little longer. But Jack [her husband] said, "Tim and his father left it for us so we can cut it down and bring it to the house." I say that we have cut Tim's father's pandanus down and so we have sinned and so we must give it to God. I have confessed it and now I will cook the pandanus.

Here we encounter an unexpected kind of sin. Jenny confesses to harvesting a pandanus fruit someone had given her as a gift. Not just any gift, this one was an explicit return for a pandanus Jenny's family had earlier shared with Tim. Pandanus is a kind of food that is paradigmatically shared through such reciprocal gifts of uncooked fruits or through reciprocal invitations to eating parties that take place among groups of various sizes. Given that pandanus is such a common item of reciprocal exchange, where can the sin possibly be in Jenny harvesting a pandanus that had been given to her as a return gift?

In fact, people routinely confess to sins that involve taking something someone has given them (Jenny herself provides another example below); it is one of the most commonly confessed types of sin. The sin arises when the recipient must collect the gift herself or himself rather than take it from the "hand" *(sigil)* of the donor. Even if the donor is present or nearby, as would be the case when the donor is tired and asks someone who is helping in her or his garden to harvest some food to be eaten collectively, the recipient will commit a sin in the act of harvesting the food. It is similarly a sin to take already harvested food that has been given to one. As long as the donor actually hands the gift to the recipient, there is no sin involved in receiving a gift, but sin ensues as soon as the recipient must collect the gift from anywhere but the donor's hand.

Based on discussions I had with various people, it seems that the idea that taking a gift in such a way is a sin follows from the fact that people tend to confess as their own sins their responses to situations that make them uncomfortable. There is great shame in taking any gift that one must collect from somewhere other than the hand of the donor, and this shame makes such action sinful. But why should taking what has been given be shameful? After all, to some extent one is only obeying the word of the donor, and obedience to others is another cornerstone of ethical behavior in Urapmin. To answer this question, we have to recognize that the Urapmin have a very strong sense of personal possession (Robbins 2003). Therefore, the transfer of goods must always be explicit if the act of receiving them is to remain above suspicion. In this connection, it is important to remember that the Urapmin put little store in the spoken word. The gift that is handed over is decisively given in action, whereas the gift that is given only verbally may not actually be given at all. Should the gift be given by a piece of mistaken or deceitful speech (both *weng famul*), then the act of taking the object would be theft. Since speech is always liable to be mistaken or deceitful, the act of taking what is only verbally given is always fraught with uncertainty. Even the feeling that one may be thieving is enough to cause the shame that makes taking verbally given gifts sinful.

While this is not a simple explanation for why taking for oneself gifts that have only been verbally given is a sin, I believe that all of the elements I have mentioned do figure in the difficulty people have with this kind of act. Even if the explanation is not accepted, however, we have to recognize that the Urapmin find such behavior deeply sinful precisely because it disturbs their inner peacefulness. It is the effect such taking has on their inner lives, more than the at worst very minimal one it might have on their social relationships, that makes it a sin.

10. [After a long pause] That must be it, or have I been running around looking longingly at things and coveting them (ai gris). Only God knows.

11. [After a long pause] I have already spoken about money. I think I have said enough. I'll go outside and then think of one I have forgotten, that's the thing.

12. [After a long pause] I helped Mike weed his big taro and sweet potato garden when he was ill. Jane said to me that tomorrow several women from Mike's village would go to Mike's garden to weed because he is sick. I thought this was true and I went to sleep in Mike's bush house, rather than ours. We were going there for the first time. We opened the door of the bush house and went inside. In the afternoon, Mike's son Donald and his family came. Before that Jack and Sheri and I thought that it was bad that no one from Mike's village had come. Then Donald's family came. We told them that we had been worrying and sitting here. Whoops, I left out a part. When we were walking on the road to the bush house we stopped and helped my sister make a garden. I was thinking that it would be bad if we were hungry and so I went and got some sweet potato from my sister's daughter's garden. They told us where the daughter's garden was and told us we could take some sweet potatoes because we had helped them. I told Jack and Sheri to wait and I went down and first I came to John's garden and checked it for sweet potatoes but it was all harvested out, so I went on to my sister's garden. I got a digging stick and poked around in an anthill. Then the stick hit a sweet potato and I harvested a very big one. I took two smaller ones too. I said to myself, "Now I am committing a sin," and I put them in my string bag. I said to myself, "Jesus I am making a big sin. I have taken enough [I won't take more]. Sin. Sin." Then I came back to the road and I told them, "We have sinned, let's go."

I brought the food to the bush house and I gave the smaller ones to Mike's wife's pigs. The big one we divided and cooked. Then we ate it and slept. In the morning Donald and his wife came. If I throw my hand into Mike's garden and grab things [i.e., harvest from it], then I make a big sin. If I just look for and pull out weeds that's all right. So I prayed about this and then I sat down and weeded the garden. In the middle of the work some other people came and helped us and we cleared out the weeds. Then Donald went and cooked taro and sweet potato in an earth oven [a very social way of cooking, a way of cooking food for group consumption, as opposed to cooking in the ashes of a family hearth] and he called us and we ate and then we slept. I came back to the village and I had sinned. I saw good taro, good sweet potato out in the open. It was a big garden and looking at it I sinned [i.e., she was covetous]. It was his garden and I went in and saw that the taro was rotting and cooked in an earth oven and ate. I walked in another person's garden and looked around and it is a sin. I thought back to when I was young and my father planted gardens. When they were ready he said they were rotten and we would cook it in an earth oven and [we would] eat. He did it the same way. I worry about my elder brother [Mike]. He is sick and lots of his taro is rotting. I was sorry about this. I looked at the huge taro and I coveted it and so I have sinned. I leave it to God. I cleared weeds in a friend's garden and I coveted the big taro and this I leave to God. I leave it to God. Will God leave my sin there, will he make me straight or leave me?

13. [After a long pause] That's all. God himself, only he sees the way I go about. Do I go about good? Don't think that I am angry, that my heart is heavy. No, I just want to talk about what I said the time that it rained on us. We went to one of our gardens and we were sleeping in the bush. Not in a bush house, just in the bush. During the night it rained on us and in the morning I told my husband, "You go make a house, I'll work in the garden." So I went to the garden and cleared weeds while he cut posts. He went down below where I was to build the house. He didn't make the house on dry ground, he made it on muddy ground. In the rain the ground there would be wet. I asked him, "Why did you make the house on muddy ground? What's stuck in your ear that you don't hear me [she laughs]. You are a man, you must think about it and make a house on the dry ground. In this swamp you will be running around like a marsupial in water trying to get to the house." I wasn't angry (<u>bel hat</u>) about this, but I said this and it was a sin. I leave it to God.

14. I think I am done. Or do I have some more? [Long pause.] I cut one of [my sister] Kim's pandanus and I put it in my house and slept. Some of it rotted, so I only brought part [to my house]. I haven't eaten it yet. In the eye of God I cut my friend's pandanus and put it in my house. And so that is a sin I committed and so I will wait [until Kim comes?] and then I will cook it in an earth oven and eat it. That is a sin, something heavy. I think . . . that's all that there is.

These last confessions provide something of a review of many of the themes considered above. The twelfth confession is yet another complex one that includes anger (over the failure of anyone from Mike's family to be at Mike's bush house when Jenny and her daughter arrived to help them with garden work) and the sinfulness of taking gifts that have been given for oneself rather than from the hand of the giver (though in this case it is complicated by the fact that they were told to harvest from the daughter's garden but ended up harvesting from the mother's). It also introduces a not yet discussed kind of sin that frequently figures in Urapmin confessions: the covetous feelings that arise when looking at ripe food in people's gardens. Urapmin like to describe in detail the desire that overtakes them when they look at good food in other people's gardens. As they say, their covetous feelings (*tiin lawut inin;* lit., "the eyes steal and eat it") make them "swallow their spit" *(mok inin)*. When people walk through other people's gardens to get to their own, they try to "walk straight" with their eyes narrowly focused on the path to avoid looking too closely at the crops all around them. But that strategy will not work when one is helping others with garden work. Jenny was bound to feel covetous as she weeded Mike's garden. Yet the fact that this response was inevitable does not render her feelings any less sinful. Even her arguments about how Mike was not eating his food quickly enough to prevent it from rotting does not exonerate her. Covetousness, like anger, is never justified.

The rest of Jenny's confession is taken up with reports of sins that are similar in kind to those we have already considered. Talking badly to someone, in this case her husband over his choice of a muddy site on which to build their bush house, is sinful even when, as here, it is done in jest and without an angry heart. The final sin, inserted at the end as if it were an afterthought, is actually the one straightforward account of a theft in this whole confession. It is clearly something that has bothered Jenny, and having unburdened herself of it she is finally ready to end her confession.

This entire confession and the discussion of Urapmin understandings of sin that I have organized around it resolves itself into one major theme: certain inner states (anger, covetousness, desire) are bad to feel and bad to act on. This second judgment holds even when others do not see the actions involved as bad (as in cases in which one person has given another the food the second person sinfully harvests). All of these inner states are directly connected to the will. This is obvious in the case of covetousness and desire, which are forms of willful energy, and anger for the Urapmin is an outcome of the frustrated will. If one has truly mastered one's will, then one will have eliminated covetousness, desire, and anger as well. At the heart of confession, then, is the effort to speak of the will so as to renounce it (cf. Carrette 2000: 41–42). But in the wake of this renunciation, questions arise as to what kind of life Christianity actually promotes and whether it is possible successfully to live such a life. These questions cannot be answered on the basis of the content of confessions alone. Any effort to explore them requires that we return to a consideration of the broader logic of the Christian moral system.

THE CHRISTIAN LIFE AND ITS IMPOSSIBILITY

As the Urapmin understand it, Christian morality unrelentingly condemns the will. For this reason, the successful Urapmin Christian lives a life that consists of virtually passive behavior that disturbs no one and aims to achieve only minimal goals of subsistence and reproduction (cf. White 1991: 177). Those who would live such a life try always to follow God's will and never their own.[7] If they succeed, they remain peaceful in all situations, refrain from "pushing" themselves or others to bend to their will, and do not feel anger themselves or make others angry.

Many people do in fact try to live in keeping with these dictates. This entails choices that sometimes cause them considerable worldly hardship. I present two brief examples of decisions made in the pursuit of a Christian life that give a sense both of what is at stake in living this way and of the efforts people actually make to do so. Both of the men whose decisions I discuss are important leaders of the church, having served for many years as deacons or other sorts of church officials. They are also reasonably successful men who have raised families and are known to be hard workers. As much as possible, they have managed to stay in the flow of sociality while also trying to achieve the passivity required by the Christian life. Here, I am interested in the choices they have made to extract themselves from that flow when they felt that it threatened to lead them into sin.

The first man, Tandi, had in 1992 just married off his only daughter. He was not unhappy with the match, yet he refused to have anything to do with either negotiating or "holding" (receiving) the bride-price he was due to receive for his daughter. He made his decision to withdraw from these activities on the basis of his belief that the tensions that always surround bride-price negotiations (which frequently unfold over the course of a year or more) would "ruin" his Christian life (bagarapim Kristin laip bilong mi). Just at the point where many men take on their most prominent public role, Tandi removed himself from the flow of public life so as to avoid having to take the kinds of willful action that create it.

Rin, the other man I discuss here, is the son of one of the leading Urapmin big men of the past several decades. His father died in 1989, and since then he has had to decide whether to try to collect on his father's debts and to work to hold together the village his father had established. Were he to undertake these two projects, Rin would move toward establishing himself as a big man. As of early 1993, however, he had decided not to pursue this path. He notes that his father often had to "push" people to conform to his desires, making some of them redeem debts when he needed what they owed him and "pulling" (pulim) others to live with him in his village. Fearing the sins of willfulness such actions require and the anger they elicit, Rin has decided not to assert himself in this way. For the same reason that Tandi does not want anything to do with his daughter's bride-price, Rin shies away from the assertion and anger that mark the career of a big man; they would, he notes, ruin his Christian life.

Tandi and Rin, and many others, try to a significant extent to live without reference to their own wills and the desires they produce. They even forgo the defense of their legitimate interests in return for a chance to live lawful, peaceful (isi) lives. Yet it is crucial to note that neither of these men has made his decision in order to feed an image that he has of himself as free from sin. On the contrary, they decided as they did because they see themselves as sinners in need of self-improvement. Rin has many young children and rarely a day goes by during which he has not been angry with one of them for their failure to perform household chores or for other reasons. He worries about this, and sometimes he lies awake in the dead of night praying to God to forgive his sins of anger so that he can be saved when the last days come. Tandi also worries that he is quick to anger, and he spends the bulk of his time living with his family in his bush houses, far from the many entanglements of village life that could arouse his temper. Like Rin, he has a keen sense of his own sinfulness.

The cases of Tandi and Rin show not only that people try hard to live Christian lives but also that even those who try hardest are bound to fail. They fail because, at least in Urapmin, the Christian life is impossible to live. There are two senses in which this is so: first, the Christian moral system conflicts with the demands of Urapmin social life in such a way as to make its breach inevitable; second, the system also in and of itself defines success in such a way as to create the conditions for people's failure to meet its demands.

I have already alluded to the contradictory demands that emanate from the Christian moral system and the traditional conception of social action: the former condemns the will entirely, while the latter demands that people exercise it in order for social life to exist. Since there is as yet no Christian replacement for the traditional Urapmin conception of social action (and this is not an area in which their Christian thought promises to provide much help in the future either), those who would live in society must do so at the cost of sinfully exercising their wills. Rin's and Tandi's cases illustrate this point well. By opting out of dealing with bride-price, collecting debts, and building villages, they are refusing to participate in the creation of some of the major contexts of Urapmin sociality (i.e., marriage, exchange relations, and villages). One result of these refusals that was evident as I was leaving Urapmin in 1993 was that the village in which they were the most prominent senior men was ceasing to function as a viable social context and was splintering into several small groupings, each planning to move to its own new site. Yet even having forgone these opportunities for creative social action, Rin and Tandi were not left feeling self-confident about their moral success. As noted above, the more mundane aspects of social life that they could not cease to engage in—raising children, keeping a family together, general village living—require enough willful assertion from them that they could not avoid falling into the clutches of sin. Like all Urapmin, they find that in the terms of the Christian moral system, their social lives, no matter how minimal, are by definition sinful.

The contradiction between the demands of Christian morality and those of Urapmin social life is exacerbated by a difference between the ways Christian and traditional moralities frame their ethical requirements. As I noted in the last chapter, traditional morality was centered on an ethic of responsibility. By taking the outcome of an action into account—asking if it was creative or destructive—that morality was able to maintain a general suspicion of the will while still supporting its exercise when socially necessary. Christian morality, by contrast, is much more an ethic of conviction; it enjoins people to seek moral satisfaction by realizing its imperatives regardless of the consequences of their doing so. If social life breaks down—if, for example, marriage negotiations should fail or a village crumble—that is of no account to those who have done what is right. And in the Christian case, doing what is right is always defined in relation to one's inner state, never in relation to the state of the world, so that no peace need ever (or can ever) be made with the social world's demands. As Soeffner (1997: 41) puts it in his discussion of Luther's Christianity, Christian moral systems that so intently focus on the inner life establish an "'impractical' reason" that "is under no obligation to the logic of action" (see also Dumont 1994: 20, passim; Buss 2000: 17). A Christian ethic of conviction focused on the inner life thus provides no basis from which to mediate contradictions that arise between its own demands and those of people's social lives.[8] In the Urapmin case, where such a contradiction is intensely felt, people are left to experience their own lives as ones of constant moral failure.

In addition to the way the Christian moral system contradicts the demands of social life, it has a second feature that also condemns the Urapmin to moral failure. One way to describe this feature is to say that the Christian moral system virtually creates the conditions that ensure people's failure to live up to its demands. Under the Christian injunction to renounce the will, the Urapmin are even more likely than most people to be aware of the sometimes subtle, fleeting ways in which their wills move. The situation is similar to the one Foucault (1978) describes surrounding the modern attention to sexuality. As he has shown, the modern concern to repress sexuality led paradoxically to an intensely exploratory attitude toward every aspect of sex and to an explosion of the number of discourses concerned with it. Similarly, the Christian concern to renounce the will has led people in Urapmin to attend assiduously to their wills and to talk ceaselessly about the problems they cause. Enjoined always to be looking for the sinful will, they are bound to find it, as is obvious in their confessions. This vicious cycle within Christian morality contributes significantly to people's conviction of their sinfulness.

At this point, I have answered the question of how the Urapmin have come to find the idea that they are sinners a convincing one. Condemned to failure by the contradictory demands of the Christian moral system and their own social life and further dogged by a vicious cycle in which the Christian renunciation of the will only makes its presence that much more evident, they routinely experience their own sinfulness. Given this experience, it is not hard for them to recognize themselves as the subject of every Christian harangue about moral weakness and every Bible verse that warns those who sin about the fires of hell. There is, in fact, no other identity besides that of sinner in which they are so secure.

The Urapmin experience of sinfulness follows, however, not just from their failure to live up to the demands of the Christian moral system but also from their loss of other moral systems in which they previously excelled. I have already discussed at length how the loss of Afek's taboos has led to a situation in which people are no longer able to turn to this system for the ethical comfort it once provided. But there is also another moral system in which the Urapmin formerly excelled, even if only for a brief time, that has been transformed in ways that have rendered it as useless as taboo for their current projects of ethical self-formation. This is the system of government law.

In Part 1 of this book, I made much of the way the Urapmin seized on the colonial discourse of lawfulness to bolster their efforts to make themselves acceptable colonial subjects. I further argued that Christianity planted itself in soil that this colonial-era project had made ready to receive it. But despite the historical relationship between colonial and Christian notions of lawfulness, people's current success at being lawful in government terms fails to assuage their feelings of sinfulness. Why is this so? To answer this question, we have briefly to consider what has happened to colonial notions of lawfulness in the era of independence and Christianity.

Much of the story of the fate of the project of colonial lawfulness in the Christian era is irrecoverable, but its basic outlines are clear enough, and they explain why government law is currently of no help in people's efforts to understand themselves as morally successful. Initially, the colonial law was assimilated, I believe, not to the traditional legal code (which it contradicted in important respects, e.g., its ban on traditional warfare), but to the two systems of taboo. By virtue of its finely woven mesh of rules that governed all aspects of everyday life and attended particularly to matters of bodily comportment (hygiene, lining for censuses, regulating the body in government work), the system of colonial law resembled both traditional taboo systems in its emphasis on regulating quotidian practice. And like the taboo systems but unlike the traditional legal system, the inner life was not part of the ethical substance it sought to regulate. Its interest was in what people did or did not do; it cared little what they felt. Finally, like the spirit-related taboos, the colonial law was a code that defined ways both to show respect to potentially dangerous others and to repair relations with those others when one had disregarded their demands (e.g., serving time in jail).

Along with these conceptual similarities, the government law was also like taboo in that it was a system with which the Urapmin had some success. They attempted to follow it with the same focused intensity they brought to the observance of their taboos, and as with the taboo systems they found themselves able to fulfill many of its dictates. We can see their success in the frequency with which patrol officers held the Urapmin up as a model of emerging colonial lawfulness. At least as the colonial legal system was administered by the patrol officers (and by this I mean relatively lightly and from a distance), the Urapmin were able to use it to constitute themselves successfully as moral subjects during the colonial era. It was, during that time, the primary new technology of the self that the whites offered to Urapmin people who were searching for novel ways to constitute themselves as fit subjects of the new order they saw emerging.

During the independence and Christian era, the role of colonial law has changed. This change has been driven from two directions. First, the government law is no longer a code that mediates between the Urapmin and powerful, unpredictable spiritlike others. Although the Urapmin respect and to some extent fear the independent government, it does not inspire the same awe as its colonial predecessor. This is not surprising, since it does not enforce most of its laws with any regularity, and its presence in the community is very slight. And along with this general loosening of enforcement, the postcolonial government has attenuated the reach of the law; it lacks the colonial government's ambition to control the minute movements of daily life through a code like the Native Affairs Regulations. To the extent that it attends at all to matters of hygiene, it frames its demands as issues of medical, not legal, necessity. Similarly, it now commands labor primarily through payment rather than through legal requirements.[9] What is left of the law is a very general code not unlike the traditional Urapmin legal code: one should not steal, fight, adulter, murder, and so on.

This general code is also, of course, much like the Christian moral code. This similarity has allowed Christianity to work as a second force for the transformation of the Urapmin understanding of the colonial law. In essence, Christianity has encompassed the government law, and the Urapmin now understand and evaluate the latter in terms set by the former. People often say that the government law and God's law are the same, and the phrase "it is wrong in the eyes of God and the government" is a staple of contemporary moral rhetoric. But despite the perception of similarity, there is no doubt that God's law is more powerful and important. After people have suffered the judgment of the courts, they never neglect to confess their legal failures as sins to God. Only confession truly ends the matter and restores a person's ethical standing. Having been encompassed by Christianity, the government legal system

no longer provides a self-contained technology of self-formation. This
means that Urapmin success in abiding by its rules is not in itself sufficient to define them as ethical subjects. It cannot provide an alternative
to the failure-ridden Christian moral scheme.

Given the difficulties produced by the Christian moral system itself
and by the way it contradicts traditional Urapmin notions of ethical social action, and given its success in evacuating or encompassing the
other moral systems with which the Urapmin are familiar, people's conviction of their own sinfulness as they try to live under it is comprehen-
sible. Attempting to renounce the will in a world in which its exercise is
required, sensitized to all of its movements, and lacking in technologies
of the self that would give it a place, their moral efforts are destined to
fail. It is, however, one of the ingenious design features of many kinds of
Christianity that they make the ever-renewed conviction of sinfulness an
important condition of salvational success; as the Urapmin say, "Jesus
came for the sinners." So what is most important is not eradicating sin
completely but trying earnestly to avoid it as much as possible and then
responding to it with contrition when, as it inevitably does, it occurs. In
the next chapter I consider the Christian ritual technologies of the self
that the Urapmin employ in their efforts to reach these goals of avoiding
sin and repenting for the failure to do so.

CHAPTER 7

Rituals of Redemption
and Technologies of the Self

To an observer, one of the most striking aspects of contemporary Urapmin life is the density of ritual behavior that marks it. Christian ritual
activity is omnipresent; people are engaged in it from morning to night,
in the village and in the bush. Never a day goes by when one does not
at least hear someone performing a prayer healing ceremony in a house
or a Spirit woman at work, and I reckon that on at least a third of the
days I was in Urapmin people attended one if not two church services.
If to this list of collective observances one adds the private prayers that
people say when they wake up, garden, hunt, and go to sleep and the
Christian songs they sing to themselves as they walk along the path, one
might begin to comprehend how deeply saturated Urapmin life is with
ritualized forms of worshipful action.

The intensity of Urapmin ritual life is rendered even more remarkable
by the fact that all the rituals that make it up are new to the Urapmin.
They only began to practice most of them after the coming of the revival
in 1977, and even those that some people had performed earlier—such
as church services and individual prayers—took on community-wide
importance only after the conversions of the late 1970s. Anthropologists
commonly note that in other parts of the New Guinea Highlands ceremonial exchange activity responded to the coming of wage labor not by
dying out, as many observers expected, but by reemerging in grander,
more extensive forms (Gregory 1982; Robbins and Akin 1999; Sahlins
1992). Among the Urapmin, who formerly channeled far more of their

energy into ritual than into ceremonial exchange, it is ritual that has effloresced, finding in circumstances of change an impetus to expand its role in their lives. And the similarity between these two postcontact explosions of activity is not merely a matter of surface commonalities; in both cases, the areas into which people's efforts have been channeled are the primary ones in which they are working out issues of change. Where exchange is the focus, its centrality follows from the fact that it is the arena in which people are negotiating key questions about how to construct selves and social relations and how to reproduce their society in the face of extensive cultural transformation (Robbins and Akin 1999). Where ritual is prominent, its importance is likewise based on its ability to constitute a site where such fundamental issues can be addressed.

As the Urapmin conceptualize it, the primary question they are facing in this period of change is the one put to them by the demands of Christian morality: how does one live as a good person while existing in the midst of a social world that routinely draws one into sin? Much of Urapmin Christian ritual performance aims to settle this issue either by helping people to control their wills, so that they can avoid sin, or by helping them to recuperate their moral status through repentance after they have sinned.

Because Christian rituals aim to help people meet Christian ethical demands by avoiding or repenting for sin, they can usefully be construed as technologies of the self in Foucault's terms, and it is in those terms that I analyze them here. Taking the most important Christian rituals, I demonstrate that both their symbolism and their processual design are shaped by the goal of helping those who practice them to overcome the difficulties of ethical self-formation. As one would expect, the focus that these rites place on the self is quite explicit. In what follows, I keep this focus in the foreground, paying particular attention to how they claim to operate on the individuals who practice them.

Before discussing the rituals themselves, I need to make two further introductory points, both of which involve the ritual of prayer. I do not want to consider the nature of Urapmin prayer in detail here (see Robbins 2001a). I do want to point out, however, that not all prayers are integral to specific ritual technologies of the self. Those that are not tend to be petitionary, asking God for success in gardening, hunting, and trade, or to prevent various misfortunes. In all of these cases, people use prayers to fill gaps left by the demise of traditional ritual life. That life was at least as much focused on issues of worldly success as it was on those of self-formation. Where its absence has left the Urapmin without any way to address worldly matters, they have turned to prayer as something of an all-purpose ritual stopgap. I do not focus on petitionary prayers in this account, for they are not central to Urapmin ritual life (a fact that is attested by their relative lack of elaboration). I mention them because they are a conspicuous part of people's daily routines, and they have allowed Christianity to insinuate itself into a wide range of areas of Urapmin concern.

The second point I want to make about prayer has to do with its role in the rituals of self-formation that I will discuss. Prayers are very much the punctuation marks of Urapmin ritual life. They mark its beginnings, endings, and transitional moments. Very often, they perform this function by spelling out verbally the nature of the ritual of which they are a part. Prayer is thus the most theologically explicit Urapmin speech genre. I exploit this explicitness in what follows by using prayers to establish or illustrate key themes in my analysis of each of the rituals I examine.

I begin with a consideration of the church service, because it is the one ritual that is performed on a fixed schedule and because it develops themes that are important in all other rituals.

INSIDE THE CHRISTIAN LIFE: THE CHURCH SERVICE AND THE DRAMA OF ETHICAL SELF-FORMATION

The Urapmin hold church services (sios sevis, lotu sevis) very frequently, at least on Saturday evening, Sunday morning, and Sunday evening. Usually, there is a service on Wednesday evening as well. People come back from their bush houses near their gardens for Saturday night services and remain in their villages at least through the Sunday morning service. Sunday afternoon is generally busy with social events. This is when young men and women play soccer and other sports and when adults spend time chatting pleasantly or discussing important community matters. These activities tend to keep people from the bush for long enough to allow them to attend Sunday night services. By Monday morning, though, most Urapmin will have left for their gardens, and it can be hard for pastors to muster enough people to hold services that evening or during the rest of the week. Whenever people are around in the villages, however, for instance, when the community is doing Kaunsil work maintaining footpaths or is involved in house building or repair, pastors will hold services most mornings and evenings. And even when the villages seem deserted, pastors may be moved by the Holy

Spirit to hold services in the church for those few who remain. Finally, there are the holidays—Christmas, Easter, and Independence—and times of millennial fervor. During these periods, people attend lengthy services in the morning and the evening for many days at a time.

To the untrained eye, Urapmin services can appear to be a chaotic mess of praying, hymn singing, speech making, and sermonizing. With the exception of the sermon, all these elements seem to appear and disappear in random fashion throughout services that last anywhere from forty-five minutes to two and a half hours. But, despite appearances, the rite has a core structure.[1] In its simplest form, a service begins when the pastor rings the "bell" (an old piece of metal pipe struck with a metal bar) to call people to church. Once people have arrived, the service begins with a prayer to "open" it, which proceeds to several hymns followed by a prayer for inspiration before reading the Bible, a sermon, another hymn, and a prayer. Sunday morning services usually add a time for "announcements" (tok save) following the first song and a healing prayer that is conducted by a small subset of the congregation after the main part of the service ends. The basic structure of a service thus has the following shape; the components that tend to appear only on Sunday are in brackets.

1. Bell
2. Prayer
3. Hymns
4. [Announcements]
5. Prayer
6. Sermon
7. Hymn
8. Prayer
9. [Healing prayer]

In practice, this basic structure often becomes distended and almost unrecognizable as extra songs and prayers are added, the announcement segment is extended to an hour or more, and a "support" section is inserted in which people speak after the sermon. Yet no matter how unwieldy the result, this basic structure is always realized. For this reason, I organize my discussion of the church service around its key elements, taking as my model the full Sunday morning version.

Kiernan (1976) has argued that the lengthy healing rituals of urban

South African Zionists evidence a dialectic of controlled and uncontrolled expression that they finally resolve through the realization of a controlled communal order (cf. Stringer 1999: 159; see also McGuire 1982 on similar issues in other charismatic churches). The Urapmin church service is organized in a similar way. The elements it opposes are not controlled and uncontrolled expression per se but the related ones of willfulness and spirit-filled lawfulness. Through its development, the service works to replace the former with the latter not only on a communal level but also, and more prominently, on an individual one. For those who participate in it, the ritual accomplishes this replacement by allowing them to display their lawful nature in increasingly obvious ways as it proceeds. When people say, as they often do, that they go to church to "strengthen their belief" (strongim bilip), it is the ability of the ritual to produce lawfulness to which they refer.

The struggle between willfulness and lawfulness begins as soon as the pastor rings the bell to begin the service. Although watches have become important status symbols in Urapmin and many middle-aged men and younger people of both sexes know how to tell time, the notion of doing things in accordance with a time schedule is still foreign to almost everyone in the community. Hence while everyone knows that there will be a service on Sunday morning, no one knows when precisely it will begin. Generally, the pastor wakes up, washes, and then rings the bell for the first time well after sunup. About twenty minutes later, he rings it again and waits in church for people to arrive. Once a small group is in attendance, they begin to sing hymns to "call" their fellow Christians to church. Yet many people dawdle in response to the call, and it is not unusual for as long as forty-five minutes to go by from the time the singing starts to the time the majority of the congregation shows up. The slow trickle of people into the church regularly leads to anger on the part of those who have had to bide their time, singing hymn after hymn while waiting for the stragglers to come. This anger, in turn, fuels haranguing speeches, given during the announcement portion of the service or in sermons, in which latecomers are accused of "wasting the church's time" or "wasting the time for church" (westim taim long lotu) and are painted as the very paradigm of willful people who follow their own desires and disregard the law. From the outset of the service, then, issues of anger, willfulness, and lawfulness are already in play.

The act of entering the church is important not only because it indexes a person's lawful commitment to the goals of the service but also because the distinction between the inside and the outside of the church

is crucial to the symbolism of the ritual. Throughout the service, many
of those who speak—whether to make announcements, pray, or deliver
or support a sermon—refer to this distinction.[2] They use it to emphasize the ideally lawful nature of life during ("while inside") the service.
They also use it to warn people that the lawful self-formation they accomplish in church will be immediately threatened when they "go outside" (go autsait) after the service and are tempted by the things of the
world. Throughout the service, the inside/outside opposition thus acts
as a symbolic register in which issues of lawfulness and willfulness are
discussed. Given this symbolism, every congregant, simply by coming
inside the church for the service, has won a first victory over the will and
entered a realm where he or she can make progress in the project of ethical self-formation.

The organization of space inside the church building also reflects the
moral concerns of the service. Men sit on the right and women on the left.
This rule is generally observed, though occasional breaches go unremarked. When asked to explain why this segregation is practiced, some
people offer no answer. Those who provide an explanation argue that
men and women are likely to concentrate better if they are not distracted
by being in close physical proximity. The seating pattern, they say, is designed to prevent the possibility that people will formulate willful desires
to have premarital or adulterous affairs. Thus in its left-right division the
seating arrangement of the service thematizes the difficulty of constructing a realm in which people can succeed in setting aside their wills.

The arrangement of seating from front to back carries other, related
messages. If the left-right division of the church recognizes the danger of
sexual will, the one between front and back sets up a contrast between
moral success and failure more generally. At the front of the church is a
low platform, raised about six inches off the main floor. The pulpit is at
the center of this platform. Male deacons generally sit on the platform
on either side of the pulpit. However, no one can sit on this platform if
they are known to have recently sinned, and deacons who have been involved in disputes or have committed other sins are noticeably absent
from their usual places. Along with other people who have committed
major sins, such as adultery, they are frequently required to sit at the
back of the church. This is appropriate, since this is where the door is
placed and thus is the part of the church that is closest to the sinful outside. Interestingly, big men also tend to sit toward the back. It is not clear
to me why they do this, but in terms of the semiotics of church seating,
their choice to do so symbolizes effectively the fact that with their fre-

Figure 6. Women praying in church. Photo by Joel Robbins.

quent displays of will and with their attention so often devoted to "out-side" worldly matters, they play out their lives closer to the edge of sin than do others. Furthermore, as we will see, they often bring "outside," worldly concerns "inside" the church by raising them during the announcement period of the service.

Once the bulk of the congregation has arrived, the leader of the service, a deacon or another person who has been chosen by them in advance to run the service, performs or calls on someone else to perform a prayer to "open" (opim) the service (see figure 6). This prayer tends explicitly to formulate the themes of the service. Here is an example of an opening prayer that was offered by a knowledgeable man in his mid- to late twenties. I use parentheses to mark alternate translations and brackets for interpolations.

> Thank you our God in heaven and on the ground. Now it is Sunday, it is your Sabbath day.
> Thank you. It is good that [you] looked after us for the seven days of the week. Father, we want to thank you for this day.
> We come and sit on your scale, father God. We want to be weighed now and so we come and sit on your scale.
> Father you can be with us and you can give us good thinking. With your knowledge you can judge each of us inside of our own lives and we can understand (receive) well your talk today on Sunday.

I want to pray to you. Everyone themselves can go to your hands and
you can be with us. Father I pray for everything; that which is not very
good, that which is not good, or that which is good. Father you be with
us, you can be with all of us, your family.

All of us who are your family come sit in the church now, father. I will
not say "you help him and you help him." About this, father, you know
about every man and about all the ways of behaving and every kind of
thing. You already know.

So father all of us go to your hand because only you can help us.

Jesus, we will get your talk and we will go out and run around. And
so I am asking. I am a sinner. I myself am calling your good name Jesus.
So you, Jesus, I come stand here because I am a sinner who has come inside. A sinful man, I myself have come inside, God, I am standing here in
your sight, here in your house holy, so father you can be with me.

My own thoughts and knowledge are not sufficient, but God your
thoughts and knowledge alone can satisfy all of us so that we can understand your talk well. We [must] do that so that we can go out and run
around until the afternoon [when there will be another service]. And so
that is why I am asking, father, I am asking you to throw out this bad
spirit and let your Holy Spirit work in each of our lives. Do that and God,
we will receive your talk and go out and run around.

And so I am calling your name, Jesus. And so all of us people who come
inside we are going over to your hand, Jesus. And so, I have asked enough
and it is true.

This is a typical opening prayer. It casts its speaker in the role of sinner, to be judged by God. It also asks that God help the congregation
understand his talk so that they will have "good thinking" and be able
to go "outside" and stay free of sin. Where the speaker says "I will not
say 'you help him'" because you already "know about every man and
every kind of behavior," he is referring to a standard list of kinds of sins
people often mention in their prayers (an example follows below). He
chooses not to mention such a list, because, he suggests, God already
understands the nature of human depravity. In asking God to throw out
the bad spirits and let the Holy Spirit enter the lives of those in the congregation, he is again asking that God help people have good thinking.
By the end of the prayer, the entire congregation has taken on the role
of sinners who have given themselves to God in the hope that he will
help them to control their wills and thereby gain salvation. Thus they
are positioned in the role they will occupy for the rest of the service.

The theme of submission to God also comes up in the prayer. Several
times, the young man praying refers to people going over to God's hand.
Because it suggests that people are putting themselves under God's
power, this is an image of people relinquishing their wills and submit-

ting lawfully to God. A similar image often mentioned in prayer involves asking God to treat the congregation like piglets and put them inside his pen. Here too the idea is that people give up the freedom to pursue their own desires in order to let God direct them in living a lawful life.

The fact of submission is not only encoded in the words of the prayer, it is also reflected in the physical act of praying. When the Urapmin pray, they close their eyes. People about to pray give fair warning and then wait for others to close their eyes before they begin. The Urapmin close their eyes because they believe that there is a very rigid Christian rule that enjoins them to do so. They do not have an explanation for why this rule exists, beyond insisting that it is biblical (the contemporary equivalent of "it is our custom").[3] But it is one of the few hard-and-fast rules of Urapmin ritual practice. Urapmin appreciate that unlike the taboos of their traditional religion, most rules of Christian ritual can be broken. Men can sit on the women's side of the church, for example, or services can be held out of doors. In good reform tradition, the Urapmin usually assume that it is the spirit in which participants perform the ritual that is crucial, not their adherence to protocol. Yet they are almost obsessively strict about making sure that people close their eyes when prayers are said. This is so, I think, because of what eyesight means to them and what giving it up thus signifies about a believer's relationship to God.

In my discussion of Urapmin epistemology in chapter 3, I pointed out the importance of sight in the acquisition of valid knowledge and noted that the Urapmin regard it as the most important human sense. Here I want to stress two other aspects of sight. The first is its protective qualities. The Urapmin rely on their vision to protect them against human and natural danger. They foreground the protective function of vision in the call to shut the door before closing their eyes to pray. After the prayer is finished, the door is reopened and must be shut again before the next prayer. People are careful to shut the door before praying because they worry that the church will be attacked while their eyes are closed. People never provided me with clear answers to the question of who it is that might attack them, though they sometimes mentioned "rascals" (raskal), the gang members of urban Papua New Guinea about whom they have heard but have never actually encountered. Probably more to the point is the idea that once inside the church, the outside is defined as a place of danger and willful violence; the sense of threat is palpable, and people rarely forget to shut the church door before they pray. When the Urapmin cannot shut outsiders out, as when they visit other communities that are known to harbor sorcerers, they sheepishly admit to keeping

their eyes open during prayer lest someone steal some item of theirs and
use it in parcel sorcery *(tamon)*. In closing their eyes in prayer, then,
people are putting their trust in God's protection and submitting their
agency completely to him.

The second meaning of closed eyes also relates to submission, but in
this case not so much of agency in general as of the will. For the Urapmin, the eyes are the organs that initiate desire; it is what the eyes see
that the will wants. Good people, say the Urapmin, keep their eyes on
the road when they are away from their village, lest they see a potential
sexual partner or a ripe taro that might lead them into desire and sin.
Domestic pigs that continually misbehave, jumping over the fences that
should hold them (kirapim banis—a phrase that also refers to human
sinning), have their eyes put out in order to extinguish their desire to
wander. Furthermore, as we have seen, to covet or want badly in Urapmin is to "steal and consume with your eyes" *(tiin lawut inin)*. Given the
strong connection between vision and desire, there is no better idiom for
surrendering one's will than closing one's eyes. In their voluntary blind-
ness, the Urapmin not only prove their trust in God's protective power
but also make an important first effort to put a stop to their willfulness
and let God guide them through his good thinking.

Once the opening prayer has set the scene, the congregation turns to
hymn singing. Everyone joins together in singing one or more hymns.
These are lyrically very simple and often borrow melodies from Western
children's songs such as "London Bridge Is Falling Down." Given their
simplicity, it is difficult to demonstrate their thematic content without
presenting a large number of them. Here I simply note that they tend to
take up issues of God's mercy, Jesus' sacrifice, and the redemption of sinners. Young women in particular tend to throw themselves into these
songs. Others do so only when they are feeling especially engaged in the
service. For this reason, pastors and others take the energy level people
bring to singing hymns to be a fairly good index of the extent to which
the congregation is free of major sin. When people's hearts are "heavy"
(hevi; see below) with sin, their singing too is heavy. When they are
"light" (lait), the singing is "spirited" (Spirit i stap wantaim ol) and goes
on for some time.

The singing is followed by the announcements portion of the service.
The length of this portion varies considerably. Those who want to speak
generally alert the leader of the service before the service begins and
their names are listed on a blackboard displayed on the raised platform
at the front of the church. The announcements they make vary in con-

tent. This is the time of the service when people report world news or tell of their dreams or visions. It is also the time for people to present testimonies (testimoni) in which they tell of "miracles" they have experienced that have strengthened their belief in God. These often consist of reports of cases in which their petitionary prayers for worldly success have been answered. An adult woman, for example, once reported that she had prayed to God for money and the next day a relative had given her some. An adult man told of a time he had prayed before hunting for wild pigs and then found a pig staring at him, standing still and allowing him to shoot it.

But the most frequent speakers at announcement periods are big men, and they tend to use them to deliver moral harangues that contain only thinly veiled references to disputes currently going on in the community. Others too bring up community problems at this time, though even issues introduced by others tend to be quickly taken up by the big men. Because they do not speak Tok Pisin and are too old to have been educated in the Bible schools, big men never preach (though they have an excellent grasp of the major Bible stories and demonstrate this in conversations outside of church). Announcement periods thus give the big men their one major role in the service, and they often exploit it to the fullest, extending this period for as long as an hour or more.

Despite the authority of the big men, the use of this time for airing community grievances is controversial, and people often accuse big men and others of illegitimately bringing "outside" problems "inside" the church. In terms of my analysis here, however, these announcements are integral to the service for the way they present the community with precisely those situations that lead them to sin. If people proclaim their sinfulness in prayer and song, it is in the tok save period that they most often prove it, both by addressing real problems and by speaking about them in heated terms.

The announcement period is the beginning of the central part of the ritual. Hymn singing and praying are repeated after the sermon, but the announcements and the sermon occur only once, in the middle part of the ritual and in a fixed order: once the sermon has been preached, people never return to discussing community problems during the same service. Given this structure of a unique center surrounded by recurring actions, the announcement period serves to begin the core part of the ritual with a display of sinful willfulness. The sermon that follows resolves this willfulness.

There is always a prayer before the Bible reading that begins the ser-

Figure 7. A man prays before reading the Bible. Photo by Joel Robbins.

mon (see figure 7). These prayers stress the need for the Holy Spirit to inspire both the person preaching, so that he can preach well, and the audience, so that they can understand what is said. The person who is going to preach is generally the one who prays, and he usually insists throughout the prayer that he himself is not capable of speaking well; only with the Holy Spirit's help can he give a sermon that "feeds" the people "nourishing" ("strong," *titil*) spiritual food that will give them the strength to avoid sin (see figure 8).

In focusing on the need to avoid sin and the consequences that sinners will face in the last days, sermons take up explicitly the moral issues that the symbolic and processual structures of the rite address. Having analyzed a sermon in chapter 6, I will not dwell on their content here. Instead, I want to examine two ways in which the performance of the sermon and the act of listening to it involve the renunciation of the will.

First, the Urapmin insist that the congregation will not be able to "hear" ("follow," "understand") a preacher who is himself currently in a state of sin. Sometimes people will publicly confess small sins (such as anger at family members) just before they preach and then pray to God for forgiveness. If since his last confession a man has committed a sin he cannot confess publicly, for whatever reason, he will abstain from preaching, even if he had been scheduled to do so. There is thus a pre-

Figure 8. A man preaching at a Sunday service. Photo by Joel Robbins.

sumption that the person delivering the moral message contained in the sermon has succeeded, at least recently, in living that message. During this part of the service, the preacher stands before the congregation as a paradigm of the ethical person, one who has, as he asks in his prayer, let God guide his life.

Second, the sermon takes up issues of lawfulness and the renunciation of the will through the efforts of pastors and others to remind people that focusing their attention on the sermon is a lawful act while letting their attention stray is willful. People sometimes sleep in church, which tends to go unremarked, but wandering eyes and side conversations are condemned. Such behavior is understood both to represent a version of the sins that people commit outside the church and to lead people to commit those sins once the service has ended. Here is part of a sermon in which an experienced pastor took up this topic:

> You say, "I don't usually understand (get) the Bible's talk, I don't hear (follow) the talk." You say, "I don't hear the talk," and you are big-headed to God. It is like here inside the church the watchman (pastor) speaks to you and you don't hear it, nothing. You come inside and you look at each other, you look over to your friend, he looks back at his friend, you move your head around, turn your head from side to side. If you do that, if you are making noise, you won't be able to receive God's talk. God's talk will not be bound (get stuck) in your heart. It will not go through. You do that

and you will have court [in the last days you will be judged], that is what he said. Just come in quietly and sit down and whatever kind of man is giving talk or news, you think about it and you be peaceful. Then he will come and take you. You Christian people, you yourselves will get heaven, God's kingdom.

This passage states that how one behaves when listening to a pastor's sermon (or other parts of the service) is a model of one's ability to act lawfully.[4] The argument unfolds on two levels. On one of them, the point is that not listening to the pastor or other speakers is itself an example of willful behavior. On the other, what is crucial is that by not listening, one robs oneself of a chance to receive God's word into one's heart. Without this word in place to stimulate good thinking, a person is destined to sin. Those who listen attentively to the sermon, by contrast, can take comfort in having successfully constituted themselves as moral persons; ones who now resemble the morally upstanding man who preaches the sermon by virtue of the way they listen to him with the same lawful attentiveness he displays toward the Holy Spirit as it guides his preaching.

The sermon is followed by more singing and then by a closing prayer. The closing prayer usually echoes the themes of the opening prayer. It draws attention to the fact that people have now "eaten" *(inin)* God's word and, having been nourished, will go "outside" where they must use their newly won strength to avoid sin.

Unlike the other prayers, the closing prayer is always collective: one person leads the prayer by speaking loudly, but everyone else prays quietly to themselves and in their own words. The excited buzz that rises is not unlike the resonant roar produced when the Urapmin play their drums. People finish their personal prayers one by one until only the leader is left praying. The leader finishes his own prayer by listing all the households that have come to church, calling out the name of the male household head and asking God to bless his family. Both the congregation's praying together and the leader's careful request for blessing each of those in attendance serves to unify the members just before they go outside. In doing this, the drama of the church service ends with the production of a Christian community. This point becomes significant in chapter 8.

Once the prayer ends, people stand up and commence to shake the hand of every other person in attendance. After a long service, a sort of relieved levity overtakes people at this point, a felt sense of the "lightness" that indexes freedom from sin. And people demonstrate their lack of anger or other willful emotions by the act of shaking hands, for despite its rather routine appearance, handshaking is a very meaningful activity in the Urapmin scheme of things.

Whenever a person encounters someone for the first time during a day, he or she must shake the other person's hand. If a person fails to offer such a greeting, it is assumed that he or she harbors anger toward the person who has been slighted. In fact, people can be taken to court for failure to shake hands, just as they can for other displays of hostility such as fighting or uttering angry words. Because this practice is monitored so carefully in the community, one cannot forgo a handshake without signifying some unhappiness. A friend and I were running home one afternoon during a downpour when we encountered a man running equally fast in the other direction. For obvious reasons, none of us stopped. As soon as we got home, my friend began to fret over the possibility that our failure to shake hands with the man we passed would be misconstrued as an expression of anger, and he was determined to forestall any misinterpretation by speaking to him about the incident the next time he saw him.

The sensitivity that surrounds handshaking means that its appearance in the final moments of the main part of the church service serves as an opportunity for everyone to demonstrate that they have achieved a peaceful heart and harbor no ill will toward anyone. With their hands extended to all, those who have participated in the service demonstrate that they have, through the ritual, become the peaceful-hearted people their Christian ethical code requires.

After the handshaking is complete and most of the congregation has gone outside, the pastor and the deacons gather near the platform with those who are "sick" (sik). "Sick" people may be suffering from a variety of physical ailments and include pregnant women who fear that *motobil* may steal their children, causing them to be stillborn. Most physical illnesses are understood to be caused by anger—either the sick person's anger or that directed at them by others with whom they are in dispute. Hence people usually confess their sins of anger in a brief discussion before the healing prayer. Once this discussion has been completed, the pastor reads James 5:14: "Might there be among you a brother who is sick? Then he must call to the leaders of the church. In the name of God they must put oil on his body and they must pray to God to help him." Then all those present lay hands on the afflicted and pray to God to heal them. In the case of a pregnant woman, the group asks God to loosen the motobil's grip on the fetus and chase the offending spirit away.

Pastors regularly conduct the same healing ritual in the homes of sick people during the week. On these occasions, pastors go through an abbreviated version of an entire church service before performing the healing prayer. Although often at speeds that render these parts of the ritual almost comical, pastors pray, sing a song, read a passage of the Bible and comment on it, and only then turn to the healing prayer. This demonstrates the extent to which the elements of the service are understood to form a whole. The healing prayer does not stand alone but gains its meaning from what comes before it.

Indeed, the healing prayer that concludes every Sunday service is the element of the ritual that most potently enacts the possibility of completely successful ethical formation that the ritual as a whole puts in play. Whereas most of the service focuses on the need to recognize and prevent sin, the healing prayer enacts the possibility of its final overcoming by asking God to cure the sick of its effects. It thereby not only looks back to the efforts that the service has taken to instill good thinking but also points toward the rituals that serve to remove the sins one has already committed. For these rituals, unlike the church service, focus less on the avoidance of sin than on the redemption of those who have sinned.

PRAYER AND THE RITUAL REMOVAL OF ANGER AND SIN

In the prologue, I touched on the traditional exchange rituals the Urapmin use to remove anger. Because the control of anger is also an important issue in Christian morality, the Urapmin continue to make use of these rituals. However, God is now understood to be the agent who removes anger from the hearts of the participants, and prayer has thus been incorporated as a part of these rituals. Sometimes the prayer is only a short prelude to the exchange. At other times, however, the prayer is the focal part of the ritual, and the exchange is relegated to a minor position. Furthermore, in many cases people actually dispense with exchange altogether and simply perform a prayer.

People have come to construe anger-removal rituals in Christian terms as rituals that remove sin. Indeed, it is perhaps better to see them as sin-removal rites in which anger is the sin being treated. People take as a pressing obligation the need to pray over those who have commit-

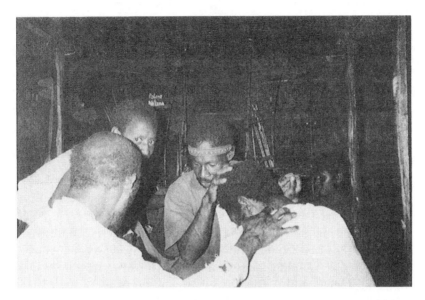

Figure 9. Laying on hands during a sin-removal ritual. Photo by Joel Robbins.

ted sins of anger. They say that if you see a "brother or sister" who has fallen into anger, you must "hold them and pray for them." The biblical passage they most often quote in support of this is, like the passage on healing, from James 5. It is line 19 of that chapter, which reads:

> My brothers, if one brother amongst you loses the true talk of God, and another brother brings him back to it, then this brother can know: if a man helps a sinner and the sinner leaves the bad road and comes back to God, then this man will take back the spirit of the sinner and he will not die. This is the way God will remove many sins.

Anger-removal rites share features both with healing and with confession rituals. During them, as during healing rites, the person or people praying will lay hands on the person whose anger is being removed (see figure 9). As in confession, the person praying will ask God to remove the sin of anger from the body of the person for whom he or she is performing the rite. The main difference between sin-removal rituals and confession is the relative informality and lack of finality of the former. Sin-removal rites can be performed anywhere and by anybody. They often take place in the house of the sinful person, but there is no rule that they must do so. And although they are frequently performed by pastors, this too is not a binding rule. Finally, unlike confessions, which can be initiated only by the person who confesses, sin-removal rites can be initiated either by the person who will pray or by the person for whom the prayer will be offered. Their flexibility allows them to be used to respond very quickly to difficulty. At the same time, however, sin-removal rites are less final than confessions, thus allowing them to be used before a sin has been handled by secular authorities. When all these features are considered, it is fair to see sin-removal rituals as something akin to the emergency room treatments of Urapmin moral ritual. As such, they are a good place to begin looking at the redemptive process that is so important in Urapmin ritual life.

I reproduce below an example of a prayer spoken during a sin-removal rite. The rite took place in the house of Tendang, a senior man who has long served as a deacon. The prayer itself was offered by Tomi, Tendang's son and the apprentice pastor whose sermon is reproduced in chapter 6. The ritual was performed for Steve, a man in his twenties who had hit his wife. Urapmin consider domestic violence a serious sin that compounds anger with physical violence and needs to be settled not only spiritually but also in the village Kaunsil's court. Tomi is married to Steve's stepsister and thus refers to him as "brother-in-law" *(bas* or *basim)*. The brother-in-law relationship is ideally one of mutual support. It is in this spirit, and in his role as a leader of the church, that Tomi undertakes this ritual.

Tomi begins by reminding Steve that the Bible says the Holy Spirit lives in our hearts. God, he says, tells us that "if a man ruins my house [the heart in which the Holy Spirit dwells] with sin, later I will ruin him." He then goes on to tell Steve of a dream that his mother had the previous night in which Tendang and another man, a pastor, had made a pigpen. The entire church was in the pigpen, but then one man broke down the fence and went out. At that point in the dream, God's Spirit said, "You must hurry up and fix the pen and put the man back inside." Tendang explains that he and his son believe his dream refers to Steve's sin. At this point, Steve begins to cry.

Last year, Tomi tells him, before he was a pastor, Tomi himself hit his wife. He was very ashamed and went to the pastor and confessed. His wife, Steve's stepsister, confirms this point. The pastors and deacons, Tomi adds, are people who can help.

Tomi then explains that he will read the Bible and then they will pray. These actions constitute the ritual proper. Before Tomi begins, however, Tendang steps in and makes sure that Steve understands that he is not to confess. Steve will still have to go to the court run by the Kaunsil to have his case settled in that forum. Only after that has been done can he con-

fess and have the pastor or deacon pray over his confession. This marks
the relative informality and lack of finality of the sin-removal rite. As I
have pointed out, the Urapmin believe that once a sin has been confessed
to God, it belongs to him and cannot be taken up by an earthly court.
For this reason, pastors and deacons are careful not to allow people to
confess sins that will need adjudication before they are settled. As the
prayer shows, there is some sense that this rite will remove Steve's sin
and cleanse his heart so that he can move on with his life until the court
case is heard. But he will still need to reckon with the consequences of
his sin both in court and in a later confession.

Tomi now reads James 5:16–19, focusing on verse 19, which is reproduced above. He preaches for a moment, explaining, "This is a clear
one. If a brother or other person sins you follow Christ's will. If you confess your sin God can forgive and cleanse you. If a man makes a sin and
stays far away, then he will feel shame. If he goes away completely, God
will not be happy." Having given this small sermon, Tendang and Tomi
grasp Steve and Tomi prays over him. This is a long prayer that explicitly
lays out the nature of the rite Tomi is performing and its grounding in the
biblical passage that he has cited. (False starts and unintentional repetitions have been removed. Numbers are used to break the prayer into several sections to aid the discussion that follows. Ellipses indicate places I
have removed material. Text in brackets indicates my interpolation.)

> 1. Okay, one, two, three. My father God, Jesus, you, my God, my Jesus,
> one of your piglets, one of your sheep . . . [has] . . . sinned. He did that.
> He is my brother-in-law Steve. He has come and we two in-laws are sitting
> together.
>
> I am preaching your story, God, the one that says that if you make a
> sin you cannot go completely away. You make a sin but you must come
> to Jesus. If you do that, God is there so he . . . he himself will clear away
> your sin. And so, he came and we two in-laws are sitting together and I
> am telling him God's story.
>
> Follow what Christ wants and follow Jesus' road. That is how it should
> be done. If a man sins but you go and bring him back, that is good. But if
> you leave and he goes away completely that is not very good. That is what
> the Bible says.
>
> 2. So father God, father God, only you are holy and clean and sweet and
> straight and so I pray to you. I send my brother-in-law over into your pres-
> ence Jesus, God. . . . His sin, his problem ("heavy"), whatever kind of thing
> he has, problem [or] sin—God, only you can clear this away. Jesus, God do
> not leave your son. God, he is your son, he is your sheep.
>
> And so I ask you Jesus to come down. It is Satan. Jesus bring down your
> heavenly knife and take Satan over to the base of a tree, to the base of a

rock [some of the places to which Afek banished the motobil now known
to be devils]. Father God, I pray to you to take this Satan far away from
him and father God you yourself stay with him, look after him. Father
God, you give him more strength and more power and more Spirit inside
of his life. Allow the Holy Spirit to work in his life.

Jesus, you send . . . [the] Spirit back down into his heart. Whatever kind
of thing he has—a heavy, the sin he makes with his wife, the accident (aksi-
dent) he gave to her that makes him heavy. This is what he is heavy over.

And Jesus only you are holy and clean. And so Jesus, only you can clean
him and wash him. Whatever kind of heavy [or] sin he has in his heart or
life, father God clean him and wash him, clear away those heavy things,
clear away those sins, dirty [things]. Jesus, only you can give him more
Spirit in his life. And Holy Spirit and the water that has life and his blood,
with these you wash him as in water and you leave him only good. His life,
his spirit, his body must be good. That is what I am asking for. So you send
the bad spirit away, the ghosts and the hidden men (bad spirits).

This is why I am asking you, Jesus, to come down. I am sending my
brother-in-law Steve over to . . . [you] . . . Jesus, God, Holy Spirit. His
name must go in your roll book, Jesus.

That is what I am asking, that you come down. My brother-in-law has
come and the two of us in-laws are sitting together. God we have been talking in this way about your story. God, we have been talking about your
story.

Do not leave your older brother Jesus' road. Follow Jesus' road and you
will become a straight man. But if you leave Jesus' road and you go completely off to the side then you will become a bad man or woman. That is
what the Bible says and so it is true talk.

My brother-in-law has sinned but he has come to you. He has cried to
you and so father God you forgive this sin of his. Whatever kind of sin or
heavy he has, you are the only one who can clear it away. That is what I am
asking for.

3. So there is his sin, but he has not confessed it to me and I have not heard
it. He will go to the Kaunsil and Komitis and confess it in their presence. He
will do that first and later he will come down to the pastors and deacons.

Jesus, you help him during this time and bring him over into the church
building. You keep doing that. You look after him and he must be good.
My brother-in-law, you look after him and he must remain good for
awhile. He must remain only good. God, he is your sheep.

4. And so, Jesus, as for me I am not like you. That is not the case. As for
me, I am a bad man, a sinner, a man who holds to adultery, coveting, disputing, anger, adultery, jealousy, all kinds of behaviors. It is me myself who
now give over to you, Jesus, my brother-in-law who has sinned and is worried and sorry and crying out. You yourself straighten him and bless him
and look after him so he will be nothing but good when he goes to the
house and sleeps. Tomorrow, God you can help him and when he eats,

walks around and washes, eats and drinks and whatever, sleeps, God you
are the one who can look after him and bless him and his wife. Please, you
do that. That is what I am asking for.

His wife . . . we people of the ground, this is our way of doing things.
Hitting wives, hitting husbands, we are people who do that. And so he was
hitting his wife and now the couple have come and are staying here. Jesus,
YOU [emphatic pronoun] be sorry for them and merciful to them. Bless
them. You are the only one who can help them.

5. This couple fell into sin. God, they are your piglets, they are your sheep.
So I am leaving them in your hands so that only you can look after them,
bless them, and you can put them inside your fence and look after them.
Please do that.

God, holy, nice father and son, I am asking this of you yourselves and I
am sending my brother-in-law over to you. Jesus, he must be put in God's
roll call area [book] in the area of your name so that you [can] look after
him and he can go on. That is what I am asking for.

Because of the heavy my brother-in-law has committed . . . , I give him
over to your presence Jesus. As for those who are good, I will not pray for
them. For the sin my brother-in-law has committed, I have asked enough in
your name. It is true.

This prayer, as is common in Urapmin, is long and repetitive. But beneath the repetition we can detect a basic movement that lends the sin-
removal ritual its structure. In section 1, as we have come to expect,
Tomi spells out the social setting surrounding the prayer and establishes
the biblical basis for the ritual. He accomplishes several additional tasks
in section 2, where he casts the sin as an effect of a satanic force inside
Steve that caused him to beat his wife. Urapmin often speak in these
terms, claiming that it is evil spirits that cause bad behavior. This is not
in any way an attempt to displace responsibility from the person who
acts, and I have never heard Urapmin use it in this way (they are too attached to their image of themselves as sinful to imagine shifting blame
in this way). The Holy Spirit causes good thinking. In the same way, evil
spirits (a category that is very ill defined, as Tomi's somewhat awkward
list of "bad spirits, ghosts, hidden men" indicates) cause bad thinking.
But in both cases, the human being who acts is responsible for allowing
the Holy Spirit or evil spirits to enter his or her life, and he or she is the
one to whom the goodness or the sin attaches. In Steve's case, this strict
attention to human responsibility means that he is currently "heavy"
and has "heavy things" (hevi, *ilum*) in his heart because he has committed the sin of hitting his wife. "Heavy" is one of two primary ways of referring to sins in Urapmin. I discuss this usage in some detail below, so

I will not say more about it here. Crucially, though, in section 2 Tomi avers that God and Jesus can wash away these heavy sins, and he asks them to do so and to leave his brother-in-law "clean." In the hope that they will do this, he sends Steve to them or, in another formulation he uses, Steve goes to them of his own accord. This is a key moment in the prayer, for it puts matters decisively in God's hands. As when eyes are closed in church, it is a moment of complete submission when penitents quiet their own wills in the hope that God will unburden them of the weight of their sins.

Section 3 shifts the topic a bit and goes back to clarifying the nature of the ritual frame. Tomi asserts that this is not a confession and that the confession is yet to come, after the Kaunsil and Komitis have settled the matter in secular terms. This section serves in an important way to situate this ritual in relation to confession; its purpose is to help Steve to live righteously during the period that will elapse before his full confession.

Section 4 is a good example of a common kind of prayer segment in which people lay out nothing less than their fundamental view of the sinful nature of man. This segment is similar to those moments during confession when the penitent leaves off discussion of his or her own sins and sets them in the broader context of the nature of human fallibility. Here Tomi points to his own sinfulness and provides a long list of the kinds of sins to which he and others are prone. In doing so, he refers to "people of the ground" *(towal diim kasel)*. The word *diim* that he uses in this construction is the same one that I translate as "presence" in those parts of the prayer in which Tomi refers to sending Steve into God's presence. So one might also translate *towal* (ground) *diim kasel* (group) as "those in the presence of the ground." Because they are in the presence of the ground, they are by definition not in the presence of God (who is sometimes referred to as "the citizen of the sky," *abiil tigen kiyaak*). Having stressed in section 2 his own efforts to send Steve to God's presence, here, as befits his theme of human sinfulness, Tomi uses the notion of people of the ground to emphasize his own, Steve's, and Steve's wife's separation from God. He calls on Jesus to be merciful, but this bleak section nonetheless foregrounds sin by stressing human estrangement from God.

Having set out the distance between God and the sinner, Tomi once again works to close it. He stresses several times that he is sending Steve into God's and Jesus' presence, taking care to focus his request by specifying that it is only Steve for whom he is praying (not all earthly people, as the theological anthropology of section 4 might suggest). The prayer ends, then, with Steve in the presence of God. Formulaically, Tomi closes by claiming that he has asked enough and he leaves it to God to remove the sin.

The emphasis Tomi's prayer places on both going away from God and coming back to him again is a gloss on the way deviance removes the deviant from the center of social life and expiation returns him closer to it. This emphasis provides a clear statement of the role of sin-removal rites in Urapmin social life. Almost explicitly, as both Tomi's and the Bible's language reminds us, they work to reintegrate the sinner into society—bringing him, as Tomi says at one point, "into the church building." Although it is a more important rite in Urapmin estimation, confession is so private, so much a matter of the relationship between an individual and God, that it cannot play this role of social reaggregation as well as can sin-removal rites. Their use as an emergency treatment, then, is based on their ability to quickly reestablish relations between the sinner and those who pray for him or her. For the sinner, the rite is a first return to society; it allows social life to go on in the periods between courts and confessions, so that one need not remain isolated and weighed down by anger and sin while one waits for the settlement of troubles. This is the import of Tomi's plea that God help Steve live well until he is able to straighten out matters in court and then in confession. Having been righted, Steve can approach these upcoming events peacefully and without temptation to compound his sin.

Only socially consequential, legally actionable sins involving physical violence, theft, or adultery will elicit the performance of a sin-removal rite. Most people most of the time do not commit such sins. For them, the routine redemptive process provides a sufficient set of technologies of ethical self-formation. That process, in which even those for whom sin-removal rites are held must participate, begins with confession.

CONFESSION

Confession is a central rite of Urapmin Christianity. Given their Baptist background, the highly institutionalized way they treat confession, and the regular communion ritual that follows it may strike some readers as surprising. Indeed, the Urapmin did not originally undertake confession in the way they do now. During the early days of the revival, people confessed their sins publicly. This is still sometimes done, but it is invariably minor sins of passing anger or major sins that have already been aired publicly in court that are confessed in this way. In the past, by contrast, people confessed major sins like adultery or theft during church services. Furthermore, those who had seen the sins of others in dreams or in visions sent by God would often confront the sinners openly during church services or community meetings. This led to a great deal of anger and shame and to a tremendous number of fights. It was in response to the havoc caused by public confession, havoc that was itself sinful, that the Urapmin developed the rite of confession that they currently practice.

One can, the Urapmin say, confess to anyone at any time and in any place. One can simply take oneself off to a quiet place in the bush and confess to God, or one can confess to one's friends. But it is church-run confession rites that are central to the redemptive process in Urapmin, and even those who also confess in other settings feel compelled to take part in these rites as well. Once a month, ideally, the pastors and the deacons arrive at church early on Saturday morning and begin ringing the church bell. Eventually, a small crowd begins to form outside the church. Inside, the pastors and deacons sit, well spread out from one another to allow a measure of privacy to the penitents who come to them. Once people begin to enter the church, each church leader sits with one penitent, listening to his or her sins and praying over him or her. Female deacons, who rarely play much of a public role during church services, figure importantly in this context, for some women are not comfortable confessing to men. As the morning winds on, many people pass through the church, and pastors and deacons go through the same routine in the afternoon and again on Sunday morning to serve those who missed the first opportunity to confess. It is their goal to have every baptized member of the church (a group that includes most children over about twelve years of age) confess. After they have come as close as possible to achieving this mark, they ring the bell for a Sunday morning service that will include a special komunion sevis (communion service).

Since the content of people's confessions have already been examined in some detail in chapter 6, I want to look more closely here at the mechanics of the rite and at how people understand it to work. Once again, the best way to gain an initial window onto the Urapmin understanding of a rite is to examine the prayers they offer during it. Once the church leader is sitting with a penitent, he begins the rite by saying an opening prayer that sets the context for what is to occur:

> Thank you God father. I pray to you now, at the time that the two of us [the speaker and the penitent] have come and sat down together in the

church. God, you have power, God, you have strength and so God I pray
to you and you can open our thoughts and clear away the garbage that is
inside of our eyes, our hearts. You can throw it out and you can put new
life [inside]. Please do that. This is why, family of God, Jesus and Holy
Spirit we come to you. I have asked enough and it is true.

This is a simple prayer. It raises themes we have seen before: the
glorification of God's power, the request that He clear away sin, and the
importance of eyes and hearts in the embodied dynamics of sinfulness.
What is new here is the request that God give the penitent "new life"
(nupela laip). If sin-removal rituals of the kind discussed in the preceding section aim to deal with a particular sin and to return good thinking
to the person for whom they are performed, the transformation intended by confession is more global in character. As we saw in Jenny's
case, the penitent is expected to confess all of his or her sins. Once all
these sins have been confessed, God is expected to allow the penitent to
begin again with a clean slate. In one prayer, a pastor expressed what is
hoped for in the following terms:

God bring down your good, heavenly water. The dirtiness she has made,
whatever kind of heavy she has put inside, only good water must run and
carry away her heavy. God, put nothing but your new life [in its place], as
one would put on new clothes. God, put your name on [her] like putting
on new clothes and she can go out.

The change of clothes, like the change of name, is an image of complete
transformation. Most Urapmin have only a few sets of clothing (most often consisting of short pants or trousers and T-shirts for men, skirts and
T-shirts for women). They very rarely acquire new pieces. Hence a
change to a new set of clothes is an important event in an individual's
life, and something everyone in the community notices. This is the sense
in which this pastor uses it here as a metaphor of a fundamental change
in the penitent's life.

The new life that confession initiates also points toward the new life
to come in heaven. Confession, even more than the other rituals examined so far, fundamentally takes its meaning from the way it places the
person who undergoes it in relation to Jesus' return. Confessions are
strictly private. Pastors are enjoined never to discuss what they have
heard in confession, and this rule of confidentiality is one that they take
seriously. But as a private rite, confession "settles" no social problems.
Indeed, it does no social work (hence the importance of the sin-removal
rites and, as we shall see, of the Spirit disko). It does not adjudicate dis-

putes or ease social tensions. This is why it cannot take the place of the Kaunsil's court. Focused on the individual, what confession does is help to ensure the individual's salvation. Only those who have recently confessed will be able to enter the kingdom of heaven when God comes.

Here is an example of a prayer that closes a confession. It very strongly emphasizes the eschatological motives at the heart of this rite.[5]

> Thank you father God. The two of us have prayed to your name, to the holy God. You are above and you sent Jesus. You are a calm, merciful man. You gave us Jesus who died on the cross and took away the sins of the two of us.
>
> Now the two of us come and sit down with you, talk with you.
>
> While we have been outside we talked all over, said all kinds of things. This thing, this dirty thing that we have been doing up until now, this thing we have done, we are ashamed of it!
>
> And the two of us must come to you. You can forgive the two of us our sins and you can make the two of us right (<u>oraitim</u>). The two of us must be holy and clean and the two of us must wait until the bugle cries for the two of us [in the last days].
>
> That is the only thing we must wait for. Jesus must come back and get the two of us. That is all. The two of us wait for Jesus to come back and take us to live in a good place.
>
> It would be bad if the two of us worked hard for nothing. Us two, inside of our work, God, we have carried your work up until now. Now, the two of us, the inside of our work cannot become nothing. And so God we are praying only to you, only you [can] help us in our work until the two of us get life . . . the two of us must get the place of life (heaven).
>
> We must do this and that is why the two of us have come and are talking with you God. The two of us combine two kinds of work: [we] do the side of work; [we] do the side of sin.
>
> The two of us have come and we are calling to God's good name. Us two, we send our sins over to God, Jesus, and the Holy Spirit; family, they must go over into your hands. That is what we think.
>
> The two of us come and sit down and father God, three-one, family of three, we come calling out to your names. So we have asked enough and it is true.

Having already noted that this prayer places confession in relation to the last days, I want to remark on two of its other features. The first is the phrasing in the penultimate paragraph, where the pastor says, "We send our sins over to God, Jesus and the Holy Spirit; family, they must go over into your hands." This idea of sending sins to God, of putting them in his hands, is expressed in every prayer that follows a confession. Although those praying rarely dwell on it, it is crucial to what the prayer accomplishes. In the language of other postconfessional prayers, penitents are "giving" their sins to God. That these sins are given to God is something pastors and deacons frequently make explicit in the course of reminding God that the penitent has not given their sins to their confessors; God must know that these sins now belong to him. Once they have been given, they no longer belong to the sinner or to the confessor. One pastor during a sermon compared confessed sins to piles of excrement that a person has deposited in the bush; one does not, he pointed out, go back to look at them. It is crucial to the new life one begins after confession that one not go back and ruminate over the sins one has given to God. Doing so will likely raise feelings of anger that will throw one immediately back into sin. This is why it is so important to state that the sins, having been sent to God, are now in his hands. This is also the basis for the rule that sins, once confessed, cannot become the subject of adjudication in secular court.

The second theme in this prayer that I want to comment on concerns work. I asked the man who spoke this prayer whether in speaking of God's work he was speaking metaphorically (tok piksa, weng do). For many years on and off he has been the primary pastor for the top Urapmin church, and one can detect a pastoral bias in the last line of his answer where he talks about the happiness of the congregation. Still, his response speaks eloquently about how the Urapmin conceptualize the role of confession in their Christian lives. He explained: "The work of God is true work. It is in reference to gardening that 'work' is used metaphorically. If you only weed a garden once in a while, it will come up bush. If you worship and pray all of the time, it [the church] will come up good. If not, the people will not be happy." I pick this theme out here because it indicates that confession is considered a crucial part of the routine work of Christian living. People who want to maintain a "clean" heart must confess regularly. Another pastor once addressed this very eloquently in a sermon:

> When we confess our sins it is because God said that if you confess your sins then your heart will be like a pot that you have washed after you have cooked greens in it and eaten. You must always do that, you must wash it all of the time. But if you leave it, if you cook in it and then leave it dirty for a long time . . . [he loses the topic for a moment and then returns to it]. . . . You must wash the inside of your heart, wash the sins, always wash the inside of your life and your heart. What he has said is that you must always keep washing the inside of your heart. So you must always confess your sins, you must get rid of the heavy things, heavy things and sins in your heart. This (your heart) is the holy house of the Holy Spirit. But if one never confesses his sins and keeps filling them up inside, treating them like

a memory and putting one on top of the other on top of the other, then you will soon be broken open on both ends like an old pot. Like a pot open on both ends that you have to throw away. That is what you will be like. He [God] said that.

The pastor is asserting here that if one does not confess regularly, one will become broken and useless like a pot that has no bottom; during the last days, God, having no use for you since you can no longer do his work, will cast you aside. The image of washing the pot is a strikingly everyday one, and it captures the extent to which the Urapmin expect themselves to orient to confession. They need to practice constant self-examination, remember their sins, and come regularly to confess them. This set of linked technologies of the self is the crucial one people deploy in doing God's work.

Given the importance of confession, it is not surprising that people ideally hope to undertake it on a monthly basis. Yet the pastors and deacons have a hard time getting people to turn up for confession that regularly. The sermon from which I just quoted, in fact, was delivered on a Saturday night after the pastor delivering it had been sitting in church all day only to have very few people show up to confess.

There are a few reasons that people are hesitant to confess regularly. The most prosaic is that they often do not like to return from their garden houses before the end of the day on Saturday. More important, people do not like to confess before they have sufficiently worked through the problems that are causing them to sin. They do not confess sins that they are still committing (such as affairs), or, as we have seen, ones that require secular settlement that they have not yet received. At the same time, however, it is important to bring up all of one's current sins (those not confessed previously) during a confession. It is better to skip confession than it is to go and not confess completely; if some sins remain, how can one receive the new life whose attainment is a goal of the ritual? Given the difficulty of offering a partial confession, at any given time when the pastors call for confession there will be people who are not ready to confess.

Successful confessions in terms of full participation tend to take place near holidays (Christmas, Easter, and Independence) or during periods of heightened millennial expectation. These are times during which Urapmin spend a lot of time in their villages and thus have many opportunities to settle their differences with one another informally or in secular courts. These are also times when people spend a good deal of time in church and are thus highly aware of their need for salvation.

Even during other times, however, pastors and deacons sometimes decide that too much time has passed since the last confession and through the force of their wills harangue people to come to confession. By making such efforts over several weeks, they will often succeed in accomplishing a confession with full participation.

After everyone has confessed, a Sunday communion service is held. These are much like regular services except that the deacons prepare small chunks of cooked taro and small glasses (of which the church has a special set) of "red water" (redpela wara, a drink made from cherry-flavored syrup). During the service, the deacons give the taro and red water to the congregants while the pastor prays. The main emphasis in these prayers is on the new life that God must send and on the "new contract" (nupela kontrak) that the people are entering into with God by virtue of their performance of this rite.[6] The notion of a new contract is one that I never heard the Urapmin talk about in other contexts. Thus its prominence in the communion service is striking. It marks the radical break with the past that the confession is supposed to have effected. It is yet another expression of the confession rite's goal of bringing about a complete transformation of the person.[7]

The theme of complete transformation is one that I have stressed, for it differentiates confession from all the other rituals of redemption so far examined. Yet there is a sense in which confession, despite the transformation it brings about, is not the final earthly, ritual step in the redemptive process. That role is occupied by the Spirit disko, a rite that in many ways needs to be seen as an extension of the confession process.

SPIRIT DISKOS AND THE END OF SIN

Spirit possession dances (Spirit disko) are without a doubt the feature of Urapmin Christian life that is most striking to an outsider encountering it for the first time. Nighttime possession dances of great energy and near-violence that go on for hours in darkened churches, they do not, to my knowledge, have parallels in Western charismatic or Pentecostal practice. Although possession by the Holy Spirit is extremely important in those traditions, as far as I know they do not hold dances expressly aimed only at achieving it. The Spirit disko is such a dance. It is not a church service during which people happen to become possessed (though people will sometimes hold a service after a Spirit disko that has ended early); there are no sermons at Spirit diskos, nor, compared to church services, are there many prayers. What there is in place of these things is possession. So central is possession to the Spirit disko that if it is not achieved in a reasonable time, those gathered halt the ritual and declare its performance a failure. To understand the Spirit disko, then, we must focus on possession and ask how it occurs and what it achieves.

As the Urapmin understand it, during possession, the Holy Spirit wrestles with the sins in one's body and ultimately "throws them out" (rausim). As some of the material quoted in the preceding section indicates, the Urapmin think of sins as physical things that accumulate in the body. The word for "sin" in the Urapmin language is *yum,* which usually means "debt"; a sin establishes a debt to God. Even more often than one hears people referring directly to sins as "yum," however, one hears people refer to them with the Tok Pisin word sin or the Tok Pisin or Urap words for "heavy" or "heavy things" (hevi, ilum). This latter usage points to the physical nature of sin. Urapmin claim that those who have sinned are "heavy" and that one can see their condition in how they carry themselves, walking as if burdened. The image suggests that should the weight of sin become too heavy, the sinner might well become completely immobilized.

As physical things that collect in the body, sins remain there until they are removed. It is this that threatens to make the heaviness of sin immobilizing. Left unattended by the sinner, sins pile up one on the other (as suggested in the sermon of the broken pot). As one pastor put it to me, unaddressed sins are like taro cuttings that one just keeps piling on top of one another without bothering to replant them. Eventually, the ones on the bottom die and begin to rot. Images of hearts full of piles of heaped up sin are common. The only way to remove sins and prevent piles from forming is first to confess them and then to participate in a Spirit disko.

There is some confusion in Urapmin representations of the process of sin removal. In their confession prayers, Urapmin ask God to clear away sins and tell him that in the act of praying they have sent the sins over to his hand. How is it, then, that the sins still remain in the sinner's body for the Holy Spirit to clear away in the Spirit disko? This is a question that I cannot answer. I have entertained images of confession leaving the body full of empty shells from which the living sins have been evacuated and the Spirit disko being the occasion for the Holy Spirit to clear the shells away. But the Urapmin neither deploy nor seem to require any such concrete imagery (cf. Needham 1983: 66 ff. on "skulls and causality"). What is clear is that confession transforms sin in some way that makes the Spirit disko possible, for it must be performed if the Spirit disko is to succeed. It is understood that the Spirit will not come if there are people with unconfessed sins who are participating. If confessions have not been held for some time, they are always held before Spirit diskos are attempted, and when a Spirit disko fails, people sometimes begin spontaneously to discuss their minor sins and make plans to hold a formal confession before another one is tried. It is obvious, then, that despite the lack of clarity about exactly how confession and the Spirit disko (not to mention the sin-removal rites) differ in the way they remove sin, Spirit diskos complete the ritual process of redemption that confession initiates.

With this background in place, I turn now to describing a Spirit disko. It, like the other rituals we have examined, begins with a prayer that sets its context and explains its goal. The relative marginality of prayer in the Spirit disko in comparison to other rites is evidenced by the fact that the singing and dancing that mark the major action of the beginning phase of the ritual have often already begun before a prayer is said and need to be stopped momentarily for one to be offered. Here is an example of a Spirit disko prayer delivered by a man in his twenties. He refers several times to "young men and women" because he is offering this prayer before many of the older people have arrived at the church.

> God I am praying to you. Now all of us come inside and we are happy. About this, do not wonder whom we are celebrating (*fiap dulubo*, we are giving happiness). We want to ask you to send your Spirit down to move us so that we can celebrate your name tonight.
> That is what I am asking you. You look at each of our hearts. Young men and young women's hearts. You have the ability to clear away the sins, heavinesses, coveting, and various bad ways that are in our hearts and take us over to Jesus, to your light and we can give happiness to you.
> That is what I am asking. So you send nothing but heaven's heat *(mamin)*, strength *(titil)* and it can come into women and men's hearts. It comes to the mothers and children, to our bodies (*angkil*, also skin) so that all of us can get hot. Jesus give your Spirit to us and we can celebrate.
> That is what I am asking. It would be bad if we tried hard at this for nothing. So we must feed this Spirit of yours. You can direct each of us people [from] inside of ourselves and we can give happiness to your Spirit until we go out and sleep.
> That is what I am asking for. The man who is coming from his house [i.e., those not yet in the church] and all of us young men and women who have come inside, Jesus, we are giving happiness to your Spirit. So we are ready and have been singing but our strength is not enough for us to sing with. So we ask you to have the Spirit alone move us and to bring down your strength and put it in our hearts so that we can celebrate your name tonight.

> That is what I am asking for. God, Jesus, Holy Spirit family your name
> is very big. The young men and women who have come inside, those who
> are in their houses, I send them straight over to your hands, your legs. I
> have asked enough and it is true.

Already the focus on the heart, on the body, and on heat is evident. So
too is the emphasis on the Spirit. In this context, God's strength appears
as only another name for his Spirit, the agency through which he enters
people's hearts directly. The frequency with which the prayer mentions
the action of "giving happiness to" or "worship" (*fiap dulumin,* ama-
masim) is yet another way the prayer marks its marginality. It turns its
focus toward the other worshipful actions that those gathered will undertake, instead of foregrounding its own efficacy as prayer.

The prayer completed, the Spirit disko begins in earnest. Its first
phase is referred to as "pulling the Spirit" (pulim Spirit, *Sinik dagamin*).
Male and female dancers begin by jumping up and down while moving
in a circle to the rhythm of Christian songs sung by women)(*bal*). These
songs borrow their melodies from traditional women's songs sung at
drum dances *(wat dalamin)*. They are far more rhythmically forceful
than the hymns usually sung in church. Their lyrics are usually in Telefol or other Min languages. Most of them were given by the Holy Spirit
during the early days of the revival. When they came to people, usually
in dreams or visions, they were sent to Telefomin where native pastors
there rendered them into the Telefol language. The ones I know best focus on being with Jesus in heaven. They express longing for salvation
more pointedly than do the songs sung during church services. Throughout the Spirit disko the loud singing continues without interruption.

Eventually, in a successful Spirit disko, some people will "get the
Spirit" (kisim Spirit) and begin to shake and flail violently and career
around the dance floor without regard for others or for the circular pattern of the dancing. This marks the second phase of the ritual.

Each new possession is greeted with celebratory whoops from the
crowd as a few people quickly move in to "control" (controlim) the possessed, allowing them to move mostly as they will but struggling to keep
them from crashing into others or into the walls (see figure 10). The violence of the possessed person is understood as an effect of the Holy
Spirit wrestling with the person's sins, striving to throw them out of the
body. People report feeling extremely hot when they are possessed in
this way, and having no thoughts beyond an overwhelming awareness of
their sinfulness.

Figure 10. At a Spirit disko. The woman on the right is possessed by the Holy Spirit and is being "controlled" by the woman holding her. Photo by Joel Robbins.

The violence of the conflict between the possessed person's sins and the Holy Spirit often hurls him or her about with a strength that the handlers cannot fully constrain. Once several people become possessed, bodies fly about wildly, and people get bumped and banged. With the dancers pounding and the possessed stomping and flailing, large slats of the church's bark floor break. Deacons and others who notice the pointed shards of bark hurl them out of the church's open windows, leaving the floor to gape with open patches on which people sometimes trip. The feeling of intense energy that pervades the dance is thus accompanied by an equally strong awareness of physical danger. Sometimes people who get bumped feel anger and must quickly find a pastor or deacon and confess so the dance can continue. Overall, a sense of violence and danger pervades the ecstasy of the rite.

After an hour or more of possession, the possessed person finally loses the Spirit and collapses limp and radiant on what is left of the church floor. When there is no longer anyone possessed, sometimes as many two or three hours after the dance began, the singing stops. Those who have not been possessed then sit down around the prone bodies of those who have been. With a prayer, and perhaps even a Bible reading and a sermon if it is still early, the Spirit disko ends.

Just as sins make one heavy, those who have been possessed and had their sins thrown out of their bodies are thought afterward to be "light" *(fong)* (see Clark 1992: 22). Indeed, they often describe feeling this way, and their slack bodies provide an image of this state. On a personal level, becoming possessed guarantees that one is at least momentarily free of sin. The final disposition of the possessed, lying limp on the church floor, is thus for the Urapmin a paradigmatic image of the person beyond the experience of sinful willfulness. It is the very picture of a yielding, lawful way of being.

Having evoked the core terms of Urapmin Christian and traditional moralities here, I want to continue this analysis by pointing out that an emphasis on suppressed or transcended willfulness is not the only way the Spirit disko addresses the theme of the will; particularly voracious willfulness is also evident in the ritual. First, there are often accusations that illicit sexuality goes on in and around Spirit diskos: some claim that young people run off to the bush while their elders are lost in the dance, or that men take the prevailing physical chaos and darkness as an opportunity to touch women's breasts. And though the Urapmin do not say this explicitly, both the physical ecstasy and the final collapse of the possessed look very sexual (see Gardella 1985), pointing to the possibility that illicit physical desire finds expression in the ritual itself.

Second, there are also ways in which willfulness not only makes a covert appearance at the Spirit disko, but is actually central to it. The action of "pulling the Spirit" that marks the first phase of the ritual is spoken of in Tok Pisin as "pulim Spirit." The less often heard Urapmin phrase is "Sinik dagamin." In both cases, the word for "pull" is the same one used to describe the efforts big men make to bring people into their villages or that young men illicitly make to turn young women's wills in marriage toward themselves. In other words, the "pulling" done in the Spirit disko is, like these other kinds of pulling, a prototypically willful action. Although addressed to the Spirit, it is not itself a Spirit-directed kind of behavior.

Third, the violent, destructive, and dangerous possessed person is a strikingly rendered picture of willfulness. As possessed people's sins of willfulness resist the Holy Spirit's efforts to banish them from their home in the human body, they smash into others, destroy the church floor, drag their handlers to and fro, and in general embody the terror of willfulness unleashed before they succumb to exhaustion. Although the Urapmin do not call this behavior caused by the Holy Spirit in its conflict with sin willful, possessed people nonetheless act out a realization of their worst fantasies of how people would behave if they completely disregarded the claims of others by lashing out violently without any respect for the lawful demands that inhere in the relationships they have with those who might be their victims. The possessed person is, in some sense, an image of the will incarnate and unfettered.

In the Spirit disko, then, Christianity appears to heighten desire and allow for the expression of willfulness at the same time that it transcends them. Christianity, in this one setting, encourages the Urapmin to cultivate an overwhelming desire for the Holy Spirit and to flail violently in the service of redemption. In giving willfulness such a positive role, the Spirit disko echoes the traditional idea that willfulness is necessary and potent even as it seeks to finally purge willfulness in the exhaustion that follows its expression. Like traditional morality, the Spirit disko recognizes that sometimes people need to pull at others to make things happen.

I would argue that the Spirit disko is redemptive for the Urapmin precisely because in this way it goes to the heart of the various contradictory relations between willfulness and lawfulness that are present within and between their two moral systems. It redeems them in Christian terms because it leaves people beyond wanting, sated beyond willfulness. Yet it does not ignore the role traditional morality gives to the will, for it also requires aggressive action and sanctions a certain amount of aggression in connection with it. Here one might argue a true structure of the conjuncture has formed, with indigenous and Christian understandings working in concert rather than at cross-purposes. It is the hint it provides of what a reconciliation between the two systems might look like that makes the Spirit disko so central to Urapmin life.

I could end my discussion of the Spirit disco here, for I think that what has been said is sufficient to explain the importance it has in the ritual process of redemption I have laid out in this chapter. But there is a final aspect of the rite that requires consideration in order to set up the discussion in the next chapter of individualism and millennialism. As the Urapmin understand it, a successful Spirit disko indicates that the Spirit has looked on their community and decided it is moral. When there is too much sin in the community, the Spirit simply will not come. In this way, the Spirit disko acts as a moral gauge for the Urapmin, telling them when things are relatively good and when they are bad for the church community as a whole.

Yet while the claim that the Spirit disko addresses the moral life of the community as a whole is quite accurate, there is also a problem with it. For while the outcome of the Spirit disko is understood to evidence the moral state of the entire church, it is also true that any given performance ends without final resolution for all of those in the majority who did not become possessed. Many people who never become possessed, among them quite a few older men, seriously wonder if their failure to do so is a sign of damnation. For the most part, they comfort themselves (and others comfort them) with the knowledge that God gives different gifts to different people. They receive dreams and visions, people say, rather than possession (see Acts 2:17). Still, a nagging worry remains at large throughout the community that perhaps a successful Spirit disko does not mean that absolutely everybody in the church is redeemed.

What is in evidence here is a largely unsettled question that haunts Urapmin Christianity: is salvation an individual or a collective matter? Can the Urapmin be saved as a community, or will some of them find heaven when Jesus comes while others will find hell? The rituals examined in this chapter all aim at redemption and salvation of the individual self, so with the partial exception of the Spirit disko none of them affect the moral condition of the community as a whole. Yet, as this discussion of the Spirit disko shows, the fate of the community is a matter of concern. We might then ask, what exactly are Urapmin Christians out to save? There is no clear Urapmin answer to this question. In posing it, we move away from the Spirit disko's fleeting promise of a reconciliation between the two moral systems with which the Urapmin live and toward a consideration of the situations in which those two systems most dramatically clash. At the same time, we turn from examining the ritual technologies of the self by which the Urapmin struggle for individual redemption to look at the attention they give to the possibility of Jesus' imminent return and how they construe its meaning for themselves as a community.

CHAPTER 8

Millennialism and the Contest of Values

Urapmin Christian rituals go a long way toward helping people face the moral challenges of day-to-day living and assuage their guilt over the sins they commit. These rituals do not, however, attenuate in the least the Urapmin sense that they are by nature sinful. This sense, as we have seen, is a product not only of Christian ideas about the fallenness of humanity. It is also a product of the contradiction between a traditional morality that values the will when it is deployed to create or positively transform social relationships and a Christian morality that categorically condemns it. It is the difficulties people encounter in trying to live between these two contradictory moral systems that give Christian ideas of fallenness their purchase on Urapmin thinking. Although the rituals of Urapmin Christianity address people's struggles to control their sinfulness and to redeem themselves when they do sin, they do not address the problem of sinfulness per se because they propose no solution to the moral contradiction that underlies it in its Urapmin guise. Focused as tightly as they are on the Christian moral state of the individual, these rituals fail to comment at all on the social demands of traditional morality. Even the Spirit disko, which offers some promise of a resolution of the contradictions between the two systems, ultimately fails to provide people with a way morally to meet the demands of their social lives: as one very committed pastor pointed out to me with real sorrow, "Even after people have been possessed in the Spirit disko, they still go outside and sin again." The resolution of the Spirit disko is thus more of a stopgap than a permanent solution to the contradictory nature of Urapmin moral life. The one place within Urapmin Christianity in which people aim for a permanent solution is their millennialism. In exploring that millennialism in this chapter, my attention thus turns to the most sustained efforts the Urapmin make to resolve their contradictory existence.

In chapters 5 and 6, I examined the tensions within and between the traditional and the Christian moral systems in terms of the different ways each understands the law, the will, and the relationship between them. That analysis was largely an ethnographic one, at least inasmuch as by adopting these terms (i.e., "law," "will") it stayed very close to the idioms in which Urapmin culture frames moral matters. To extend my analysis, I need to reframe my account of the conflict between the two moral systems in a language that both abstracts from specific Urapmin debates to capture their struggle at a more general level and locates my own argument more explicitly in theoretical terms. In this reframing, the contradiction the Urapmin are contending with becomes one between two paramount values: relationalism and individualism.

The notion of a paramount value comes from the work of Dumont (1980, 1986). He uses it to point to that aspect of a culture that most forcefully structures the relations between the elements that make it up (Dumont 1986: 231; Robbins 1994: 28).[1] Those aspects of a culture (the "representations" that constitute it) that accord with its dominant value will be the most fully developed; those that contradict it in some way will be less elaborated and will figure importantly only in limited, carefully defined contexts ("levels"). Thus to give an example that relies on widely known Dumontian terms that I define more fully below, in modernWestern culture individualism is a paramount value. Representations that accord well with individualism—such as those that make up our psychological theories, or those that underlie most of our models of evolution—are highly elaborated and widely applied. Holism, by contrast, is only a value in a few limited contexts, like that of the family when it is considered as a whole whose existence is more important than that of the individuals who make it up. To the extent that the family is understood holistically, and it is arguable that this understanding is on the wane (Birken 1988), representations of it are neither as widely applied nor as richly elaborated as are those of the nature of the individual mind or of existence as a struggle between individuals for survival. Holistic images of the family do not, for example, govern our perception of the highly valued realms of the economy or of work to the extent that representations of individual psychology and evolutionary process do. This

is so because the paramount value of individualism determines that holistic representations can appear and be elaborated only in contexts in
which they do not directly contradict representations that are more fully
in accord with it.

It is widely assumed that Dumont insists that individualism and
holism are the only two paramount values that can govern human cultures. It is true that he himself never discussed any other paramount
value, as I mentioned in the introduction, but he did some time ago confess that the cultures of Melanesia were as "badly described" from the
point of view of holism as from that of individualism, thus suggesting
that some other paramount value must be operative there (1986: 215–
16). Given this admission, it is appropriate to ask what value might
characterize the cultures of the region. In seeking an answer to that
question, it is useful first to define individualism and holism and consider how they fail to describe those cultures.

As paramount values, individualism and holism do not simply define
what is good. More fundamentally, they determine what cultural form
something has to take in order even to be eligible to be reckoned as good
(Robbins 1994: 31). In holist cultures, which can be understood as ones
in which the paramount value is placed on achieving certain states of the
social whole, only states of that whole can be evaluated as good. The action of any person or element cannot be reckoned as good on its own
but only in relation to the contribution it makes to achieving a valued
state of the whole. In individualist cultures, it is only persons or elements
considered as individuals that can be evaluated successfully, and they are
so evaluated from the point of view of how their actions bear on their
own self-determined projects rather than on the state of a larger whole.

When they are understood in these ways, it is not difficult to see why
Dumont argues that neither individualism nor holism is the dominant
value in Melanesian cultures (Robbins 1994: 37 ff.).[2] The case for
Melanesian cultures as individualist falls afoul of the often reported fact
that Melanesians tend to regard the person not as a discrete individual but
as "a microcosm of relations" (Strathern 1988: 131; emphasis removed).
People's actions are less often understood as self-determined than as
elicited by the requirements of the relationships that they have (Strathern
1987: 295; Wagner 1974, 1986). Furthermore, those who do disentangle
themselves from their relationships are not heroic individuals but "rubbish men"; that is, they fall out of the arena of potential positive evaluation altogether by failing to take the appropriate form (Burridge 1975;
McDowell 1980). And as hard as it is to argue for individualism as the

paramount Melanesian value, the case for holism is equally difficult to prosecute. I argued at some length in chapter 5 that Melanesian cultures do not contain explicit models of the social whole and its structure that people are represented as enjoined to realize. This absence of an overarching model of society renders it impossible for Melanesian cultures to be holist, since there is neither a recognized whole whose state can be evaluated nor an ideal that can serve as a standard against which such an evaluation could be made.

If Melanesian cultures neither recognize the autonomous individual nor the social whole, what do they recognize and evaluate? The answer that is most widely supported by the literature is that they recognize relationships and that, in terms of paramount valuation, they should be seen as "relationalist." Several of the most important synthetic works in Melanesian anthropology support this claim (Wagner 1981; Gregory 1982; Strathern 1988), as do numerous ethnographies of particular cultures (see Robbins 1994: 37 ff. for a discussion of some of these). What they demonstrate is that, as relationalist, Melanesian cultures value the creation of relationships over that of other cultural forms (e.g., individuals, wholes) and that they reckon the value of relationships rather than of the individuals who make them up or the larger structures of which they may empirically be a part.

In the Urapmin case, the logic of their traditional morality attests in particularly clear terms to the relationalism of their culture. That morality, as we have seen, strongly enjoins lawfulness, which it defines as showing respect for the dictates of existing *relationships*. It is more ambivalent when it comes to the matter of the will. When the will is destructive of relationships—as when it pushes people to eat without sharing (to "eat nothing," without putting food to use in producing relationships) or to have adulterous sexual encounters that do not lead to the establishment of recognized social bonds—traditional Urapmin morality condemns it. But when the will is productive of new relationships or of the positive transformation of older ones—as when women call the name of men in marriage, or people share food or wealth items with relatives or trade friends, or big men persuade people to join their villages—traditional morality supports it, even to the extent of condoning its exercise despite the tensions generated by the way the paradox of lawfulness ensures that every piece of relationship building will look from the standpoint of other relationships to be somewhat unlawful. That traditional morality judges actions primarily by the way they effect relationships is sufficient to indicate the existence and nature of a kind of relationalism that has until recently been the only paramount value in Urapmin culture (cf. Faubion 2001: 90; Strathern 1997: 146). Indeed, the logic of the traditional moral system provides a clear example of the way a paramount value can control how and where a representation that does not fully accord with it can appear: Urapmin relationalism determines that the will can only act morally when it is in service of the creation of relationships; when it acts otherwise, it is condemned.

With the coming of Christianity, the traditional relationalism of Urapmin culture has been severely challenged. This is so because Christianity is unrelentingly individualist. As Dumont (1986) has argued at length, the individualism that dominates Western culture first developed in Christianity (see also Dumont 1980, 1994; Burridge 1979; Morris 1972; Shanahan 1992; Soeffner 1997). Its most explicit expression is that religion's insistence on the individual as the sole unit of divine judgment; as Christians see it, families, churches, denominations, and towns do not get saved, only individuals do. This individual alone before God is the paradigm of "the independent, autonomous, and thus essentially nonsocial moral being, who carries our [the West's] paramount values" (Dumont 1986: 25). The Urapmin, as I will show, well understand Christianity's individualist emphasis. Hence, with Christianity's arrival, relationalism has lost its right to occupy without question the paramount slot in Urapmin culture.

The tensions that hold between relationalist and individualist values in Urapmin are apparent when one examines from a Dumontian point of view the contradictions that hold between traditional and Christian morality. In traditional Urapmin morality, willfulness is evaluated in connection with its effects on relationships. Depending on its effects, it can be judged either good or bad. For Christianity, however, the only issue is whether an individual acted willfully. If he or she did so, he or she sinned, regardless of the relational consequences of his or her willfulness. All willfulness is condemned because it is evaluated as a condition of the individual heart considered as the innermost essence of the individual, not as a social force (Dumont 1986: 244). Simply to experience it, or any of the emotions that follow from it, is enough to spoil that heart. Since the individual is evaluated without regard to his or her relationships, it is also possible to know in advance which states or actions of that individual will be good and which will be bad. This is why Christianity can condemn the will categorically, instead of on the basis of specific cases.

This brief introductory analysis has established that the tensions between traditional and Christian morality, tensions I previously analyzed in terms of the different understandings and evaluations of the will and the law, can also be understood as a conflict between the paramount values of relationalism and individualism. At the outset of this discussion, I described this reanalysis as an abstraction from terms the Urapmin would find experience near. But while the conflict between relationalism and individualism is not one that Urapmin culture conceptualizes in terms as concrete as those it uses to represent the conflict between the law and the will, it is not difficult to demonstrate that Urapmin people do take it up. I establish this in ethnographic terms in the next two sections and then go on to examine how millennialism serves as a response to the questions posed by this conflict.

INDIVIDUALISM AND URAPMIN CHRISTIANITY

The Urapmin understanding of individualism as a value is most evident in their model of Christian salvation. A particularly good illustration of this model and of its individualism is contained in the Urapmin interpretation of a specific biblical parable that they often discuss. Taken from the Gospel of Matthew, this is one of Jesus' well-known "eschatological parables."

PARABLE OF THE TEN YOUNG WOMEN

When the kingdom of heaven comes it will be like [the case of the] ten young women. A bridegroom was about to come and these ten young women had taken oil lamps to go on the road to find him and bring him back. Five of them were foolish and five of them were smart. The foolish ones brought their lamps, but they did not bring any oil. But the smart women filled bottles of oil and brought them along with their lamps. When the bridegroom did not come quickly, the women got tired and fell asleep.

In the middle of the night a cry rang out: "The bridegroom is coming. You go meet him on the road and bring him here." So these young women woke up and started to get their lamps ready. The foolish women said to the smart women, "You give us some of your oil. Our lamps are ready to go out." But the smart women answered them, "No. This oil won't be enough for us and for you too. It would be better if you went to the store and got some of your own." After the foolish women had left to go buy oil, the bridegroom came. All of the women who were ready went in the house with him to the big marriage feast. And then the door was shut.

Later the other young women came and they said "God, god,[3] you open the door for us." But he answered "I tell you the truth, I do not know of you." So you must watch out good. You do not know the day or the hour. (Matt. 25:1–13)

As they do with the other eschatological parables from Matthew's gospel, Western readers tend to interpret this parable as emphasizing the need for Christians to be ready for the Second Coming and the fact that those who are not ready when it comes will miss out on the kingdom of heaven. "The point of the parable," according to one popular Western commentary, "is that the disciples are to be prepared, and be ready when the Lord comes and thus enter the kingdom" (Fenton 1963: 396).

Read in this way, this parable ought to present no interpretive problems for the Urapmin; they are well versed in the art of determining the eschatological import of passages from the Bible. Yet unlike other blatantly eschatological passages that they find more or less transparently clear, the Urapmin do not find this one easy to work with. In fact, the attention they give it seems to follow less from any confidence they have in their grasp of its message than from the way it raises the problem of how to define the appropriate unit of salvation. The following elegant example of the interpretation the Urapmin tend to make of this parable demonstrates this in striking terms.

One night I went to Rom's house well after midnight and found him studying (stadi) the Gospel of Matthew. He explained to me the import of the Parable of the Ten Young Women in the following way:

> The oil is a metaphor for belief. The foolish women do not hear what God says and they do not believe. The bridegroom is Jesus. But they [the foolish women] come running when Jesus comes. Then they want oil, but the other women say we only have enough for ourselves. The Bible says each person has their own belief. My wife can't break off part of her belief and give it to me. The same holds for me, I can't give her some of mine. It is a hard thing to give. These five women ask for a piece of belief but there is not enough to give some to them. They want to believe but it is too late. Pastors often preached it to them, but they did not hear it: a man can't give a piece of belief to his wife or children. Each has their own. Its not like [what happened with] the plane ticket, where I was short of money and you helped me. Belief is a big thing.

For Rom, the parable is about the limits of sharing and the limited value of relationships based on it. It asserts that each individual is responsible for his or her own belief. If one should fall short of belief when Jesus comes, no one, not even one's closest relatives, will be able to lend one moral credibility. The individual alone is the unit of salvation. Here surely is Dumont's "independent, autonomous, and thus essentially nonsocial moral being" who as the "the-individual-in-relation-to-God" is the subject of Christian salvation (Dumont 1986: 27, after Troeltsch). Rom's interpretation of the parable is a common one in Urapmin, and in making it, he and others demonstrate that they have a sophisticated understanding of the Christian version of individualism.

The Urapmin also display their grasp of Christian individualism in the tropes they use to gloss the process of seeking salvation. The realm of competitive contests, for example, provides a fertile source of imagery for people to use when speaking metaphorically about the individual nature of salvation. The Urapmin often gloss the attempt to gain salvation as a "race" (<u>resis</u>) and state that success in salvation comes when a person "wins" (<u>win</u>) such a race or some other contest. They similarly use high school entrance examinations, another kind of contest that only the best are understood to win and that individuals pass or fail on their own, as metaphors for gaining or losing salvation. Beyond the realm of verbal metaphor, people also frequently dream of watching contests in which some people succeed and others fail, and they interpret these dreams as bearing on the theme of salvation. The dream of a log-jumping contest that I discussed in chapter 4 is an example. The origin of people's use of contests to represent salvation may rest in a historical relationship between competition and Christianity in Urapmin. Recall that it was Lemkiknok, the first Telefolmin evangelist to come to Urapmin, who introduced the Urapmin to competitive sports. To a culture that had not had any competitive games, he brought soccer, basketball, and volleyball, all of which have become very popular. In testing people before sending some of them on to the mission school at Telefomin, he was also the first to introduce examinations. But as illuminating as this connection is of the interplay between Christian ideas about salvation and notions of contest, it is also telling that it is not the team sports that Lemkiknok introduced that the Urapmin use to refer to salvation. Instead, they most often refer to races that have only one winner, or to contests like the log-jumping one or school examinations in which each individual succeeds or fails on his or her own. In all of these cases, the individual nature of the victory is foregrounded.

Leaving the domain of contest, there is another metaphor that the Urapmin commonly use for salvation that similarly highlights its individualist nature. This metaphor figures salvation as the possession of a plane ticket. As Urapmin well know, each individual needs his or her own ticket to travel. A ticket is not something that can be divided and shared with others (though others can help an individual buy one, as Rom notes in his interpretation of the parable). Because this is true, most people travel to Tabubil or other Min areas unaccompanied by members of their families; they travel, that is, as individuals.[4]

The biblical interpretation and the metaphorical usages already considered indicate that the Urapmin have an intellectual understanding of the individualism inherent in the Christian model of salvation. This understanding also finds institutional expression, most notably in the practice of confession (cf. Abercrombie, Hill, and Turner 1986: 43 ff.). Several aspects of confession evidence the individualism of Urapmin Christianity. Turning first to the formal aspects of the confession ritual, it is immediately noteworthy that individuals confess their sins privately and one person at a time. Furthermore, the confession affects only the individual. Unlike court cases or sin-removal rites, other contexts in which people often admit to wrongdoing, confession is not part of a process of restoring broken relationships. Instead, it acts only on the "heart" of the person who confesses. Indeed, because the pastors and deacons take seriously the confidentiality of confessions, the information conveyed in them is socially invisible. And because a confession affects only the person who makes it and the person's relationship to God, one cannot confess for another. When, during the early days of the revival, the Urapmin allowed those with the gift of discernment to reveal the sins of others, they in effect entertained the idea that something like confession for another was possible. But they blocked this possibility when they took action to prevent those people with powers of discernment from revealing the sins of others and thus forced all sinners to confess for themselves. Today, the individualism of Urapmin confession is so strict that even young children of nine or ten, if they have been baptized, are expected to make their own confessions. Nothing that their parents or others can do will guarantee that God will take away their sins.

The prayer that follows a confession is a final formal aspect of the rite that bespeaks its individualism. Recall that in this prayer, the pastor or deacon makes it clear that the penitent has given his or her sins not to the church official offering the prayer but to God. They take great care to make this point clearly so that the sins are not transferred to themselves. There is in this prayerful special pleading a strong indication that confession should not be seen as the formation of a relationship between the person confessing and his or her confessor. This is especially clear when one takes into account the regular use of gifts to make relationships in Urapmin. In this case, the gift is explicitly refused. Although the confessor is there to offer "support" (*dongdagalin*, <u>sapot</u>) to the sinner, confession is very much a matter of the individual facing his or her God and working to ensure his or her own individual salvation. It is the penitent's work in confessing fully and honestly, not the bonds he or she forms with the church official, that underlies the success of the rite.

Along with these formal aspects of the rite that clearly indicate its individualism, the content of people's confessions also bears it out. Rather than review in detail my earlier discussion of the content of confession, let us simply recall how penitents handle issues of anger. Even if one's anger "arises" *(tabemin)* in response to the fault of another person, the experience of it is one's own sin. During her confession, Jenny reported that she had been angry at her son and daughter-in-law for stealing money her husband had earned working in Telefomin and had given them to bring to her. Nowhere in her confession did she suggest that her son and daughter-in-law were not at fault in this case. But in spite of their guilt, she still insisted that her anger over their actions was her own sin. Here we see a crucial aspect of the individualism of confession in Urapmin: even those sins of anger that quite obviously stem from negative states of particular relationships, states that have been brought about by the actions of others, and even when anger is an expected response to the abuse of the law governing such relationships, that response is reckoned as one for which the individual who experiences it is responsible. One's response to the world is one's own responsibility. Thus disengaged from the relationships that make up the social world, the confessing subject in Urapmin is a perfect example of the "nonsocial" yet still moral individual of Christian individualism.

INDIVIDUALISM AND ITS DISCONTENTS

Although Christian individualism has become an important part of Urapmin culture, this does not mean that the Urapmin are untroubled by it. On the contrary, their simultaneous commitment to their culture's traditional relationalism makes Christian individualism very difficult for them to accept. The image of the person at once wholly responsible for himself or herself and utterly unable meaningfully to help others squares so poorly with their own social understanding and experience that they find it difficult to keep in focus, much less embrace. Their difficulty on this score comes out clearly in Rom's interpretation of the Parable of the Ten Young Women. On the one hand, he obviously takes the individual nature of belief to be a normative part of Christian doctrine and as such "a big thing." On the other hand, he suggests the anomalous nature of such individualism by implying how poorly it fits with the constant sharing and support that characterize the Urapmin household—a unit of both production and consumption that is deeply committed to generalized reciprocity among its members. It is as if Rom is saying even though we share everything and are always helping each other, when it comes to this big thing somehow this will not work. Like other Urapmin, he understands the individualism at the heart of this parable but also finds its message extremely difficult to integrate into his understanding of his life. The Urapmin keep coming back to this parable precisely because it is difficult for them in this way.[5]

The apocalyptic dreams that people often have also express their difficulties accepting individualism as a paramount value. All of these dreams have a similar structure. In them, the community is split between those who are saved and those who are damned. In some dreams, the imagery is straightforward: the dreamer actually witnesses the Second Coming and sees Jesus take some Urapmin people to the sky while leaving others to sink to hell. In other dreams, the same point is made metaphorically, as in the case of those in which dreamers report seeing a fence inside of which only some Urapmin stand, or, as mentioned above, a contest that only some Urapmin win. But in all of the scores of cases I have heard, the message is the same: only some Urapmin will be saved.

The splitting of the community that these dreams image quite obviously raises the issue of the individual nature of salvation; dreamers always see specific individuals being saved, never relational units such as families or groups of affines (see below). But a closer look at the details of these dreams provides us with another clue to the nature of the social experience that makes this individualism difficult for the Urapmin to comprehend. In these dreams, the dreamer invariably sees that only very few people are saved. Usually, foremost among the saved are the pastors and the deacons of the local church. The point of these dreams, then, is that you cannot count on these church officials to save you. Although pastors and deacons work for the community and although they can encourage others to believe, in the end they can only save themselves. Based on experience in other areas of their lives, especially in traditional religion (in which male ritual leaders claimed to practice much of the religion by themselves but to do so on behalf of everyone), and also in those areas of production marked by the gendered division of labor, people are used to having others work for the good of the family or some other (often shifting) social group (Strathern 1988). But in matters of salvation, the work of the specialist cannot be shared. Rom noted that in the Parable of the Ten Young Women the pastors had many times told the foolish women they needed their own oil, but their preaching fell on deaf ears; and the effects of this deafness were devastating, because it is not enough to listen to the pastor, one must also act for oneself. The import of these dreams is similar: even if your relationalist thinking might lead you to imagine that the pastors can secure salvation for you and for others with whom they have relationships, in truth only you can save yourself.

In all these examples, the relationalist nature of Urapmin conceptions of social life creates problems for people's understanding of Christian individualism. In his reading of the parable, Rom expresses the relationalist ideas that he is working with when he implies that one would expect that husbands and wives, and parents and children, ought to be saved together. In their dreams, people suggest in the same way that it makes sense to them that pastors and their congregants should be saved together. Rather than individuals, from the point of view of relationalism it is these relationships that ought to be the unit of evaluation.

Contemporary Urapmin culture is deeply marked by the contest between their traditional relationalism and the individualism they confront in the Christianity to which they are also committed. These few examples are meant only to suggest the nature of the problem faced by Urapmin thought. In the next section, I lay out the ways relationalism enters into Urapmin understandings of Christianity and then consider how this contest is played out within Christianity itself through Urapmin practices of millennialism.

RELATIONALISM AND THE URAPMIN CHURCH

The Urapmin have a keen grasp of the individualist nature of Christian salvation, yet they are also inclined to view their church in relationalist terms. This view of the church provides the focus of their apocalyptic attempts to construct a nonindividualist model of salvation. In this section, I examine the way the Urapmin perceive relationships in order to show how they are able to understand the church as a relational unit.

When speaking to or of a group of two or more people, the Urapmin most often employ a special set of terms whose cognates in the Telefol language the linguist Alan Healey (1962: 19) calls "kin group terms." Oates and Oates (1968: 166 ff.) discuss a similar set of terms in their work on the Kapau language of Papua New Guinea and refer to them as "group pronouns." However, the fullest discussion I have found of such terms comes not in work from Melanesia. It appears in Merlan and Heath's (1982) study of what they call the "dyadic kinship terms" of several Australian languages of the Northern Territory.[6] As they define them, dyadic terms are ones "in which the kinship relationship is between the two referents internal to the kin expression" (1982: 107). As examples, they offer English expressions such as "(pair of) brothers" and "father and child." As we will see, in the Urapmin case these terms refer to affinal as well as kin relations, and in at least one instance a term may be triadic rather than dyadic in its references (picking out three relationships between three or more people). But a primary implication of Merlan and Heath's definition holds in Urapmin as well: these terms refer primarily to the relationships between people in a group rather than to the individuals united. In effect, they name groups that are understood as bundles of relationships. For this reason, setting aside the dyadic/triadic issue, I am inclined to call them "relational terms" and to use them as evidence of the relational image of the social world that is central to Urapmin culture.[7]

Urapmin relational terms form a fairly simple paradigm that assimilates groups parsed along the dimensions of relative age, kin or affinal connection, number of members, and gender into one of a small number of kinds of relational units. Thus age-mates are treated in all cases as if they were related either as "siblings" (ningkil),[8] "a group of married couples" (akmal), or "a group of affines" (amdimal). Women with children (aptil) or men with women and/or children (alimal) are treated in all cases as if they were parents and children.[9] All of these groupings are also distinguished from similarly constituted groups involving only two people. Thus among age-mates a single pair of siblings is alep, a single couple is agam, and a single pair of affines is kasamdim. Among cross-generational groups, a woman with one child is awat and a man with one child is alim. It should be noted that the terms referring to groups of three or more people that involve cross-generational relationships do not distinguish whether it is "children" or "parents" that are multiply present. Thus alimal can mean a man and two children or a man, a woman, and a child.

In saying that these terms refer to relationships, I am arguing that they do not, like kinship terms, refer to fixed statuses that individuals are understood to hold. In fact, they are never used to refer to single individuals. People use these terms when they want to refer to or address the group, but they do not speak of individuals being members of such groups. A mother of two children, for example, would not be referred to as part of an aptil (though, using kinship terminology, she could be referred to or addressed as alamon, "mother"). One would apply this

term to her and two of her children only when referring to or addressing them as a group bound by the mother-child relationship. Similarly,
people do not use relational terms to refer to groups that they as individuals belong to: that is, one does not say "my ningkil" or "my alimal"
(Healey 1962: 25).

The importance of these terms for the present argument follows from
the way they allow the Urapmin to speak in relational terms about the
constantly shifting social world around them. They filter out the great
variety of that world, a world kept in perpetual kaleidoscopic motion by
the Urapmin commitment to will-driven rather than structure-driven social action, by rendering all of the various collocations of people that life
presents as one of a limited number of kinds of groups founded on a limited set of kinds of relationships: age-mates are always groups of siblings, couples, or a single kind of affine; cross-generational groups always consist of parents and children. Although the kinship system
makes use of classificatory extension, especially in the descending gen-
erations where ego can refer to many people as "my child" (nimi man),
it still discriminates relationships far more carefully than does this system of relational terms. Given this, it is noteworthy that the Urapmin use
the relational terms ubiquitously and more rigorously than they use kinship terms (which are very often replaced in address with the simple
nimi lakon, "my friend"). This is so, I would argue, because the relational terms more accurately reflect the social ontology of their culture.
This ontology assumes a social world made up of constantly shifting
groups all of which are constituted by people who are, in whatever configurations they appear, bound by particular relationships. No one ever
appears as an individual outside of relationships. At the same time, however, in the world these terms figure, no one ever appears as part of an
overarching social whole such as might be constructed by a system of
unilineal descent groups and prescriptive marriage alliance. The terms
parse the social world not as something that is made up of individuals
or that constitutes a structured whole but rather as an ever-changing
pageant of relationships.

On the basis of this relational social ontology, the Urapmin recognize
their church as a kind of relational group. It is an alimal—a group of
husbands with their wives and children (who are related as siblings).
Pastors and others who preach address the congregation as "church alimal" (sios alimal) or simply as "alimal." During the closing prayer that
ends each church service, the prayer leader asks God to bless each of the
alimal in attendance at church: "God please bless John alimal, Stendi al-

imal," and so forth. But in combining these smaller alimal, the congregation does not become some whole of a different order. It remains an
alimal—a group of people related as husbands and wives, parents and
children, and brothers and sisters. When the Urapmin try to save not individuals but something else, this is the relational unit on behalf of
which they work.

MILLENNIALISM AND RELATIONAL SALVATION

It is through their millennial practice that the Urapmin attempt to save
their church in a way that honors their relationalism while skirting the
demands of Christian individualism. This is especially evident in the way
their millennialism modulates between everyday and heightened forms.

Everyday millennialism, which consists of a constant round of talk
about the imminence of Jesus' return and the moral vigilance needed to
make one ready for his arrival, is an enduring aspect of Urapmin life.
Every so often, however, it gives way to a heightened millennialism in
which an upsurge of millennial talk is accompanied by a dramatic increase in ritual practice. As talk of signs of the Second Coming becomes
abundant, with many more people than usual reporting dreams and visions of eschatological import, and as the community begins to spend
much of its time in church praying, reading the Bible, and engaging in
Spirit diskos, the Urapmin appear during periods of heightened millennialism as if they were in the midst of a full-fledged millennial "movement."

In what follows, I argue that the oscillation between everyday and
heightened forms of millennialism is kept in motion by the fact that the
two forms treat differently the conflict between paramount values that
besets Urapmin culture. Everyday millennialism expresses the problems
the Urapmin have with Christian individualism, but, because it cannot
solve those problems on its own, it ultimately compromises with that
paramount value. Heightened millennialism then becomes necessary by
virtue of the way it "solves" these problems and restores relationalism
to its place of paramountcy. But because it solves them only by ignoring
Christian individualism altogether in an attempt to work out a nonindividualist model of salvation, it in turn opens the door to the reemergence
of the everyday millennial accommodation to individualism.[10]

There is an important Urapmin cliché that captures succinctly the
way in which their everyday millennialism puts Christian individualism
in question. People say, "I will find out if I am saved when I die or when
Jesus comes back." The two possibilities offered by the cliché appear

nicely to balance Christian individualist and Urapmin relational views of salvation: death and the judgment that it brings are events suffered by individuals (LiPuma 2000: 250); Jesus' return, by contrast, will be an event that the church faces as a relational unit. There is, of course, an individualist streak even in the relational apocalyptic scenario, since individuals will still be judged on their own merits. But at least, as the Urapmin see it, the whole church will learn at once if it can stay together in heaven or if some of its members will be lost.

Given the relationalist nature of the millennial model of salvation, the way the Urapmin behave in contradistinction to what this cliché would lead us to expect is very telling. The cliché makes use of a balanced parallelism by means of which it gives equal weight both to death and to Jesus' return. Yet it would be wrong to assume from this that people actually accord both of these phenomena equal salvational importance. On the contrary, in their thinking about matters of salvation, they overwhelmingly focus on the coming apocalypse. This is evident not only during periods of heightened millennialism but also in the constant hum of their everyday millennial talk; at all times Jesus' return far outstrips death in it importance for Urapmin salvational thinking. Indeed, the eclipse of individual death as an important religious moment is strikingly apparent not only in its absence from people's conversations but also in the currently paltry and disorganized state of Urapmin funerals, which are desultory affairs that unfold according to no fixed pattern. If death is the crucial moment in the model of salvation as an individualist issue, then its eclipse by the collective apocalyptic imaginings of everyday millennialism puts the dominance of that model into question.

Throwing all of the emphasis on the coming apocalypse does not, however, completely solve the problem of how to be Christian without being individualist. Even when the moment of salvation is a collective one, people are still judged and saved as individuals. There seems no getting around this point, at least from the vantage of everyday millennialism. Thus, in the last analysis, everyday millennialism is forced to accommodate itself to Christian individualism.

This matter of individual judgment is the one over which heightened millennialism attempts most strenuously to differentiate itself from its everyday counterpart, and in making this attempt, it proposes a solution to the dilemma of how to have a nonindividualist Christianity. Its solution is based on having everyone work collectively toward salvation so that everyone can be saved together. In this way the Urapmin imagine that they might be able to make salvation an event in which the entire church alimal is saved at once.

During periods of heightened millennialism, the church alimal undertakes several kinds of such collective action. Constant church services, for example, work toward the salvation of the entire congregation. I have already discussed how the church is understood as a relational unit. That it should also be the unit of salvation is confirmed in the closing prayer in which the prayer leader asks God to bless all the families in attendance. After this prayer, everyone in the church shakes hands with everyone else and thereby reaffirms the relationships that bind them. In the preceding chapter, I interpreted this handshaking from the point of view of its bearing on each individual's effort to demonstrate lawfulness. From the point of view of the present argument, it can be examined for what it reveals about the constitution of the church alimal; for it is a recognition by all involved of the ties that bind them as members of the same congregation. Although people enter the church one or two at a time, many displaying the willfulness that leads to sin by arriving late, they leave as one, having become tied together as an overarching alimal in which everyone recognizes with a handshake the lawful demands embedded in their relationships to everyone else. During periods of heightened millennialism, the constitution of this overarching alimal and the reaffirmation of its unity-in-devotion is reenacted twice a day, at the end of both the morning and the evening services.

Even more striking in its suggestion that salvation might be a collective matter is the Spirit disko. Indeed, it is through this institution that the Urapmin most fully elaborate their vision of collective salvation. Remember that the success of the Spirit disko indicates that the Holy Spirit has at least for a moment judged the entire congregation to be spiritually healthy. While only a few dancers become possessed, people take the possession of a small group of dancers as a sign that the Holy Spirit has found the collectivity as a whole morally sound.[11] In chapter 7, I raised the question of what it means for the Urapmin notion of salvation that Spirit diskos are understood to reveal the spiritual state of the entire community, while at the same time only some dancers in them become possessed. Here, I can offer an answer in terms of the notion of alimal. The prototypical referent of the term "alimal" is a nuclear or extended family that lives in one household. Because they are structured by a clear division of labor by age and gender, Urapmin families are relational units that are marked by a strong interdependence of their members; the success of the relational unit depends on the contributions of all its parts. In the Spirit disko, the church alimal is similarly a relational unit that depends on the contributions of all its parts to reach its goal. Recall that if everyone in attendance has not confessed their sins to a pastor or deacon before the dance begins, no dancers will become possessed and the Spirit disko will fail. Even if the Spirit comes only to individuals, then, readiness to receive that Spirit is a state of the alimal. This is why the Spirit disko is able to act as a gauge of the spiritual state of the alimal. Dependent as its outcome is on the state of the alimal, the very end of a successful Spirit disko is a moment when the Urapmin feel themselves to have achieved a glimpse of the kind of collective salvation that their social experience leads them to seek and to value.

A final indication of the extent to which the Urapmin imagine that in the last days it is groups of related people that should be able to help each other attain salvation is the way they waited for my mail from home as eagerly as I did (Robbins 1997b). This followed less from any concern for me, though this was abundant in other contexts, than it did from people's assumption that my parents and sister, who lived in America, and my wife, who lived there for part of the time I was in Urapmin, would not fail to send me any information they might learn about the coming apocalypse. My family would want to tell me of this information to strengthen my belief; they would want to help me to be saved along with themselves. Some also suggested that my parents would probably want me to be home if they thought that the last days were imminent (and were thus themselves entering into a state of heightened millennialism). Salvation is something that families should work toward together. At least in its millennial guise, salvation is a relational event.

This relational kind of salvation is what the Urapmin aim for when they act on the basis of intense millennial concern. As millennial fears heighten, the collective efforts of church services and Spirit diskos abound, and people stay in the villages to be able to participate in them and, one senses, simply to be close to one another and help each other to be prepared so that Jesus will take them all together.

Yet to this point, Jesus has not come. In practice, this has meant that all periods of heightened millennialism have, after runs of two or so weeks, given way to a return of the everyday form of eschatological expectation. The terms in which Urapmin pastors encourage such transitions speak rather eloquently of the passage from relationalism to individualism that is central to them. During periods of heightened millennialism, people ignore their gardens, leave off hunting, and forgo the routine "maintenance" work their houses and possessions constantly require. In response to this, as the days of unending ritual practice drag on, pastors begin to preach that people need to return to their gardens. The rationale they offer is always the same: if you do not go back to your gardens and Jesus does not come, you will have to steal food to eat and by doing so you will sin. Jesus, the pastors go on to add, would be more than happy to find you at work in your garden when he returns. With this argument, pastors send people back to their daily lives on patently individualist grounds. If they continue to work as an alimal for the goal of collective salvation, they put each of their individual souls in peril. Better they should work for their own individual sustenance (or, at most, the sustenance of their households) and, in doing so, protect themselves individually from sin. It is on this basis that the heightened millennial project of relational salvation is regularly sublimated into an everyday millennialism that, by virtue of its compromise with individualism, will eventually bring the Urapmin back around to try the heightened form again.

URAPMIN REJECTIONS OF THE WORLD AND THEIR DIRECTIONS

In my initial discussion of Urapmin millennialism in chapter 4, I argued that it lent their culture a strong strain of world rejection.[12] In a note in chapter 7, I pushed my discussion of this topic a step further by arguing that the millennial strand of world rejection was complemented by another one based on the way the Christian ethic of conviction made it impossible for people both to remain committed to their social lives and to construct themselves as moral persons. Building on these discussions, I now want to add that these two types of world rejection take different forms. The ethical type leads to individual withdrawal from the world, whereas the millennial one leads to collective withdrawal on the part of the church alimal as a whole. In this section, I consider how the differences between these two forms of withdrawal might shape the future of the Urapmin efforts to mediate between relationalism and individualism.

In taking up the issue of Christianity's role in shaping social change in the West, Dumont (1986) does not argue that Christianity in its original formulation immediately produced modern individualism. Instead, he claims, it first produced outworldly individuals who, like Indian renouncers, became individuals precisely by stepping outside of the social whole to which they belonged. It was not until the church made its accommodation with the state, the culmination of a slow process that reached its fullest expression only during Charlemagne's rule, that holism gave way to modern, inworldly Christian individualism. If we looked only at the withdrawal driven by their individualist ethic of conviction—the kind of withdrawal Rin and Tandi sought in their disengagement from some of the crucial contexts of their social lives—we might imagine that the Urapmin were on this path and would eventually settle for a relatively untroubled inworldly individualism.

This prediction would not on the face of it be too far-fetched, for Christian inworldly individualism does exist elsewhere in Papua New Guinea. One can find it, for example, in Errington and Gewertz's (1995) well-known work on Karavar evangelicals. Contemporary Karavaran Christians, in their belief that individuals can make decisive changes in social life and in their insistence that they have the state's backing for their efforts to make such changes, clearly subscribe to an inworldly individualism. It is notable, however, that most of these evangelicals have spent a significant part of their lives working in the cash economy and living in urban Papua New Guinea (Errington and Gewertz 1995: 112). Their individualism clearly has roots sunk deeply not only in Western Christian ideas but also in experiences of Western social life. It is this experience of Western social life, I would argue, that allows for the final transformation of relationalism to a clearly delineated inworldly individualism.

The Urapmin case is different from the Karavar one. None of the leading Urapmin Christians have extensive experience of Western social forms. Correlatively, their individualism remains outworldly, and they also strenuously devote themselves to the salvation of an outworldly relational collectivity. The imagined heavenly community of the Urapmin is in fact a relational analog of the outworldly rather than the inworldly individual. In both cases, it is not things of this earth (*towal diim mafak-mafak;* samting bilong graun) that matter, only those of heaven. But in its denial of the individual as a value, the Urapmin eschatological vision of relational salvation posits an outworldly analog that decidedly rejects Christian individualism. And this vision of collective withdrawal exists not only in Urapmin minds, for it is also given concrete expression in the heightened form of Urapmin millennialism. During periods of heightened millennialism, it is the church alimal, not the individual, that withdraws from the world, leaving behind its gardens and other this-worldly concerns for a single-minded dedication to Christian worship.

This much follows from what has already been said, for it is simply a millennial extension of the idea that the alimal as a relational unit is, for the Urapmin, an important subject of salvation. But while the salvational emphasis on the alimal is clear enough in Urapmin millennialism, careful examination shows that in its Christian guise the notion of the alimal is also undergoing some fundamental changes that threaten its relationalism and move it toward accommodation with individualism as a value.

I have to this point presented the alimal as one of the relationally constituted groups that populate the social landscape posited by Urapmin relationalism. As such a group, the alimal cannot be understood in either individualist or holist terms. Yet as the Urapmin begin to imagine the alimal in Christian terms, their thinking about it takes on the cast of what Dumont (1986) calls a "pseudo-holism." If real holism is a kind of self-conscious organic solidarity in which all of the parts of a whole have and recognize themselves as having different functions in relation to the success of that whole, pseudo-holism refers to conceptions in which people are imagined to constitute a whole only by virtue of some supremely important characteristic they all share. Dumont argues that pseudo-holism comes about when individualist ideologies try to integrate into themselves aspects of holistic thinking. But, despite its relationalist origins, it seems that the Christian alimal can also to some extent be understood as a pseudo-holism, for what will link people when Jesus comes is not their relationships to one another but the fact that all of them are alike in that individually each is free from sin. As they work together to help each other to attain salvation—by praying for and with one another, by preaching to one another, by holding Spirit diskos together—the Urapmin operate with a traditional relational notion of the alimal in which people who are related to one another are on that basis part of one another's salvational project; indeed, everyone's salvational project is defined relationally. But when Jesus comes, the best they can hope for is that that alimal will be saved not on the basis of the quality of the relationships that compose it but rather on the pseudo-holist grounds that each individual within it is equally morally pure. At the moment when it falls under the gaze of the returned savior, the church alimal will perforce be transformed from a relational unit into a pseudo-holist one.

This notion of a pseudo-holist collectivity, in which specific relationships lose their distinctiveness and solidarity begins to be based on the similarity of individual elements (in this case, a similarity born of equally good moral standing), is ultimately a step toward individualism. Its focus on the attributes of individuals cannot help but support the individualist trends already apparent in Urapmin Christian thinking. Ironically, then, a millennialism that begins as a subversion of individualism in favor of the traditional value of relationalism ultimately serves to subvert relationalism all the more thoroughly. In dreaming that they can all go to heaven together, the Urapmin preserve the image of the alimal as a set of relationships that have value in themselves. But when they imagine what will happen when Jesus arrives, they can only think of other Urapmin as individuals who either are or are not saved. It is not far from that perception to one in which the Urapmin see each other as individuals each with his or her own problems. These will be problems that are, as they say, each individual's "own business" or "own will" (both *ilimi san*).

In the most important early discussion of the revival of 1977 in the Min region, Jorgensen (1981a) paints a picture of a Telefolmin community seemingly on the verge of making this final transformation to an uncontested individualism. He argues that the revival was crucial for the Telefolmin because in doing away with the men's cult that previously dominated religious activity in the region, it sundered extra-household links of material reciprocity and left the household to function as the primary unit of consumption. It did this just as the cash economy was becoming more important among the Telefolmin, and thus it allowed Telefol families to control the flow of their earnings. It is hard to miss a perception of rising individualism in Jorgensen's account—the revival providing a rationale for people to avoid sharing and neglect the work of building relationships.

The situation in Urapmin has not progressed that far. The household is important as a unit of consumption, but it also lends its character as an alimal to the church congregation as a whole. The Urapmin have developed a dense web of sharing within this congregational family. They pray daily in each others' houses and watch out for each others' moral health, and when the church becomes actively millennial they work together toward salvation in all the ways I have mentioned. Will the Urapmin future thus unfold in a different direction from that taken by the Telefolmin?

Like the Karavar, the Telefolmin have had a far more significant engagement with Western social life than have the Urapmin. Thus a similar argument also accounts for the difference between the Telefol and the Urapmin cases. The Karavaran familiarity with Western social forms has allowed them to work comfortably with Christian individualism. The Telefolmin are also developing such familiarity and modifying their social life accordingly. The Urapmin, by contrast, are not very familiar with most Western forms of social life. Although they are, of course, well acquainted with Christianity and its individualism, they have not had much chance to observe how Westerners build a social life around that paramount value. And the Protestant Christianity to which they subscribe has not made up for this lack of familiarity, for on its own it does not provide them with a model of society that they might use to replace the one that is founded in their relationalism. In fact, with its focus on sin and the inner life, Christian individualism offers the Urapmin little in the way of tools with which to craft a viable *social* life in any form (Robbins n.d.; Soeffner 1997). Perhaps this is why it tends to work best when it counsels a withdrawal from this world and encourages the Urapmin to take the first step in this direction either through individual quietism or collective millennial fervor. In any case, however, it is because it cannot by itself succeed in replacing the relational structure of their cultural conception of sociality that Christianity fails to ensure the final victory of the individualism that it has introduced into Urapmin life. It would, I think, take the dominance among the Urapmin of those social forms through which Western individuals succeed in inhabiting *this* world, especially the capitalist market, for individualism finally to be completely at home there.

Conclusion

Christianity, Cultural Change, and the Moral Life of the Hybrid

Most Urapmin are troubled. Not broken, paralyzed, or without moments of relative comfort—but troubled. More than anything else, they are troubled. The heavy Christmas with which I began should have been enough to intimate this. For in its awkward way, as an inverse celebration, the heavy Christmas represented a sort of luxuriating in trouble; an elaborate text of trouble that no one who was not already troubled would struggle to read over the shoulder of his or her fellows, much less stick around to write. And the solution to heavy Christmas, the Kaunsil's inflationary innovation on the old dispute-resolving exchange ritual, while it put things right side up again, could never dissipate the trouble completely. At its heart the solution was an old-fashioned fix for a new kind of problem: a new kind of problem that arose at exactly the point at which old-fashioned fixes failed to meet new kinds of demands. A brilliant piece of bricolage in the moment, the outsized exchange ritual, like so many contemporary Urapmin fixes, was not built to last. The Kaunsil never filed the pig law for people, which would have been a victory for Urapmin Christian morality (the draconian terms of which the law echoed) over their traditional moral system. So even while the exchange fixed the disputes at hand, the old and new moral systems both remained in play and the Urapmin remained troubled.

Troubled though they are, however, the Urapmin are not troubled in the way anthropologists have come to expect people to be troubled.

They are not poor. They have not been wrenched out of a workable subsistence by an ultimately unforgiving market economy. They are not fighting ethnic or tribal wars. It is true, as Appadurai (1996) predicts, that Urapmin imaginations can go places they never went before, places that sometimes make people feel like the problems and promises of poverty, wage work, market consumption, and tribal strife might someday be theirs. But none of these imaginings has broken them or destroyed the grounds of their living together. More often than not, they have instead energized the Urapmin; they have filled the Urapmin with hopes of change they sometimes think are tantalizingly close to realization, or with fears they believe they can mobilize to address. So neither these imaginings nor more concrete versions of the political-economic dislocations they portend are at the heart of the Urapmin troubles.

What troubles the Urapmin is rather to some extent an outcome of their very success in reproducing the traditional grounds of their lives: their families, their gardens, their hunting territories. What troubles them is trying to live with the culture that supplies those grounds and another culture, a Christian one, at the same time. Living with the counterposed paramount values of these two cultures is what troubles them and makes their experience of cultural change so wrenching. I have written this book to make the nature of this trouble evident. In conclusion, I want to make some more general points about the broader relevance of the way this study has approached morality, Christianity, and cultural change.

MORALITY

It is not an accident that so much of the Urapmin struggle to live caught between two cultures is fought out over issues of morality—over questions of how to live as good people. Several anthropologists, seemingly working in isolation from one another (since with only one exception none of them references the others), have recently converged in an attempt to argue that the study of morality and ethical thinking should have an important place in anthropology (Evens 1999; Faubion 2001; Laidlaw 2002; Lambek 2000; Myhre 1998; Parish 1994). For all of these authors, ethical reasoning and action are situated between the extremes of those forms of practice that follow from rigid cultural compulsion (usually figured as operating on an unconscious or completely naturalized level) and those that are grounded in naked self-interest (however this is culturally defined). Ethical reasoning and action avoid either of these extremes by virtue of the way they are culturally defined as forms of practice in which on the one hand values provide some "directive force" (Parish 1994: 287–88) but on the other actors are also explicitly understood to have some choice in how to respond to that force. The ethical is a field of values, as Faubion (2001: 90) similarly puts it, that "actors are less obliged than encouraged to realize." Because actors who would be ethical must feel the directive force of these values, must recognize themselves as encouraged by them, the ethical field cannot be one governed by unconscious cultural compulsion. At the same time, because people must orient to these values in their decision-making process, even if only to flaunt them, it is also a field in which naked self-interest cannot simply run the table. In cultural terms, it is a field left open in significant ways, but not in all ways, to choice (Laidlaw 2002: 323).

Because so much anthropological energy has been devoted either to waging battles between the extremes of cultural replication and self-interested scheming or to constructing syntheses between them, the moral realm has been left relatively unconceptualized in anthropological theory and has not often been a focus of research (Howell 1997: 6; Laidlaw 2002: 311). Yet the nature of the ethical domain has been carefully delineated by philosophers, and the authors I cited above (with the exception of Evens and Parish) all draw on Aristotle's (1980) discussion of *phronesis* (often translated as "practical wisdom") in describing the kind of thinking that underlies ethical practice. These anthropologists suggest that by following the philosophical tradition in recognizing the unique qualities of ethical practice as a kind of practice and by developing ways to make those domains of culture that require such practice central to our cultural analyses, we can open up new angles on a variety of issues of anthropological concern. I agree with this broad assertion, and within the confines of the themes of this book I want in particular to indicate how attending to the moral domain can advance our understanding of cultural change.

Having defined the moral domain as one in which actors are culturally constructed as being aware both of the directive force of values and of the choices left open to them in responding to that force, we have to recognize that it is fundamentally a domain that consists of actions undertaken consciously. As Strathern (1997: 142) has noted, in Papua New Guinea when actions that should be considered open to moral evaluation are undertaken unconsciously, as when people have been driven to act by sorcery or by having their minds changed by magic, those actions are generally taken out of the moral domain and regarded as amoral rather than immoral. Other cultures make similar distinctions (think of the Western discourse on the relationship between sanity and responsibility). Consciousness of the issues involved is thus a criterion of moral choice.

It is as a domain of conscious deliberation and considered action that the moral takes on a special role in processes of cultural change. Put most simply, because the moral domain is a conscious one, it is also the one in which the fact of change is most likely consciously to register for those involved in it. It is in moral terms that the differences between the values promoted by an old culture and by a new one, and the differences between the choices these values leave open to people, are most likely to be consciously recognized. And because of the necessity of choice in the moral domain, these differences are also likely to be felt as pressing contradictions; as problems that need working out rather than as ones that can be safely ignored. The Urapmin situation—where so much energy has gone into moral self- and social reconstruction both through reframing people's understandings of themselves and through their creation of an elaborate new set of ritual technologies of self-formation—makes this point with great clarity (for another detailed case from Papua New Guinea, see Tuzin 1982, 1997).

It must be added, however, that had I chosen to concentrate on other domains (ones that were less an explicit focus of Urapmin attention), I might have described cultural change in Urapmin in a very different way. As a domain characterized by a conscious reckoning with the need for choice, in situations of cultural contact the moral domain is destined to be one in which people can recognize and confront the problems of working with two cultures at once. It is thus set up to produce situations of the kind I have tried to capture through the model of adoption. Had I focused not on the moral domain but rather on other domains of Urapmin culture, other of the models I have drawn from Sahlins's work would have applied.

Take, for example, the domain of magic. Magical practices *(serap)* are ones that the Urapmin define as largely self-interested. The Urapmin understand Christianity to condemn all of these practices, and one of the things people did during the revival was burn or otherwise dispose of most of the objects used in magic. Some people still resort to magic, albeit mostly very secretly, but the general perception is that people rarely use it anymore. If one looks, however, at the kinds of self-interested ends toward which people once employed magic—to ensure hunting and gardening success, for example, or to make sure sojourns to other communities to collect shell money were successful—one discovers that people now pray to God for help in attaining them. This is a case in which Christian practices have been neatly slotted into traditional categories, along the lines suggested by the models of assimilation and transformation. To choose which model is most appropriate, one would have to analyze whether the Christianization of magical practice has transformed the relation between these categories of self-interested activity and other kinds of activity (in which case transformation would be the appropriate model) or had rather left those relations untouched (in which case the model of assimilation would fit). In the current context, however, it is less important to carry out such an analysis than it is to indicate how the possibility of doing so illustrates the theoretical point that in other domains of Urapmin culture change has proceeded along lines different from those it has followed in the moral domain.

I have focused on morality in this book in part because moral transformation is the overriding preoccupation of contemporary Urapmin life. To write an ethnography of the Urapmin that did not focus on it would be to betray their sense of what is most important in their lives. But I have also focused on it because, as I have tried to argue here, I do not think the Urapmin preoccupation with morality is a contingent one. It is determined first, as this section has suggested, by the nature of the moral domain as one that brings change to consciousness. It is also shaped by a second factor at play in the Urapmin situation, and in many other situations of change as well: the way the cultural content of Christianity foregrounds issues of moral change. Having considered how the Urapmin concern with morality sheds lights on more general processes of cultural change, I now want to make a similar argument about the more general points that can be made on the basis of their encounter with Christianity.

CHRISTIANITY, LAW, AND INDIGENOUS PEOPLES

As I have analyzed Urapmin history, the colonial encounter was crucial in putting issues of lawfulness on the table. The patrol officers who visited the Urapmin repeatedly told them that they were lawless and needed to learn to control themselves. Furthermore, they put into a place a system of laws, the Native Affairs Regulations, designed to regiment most areas of Urapmin life. All of this was done in an atmosphere suffused with threat and occasional terror. For their part, the Urapmin were

quick to grasp the importance of the law, recognizing in it something
akin to the system of taboos that governed their relationships with nature spirits and with the ancestress Afek. Behaving lawfully promised
them the possibility of working out a similar modus vivendi that would
allow them to create workable relationships with the colonists and escape the worst of the punitive apparatus they had put into place. Because
it was so central to the early colonial encounter, the law was already the
idiom of Urapmin engagement with the West at the time Christianity
arrived.

Yet once Christianity joined the conversation on the law already taking place in Urapmin, it profoundly changed the terms of the discussion.
It did so by driving a wedge between the law and traditional ideas of
taboo, and by setting itself up against the traditional legal code that
aimed at balancing law and will. To a great extent, the Urapmin welcomed these changes. They have found the end of the taboo system, figured as the advent of free time, a liberation. The Christian system that
straightforwardly condemns the will has also appealed to them, in this
case as a powerful tool they can use in their continuing efforts to construct themselves as the kind of moral subjects the colonial and postcolonial orders seem to them to have demanded they become. At the
same time that the Urapmin welcome these changes, however, there are
aspects of them that they find troublesome. First, the abrogation of
Afek's taboos has robbed them of the one realm in which they previously
experienced a satisfying sense of moral success. Second, and of even
more consequence, the Urapmin have been unable to reconcile the contradictions between those aspects of their traditional moral system they
cannot jettison because they are central to their social life and the requirements of their Christian morality. It is these aspects of the way the
Christian conversation on the law has gone on among them that have
left the Urapmin feeling so deeply sinful.

Like all ethnographic cases, the Urapmin one is in some ways unique.
Yet I have presented this summary of the cultural dynamics at the heart
of this book in the hope that seeing them laid out synoptically like this
might indicate the extent to which they also tell us something more general about one of the ways Christianity has often made itself felt during
times of cultural change, and also about why it has so often succeeded
in making itself central during such times.

It is to some extent true to say that Christianity has been central to
processes of cultural change in various places the world over simply because Western colonizers, or missionaries working in colonial and post-

colonial situations, have brought it to those places. But while having agents such as these to carry it throughout the world has been a necessary condition of Christianity's impact, it is not sufficient to explain why that impact has been so profound. People could, after all, reject the Christianity these agents bring, as they sometimes do and as they often reject other Western cultural imports, or they could give it only slight play in their lives. But very often, Christianity's impact has been deep. To explain the depth of this impact we need to do more than document the way it was brought places by powerful outsiders. We also need to examine what it is about its cultural content that makes Christianity attractive to people facing significant cultural change.

Speaking generally for a moment—which is to say pitching the discussion at a level that ignores the differences that distinguish Christian denominations from one another—it is important to note that Christianity in most of its guises offers those who take it up both a set of ideas about moral change and the conceptual materials they need to establish a set of institutions (churches, rituals, roles of religious leadership and followership, etc.) that allow them to put those moral ideas into practice. Furthermore, the moral transformation Christianity demands is not only personal, though certainly it is that, but also cultural. Christianity first established itself as a church through Saint Paul's claims that its moral system superseded that of the Jewish law, at least for its gentile adherents.[1] With the arguments it brought to this crucial encounter with Judaism embedded in its canonical doctrine, especially in the Pauline writings, Christianity always comes to new situations equipped with a set of arguments for why people need to throw over an inadequate traditional moral system in favor of the new one it can provide. For the Urapmin and many others whose traditional moral systems involved taboos that have much in common with the Jewish laws that early Christians found most in need of abrogation, these canonical arguments hit home with particular force, as evidenced in the Urapmin embrace of what they call free time. But even for those whose traditional moral systems are not taboo-like in their multiplicity, specificity, and insistence on the value of good practice in its own right, Christianity cannot help but present itself as a discourse that demands changes not only in personal morality but also in the shared ethical codes that constitute an important part of a people's culture.

Given this emphasis on the need for moral change, Christianity makes itself immediately useful to those shaken out of their traditional lives by contact, colonization, or other forms of cultural dislocation. If the moral domain is the one in which change most readily becomes a conscious process, then it is also the domain in which people caught up in change are most in need of new ideas and the raw materials to establish new institutions. Christianity offers these ideas and raw materials. That it does so is at least part of the secret of the impact it has so often had on processes of cultural change.

While the centrality within it of moral discourse is a quality of the Christian tradition broadly understood, we might also consider whether the subtradition that has most influenced the Urapmin displays any particular qualities in this area that render its influence on processes of cultural change distinctive. Approaching this issue is difficult, for the anthropology of Christianity is in its infancy and we have as yet no anthropologically useful way of parsing the broad Christian field into a set of subtraditions. In some cases denominations might work for this purpose (as they have often worked in the sociology of religion), or even particular mission organizations (which have often worked for historians of religion), but the point I am aiming to make here requires a somewhat broader category. The category I have in mind might be characterized as one made up of churches in the revivalist tradition that includes the Pentecostal and charismatic churches that trace their origins back to Methodism and the holiness movement it spawned (Carwardine 2000; Smith 1957; Synan 1997). What churches in this tradition share are the convictions, held in contradistinction to the Calvinist tradition, that everyone can be saved, that people through their faith play a role in their own salvation, and that it is the gifts of the Holy Spirit in various forms that make it possible for people to play that role successfully.[2] What I want to argue here is that when they enter into situations of cultural change, churches in this lineage tend very often to set up the kinds of highly fraught moral conflicts between old and new traditions that we have seen in the Urapmin case.

Two examples from different parts of the world can serve to indicate that the moral struggles the Urapmin face are not, in their basic structure, unique among those exposed to the revivalist tradition. Austin-Broos's (1997) sensitive account of Jamaican Pentecostalism provides a first example. In bare summary, the story of one of the main lines of her complex analysis can be told as follows. American Pentecostal churches were willing to ordain poor and relatively uneducated Jamaicans, no doubt trusting in the Holy Spirit to guide these new pastors in the discharge of their religious duties. Poor Jamaicans have used the authority ordination gave them, and the promise of spiritual perfection these new pastors offered their congregants, first to escape the lowly place they occupied in the colonial status order (Austin-Broos 1997: 82) and second to establish churches that address their own most pressing moral problems.

Foremost among the moral problems Pentecostal churches address are those caused by the Jamaican tradition that allows casual unions and concubinage to exist alongside monogamous marriage. Tightly coordinated with the racial and class hierarchies that give form to Jamaican society, the system that allows both monogamous marriage and "the sweetheart life" to coexist as options in a single social field is a core element of the lower-class Jamaican social order. Pentecostalism's strict moral code condemns the sweetheart life as sinful, but it reaches out to those engaged in it, especially to women. It also provides it adherents with one very important tool to use in addressing the sin of fornication (the rubric under which it recognizes the sweetheart life): as ordained clergy, Pentecostal pastors can perform officially recognized marriage rites, something poor Jamaican clergy in other denominations are unable to do. When pastors perform these rites, they solemnize unions between congregants and thereby succeed in rendering them no longer sinful.

As powerful as this ritual tool is, however, Pentecostalism has not been able to eradicate the sweetheart life among its members: that life is too deeply embedded in the Jamaican social order to be easily done away with. Hence the sweetheart life persists among Pentecostals, and its persistence leaves them caught between two moral systems, one traditional and one Christian, that seek to govern sexuality, procreation, and marriage in different ways. The Pentecostal struggle to live between these moral systems is central to Austin-Broos's discussion; so central, in fact, that in part in reference to it she subtitles her book *Religion and the Politics of Moral Orders*.

This subtitle also refers to another, more wide-ranging moral conflict, one that underlies that between Pentecostal and traditional Jamaican understandings of sexual and marital morality (Austin-Broos 1997: 199). Austin-Broos (1997: 249) describes this broader conflict as one between what she calls the Jamaican commitment to the eudemonic, an earthly experience of ecstasy in "rite and performance," and the Pentecostal emphasis on a morally strict, essentially ascetic code of behavior. The key Pentecostal move in its argument with the eudemonic is to make a place for the eudemonic by encompassing it in its own possession, dancing, and healing rites (e.g., Austin-Broos 1997: 80, 144). In effect, the Jamaican Pentecostal churches sanctify the eudemonic by making it serve Christian ends; in doing so, they bring the eudemonic "into the church" (Austin-Broos 1997: 71, 199). There is a certain move to-ward reconciliation in this encompassment, but at the same time it keeps the eudemonic alive in a church whose primary emphasis on moral strictness condemns all of its secular expressions. One senses that by keeping alive a tradition that it in so many other ways attempts to erad-icate, the reconciliation Jamaican Pentecostalism makes with Jamaican culture proves itself far from complete.

Similar issues arise among the urban Zulu Zionists of South Africa who Kiernan (1994, 1997) has studied. These churches trace their ori-gins to John Dowie's Christian Catholic Apostolic Church, an American church that in its millenarianism, emphasis on healing, and hopes of re-storing something like the primitive Christian community was "an im-portant forerunner of Pentecostalism" and thus squarely in the Pente-costal and charismatic category as I have defined it (Blumhoffer 1988: 249; Comaroff 1985; Kiernan 1994: 73). The Zulu Zionists subscribe to a "Puritan" morality marked by "the severity" of its "prohibitions" (Kiernan 1997: 243). In the urban context in which the Zionists live, this Puritan morality, one that focuses on individual self-control aimed at self-development, exists in tense dialogue with a traditional African morality of uniformity and egalitarianism (Kiernan 1997: 245). For Zionists, the traditional morality is always a force, its claims insistently made by the sorcerers who defend it by attacking those whose self-control has allowed them to develop themselves in ways that make them stand out from those around them (Kiernan 1997: 245). Unsurprisingly, Zionists, devoted as they are to Christian moral standards of self-control and self-development, often see themselves as in violation of the traditional moral code and hence as targets of sorcery (Kiernan 1997: 247). Their fear of sorcery constantly threatens to entice them back into the fold of traditional morality. Living between the Christian and the traditional moral systems, the Zionists ultimately find themselves con-demned to negotiate a situation in which what is moral from the point of view of the Zionist system is immoral from that of the traditional one. Like the Jamaican Pentecostals, they find themselves inescapably en-meshed in a religious politics of moral orders.

Equally noteworthy in the Zulu Zionist case is the extent to which the church's members confront within their Christian culture an emphasis both on ascetic self-control and what Austin-Broos would call eude-monic freedom and release. As Kiernan (1994: 77) notes, the Zionist's Puritan code is counterbalanced by the way "[e]very Zionist has some access to the Holy Spirit and nobody can be held to account for what is said or done when under the inspiration of the spirit; this encourages the free expression of social and personal concerns. In this respect, the activation of the Holy Spirit promotes the unbridling of normative constraints." In the article I am quoting from, Kiernan (1994: 77–78) explains away the apparent contradiction between the asceticism of the Puritan code and the freedom of the inspired believer by pointing out that Zionist asceticism also gains its adherents a certain kind of freedom, in this case from the socioeconomic system that oppresses them and that they use their asceticism to opt out of to the extent their lives allow. Yet I am not sure the two kinds of freedom are really equivalent: one is negative, as it were, a freedom to withdraw in order to embrace a project of self-control; the other is a positive freedom to act beyond the boundaries of a moral code in some ways felt to be restrictive. In a later article, Kiernan (1997: 247–49) mentions that at least for Zionist preachers (though perhaps less so for lay members), the image of Satan represents the ever-present possibility of a loss of self-control in the face of the attractions of the second, positive kind of freedom. There is, then, a real concern on the Zionist part that the freedom of self-expression the Spirit gives not be allowed to lead on to the more general "unbridling of normative constraints" it might be taken (by those who experience it) to foreshadow.

The Jamaican and Zulu Zionist cases turn on a number of issues that are central to the Urapmin case as well. There is, first, a localization of religious authority through the open ecclesiastical "structure" of the Pentecostal and charismatic churches and the role of the Holy Spirit in guiding the hand of local church leaders (although I did not highlight this point in my discussion of Zulu Zionism, it holds for them as well). Second, there is an enduring conflict between Christian and traditional moral systems that is recognized in these terms by adherents themselves. This follows from the way "Pentecostally oriented churches continuously dwell on the boundary between Christianity and 'heathendom'" (Meyer 2001: 117) and rail against any compromise between them. It also follows from the way churches in this tradition insist that every individual must meet the demands of the Christian moral code on their own; there is no room to attenuate the conflict between the two codes by having one social class or gender, for example, meet the demands of the Christian system while another meets those of the traditional one, or by having one code apply only in some cultural domains and the other apply only in others (Barker 1993; see below).

Third and finally, there is a tension within both the Zionist and Jamaican Pentecostal churches between ideas and practices that seem to foster liberation and those that emphasize strict self-control. This tension, one that showed up in the Urapmin case in their ambivalent relationship to free time as an era both of freedom and of uncontrolled license and in the Spirit disko's way of both allowing the will expression and attempting to overcome it, turns up routinely in cases in which Pentecostalism shapes social change.[3] It can be accounted for in two ways, and both accounts probably apply in most situations. The sense of liberation revivalist Christianity fosters, and the openness of revivalist ritual and discourse to images of liberation despite their general emphasis on moral strictness, is born out of the promise that revivalist religions make to free people from the demands of their traditional moral systems. It is freedom from these demands that is experienced as liberation. Even when elements of the traditional culture are brought into revival Christianity, as is the case with the eudemonic in Jamaica, the theme of liberation is ultimately grounded in the way these elements are jarred loose from traditional moral constraints. Equally important, however, as a cause of the Pentecostal and charismatic elaboration of the tension between freedom and constraint is the way this tension serves these churches as an idiom in which to comment on the dual moral situations it so often sets up: in such dual situations, every act is at least potentially both a transgression of the constraints of one system and a capitulation to the constraints of the other. By keeping images of liberation and constraint constantly in the foreground, Pentecostal and charismatic Christianity speak eloquently to the trials of those they catch up in such struggles to live between cultural logics.

I have argued here both that because of its cultural content Christianity in general enters situations of cultural change as a discourse about moral transformation and that Pentecostal and charismatic Christianity, because of some of those parts of their cultural content that make them unique within the Christian tradition, do this in a particular way. These two arguments can be brought to conclusion through a brief consideration of another case from Papua New Guinea. This case is drawn from Barker's (1990b, 1993) rich ethnographic work among the Maisin of Uiaku village on the northern coast of Papua New Guinea. The Maisin are Anglicans and have been since the early 1920s (Barker 1990b: 193). As we would predict given my argument about Christianity in general, the Maisin have seen Anglicanism as the source of a new moral order that is in many ways different from their traditional one. As Barker (1993: 204) puts it, for the Maisin the Anglican and the traditional systems constitute two "practico-moral environments" characterized by "variant values." In this respect, the Maisin share much with the cases of Pentecostal and charismatic Christianity I have just discussed.

But Anglicanism is not a form of Pentecostal or charismatic Christianity, and the dual moral situation of the Maisin has played itself out in ways very different from those of the Urapmin, the Jamaican Pentecostals, and the Zulu Zionists. Since the coming of the mission in the early part of the twentieth century, the Maisin have recognized not only a moral bifurcation of their world but a spatial one as well. Anglicanism belongs to the mission station, which houses the main church, whereas traditional life is carried out in the village. Likewise, each moral system applies in the space appropriate to it. Maisin Anglicanism has not worked to overcome the spatial side of this separation, for example, by democratizing religious authority in the Pentecostal and charismatic style and thus allowing all believers to act with such authority in their daily lives within the village. Instead, Anglican clergy are still today seen as specialists and as "strangers," and their authority does not extend beyond the station (Barker 1990b: 182). Neither has Maisin Anglicanism worked to overcome the moral side of the bifurcation by demanding that people look beyond the spatial segregation of the two moral systems to confront the contradictions that would appear if both were to apply in the same contexts. As a result of the stability of the spatial divide, then, the moral divide in the Maisin case appears stable in a way it does not in any of the Pentecostal and charismatic cases. As Barker (1990b: 183) notes, the Maisin "seem comfortable with their biculturalism." They live with both systems "without experiencing sharp contradictions" (Barker 1993: 225). Among the Maisin, there is little in the way of the Pentecostals' and charismatics' unyielding sense of personal sinfulness to drive an attempt at synthesis.

In the present context, the Maisin case is valuable for the way it at once illustrates both the general tendency of Christianity to enter situations of change by proclaiming the need for people to adopt a new morality and, by serving as an example that stands in contrast to the Pentecostal and charismatic cases I presented above, the extent to which their way of bringing this proclamation to bear has its own unique features. What all of the cases considered here have aimed to establish is that the cultural content of Christianity decisively shapes the role that religion plays in cultural change. Considered historically and sociologically, the Jamaican, Zulu Zionist, and Urapmin cases are very different from one another: the first two are urban, the third is rural; the Jamaicans and Zulu Zionists have long been engaged with the capitalist economy, though in different ways and with different effects on their modes of social organization, while the Urapmin have hardly participated in it at all; and all three groups come from different pre-Christian cultural backgrounds. Yet their conversion to churches in the Pentecostal and charismatic tradition has meant that cultural change among them has turned on similar issues of how to coordinate a life lived between two moral systems and how to negotiate the way their new religion responds to this situation by promoting both liberation and ascetic self-control. Having encountered a different branch of the Christian lineage, the Maisin stand out from all of these other groups, though on a general level they are similar to them by virtue of the central role they too give to issues of morality in their attempt to understand their contemporary lives. To understand the similarities between the first three cases and the way they differ from the Maisin one, we need to attend to the cultural aspects of Pentecostal and charismatic Christianity. To understand what connects all four cases, we need to attend to the cultural aspects of Christianity more generally. And as a general theoretical matter, it is fair to say that the if the anthropology of Christianity is to flourish, it will have to attend to the cultural content of all kinds of Christianity. The Urapmin case along with those I have cited here and others that are beginning to fill the anthropological literature demonstrate that converts routinely come to understand and grapple with that cultural content—as they do so, they deserve and require an anthropology that is not blind to it.

Viewed in the context of an understanding of the way the cultural content of Pentecostal and charismatic Christianity has expressed itself in a wide range of cultural milieus, it is not hard to appreciate the extent to which the Urapmin problem of living caught between two different cultures and finding themselves at once liberated and troubled by that experience is not unique to them. It is but one example of a more widespread dynamic of cultural change. Having moved from an argument about the centrality of the moral domain in cultural change to one about why Christianity, because of its cultural content, is likely to be attractive to those caught up in moral change, I thus come finally to a consideration of what the Urapmin case can teach us about what is involved in studying change as a cultural process.

CULTURAL CHANGE

Throughout this book, I have described what is going on in Urapmin as a kind of cultural change. While one might consider this an obvious description of what has been happening there, I have had to train myself to discuss it consistently in these terms. The need for discipline in this regard follows from a peculiarity of anthropological usage: anthropologists, even those committed to the study of culture, much more frequently employ the phrase "social change" than they do "cultural change." Often enough, they employ the more popular phrase while discussing matters that quite evidently actually are ones of cultural change, but the fact remains that no matter how regularly anthropologists take up issues of cultural change, the phrase "cultural change" is not really an established one in the anthropological lexicon.

One does not want to make too much of a linguistic fillip of this sort. At the same time, however, I want to note that I have endeavored to be rigorous in my use of the phrase "cultural change" because one of my primary goals has been to argue for the value of developing a set of models that allow us to study cultural change as a cultural process rather than as a simple reflex of social or psychological changes taken as somehow more fundamental. Toward that end, I have couched my analysis of the history and present nature of the troubled Christian lives the Urapmin lead in an explicitly cultural idiom derived from the structuralist tradition, particularly as it has been extended by Sahlins and Dumont. Through the application of models derived from this tradition, I have arrived at an analysis that argues that the fundamental cultural fact of contemporary Urapmin life is that it is lived caught between two cultures; what is most distinctive about the Urapmin case from the point of view of cultural theory is the way people there are guided by two cultural systems that have in many ways remained distinct and between which exist many contradictions that have yet to be smoothed out through successful processes of synthesis.

In discussing the Urapmin case in these terms, I find myself in the unexpected position of having written an ethnography of an unfashionably remote and geographically contained group of people that raises issues—issues of how cultures come together—that are at the center of a much in vogue theoretical discourse focused on populations that are far better integrated into the world economy and that are often to some or other degree geographically displaced. The primary watchword of this theoretical discourse is "hybridity," a term that well captures the nature of the Urapmin predicament. Yet much of the literature on hybridity is distinctly disappointing in its handling of matters of cultural theory. In closing, I want to examine the limitations of some theories of hybridity and argue that a fully cultural approach to this topic, an approach of the kind I have tried to carry out here, has much to offer discussions of globalization and the complex cultural configurations it leaves in its wake.

As a phenomenon that has gained a wide currency as the point of contact between discussions of globalization and those of postcolonialism, hybridity has been theorized from a variety of perspectives. While those working from most of these perspectives at least make a nod toward the cultural aspects of hybridity, few of them go on to investigate it in ways that can be considered, at least from an anthropological point of view, sophisticated in their handling of culture. What might be lost to our understanding of hybridity as an outcome of this tendency to theorize it in other than cultural terms is made evident in Nederveen Pieterse's (1995: 55) recent call for a more rigorous theorization of hybridity in general. "Ironically," he points out, any theory of hybridity would "have to prove itself by giving as neat as possible a version of messiness, or an unhybrid categorization of hybridities." Assuming that this is true, the key questions become, where should we look for order in the mess, and how should we categorize hybridities? A cultural theory of hybridity, I want to argue, would be one that looked for order on the level of culture and that categorized hybrid formations in terms of the different ways two or more cultures interacted to construct them.

While we have as yet little in the way of a categorization of different kinds of hybridities, we do have several ways of analyzing their internal orderings. The three acknowledged masters of hybridity theory — Bhabha, Hall, and García Canclini — each locate the ordering of the phenomenon in a different place. For Bhabha (1994), the ordering of hybridity ultimately occurs intrapsychically, and he relies on Lacanian psychoanalysis to explain its vicissitudes and to register its impacts. To the extent that Lacanian theory and postmodernism more generally involve Bhabha with semiotic issues, he appears at times to make pronouncements about culture, but in the end the location of culture is for him in the psyche, and it is in psychoanalytic terms that hybrid cultures make sense (Kraniauskas 2000: 238, 245; Moore-Gilbert 1997: 140–51). Hall (1992, 1994, 1996), by contrast, concerns himself with the political ordering of identities. Hybridity is ordered on the basis of the political logics by which people come to take up particular identities and combinations of identities. As with Bhabha, various semiotic theories play a role in Hall's work and lend it the appearance of a kind of cultural analysis. But to analyze what Hall (1994: 395) calls the "points of identification" that connect people to culture is not to analyze culture itself, and thus he too fails to come to grips with what hybridity might mean as a relationship between elements of two or more cultures.

Unlike Bhabha and Hall, García Canclini (1995) does approach hybridity as a largely cultural issue. His primary focus is on the distinctions that organize the understanding of expressive culture, and he traces changes in the ways artistic, popular, and mass cultural production, as well traditional and modern art, have been distinguished from one another in Mexico and Latin America more generally. The hybridity that most concerns him is the kind that follows from the collapse of the boundaries between these terms. There are many helpful pointers toward a cultural theory of hybridity in his work. For example, his claim that we need to study not hybridity but processes of hybridization usefully throws emphasis on the extent to which it is the dynamics of cultural change that are at issue (García Canclini 2000: 43). Likewise, some of the mechanisms by which he suggests hybridization occurs—such as reconversion (2000: 43) and decollection (1995: 223–28)—are suggestive. Yet one comes away from his work without a sense of having encountered a hybrid culture in the rich sense one expects to in an ethnography. In fact, it is precisely a discussion of the cultural ordering of hybridization that is finally missing in his major work, *Hybrid Cultures*: the fragments of analysis he presents are elegant, and there is no doubting a major ethnographic talent at work, but the broader cultural processes that would order these fragments remain elusive.

A crucial moment for the cultural theorization of hybridity arrives at precisely this point, for it is here that the question arises of whether I am asking too much in seeking a cultural order underlying the hybrid fragments that feature in an account such as García Canclini's. Perhaps García Canclini's failure to present an overall cultural ordering of the various hybrid zones he discusses is an expression of the truly fragmentary, relatively disordered nature of the situation he is studying. Many anthropologists would likely agree that this is the case—not only in García Canclini's Mexico, but everywhere—and they would suspect that I am misguided in requiring us to find an internal cultural ordering of elements in situations of hybridity. In fact, for many, this requirement is founded on an image of the ordering capacity of culture that it is the very purpose of the notion of hybridity to render obsolete.

Those who hold this position argue that the culture concept is now of little use: our recognition of the ubiquity of hybridity teaches us that no one, or only very few people living in small, very remote groups, live culturally ordered lives anymore. Wicker (2000: 39) tells this common story in a particularly straightforward and self-confident way, and takes from it the lesson that any adequate concept of culture "must do without grammar or syntax, as these would merely serve to imply the existence of a coherent logic." With these prohibitions in place, one wonders why one should bother to have the concept at all, and in fact Wicker's (2000: 39) bottom line is that we should shift away from the "perception of culture as something in itself, towards those dynamic and complex fields of negotiation, invested with various degrees of defining power, which emerge from partly divergent and contradictory lines of exploration and discourse." Assuming that Wicker does not want the notion of discourse to play the role of culture in this argument, as it sometimes does in others, then we are, on his account, well and truly done with the notion of culture.

One might find reason for caution in the way Wicker's attack on culture seems to leave us, as do so many of the theories of practice and contention on which he draws, with little more to account for the shape of social life than the kinds of individuals and their projects that make up Western common sense (Robbins 2002; Graeber 2001: 30). Indeed, having recognized this tendency for hybridity theorists to revert to basic Western assumptions, van der Veer (2000: 95), writing in the same volume as Wicker, worries about the American-style individualism that haunts many critiques of the culture concept they produce.[4] If we were to accept these critiques as adequate, we would fall prey to a danger that Tsing (2000) argues threatens globalization theory in general: accepting at face value globalizing Western culture's claims to apply the world over rather than analyzing the cultural embeddedness of those claims and the limitations on their spread. Structuralism was, I think, the last anthropological theory that did not flatter Western common sense in the way this kind of hybridity theory does. That is one reason I think it is worth pushing the idea of a fully cultural theorization of hybridity carried out in structuralist terms.

Yet the desire to step back from a theory that reproduces too many pat Western assumptions is not the only motive I would suggest ought to motivate a turn to culture in the theorization of hybridity. Equally important is a fundamental flaw in the way hybridity theorists and other kindred spirits have attacked the notion of culture. As Brightman (1995) has shown in a painstaking review of many of the streams of argument that lead into the hybridity critique, their proponents generally attack a caricatural notion of culture. The scholars who have developed these arguments have, he shows, an alarming tendency to treat cultural theory as if it is limited in precisely those respects that they suppose the traditional notion of culture has been limited. That is to say, they treat the way anthropologists have used culture as unchanging, clearly bounded, and free of contradiction. In doing so, they produce "invented images of culture" that are "both arbitrary and partial with respect to a much more diverse and versatile field of definition and use" (Brightman 1995: 541). Tsing (2000: 339–40) makes a similar point, though perhaps a tad less critically than Brightman, when she notes that globalization theory "renews stereotypes of the anthropological past in order to confront them." Looking beyond these stereotypes, it is clear that anthropologists employing the notion of culture have always, and in recent decades regularly, been alive to cultural contradictions, to the cultural patterning of historical change and to the ways cultures coordinate issues of boundary making and breaking. One might want to see more of this, but to claim that anthropological theorizations of culture do not provide resources for addressing these topics is badly to misread the theoretical history of the discipline.

While Brightman's and Tsing's arguments are aimed at a variety of positions from which anthropologists have demanded that we "forget culture" (a phrase taken from Brightman's title), Friedman (2000) has proffered a similar complaint in relation to the hybridity critics in particular. Such critics, he asserts, begin with the misguided assumption that cultural "coherence lies in origins, authenticity, and purity itself" (Friedman 2000: 80). But even if some proponents of culture have assumed that, and surely very few have in recent decades (Brightman 1995: 540), it is not something those who would use the concept need necessarily assume. We are once again in a position of watching theorists fight their way out of a thicket of outdated stereotypes they themselves have raised again from by now ancient seeds. Even the majority of diffusionists, not to mention more contemporary proponents of the anthropological study of culture, would have agreed with Friedman's (2000: 81) claim "it is not the origin of its elements but the way they are synthesized that is the specificity of a culture." Once this is recognized, it is clear that the hybridity theorists are attacking a straw man.

Some might sense in Friedman's use of the word *synthesis* a return to ideas of *integration* (a term he does use in the next sentence) and coherence that they might have hoped to get beyond. But what do these terms mean exactly? What do they mean for a cultural theory that has long recognized issues of change, contradiction, and cultural porousness, as Friedman's certainly has (e.g., Friedman 1994)? They mean something about the ways people live amid systems of meaning that at once constrain and enable their practice, and they mean that those systems can be studied in ways that bring out their systematic character. Brought into a cultural theory of hybridity, they mean that we should at least begin our analyses with the assumption that cultural hybrids too, if they are to provide the grounds for meaningful human lives, are also in important respects systematic. What I have tried to do in this book is bring out the systematic character of one kind of hybrid situation—one in which two cultures operate among the same people without in key respects being synthesized.

The systematic character of the Urapmin cultural hybrid is one that is only apparent when we examine it from the point of view of its values and in doing so recognize that it is structured by the competition between two values—relationalism and individualism—that both aim to claim paramountcy. It is the lack of compromise between these two values that prevents synthesis in many domains. To say that the hybrid that results from the relationship between these two values and between the elements of the two cultures they give shape to is systemic does not mean that it is finally settled or unchanging. Rather, "systematic" here refers to a certain predictability in the issues this hybrid formation presents to the Urapmin and in the ways they find them hard to resolve: the logics of the two cultures contradict each other and repel efforts at synthesis in predictable ways. This predictability in turn gives shape to a systematic ritual life—systematic both in terms of predictability and in terms of the integration of its parts toward a single goal of ameliorating the sense of moral failure that follows from the inability of the Urapmin to resolve the contradictions that hold between their conflicting paramount values. The interplay of cultural elements that gives this system its shape could shift at any time, both for reasons generated internally by the way the Urapmin live with the system and its contradictions or because of changes in the outside forces that bear on their lives. Yet for the moment their lives do have a routine quality, and this hybrid cultural system is its foundation.

Returning briefly to the issue of categorization, I submit that the unsynthesized duality of the Urapmin cultural system—the way it is constructed out of the relationship between two cultural logics that remain largely distinct—constitutes one kind of cultural hybridity. Doubtless there are other kinds of cultural hybridity to be found as well. One surely can, for example, find cases in which one culture and its values are clearly paramount and elements of a second culture are brought in only when they do not conflict with them. One can also find cases in which the liberal value on individual creativity is paramount and, as long as that value is respected, each individual is encouraged to knit together various cultures in his or her own creative synthesis (an important position in discussions of the hybridity of migrant culture; see Papastergiadis 2000). Or one could even make distinctions within these broad types. For example, within the category of cases in which two cultures remain unsynthesized, one can distinguish those in which they are mired in conflict (the Urapmin and the other Pentecostal and charismatic cases discussed in the previous section would fit here) from those in which there is little conflict (the Maisin case). These and other configurations all warrant study, and hybridity theory will take an important step forward when we are able to develop models to account for why some configurations show up in some situations and others show up in others . However, the burden of my argument here is not to enumerate every possible configuration or to account for their distribution but only to suggest that they can and should be discussed culturally. To discard the concept of culture at this point would to be give up on one of the most powerful tools we have for understanding how different hybridities are internally organized and for delineating the differences among various kinds.

I have argued that in situations of cultural change, issues of morality are likely to be very salient for people. Hybridities in which cultures are brought together but not reconciled are marked by a permanent openness to change: they put in play processes in which is it clear that things are not at rest. As such, they are bound to be cultural hybridities whose force is particularly felt in the moral domain. They are, we might say, moral hybridities. The Urapmin have made of their hybrid situation lives fraught with a sense of moral failure but also driven by a profound moral hope vested in the promise of a more perfect future. In this book I have tried to give an account of the grounds of that sense of failure by means of an analysis that does not discount the hopes that underlie that sense of promise. An account, that is, that recognizes the difficult nature of where the Urapmin have been but that also conveys the depth of their commitment to the places their hybrid culture is taking them.

Notes

PROLOGUE

1. Terms in the Urap language are given in italics; those in Tok Pisin, the primary lingua franca of rural Papua New Guinea, are underlined. I discuss the Urapmin use of these two languages in the introduction.

INTRODUCTION

1. There was a two-year period in the early 1980s when the mining town was being built during which many Urapmin men went there to work. I discuss this period more fully in chapter 2. In the present connection, it is important to note that this brief period in which wage labor was abundantly available to many Urapmin men occurred *after* the onset of the revival and thus the effects of this period cannot be used to explain the revival's success.

2. Sahlins sometimes writes as if every act of referring to the world results in change. Thus, for example, the statement, "Every reproduction of a culture is an alteration, insofar as in action, the categories by which a present world is orchestrated pick up some novel empirical content" (Sahlins 1985: 144). I find it useful, however, to consider cases in which the categories people deploy manage to bend the world to their terms, as they often do, as limit cases in which persistence is more pronounced than change. Nothing in Sahlins's analytic practice precludes this way of employing his approach.

3. Despite Sahlins's focus on modernization, the relevance of this model of cultural change is not limited to cases in which non-Western cultures come into contact with Western ones. Tuzin's (1997) account of the way the Ilahita Ara-

pesh responded to the growing military prowess of their neighbors the Abelam by adopting the Abelam men's cult, a move that created extensive revision and contradiction in traditional Ilahita understandings of gender relations, provides an excellent example of a similar process at work entirely outside the sphere of Western influence.

4. Although Sahlins does not make this point explicitly, in his first discussion of the ideas that would become his model of modernization he implies it in the course of an analysis of Chinese interest in development (Sahlins 1990).

5. Sahlins regularly speaks of the value of specific categories, but he uses this term in the Saussurian sense to refer to the meaning a term has by virtue of its relations to other terms in a system. It will be clear in what follows that the notion of value I am using here is somewhat different.

6. In Dumont's (e.g., 1986: 249) terms, the fact that I speak of categories and values as different things, rather than conjoining them in a single expression as he does with value-ideas, would bespeak my entanglement in specifically modern notions of the separation between facts and values. For Dumont, all ideas contain values as part of their composition. I do not dispute this point. But it is also clear that some ideas appear within a culture primarily as values and serve to coordinate the relations between other elements. Other ideas, in fact the bulk of ideas, borrow their value components from their relation to those ideas that are primarily values. To take one of Dumont's favorite examples, left and right are ideas whose value component is not primary. Their value derives from the more value-laden idea of the integrity of the body. I distinguish between ideas whose values are secondary or derived (which I call "categories") and those whose value component is primary (which I call "values") because the two kinds of ideas clearly play different roles within culture. This is something Dumont implicitly recognizes in his focus on paramount values, which are values in the sense that I use the term, and the way their evaluative force shapes other value-ideas.

7. I realize that I am here treating in passing social structure as a part of culture rather than as a separate system or entity. In chapter 5 I discuss Urapmin social structure in more detail and lay out on a theoretical level my reasons for treating social structure in this way.

8. I follow Jorgensen (1981b) in using the phonetically more accurate "Telefolmin" to refer to the Telefol people. When I am talking about the place, which in this book I do primarily in discussing its importance as a government and mission center, I retain the official government spelling, Telefomin. When citing from patrol reports throughout the first part of the book, I retain the spellings used in the original sources.

9. The residential situation in this area was actually more complex that I can discuss here, with several hamlets caught in the process of deciding whether to return to an earlier fusion with Makalbel. But for our purposes here, it suffices to recognize Makalbel as the major village in this area.

10. By my census in 1992, there were 43 Urapmin under five years of age (20 male and 23 female), 122 between the ages of six and seventeen (70 male and 52 female), 194 between the ages of eighteen and forty-five (109 male and 85 female) and 37 over forty-six years of age (19 male and 18 female). As the gender

imbalance would lead one to expect, bachelors are a relatively frequent feature of the Urapmin social landscape. But the situation is not as extreme as these numbers might suggest, for there are also quite a few widowers in the population. I was not able to determine reasons for the general gender imbalance, beyond the significance of death during childbirth as a factor in female mortality.

11. In making this statement, I have not included several works focused on missionaries in Papua New Guinea rather than on local appropriations of Christianity (Huber 1988; Langmore 1989).

1. FROM SALT TO THE LAW

1. There are of course exceptions to this observation, perhaps most notably in the cargo cult literature (e.g., Burridge 1960; Lawrence [1964] 1971; Worsley 1968), but it remains the case that until recently it has been a generally accurate one.

2. I find Errington and Gewertz's term "emulation" preferable to the more common "mimesis" for describing the Melanesian situation because it suggests a *conscious* effort to take over white practices, whereas mimesis carries too many connotations of unconscious, even childlike mimicry. Indeed, it may be no accident that so many accounts of mimesis focus on traditions of spirit possession, a practice that itself carries connotations of passivity (Atkinson 1992). I use "incorporation" here to highlight the extent to which the Urapmin wanted to bring whole colonial institutions into their community rather than simply take over certain general styles of action (e.g., cooperation) or possession of specific resources.

3. The Urapmin *min* can be affixed to social category and tribal names, meaning the same thing as the Telefolmin *min*—"person/people of certain named clan/locality" (Healey and Healey 1977: 127). But the Urapmin *min* is also affixed to the generic names of certain types of spirits (e.g., *utungmin, nuk amin*), and so its use to refer to whites does not indicate whether the Urapmin were at that time thinking of whites primarily as humans or as spirits.

4. *Tabalasep* was actually in use in Telefomin proper by the time of the Karius and Champion patrol in Telefomin. It may well be true, however, that the Urapmin did not learn it until later because the power of names is such that people often keep them secret, especially when they refer to beings of extraordinary power.

5. I examined these patrol reports in the National Archives of Papua New Guinea. Reference to reports follows the numbering of reports themselves, thus "2 of 48/49" is the second report for the 1948–49 period. Where I am making a number of serial references to the same report, I give just the page ("sheet") number.

6. Wheatcroft (1976: 50) disputes a claim that he attributes to Cranstone, an early anthropological visitor to the Min area, that warfare between the Urapmin and the Tifalmin ceased by 1950, noting that his own "calculations put the date of cessation of hostilities at approximately 1955, not any earlier." As he does not detail the disputes that took place after 1949, it is impossible for me to check his assertion against incidents reported to me by the Urapmin, none of which they

placed after the beginning of the administration presence. The patrol reports, no doubt not fully reliable on this score, mention no warfare between the Tifalmin and the Urapmin after 1949. The lack of fighting does not mean that tensions did not run high. In his third report Rogers mentions that some Atbalmin had apparently attempted to encourage hostilities by spreading rumors among the Urapmin that the Tifalmin had killed a young Urapmin man (4 of 48/49). In a report from late 1950, West mentions in passing that a "large number of armed Tifalmin natives surrounded camp during night as a result of rumors concerning the purpose of the census emanating from the URAPMIN carriers, who are traditional enemies of the TIFALMIN, but dispersed when reassured about the patrol's motives" (2 of 50/51, p. 4). It is impossible to discern here whether the Urapmin were "egging" (*wiitmolin*—a common cause of Min violence) the Tifalmin into a conflict that would surely be to their detriment, or if they were just sharing their own anxieties about the census. Later in the report, in any case, West reasserts the Administration understanding that "organized tribal warfare . . . seems to have disappeared with the establishment of friendly relationships between the Urapmin and Tifalmin groups" (10). With treachery, ambush, and individual murder playing a large part in Urapmin warfare, incidents surely could have occurred without administration awareness, though I have no evidence to suggest that they did.

7. As I discuss in chapter 5, the Urapmin claim that women have always chosen their own mates. In Urapmin, it was husbands, not fathers, who shot their wives' legs, and they did so when wives tried to leave a marriage they themselves had initiated. A woman who had been shot would stay in the house she shared with her husband while the wound healed. When the wound finally healed, Urapmin say, the woman would be tightly fastened (pas) to her husband.

8. Urapmin people endlessly exchange foodstuffs with each other that neither party needs, having grown their own. So simply having enough of something is not, as the patrol officers thought it was, a reason that the Urapmin would back out of trade relations that were proceeding satisfactorily on social grounds.

9. Nolen's name appears as "Nolan" on the cover sheet of this report and is spelled in both ways in the literature. In the part of the report that he undoubtedly typed himself, his name appears as Nolen, and I use this spelling throughout my discussion.

10. In a carefully observed article on the colonial experience of the Faiwolmin, one of the Southern Min groups whose colonial history differed in some respects from that of the groups around Telefomin, Polier (1995: 264) also emphasizes the important role played by violence and fear in the colonization process.

11. Morren (1981: 54) has noted a lack of rancor on the part of the Mianmin in recounting what they allege was a massacre of their people on the part of Taylor and Black's Hagen-Sepik patrol. Rather, he argues, the Mianmin "were pragmatic and optimistic in pursuit of their developing contact with whites and the rest of the non-Miyanmin world." In the 1960s, he goes on to add, they embraced the white world and "civilization" wholeheartedly. In many respects this

description would apply as well to the Urapmin. However, given Urapmin reluctance to engage distant hurts and anger by speaking emotionally in the present, I think it is also true that one has to attend carefully to any statements of past unhappiness or aggression, no matter how mild. Claims that early contact was "a hard time," or that the patrol officers and police were "wrong" in what they did, despite being extremely understated, represent strong rebukes in the terms of their culture.

12. See Morren (1981: 52) and Poole (1976: 222) for discussions of the strong impression made by the effect of bullets on human bodies among the Mianmin and the Bimin Kuskusmin respectively.

13. Kaunsils had this authority in Urapmin because the village court magistrate system introduced in many other parts of Papua New Guinea was never put in place in the Telefomin area (for accounts of the village court magistrate system, see Scaglion 1990; Westermark 1986). In early 1993, just before I left Urapmin, people had appointed a magistrate-in-training with the understanding that the system would soon be introduced in their area.

2. CHRISTIANITY AND THE COLONIAL TRANSFORMATION
OF REGIONAL RELATIONS

1. Rambo (1993) offers a review of the literature on conversion that evidences both the diversity and the poor integration that beset it.

2. I have not considered the details of Horton's intellectualist account of African conversion here, for it relies on claims about traditional African cosmologies that are not as portable as the broader theoretical background on which they rest. But I should note that in his discussion of the African material, Horton (1971: 102–4) suggests that the cultural content of Christianity and Islam played little role in the conversion process, with converts picking up only those parts of their doctrines that fit with changes that had already occurred in their own cosmologies. His position is subtler than I can convey here, but at times it comes close to begging the question of why people would need to convert for intellectualist reasons if their own cosmologies had already changed sufficiently to explain the new circumstances they found themselves in. Furthermore, to the extent that Horton's argument overlooks, as Gray (1978: 96) puts it, "the possibility that world religions may have introduced completely new concepts to the African religious repertory," I would want to distance myself from it for the same empirical reasons I am led to reject other approaches that minimize the role of Christian doctrine (for another discussion of this aspect of Horton's theory, see Fisher 1973).

3. There are almost certainly other reasons why the land-hungry Telefolmin never overtook the Urapmin. Afek's sacred narrative (weng awem) enjoins the Telefolmin and the Urapmin to be allies in their battles against the Feramin and the Tifalmin respectively. Furthermore, the Urapmin served as a protective buffer between the Telefolmin and the Tifalmin, a much larger group than the Urapmin. Still, one imagines that it was the unique place the Urapmin occupied in the ritual system that made their elimination unthinkable to the Telefolmin.

4. Personal communication from Eytan Bercovitch suggests that at least some other Min groups, in their secret traditions, also assert that their origin is at Wim Tem.

5. Smalley's estimation of the development potential of the Urapmin and their neighbors remains the consensus today in spite of the opening of the Ok Tedi mine to their south. A recent authoritative report notes that most people in the Sandaun (West Sepik) Province in which the Urapmin live "are strongly disadvantaged relative to people in other districts of PNG [Papua New Guinea]. The most disadvantaged people live in the southern mountains in such places as Telefomin. . . . In these areas, large numbers of people are constrained by low potential environments, very low incomes and poor access to services. They have few opportunities to improve their livelihoods" (Hanson et al. 2001: 229). The authors go on to conclude that Telefomin is one of the two "most disadvantaged" districts in Papua New Guinea (304).

6. Haiden (heathen) is the Tok Pisin term the Urapmin use to refer to non-Christians. I retain it here to conform to their usage, though they are by and large more tolerant of non-Christians than the English connotations of the term suggest.

7. Polier (1995: 266 ff.) discusses in detail the case of a Faiwolmin boy who, frightened during an initiation, ran away and took shelter with the government officers, eventually becoming an important liaison between his people and the administration and Catholic mission. In less dramatic terms, many of the early mission students from Urapmin made a similar choice.

8. Knamti was speaking Tok Pisin when he told me this. In Urapmin, which he would have spoken to his brother in the 1960s, sibling terms express relations of relative age. Thus Knamti would have said "you are my *older brother [fik]*" in the statement he is reporting.

9. The village book actually suggests that two men had gone to Rabaul to work in 1959. I believe one of these men remained in Rabaul. The other did return and then went out again with the 1965 group. The larger 1965 group, in any case, figures more importantly in Urapmin history.

10. I am not arguing that these men may not have also had a variety of other motives for opting out of the initiation system. What is clear, however, is that their publicly meaningful motive was one expressed in Christian terms. It is the fact that Christianity had become an "official" motive in this way that is important here.

11. I present another, similar life history in Robbins 1998a: 190–91.

3. REVIVAL, SECOND-STAGE CONVERSION, AND THE LOCALIZATION OF THE URAPMIN CHURCH

1. Morren (1986: 302) argues a related point for the Min region as a whole, and Bays (1993: 175) contends that the localization of religious authority is a general feature of revivals in "non-Western cultures." Smith (1957: 80) suggests that mid-nineteenth-century revivalism in the United States had a similar effect of expanding "lay participation and control" in many Protestant churches.

2. The revival these men told Diyos about was both an important one in the

long revival history of the South Sea Evangelical Church (SSEC) of the Solomon Islands (Burt 1994: 241) and one that influenced not only the Min revival but also many of the other revivals of the 1970s and 1980s in Melanesia (Barr 1983b: 112). I discuss the influence of the SSEC on the Min and other revivals in more detail in Robbins 1998a: 223–26.

3. I discuss these visions and Diyos's life history in greater detail in Robbins 1998a: 200–240.

4. The last few cohorts of Urapmin to train for pastoral and evangelical roles outside of Urapmin would be educated at Diyos's college. The Urapmin view it as the most rigorous of the schools any of them attended and accord its graduates great respect.

5. I consider Diyos's sermon on this story and the way it framed the situation at the college by acting as a "living myth" (Young 1983) in Robbins 1998a: 229–37.

6. Diyos's statement that revival broke out "all over the land of the Min people" accords well with Jorgensen's (1996) claim that the Min understood the revival in regional terms and that this understanding was important in consolidating their regional identity. It should be noted, however, that Diyos's account of the places the revival reached during these early days may not be correct in all of its specifics. I thank Mike Wesch, who notes that a revival did not occur in Tumobil until 1985, for alerting me to this point.

7. These trances are different from those that people who are not Spirit women go into when possessed by the Holy Spirit. Only Spirit women see pictures and are able to reveal hidden knowledge and learn what will happen in the future.

8. In the past, men who were known as "diviners" (usong tanum) played a similar role in healing, though they did not actually see the spirits or become possessed by any supermundane agency. There was traditionally no tradition of possession among men or women in Urapmin and no important "religious" role for women in the healing process.

9. Barth's account of Baktaman epistemology was extended to other Min groups and considerably enriched by others, including Jorgensen (1981b), Bercovitch (1989), and Poole (1976).

4. CONTEMPORARY URAPMIN IN MILLENNIAL TIME AND SPACE

1. The works that have shaped my discussion of time include Carr 1986, 1991; Kermode 1996; Ricoeur 1981, 1984; White 1987. For the narrative construction of space I have relied on discussions of narrative and nationalism (Bhabha 1990; Borneman 1992; Foster 1995a; Gupta 1992). Bakhtin's (1981) notion of the chronotope has also influenced my attempt to link the narrative constructions of time and space in a single account. I discuss these sources and my reading of them in more detail in Robbins 1998c, 2001c.

2. This "someone" is also at times called simply "a man" or a "wild animal" (wel abus) from the Tok Pisin Bible's translation of "beast." At other times, the Urapmin do not talk of a single figure at all but refer instead only to the rise of "a new government."

3. In orthodox Dispensational theology (see below), God's judgment takes place only after the rapture and millennium that follows it. The Urapmin, however, tend to run the rapture and God's judgment together, imagining that they are essentially a single event.

4. I discuss the distinction between heightened and everyday millennialism and its role in studies of millenarianism more fully in Robbins 2001c.

5. Those interested either in the history of Dispensational doctrine or in the arguments offered by Dispensationalists to support the positions I am about to review should consult Boone 1989; Boyer 1992; Brummett 1991; Harding 1994; Weber 1987.

6. This point is strikingly illustrated between pages 5 and 6 of Larkin's (1920) book.

7. The notion of an episodic view of time comes from Gellner (1964). McDowell (1985, 1988) and Errington (1974) have put it to use in their discussions of cargo cult movements, arguing that it describes an indigenous Melanesian conception of time and change. I argue elsewhere (Robbins 2001c) that this claim does not fit the Urapmin case. More broadly, it seems quite possible that less complex episodic constructions of time elsewhere in Melanesia are not indigenous but have instead been influenced by experiences of contact and colonialism and by encounters with Christian ideas (cf. Thomas 1994).

8. Speakers who believe on the basis of world news that the last days have begun also use this phrase to mark the break between the recent, Christian past and the present final age (see Jimi's speech reported below for an example). It serves, then, as something of an all-purpose episodic marker.

9. Many scholars have argued that nationalism is weak in Papua New Guinea (e.g., Clark 1997; Jacobson 1995; Kelly 1995; Worsley 1996). I discuss the theoretical import of the Urapmin case as regards this literature more fully in Robbins 1998c.

10. Perhaps the only early studies to have given serious consideration to the kinds of "racial" ideas I discuss here were the early studies of cargo cults by Burridge (1960) and Lawrence ([1964] 1971). This is not the place to consider the usefulness of the Western term "race" to discuss Melanesian ideas; I rely on it here not only as a heuristic but also to remind readers of the colonial background of these ideas. We badly need a study of how Australian racial ideologies (and where relevant those of the earlier colonizers) were conveyed to Melanesians. For too long, we have assumed that the black/white contrasts drawn by Melanesians were based solely on their "observations" of on the one hand differences in skin color and on the other the material and technological superiority of the colonizers. It strikes me as far more likely that European racist ideas helped to shape Melanesians' "observations" into the elaborate racial schemes we currently find among them. Urapmin stories of how Australian government officers berated them by telling them that their ancestors were cassowaries and wild pigs give a glimpse of the sorts of colonial practices that have surely influenced the developing Melanesian racial consciousness.

11. For works that suggest that the Urapmin sense of black inferiority exists in many Melanesian societies, see Kulick 1992; Lattas 1992; Smith 1994; Trompf 1994. In an interesting recent article, Wood (1995), while presenting

some evidence of ideas of inferiority similar to those I discuss here (e.g., Wood 1995: 33), argues that the Kamula have largely been able to "incorporate" whites by bringing them into their domain and understanding some of them as their own dead reincarnated.

12. While their relationships to Jesus are extremely important to Urapmin, it is also true that he is a very distant figure when compared with the Holy Spirit and with God, both of whom are "colorless." It is the Holy Spirit that possesses the Urapmin, physically cleanses away their sins, and gives them signs of the future. God too, constantly addressed as "father" (a role that for the Urapmin symbolizes care and protection) is a very vivid, relationally present figure with whom one makes contact daily through prayer. In contrast, the Urapmin rarely address Jesus directly or expect to have contact with him before his Second Coming. Urapmin have theological reasons for treating these different figures as they do: God is the all-powerful creator who sent the Holy Spirit as a "replacement" (senis) for Jesus when the latter could no longer communicate directly with humans. Yet while this theological understanding accounts for the roles played by the three figures of the Trinity in Urapmin life, it is tempting to interpret Jesus' distance as also following from his whiteness. As much as Urapmin want meaningful relations with whites, they have also repeatedly experienced the limits of those relations, and these limits must influence the kinds of connection they can imagine themselves having with the white Jesus. This point does not vitiate my argument in this paragraph that Jesus is by far the most available and solicitous white person the Urapmin have "met." Instead, I raise it here to demonstrate again the mundane sense in which Jesus is white: as is the case with other whites, there are limits to the relationships the Urapmin can form with him.

13. There are Urapmin and Tok Pisin words for "friend" (dup, dufin, poroman, pren) that people sometimes use to describe their relationship to Jesus, especially when preaching. Yet the Tok Pisin word that comes closest to carrying the sense of the English "friend" I am evoking here is actually bilip, the word for "belief." By "belief" in Jesus, Urapmin refer to their confidence that he will deliver to them what he has promised to give them in return for their acts of fidelity to him. That is, belief is not itself what is given,but is rather a faith that what is given (primarily obedience) will be reciprocated. In this sense, what the Urapmin believe is that Jesus will repay their friendship along the kinds of reciprocal lines the Urapmin use to repay each others' friendship. Other whites often ignore their obligations in these matters.

14. I discuss the theme of self-control in greater detail in chapter 6.

5. WILLFULNESS, LAWFULNESS, AND URAPMIN MORALITY

1. "To remember," another cognitive process, similarly appears as a verb with aget as its subject (aget funang).

2. Urapmin claim that their marriages have always been initiated by women expressing their wills. Jorgensen (1993: 67–68) notes that before the colonial period, Telefol parents, in an effort to balance marriages as sister exchanges, would name potential suitors for their daughters. It was not until the colonial

period that the rule of <u>laik bilong meri</u> ("what the woman wants") was insti-
tuted in Telefomin (Jorgensen 1993: 68). In the Urapmin case, the existence of
ritualized and highly coded ways for women to reveal their will combined with
discussions with older people about their marital histories indicate unambiguously that the central place of the women's wills in the making of marriages predates the imposition of colonial rule.

3. Throughout this discussion, I use the phrases "new relationships" and
"the creation of relationships" to indicate not only the creation of relationships
ex nihilo, as when a woman calls the name of a man, but also the transformation of existing relationships from a dormant to an active state (as when, for example, brothers who have not lived or worked together for years begin to make
a garden together).

4. I discuss the Urapmin case in relation to Godelier's (1986) distinction between big men and great men more fully in Robbins forthcoming.

5. I discuss these ideas and also the anger removal rituals I am about to mention more fully in chapter 7.

6. Two of the contemporary big men are brothers who live next to each
other. Their followers might be said to have two big men, but in fact the brothers function as a unit. No one follows only one of them, and hence neither of
them has followers of his own who are not also followers of the other.

7. Given that living with or near a big man is an important part of being his
follower, this practice of dual residence might seem to contradict the claim that
each person has only one big man. In the cases of dual residence I know of, however, one of the residences has been in a village with no big man of its own.

8. I once made this point in conversation with Dan Jorgensen, who worked
with the neighboring Telefolmin. He thought that for the Telefolmin <u>lukautim</u>
and <u>bosim</u> were not quite synonyms. To clinch his point, he said that although
Telefolmin, like Urapmin, use a cognate of *tiinmolin* as the verb describing what
children do for elderly parents, he could not imagine them saying children <u>bosim</u>
rather than <u>lukautim</u> their parents. In Urapmin, however, I have heard precisely
this usage, "em i bosim momapopa bilong en."

9. Deaths, except those of infants, are never blamed on the spirits. Instead,
they are seen as caused by sorcerers from neighboring groups.

10. The one exception to this generalization involves what seems to have
been a quite standardized practice by which men sometimes shared morsels of
food from men's feasts with women and children to whom they were taboo (see
also Whitehead 2000). But this practice seems to have been traditional in its own
right, and in participating in it, it is not clear that men saw themselves explicitly
as violating a taboo. In fact, to some this practice was seen as in itself moral. As
I was told several times, breaking this one "taboo" was precisely what "good
men" did.

6. DESIRE AND ITS DISCONTENTS

1. Aunger (1996: 213) finds Christians preaching a similar message in the
Ituri forest of Zaire.

2. It is worth emphasizing that when Christianity enjoins the Urapmin to

disregard the taboos, it does not understand itself to be promoting willfulness. To do this would be to contradict the thoroughly negative evaluation of the will that is at its center. It rather sees itself as demanding fidelity to the laws of God. When the Urapmin view taboo abrogation from the point of view of their traditional understandings of such matters, however, they cannot help but construe it as willful.

3. It is common for the person who is preaching either to read out loud or to have others read out loud the Bible verses on which he (or very rarely she) will be preaching. In this case, for the reader's convenience, I have indicated where the verse is read in the transcript but have given it, along with my English translation of the Tok Pisin text, just before the sermon itself.

4. This text is based on a transcript made from a tape recording with the help of several Urapmin. I have removed from the text two kinds of repetition: false starts, the inclusion of which would make the text far more difficult to read; and the repetition of Tomi's saying something first in Tok Pisin (the language of the Bible) and then in Urap. Sermons that stay close to the text, as does Tomi's, do a lot of this running translation. To include such material would give a false sense of emphasis at certain points. Wherever repetition is being used for emphasis, I have left it in the text. I use brackets to enclose alternate translations or added words that make the text easier to follow. Ellipses are used to indicate pauses. Each paragraph is numbered for ease of reference.

5. See Fung 1988: 267 for a discussion of the meaning of the Greek word *makrothymia* that accords with the Tok Pisin Bible's translation of this virtue as "larim ol i rongim yumi" (leaving those who wrong us alone).

6. Although it cannot count as a full explanation of why the Urapmin favor peacefulness over these other two inner states in their ethical thinking, it is worth noting that as they conceptualize them, both concern and happiness are transitive states that relate one to others (the Urapmin rarely speak of happiness [ifal tabemin], and when they do it is usually in constructions that refer to "giving" happiness to someone else). Peacefulness, by contrast, is understood as a nontransitive state of a person's heart.

7. One might imagine that Urapmin Christianity does enjoin people to follow their own wills in at least one situation—when their will is to follow God's will. Although such a construction would perhaps be logical within their Christian thinking, it is not one that they make. They have a variety of ways of talking about how one comes to follow God's will: most important, one does so by having the Holy Spirit in one's heart; one can also do so by having the "good thinking" that the Spirit gives; or one can make room for it to happen by "suppressing your will" *(daunim laik bilong yu yet)*. Note, however, that none of these ways of construing the process of following God's will frame it explicitly as something that is brought about by a positive use of the human will. While one might want to interpret the suppression of the will as a case of using the will positively in the service of its own elimination, the very fact that the Urapmin do not think of it in this way indicates the extent to which their Christian thinking has stripped the will of any positive function.

8. In chapter 4 I discussed the thread of world rejection that runs throughout Urapmin Christianity. We can see now that this thread is woven of two

strands. One is the apocalyptic telos of the Christian life, as I discussed it in that chapter. The second stems from Christian morality's refusal to brook any compromise with the demands of social life; by making social life impossible, Christian ethics supports its rejection. I take up world rejection again in chapter 8.

9. The institution of council work, whereby people are required to work on local civic projects, is understood to have government backing, but it is administered locally and can be modified to suit local needs.

7. RITUALS OF REDEMPTION AND TECHNOLOGIES OF THE SELF

1. Stringer (1999: 141 ff.) discusses the general difficulty of identifying the order in services held by charismatic-type churches.

2. The Urapmin term for both "outside" and "inside" is the same. It is *tam* (see also Healey and Healey 1977). There is important conceptual ground related to this that turns on the way the full/empty opposition seems to encompass that between inside and outside in Urapmin thought. I do not, however, have space to consider this issue here. In Urapmin Christianity, the Tok Pisin terms insait and autsait are regularly used, and it is these I am referring to throughout this chapter.

3. The Sumbanese Protestants studied by Keane (2002: 77) explain that they close their eyes in prayer because prayer is supposed to come from the inside of the person. Although they might well agree with this interpretation if it were presented to them, the Urapmin did not offer it.

4. Although the Christianity of the Gebusi whom he studies is somewhat different from that of the Urapmin, Knauft's (2002: 146) observation that their church services are "a microcosm of patient waiting, deference, and self-denial" bears comparison with my point here.

5. The pastor performing this prayer refers throughout to "the two of us," as if he were praying not only for the penitent but also for himself. This is not common in confession prayers. I asked the pastor why he did this, and he responded, "It is not that she is a sinner and I am clean, both of us are sinners." In all contexts, those who pray are generally careful to remind God that they see themselves as sinners and do not have the hubris to imagine that they have some special claim to his attention. This seems to be part of the pastor's motive for including himself here. Equally important, I think, is the fact that the pastor is here praying for a woman who is very much his peer in age. His inclusive language seems to index his identification with her.

6. The new contract in question refers in Urapmin usage not to God's offer, through Jesus, of a new covenant to all humanity, different from his previous one with the Jewish people, but rather to the renewal of the contract each Urapmin has with him.

7. The prominence of the new contract theme in the Urapmin practice of communion stands out for the way it eclipses the theme of sacrifice so prevalent in the communion rites of other Christians. Neither Jesus' sacrifice nor the congregation's (for collection is taken at communion services to pay for the cherry-flavored drink mix that must be bought in Telefomin) is an important theme of the service. The new contract theme also completely overshadows any emphasis

on communion between members of the church: the bond in question is between the individual and God. For comparative work on the meaning of communion, see Bossy 1983; Hastings 2000.

8. MILLENNIALISM AND THE CONTEST OF VALUES

1. I have elsewhere documented the following account of Dumont, and discussed the way the notion of relationalism draws on his work, through a close reading of his major writings (Robbins 1994). Instead of reproducing the documentation (and length) of that article here, I will content myself with simply laying out those of its conclusions that bear on my present argument. Citations to that article give page references for those who are interested in a step-by-step development of various parts of the argument.

2. I write of "Melanesian cultures" in general in this and the next few paragraphs. Both Dumont and the Melanesianists who have most inspired this part of my argument (Wagner [1975] 1981; Gregory 1982; Strathern 1988) argue in these broad terms when their primary goal is to develop theoretical constructions. Although it would be well worth explicitly defending the advantages of phrasing an argument in these terms (and Strathern [1988] does this to some extent), to do so here would take me too far off course. I would, however, ask those who find such broadly framed arguments indigestible to read the next few paragraphs purely for their conceptual content and then judge the ethnographic value of their arguments in the present context only when I come to apply them to the Urapmin case (i.e., in effect substitute "Urapmin" for "Melanesia" in the next few paragraphs).

3. The Tok Pisin translation has "Bikpela, bikpela" here, which in Urapmin cannot refer to a worldly social status in the way that "Lord" (in the King James Version) or "Sir" (the New English Bible) do. Urapmin can only read "Bikpela" as "God" or as unclear (the fact that the second use switches to lowercase would not be significant for Urapmin). In this context, the reading of it as "God" only serves to reinforce the apocalyptic message of the parable, since, as the Urapmin understand it, it is God who will refuse to open the heavenly door for those who are damned in the last days.

4. With the days of plantation contracts long past, people never travel to places where they will not be in relationships when they arrive (e.g., Tabubil, where there are other Urapmin living, or other Min areas where histories of intermarriage allow them to trace kinship links). But because of the cost of tickets, they often fly without any relatives to accompany them, in planes piloted by expatriates who are completely outside their system of relationships. It is thus, I imagine, in transit that people most nearly experience themselves as individuals or, as they say, "one piece" (wan pis).

5. Knauft's (2002: 147, 149, 158, 164) quotation from a Gebusi sermon and his discussion of Gebusi Christianity indicate that they too have a sophisticated grasp of Christian individualism very much like that of the Urapmin. Although this is not the place to elaborate on this point, one wonders whether individualism stands out so clearly to people like the Urapmin and the Gebusi because it squares so poorly with their traditional ideas. We tend to imagine that people

are most likely to grasp new ideas that are similar to ones they already have, but this case (and in some sense the elaboration of the adoption model throughout this book) indicates that the opposite might also be true.

6. To some extent, the terminological divergence evident here is a simple product of the lack of wide discussion of these terms. But beyond that, it is also a result of the authors' different determinations of the nominal (Healy, Heath and Merlan) or pronominal (Oates and Oates) status of the terms in the languages they study. Matters become even more complex when we factor in Phyllis Healey's (1965: 16 ff., 51 n.12) claim, published several years after Alan Healey's article, that the Telefol terms are not in fact nouns but of a class of quantifiers she calls "kin quantifiers." My own sense of the Urap terms is that they function as nouns, though my studies of the language are not as thorough as the Healeys' studies of Telefol. In any case, the following argument does not hinge on our assignment of the terms to a particular category.

7. This discussion of Urapmin relational terms is similar in spirit to other recent accounts by Sahlins (1985), Merlan and Rumsey (1991), and, in particular, Rumsey (1998, 2000) that relate linguistic usages to the construction and reproduction of social ontologies. I should also add that one could provide evidence of Urapmin relationalism by looking at other of their person-reference practices (e.g., the pervasive use of teknonymy and the prevalence of kin-term constructions that specify explicitly the prior relations that produced a relation in question, as in the use of *en man, neng man* ["older sister's child, younger sister's child"] to refer to parallel cousins). I focus on their use of relational terms here because of the important role these terms play in Urapmin conceptualizations of their church. Stasch (2002) considers a host of related issues in his discussion of what he calls "dyad-centric personhood" among another Melanesian group.

8. The Urapmin point out that while the Telefolmin distinguish these sibling groups in terms of whether they are single or mixed sex, they themselves do not (see Healey 1965: 17).

9. This is the one term we might take to be triadic, since it links at least three people and sometimes involves three relationships: husband and wife, mother and child, father and child.

10. For a very different, cognitive psychological rather than cultural analysis of an oscillation that, at least in its surface features, is very similar, see Whitehouse 1995.

11. There is a bit of individualist thinking incorporated even into the Spirit disko. Those women who are known as Spirit women are very often the first to become possessed at Spirit diskos. If only these women become possessed, the Urapmin consider a Spirit disko a failure. Just as the pastor cannot save the whole community through his actions, so too the Spirit woman cannot prove its salvation through her possession. However, even if only a few people who are not Spirit women do become possessed, people consider the dances to have been successful.

12. My indebtedness to Weber (1946) extends beyond this section's titular reference. As it appears in this section, however, it is mediated through Dumont's work. As I suggested in the introduction, I have for some time thought

that the strongest account of Dumont's importance would be one that emphasized his singular accomplishment in bringing together the best of the French tradition (Mauss, of course, but also Durkheim and Lévi-Strauss) with a deep appreciation of Weber's theories of value and of the nature of the conflicts that arise between value spheres. A full discussion of this point, however, is something for another venue.

CONCLUSION

1. The exact nature of Paul's arguments concerning the difference between the Christian and the Jewish moral systems is currently a topic of extensive debate (see Westerholm 1988 for a book-length review and Thielman 1994 for a shorter, less detailed but more recent account). In particular, many have come to question the veracity of Luther's reading of Paul as a proponent of a straightforward doctrine of justification by faith alone. Regardless of where one comes down on these debates, however, it is clear on any reading of Paul that he thinks that the Christian moral system is different in some way from the Jewish one. This is all that is required by my argument. More to the point, perhaps, is that the bulk of Protestant missionaries through history have probably retailed some version of the strong Lutheran argument to those they have proselytized.

2. As Mason (2000: 41) notes, most lay Protestants now subscribe to broadly Arminian assumptions about the possibility of salvation for all and the role of the individual believer in making himself or herself worthy of salvation through his or her faith. The revivalist tradition I am singling out here most stands apart from the general run of Arminian churches for the role it gives to the Holy Spirit and to ecstatic experience.

3. Meyer (2001: 28), whose work on Ghanaian Pentecostalism could have been included here as another case that bears out the main lines of this analysis, argues that in contemporary Ghana Pentecostalism's appeal is based on the way it allows people to entertain elaborate fantasies about the liberations modernity promises to them while also offering to help them avoid the dangers of this liberation through ritual practice and, although she does not spell this point out as fully, the provision of a moral code attuned to the dangers of these temptations. We find here once again that Pentecostalism appeals by allowing people some experience of liberation while also preaching extreme self-control. Comaroff (1985: 132–35), in a historical account, discusses the Methodist roots of the revivalist emphasis on both "emotionalism" and "repression" that I am highlighting here.

4. While it deserves a more substantial critique than I can give it here, it is worth noting that Ferguson's (1999) claim that in many situations we need to abandon the culture concept in favor of one of identity strikes me as raising the same problems as Wicker's approach. The richness of Ferguson's work, I would argue, is a product of the extent to which he ignores his own injunction and deploys without theorizing or calling attention to them many of the basic techniques of cultural analysis.

References

PATROL REPORTS CONSULTED

All of these patrol reports are from Telefomin, Sepik District. They are held in the National Archives of Papua New Guinea, Waigani. Not all of these reports concern patrols to the Urapmin; some are listed because they address issues I discuss in this book. I have listed only those reports that I have drawn on directly in writing this book.

NUMBER AND YEAR	DATE PATROL BEGAN	PATROL CONDUCTED BY
1 of 1948/49	January 1, 1949	a/ADO D. Clifton-Bassett
2 of 1948/49	March 3, 1949	PO J. M. Rogers
3 of 1948/49	April 4, 1949	PO J. M. Rogers
4 of 1948/49	June 3, 1949	PO J. M. Rogers
1 of 1949/50	October 25, 1949	a/ADO D. Clifton-Bassett
2 of 1950/51	August 7, 1950	PO H. W. West
1 of 1951/52	August 3, 1951	PO L. J. Doolan
2 of 1951/52	February 5, 1952	PO L. T. Nolen
3 of 1951/52	May 23, 1952	CPO J. A. Gauci
2 of 1952/53	February 2, 1953	CPO K. Graham
3 of 1952/53	April 14, 1953	PO L. T. Nolen

(Continued)

NUMBER AND YEAR	DATE PATROL BEGAN	PATROL CONDUCTED BY
Special Report	June 1954	ADO F. D. Jones
1 of 1955/56	July 18, 1955	CPO N. J. Grant
7 of 1955/56	May 29, 1956	PO G. F. Booth
1 of 1956/57	August 29, 1956	PO G. F. Booth
3 of 1956/57	November 28, 1956	PO G. F. Booth
5 of 1956/57	April 4, 1957	PO G. F. Booth
1 of 1957/58	July 7, 1957	a/ADO R. T. Neville
2 of 1957/58	August 9, 1957	PO G. F. Booth
5 of 1957/58	April 22, 1958	a/ADO R. Aisbett
6 of 1957/58	May 23, 1958	a/ADO R. Aisbett
3 of 1958/59	November 19, 1958	a/ADO R. Aisbett
5 of 1958/59	March 10, 1959	a/ADO R. Aisbett
1 of 1959/60	August 27, 1959	ADO W. T. Brown
2 of 1959/60	September 21, 1959	ADO W. T. Brown
3 of 1959/60	October 20, 1960	ADO W. T. Brown
5 of 1959/60	April 2, 1960	ADO W. T. Brown
8 of 1959/60	June 24, 1960	ADO W. T. Brown
1 of 1960/61	July 8, 1960	PO J. F. Tierney
4 of 1960/61	January 20, 1961	a/ADO R. A. Calcutt
6 of 1960/61	February 20, 1961	a/ADO R. A. Calcutt
6 of 1961/62	January 11, 1962	PO J. F. Tierney
9 of 1961/62	June 6, 1962	PO J .P. Kelly
4 of 1962/63	October 4, 1962	PO J. P. Kelly
11 of 1962/63	May 22, 1963	CPO M. Briar
5 of 1963/64	January 31, 1964	CPO K. N. J. Allen
6 of 1963/64	February 14, 1964	CPO K. N. J. Allen
2 of 1964/65	October 1, 1964	ADO J. R. Cochrane
3 of 1964/65	October 27, 1964	CDO M. J. Edgar
5 of 1964/65	January 15, 1965	PO H. W. Gill
8 of 1964/65	April 27, 1965	PO H. W. Gill
2 of 1965/66	August 10, 1965	CPO I. F. S. Smalley
3 of 1967/68	February 26, 1968	PO M. J. Lowe
2 of 1968/69	September 5, 1968	LGA G. Bundari
3 of 1968/69	October 25, 1968	CPO K. E. Murphy

5 of 1968/69	January 28, 1969	ADO B. M. Fischer
6 of 1968/69	March 5, 1969	LGA G. Bundari
1 of 1969/70	July 21, 1969	LGA G. Bundari
2 of 1969/70	July 29, 1969	PO K. S. Black
3 of 1969/70	September 11, 1969	AFO H. Wura
4 of 1969/70	December 15, 1969	ADO B. M. Fischer
6 of 1969/70	February 16, 1970	PO K. S. Black
7 of 1969/70	February 19, 1970	ADO B. M. Fischer
8 of 1969/70	March 23, 1970	ADO B. M. Fischer
9 of 1969/70	June 18, 1970	ADC K. R. Kelly
1 of 1970/71	August 10, 1970	PO N. L. Mitchell
2 of 1970/71	August 25, 1970	PO K. S. Black
5 of 1970/71	December 10, 1970	ADO K. R. Kelly
9 of 1970/71	March 10, 1971	PO G. M. Henke
10 of 1970/71	March 5, 1971	PO K. S. Black
11 of 1970/71	March 5, 1971	APO B. M. Vaninara
12 of 1970/71	March 21, 1971	PO K. S. Black
6 of 1971/72	June 22, 1972	PO P. Sireh
8 of 1972/73	March 7, 1973	PO H. H. Sauka
7 of 1973/74	January 22, 1974	APO S. Ebuc

WORKS CITED

Abercrombie, Nicholas, Stephen Hill, and Bryan S. Turner
    1986 *Sovereign Individuals of Capitalism.* London: Allen & Unwin.

Akin, David
    1999 "Compensation and the Melanesian State: Why the Kwaio Keep Claiming." *Contemporary Pacific* 11(1): 35–67.

Amselle, Jean-Loup
    1998 *Mestizo Logics: Anthropology of Identity in Africa and Elsewhere.* Trans. Claudia Royal. Stanford: Stanford University Press.

Anderson, Benedict
    [1983] 1991 *Imagined Communities: Reflections on the Origin and Spread of Nationalism.* London: Verso.

Anonymous
    1978 *Nupela Testamen na Ol Sam.* Port Moresby: Bible Society of Papua New Guinea.

Appadurai, Arjun
    1996 *Modernity at Large: Cultural Dimensions of Globalization.* Minneapolis: University of Minnesota Press.

Aragon, Lorraine V.
1996 "Twisting the Gift: Translating Precolonial into Colonial Exchanges in Central Sulawsi, Indonesia." *American Ethnologist* 23(1): 43–60.
Aristotle
1980 *The Nicomachean Ethics*. Trans. David Ross. Oxford: Oxford University Press.
Atkinson, Jane Monnig
1992 "Shamanisms Today." *Annual Review of Anthropology* 21: 307–30.
Aunger, Robert
1996 "Acculturation and the Persistence of Indigenous Food Avoidances in the Ituri Forest, Zaire." *Human Organization* 55(2): 206–18.
Austin-Broos, Diane J.
1997 *Jamaica Genesis: Religion and the Politics of Moral Orders*. Chicago: University of Chicago Press.
Bakhtin, M. M.
1981 *The Dialogic Imagination*. Trans. Caryl Emerson and Michael Holquist. Austin: University of Texas Press.
Barker, John, ed.
1990a *Christianity in Oceania: Ethnographic Perspectives*. Lanham, Md.: University Press of America.
Barker, John
1990b "Mission Station and Village: Religious Practice and Representations in Maisin Society." In *Christianity in Oceania: Ethnographic Perspectives*, ed. J. Barker, 173–96. Lanham, Md.: University Press of America.
1992 "Christianity in Western Melanesian Ethnography." In *History and Tradition in Melanesian Anthropology*, ed. J. G. Carrier, 144–73. Berkeley: University of California Press.
1993 "'We are Ekelesia': Conversion in Uiaku, Papua New Guinea." In *Conversion to Christianity: Historical and Anthropological Perspectives on a Great Transformation*, ed. R. W. Hefner, 199–230. Berkeley: University of California Press.
Barnes, John A.
1962 "African Models in the New Guinea Highlands." *Man* 62(2): 5–9.
Barr, John
1983a "Spiritistic Tendencies in Melanesia." In *Religious Movements in Melanesia Today*, ed. W. Flannery, 1–34. Garoka: Melanesian Institute.
1983b "A Survey of Ecstatic Phenomena and 'Holy Spirit Movements' in Melanesia." *Oceania* 54(2): 109–32.
Barth, Fredrik
1975 *Ritual and Knowledge among the Baktaman of New Guinea*. New Haven: Yale University Press.
1987 *Cosmologies in the Making: A Generative Approach to Cultural Variation in Inner New Guinea*. Cambridge: Cambridge University Press.

Bashkow, Ira R.

1999 "'Whitemen' in the Moral World of the Orokaiva of Papua New Guinea." Ph.D. dissertation, University of Chicago.

Battistella, Edwin L.

1990 *Markedness: The Evaluative Superstructure of Language*. Albany: State University of New York Press.

Bays, Daniel H.

1993 "Christian Revivals in China, 1900–1937." In *Modern Christian Revivals,* ed. E. L. Blumhofer and R. Balmer, 161–79. Urbana: University of Illinois Press.

Bennett, Keith, and Lindsay Smith

1983 "A Revival Movement among the Telefomin Baptist Churches." In *Religious Movements in Melanesia: A Selection of Case Studies,* ed. W. Flannery, 127–40. Goroka: Melanesian Institute for Pastoral and Socio-Economic Service.

Bercovitch, Eytan

1989 "Disclosure and Concealment: A Study of Secrecy among the Nalumin People of Papua New Guinea." Ph.D. dissertation, Stanford University.

1994 "The Agent in the Gift: Hidden Exchange in Inner New Guinea." *Cultural Anthropology* 9(4): 498–536.

Bhabha, Homi K.

1990 "DissemiNation: Time Narrative, and the Margins of the Modern Nation." In *Nation and Narration,* ed. H. K. Bhabha, 291–322. London: Routledge.

1994 *The Location of Culture*. London: Routledge.

Biersack, Aletta

1980 "The Hidden God: Communication, Cosmology, and Cybernetics among a Melanesian People." Ph.D. dissertation, University of Michigan.

Birken, Lawrence

1988 *Consuming Desire: Sexual Science and the Emergence of a Culture of Abundance, 1871–1914*. Ithaca: Cornell University Press.

Blumhofer, Edith L.

1988 "Dowie, John Alexander." In *Dictionary of Pentecostal and Charismatic Movements,* ed. S. M. Burgess and G. B. McGee, 248–49. Grand Rapids: Regency.

Blumhofer, Edith L., and Randall Balmer

1993 "Introduction." In *Modern Christian Revivals,* ed. E. L. Blumhofer and R. Balmer, xi–xvi. Urbana: University of Illinois Press.

Boone, Kathleen C.

1989 *The Bible Tells Them So: The Discourse of Protestant Fundamentalism*. Albany: State University of New York Press.

Borneman, John

1992 "State, Territory, and Identity Formation in the Postwar Berlins, 1945–1989." *Cultural Anthropology* 7(1): 45–62.

Bossy, John
　1983 "The Mass as a Social Institution: 1200–1700." *Past and Present* 100: 29–61.
Bourdieu, Pierre
　1977 *Outline of a Theory of Practice.* Trans. Richard Nice. Cambridge: Cambridge University Press.
Boyer, Paul
　1992 *When Time Shall Be No More: Prophecy Belief in Modern American Culture.* Cambridge, Mass.: Harvard University Press.
Brightman, Robert
　1995 "Forget Culture: Replacement, Transcendence, Relexification." *Cultural Anthropology* 10(4): 509–46.
Brison, Karen
　1995 "Changing Constructions of Masculinity in a Sepik Society." *Ethnology* 34(3): 325–55.
Brown, Paula
　1995 *Beyond a Mountain Valley: The Simbu of Papua New Guinea.* Honolulu: University of Hawai'i Press.
Brubaker, Rogers
　1984 *The Limits of Rationality: An Essay on the Social and Moral Thought of Max Weber.* London: Routledge.
Brumbaugh, Robert
　1980 "A Secret Cult in the West Sepik Highlands." Ph.D. dissertation, State University of New York at Stony Brook.
　1990 "'Afek Sang'": The Old Woman's Legacy to the Mountain-Ok." In *Children of Afek: Tradition and Change Among the Mountain-Ok of Central New Guinea,* ed. B. Craig and D. Hyndman, 54–87. Oceania Monograph 40. Sydney: University of Sydney.
Brummett, Barry
　1991 *Contemporary Apocalyptic Rhetoric.* New York: Praeger.
Brusco, Elizabeth E.
　1995 *The Reformation of Machismo: Evangelical Conversion and Gender in Colombia.* Austin: University of Texas Press.
Burridge, Kenelm
　1960 *Mambu: A Study of Melanesian Cargo Movements and Their Social and Ideological Background.* New York: Harper and Row.
　1975 "The Melanesian Manager." In *Studies in Social Anthropology,* ed. J. H. M. Beattie and R. G. Lienhardt, 86–104. Oxford: Clarendon Press.
　1979 *Someone, No One: An Essay on Individuality.* Princeton: Princeton University Press.
　1987 "Revival and Renewal." In *The Encyclopedia of Religion,* ed. M. Eliade, 12:368–74. New York: Macmillan.
Burt, Ben
　1994 *Tradition and Christianity: The Colonial Transformation of a Solomon Islands Society.* Chur, Switzerland: Harwood Academic Press.

Buss, Andreas
2000 "The Evolution of Western Individualism." *Religion* 30(1): 1–25.

Campbell, Stuart
1938 "The Country between the Headwaters of the Fly and Sepik Rivers in New Guinea." *Geographical Journal* 92: 232–58.

Carr, David
1986 *Time, Narrative, and History.* Bloomington: Indiana University Press.
1991 "Contribution to 'Discussion: Ricoeur on Narrative.'" In *On Paul Ricoeur: Narrative and Interpretation,* ed. D. Wood, 160–74. London: Routledge.

Carrette, Jermey R.
2000 *Foucault and Religion: Spiritual Corporeality and Political Spirituality.* London: Routledge.

Carrier, A. H., and J. G. Carrier
1991 *Structure and Process in a Melanesian Society: Ponam's Progress in the Twentieth Century.* Chur, Switzerland: Harwood Academic Publishers.

Carwardine, Richard
2000 "Revivalism." In *The Oxford Companion to Christian Thought: Intellectual, Spiritual, and Moral Horizons of Christianity,* ed. A. Hastings, A. Mason, and H. Pyper, 622–23. Oxford: Oxford University Press.

Champion, Ivan F.
1966 *Across New Guinea from the Fly to the Sepik.* Melbourne: Lansdowne Press.

Clark, Jeffrey
1992 "Madness and Colonisation: The Embodiment of Power in Pangia." *Oceania* 63(1): 15–26.
1997 "Imagining the State, or Tribalism and the Arts of Memory in the Highlands of Papua New Guinea." In *Narratives of Nation in the South Pacific,* ed. T. Otto and N. Thomas, 65–90. Amsterdam: Harwood Academic Publishers.
2000 *Steel to Stone: A Chronicle of Colonialism in the Southern Highlands of Papua New Guinea.* Oxford: Oxford University Press.

Clay, Brenda Johnson
1977 *Pinikindu: Maternal Nurture, Paternal Substance.* Chicago: University of Chicago Press.

Clifford, James
1986 "On Ethnographic Allegory." In *Writing Culture: The Poetics and Politics of Ethnography,* ed. J. Clifford and G. E. Marcus, 98–121. Berkeley: University of California Press.

Comaroff, Jean
1985 *Body of Power, Spirit of Resistance: The Culture and History of a South African People.* Chicago: University of Chicago Press.

Comaroff, Jean, and John Comaroff
1991 *Of Revelation and Revolution: Christianity, Colonialism, and Consciousness in South Africa.* Vol. 1. Chicago: University of Chicago Press.

Comaroff, John L., and Jean Comaroff
1992 *Ethnography and the Historical Imagination.* Boulder: Westview Press.
1997 *Of Revelation and Revolution: The Dialectics of Modernity on a South African Frontier.* Vol. 2. Chicago: University of Chicago Press.

Cox, Harvey
1995 *Fire from Heaven: The Rise of Pentecostal Spirituality and the Reshaping of Religion in the Twenty-first Century.* Reading, Mass.: Addison-Wesley.

Craig, Barry
1990 "The Telefomin Murders: Whose Myth?" In *Children of Afek: Tradition and Change among the Mountain-Ok of Central New Guinea,* ed. B. Craig and D. Hyndman. Oceania Monograph 40. Sydney: University of Sydney.

Crook, Tony
1997 "Growing Knowledge: Exploring Knowledge Practices in Bolivip, Papua New Guinea." Ph.D. dissertation, Cambridge University.

Davidson, Arnold I.
1986 "Archaeology, Genealogy, Ethics." In *Foucault: A Critical Reader,* ed. D. C. Hoy, 221–33. Oxford: Basil Blackwell.

Dombrowski, Kirk
2001 *Against Culture: Development, Politics, and Religion in Indian Alaska.* Lincoln: University of Nebraska Press.

Douglas, Bronwen
1995 "Power, Discourse and the Appropriation of God: Christianity and Subversion in a Melanesian Context." *History and Anthropology* 9(1): 57–92.
1998 *Across the Great Divide: Journeys in History and Anthropology.* Amsterdam: Harwood Academic Publishers.
2001 "From Invisible Christians to Gothic Theatre: The Romance of the Millennial in Melanesian Anthropology." *Current Anthropology* 42(1): 615–50.

Draper, Norm, and Sheila Draper, eds.
1990 *Daring to Believe.* Hawthorn, Victoria: Australian Baptist Missionary Society.

Dumont, Louis
1977 *From Mandeville to Marx: The Genesis and Triumph of Economic Ideology.* Chicago: University of Chicago Press.
1980 *Homo Hierarchicus: The Caste System and Its Implications.* Trans. Mark Sainsbury, Louis Dumont, and Basia Gulati. Chicago: University of Chicago Press.
1986 *Essays on Individualism: Modern Ideology in Anthropological Perspective.* Chicago: University of Chicago Press.
1994 *German Ideology: From France to Germany and Back.* Chicago: University of Chicago Press.

Dundon, Alison
2002 "Dancing around Development: Crisis in Christian Country in Western Province, Papua New Guinea." *Oceania* 72(3): 215–29.

Englund, Harri, and James Leach
2000 "Ethnography and the Meta-Narratives of Modernity." *Current Anthropology* 41(2): 225–48.

Errington, Frederick
1974 "Indigenous Ideas of Order, Time, and Transition in a New Guinea Cargo Movement." *American Ethnologist* 1(2): 255–68.

Errington, Frederick K., and Deborah B. Gewertz
1995 *Articulating Change in the "Last Unknown."* Boulder: Westview Press.

Evens, T. M. S.
1999 "Bourdieu and the Logic of Practice: Is All Giving Indian-Giving or Is 'Generalized Materialism' Not Enough?" *Sociological Theory* 17(1): 3–31.

Eves, Richard
1998 *The Magical Body: Power, Fame, and Meaning in a Melanesian Society.* Amsterdam: Harwood Academic.

Eyre, Stephen L.
1988 "Revival Christianity among the Urat of Papua New Guinea: Some Possible Motivational and Perceptual Antecedents." Ph.D. dissertation, University of California, San Diego.

Fardon, Richard
2000 "Metissage or Curate's Egg." *Africa* 70(1): 144–51.

Faubion, James D.
2001 "Toward an Anthropology of Ethics: Foucault and the Pedagogies of Autopoiesis." *Representations* 74: 83–104.

Fenton, J. C.
1963 *Saint Matthew.* Baltimore: Penguin.

Ferguson, James
1999 *Expectations of Modernity: Myths and Meanings of Urban Life on the Zambian Copperbelt.* Berkeley: University of California Press.

Fisher, Humphrey J.
1973 "Conversion Reconsidered: Some Historical Aspects of Religious Conversion in Black Africa." *Africa* 43(1): 27–40.
1985 "The Juggernaut's Apologia: Conversion to Islam in Black Africa." *Africa* 55(2): 153–73.

Fitzpatrick, Peter
1980 *Law and State in Papua New Guinea.* London: Academic Press.

Flannery, Wendy, ed.
1983a *Religious Movements in Melanesia Today (1).* Goroka: Melanesian Institute for Pastoral and Socio-Economic Service.
1983b *Religious Movements in Melanesia Today (2).* Goroka: Melanesian Institute for Pastoral and Socio-Economic Service.

1983c *Religious Movements in Melanesia: A Selection of Case Studies and Reports*. Goroka: Melanesian Institute for Pastoral and Socio-Economic Service.

1984 *Religious Movements in Melanesia Today (3)*. Goroka: Melanesian Institute for Pastoral and Socio-Economic Service.

Foster, Robert J.

1995a "Introduction: The Work of Nation Making." In *Nation Making: Emergent Identities in Postcolonial Melanesia*, ed. R. J. Foster, 1–30. Ann Arbor: University of Michigan Press.

1995b *Social Reproduction and History in Melanesia: Mortuary Ritual, Gift Exchange, and Custom in the Tanga Islands*. Cambridge: Cambridge University Press.

Foucault, Michel

1978 *The History of Sexuality. Volume I: An Introduction*. Trans. Robert Hurley. New York: Vintage Books.

1990 *The Use of Pleasure*. Trans. Robert Hurley. New York: Vintage Books.

1997 *Ethics: Subjectivity and Truth*. Vol. 1. New York: New Press.

Friedman, Jonathan

1994 *Cultural Identity and Global Process*. London: Sage.

1999 "The Hybridization of Roots and the Abhorrence of the Bush." In *Spaces of Culture: City, Nation, World*, ed. M. Featherstone and S. Lash 230–56. London: Sage.

2000 "Global Crises, the Struggle for Cultural Identity and Intellectual Pork-barrelling: Cosmopolitans versus Locals, Ethnics and Nationals in an Era of De-hegemonisation." In *Debating Cultural Hybridity: Multi-Cultural Identities and the Politics of Anti-Racism*, ed. P. Werbner and T. Modood, 70–89. London: Zed.

Fung, Ronald K.

1988 *The Epistle to the Galatians*. Grand Rapids: Eerdmans.

García Canclini, Néstor

1995 *Hybrid Cultures: Strategies for Entering and Leaving Modernity*. Trans. Christopher L. Chiappari and Silvia L. Lopez. Minneapolis: University of Minnesota Press.

2000 "The State of War and the State of Hybridization." In *Without Guarantees: In Honour of Stuart Hall*, eds. P. Gilroy, L. Grossberg, and A. McRobbie, 38–52. London: Verso.

Gardella, Peter

1985 *Innocent Ecstasy: How Christianity Gave America an Ethic of Sexual Pleasure*. New York: Oxford University Press.

Gardner, Donald

1981 "Cult Ritual and Social Organization among the Mianmin." Ph.D. dissertation, Australian National University.

1987 "Spirits and Conceptions of Agency among the Mianmin of Papua New Guinea." *Oceania* 57(3): 161–77.

Geertz, Clifford

1973 *The Interpretation of Cultures*. New York: Basic Books.

Gellner, Ernest
1964 *Thought and Change*. Chicago: University of Chicago Press.

Gewertz, Deborah B., and Frederick K. Errington
1991 *Twisted Histories, Altered Contexts: Representing the Chambri in a World System*. Cambridge: Cambridge University Press.

Godelier, Maurice
1986 *The Making of Great Men: Male Domination and Power among the New Guinea Baruya*. Trans. Rupert Swyer. Cambridge: Cambridge University Press.

Goodwin, Jeff
1996 "How to Become a Dominant American Social Scientist: The Case of Theda Skocpol." *Contemporary Sociology* 25(3): 293–95.

Graeber, David
2001 *Toward an Anthropological Theory of Value: The False Coin of Our Own Dreams*. New York: Palgrave.

Gray, Richard
1978 "Christianity and Religious Change in Africa." *African Affairs* 77(306): 89–100.

Gregory, C. A.
1982 *Gifts and Commodities*. London: Academic Press.

Gupta, Akhil
1992 "The Song of the Nonaligned World: Transnational Identities and the Reinscription of Space in Late Capitalism." *Cultural Anthropology* 7(1): 63–79.

Hall, Stuart
1992 "The Question of Cultural Identity." In *Modernity and Its Futures,* ed. S. Hall, D. Held, and T. McGrew, 273–325. Cambridge: Polity Press.
1994 "Cultural Identity and Diaspora." In *Colonial Discourse and Post-Colonial Theory: A Reader,* ed. P. Williams and L. Chrisman, 392–403. New York: Columbia University Press.
1996 "New Ethnicities." In *Stuart Hall: Critical Dialogues in Cultural Studies,* ed. D. Morley and K.-H. Chen, 441–49. London: Routledge.

Handler, Richard
1988 *Nationalism and the Politics of Culture in Quebec*. Madison: University of Wisconsin Press.

Hanson, L. W., et al.
2001 *Papua New Guinea Rural Development Handbook*. Canberra: Australian National University.

Harding, Susan
1991 "Representing Fundamentalism: The Problem of the Repugnant Cultural Other." *Social Research* 58(2): 373–93.
1994 "Imagining the Last Days: The Politics of Apocalyptic Language." In *Accounting for Fundamentalism: The Dynamic Character of Movements,* ed. M. E. Marty and R. S. Appleby, 57–78. Chicago: University of Chicago Press.

2000 *The Book of Jerry Falwell: Fundamentalist Language and Politics.* Princeton: Princeton University Press.

Harkin, Michael E.
1997 *The Heiltsuks: Dialogues of Culture and History on the Northwest Coast.* Lincoln: University of Nebraska Press.

Harrison, Simon
1985 "Concepts of the Person in Avatip Religious Thought." *Man,* n.s., 20(1): 115–30.

Hasluck, Paul
1960 *Australian Policy in Papua and New Guinea: Statement in the House of Representatives, Canberra.* Canberra: Commonwealth Government Printer.
1976 *A Time for Building: Australian Administration in Papua and New Guinea, 1951–1963.* Melbourne: Melbourne University Press.

Hastings, Adrian
2000 "Communion." In *The Oxford Companion to Christian Thought: Intellectual, Spiritual, and Moral Horizons of Christianity,* ed. A. Hastings, A. Mason, and H. Pyper, 126–27. Oxford: Oxford University Press.

Hayward, Douglas James
1997 *Vernacular Christianity among the Mulia Dani.* Lanham, Md.: American Society of Missiology and University Press of America.

Healey, Alan
1962 "Linguistic Aspects of Telefomin Kinship Terminology." *Anthropological Linguistics* 4(7):14–28.
1964 "The Ok Language Family in New Guinea." Ph.D. dissertation, Australian National University.

Healey, Phyllis, and Alan Healey
1977 *Telefol Dictionary.* Vol. Ser. C—No. 46. Canberra: Australian National University.

Healey, P. M.
1965 *Telefol Noun Phrases.* Vol. 4. Canberra: Australian National University.

Horton, Robin
1971 "African Conversion." *Africa* 41(2): 85–108.
1975a "On the Rationality of Conversion, Part I." *Africa* 45(3): 219–35.
1975b "On the Rationality of Conversion, Part II." *Africa* 45(4): 373–99.
1993 *Patterns of Thought in Africa and the West: Essays on Magic, Religion and Science.* Cambridge: Cambridge University Press.

Horton, Robin, and J. D. Y. Peel
1976 "Conversion and Confusion: A Rejoinder on Christianity in Eastern Nigeria." *Canadian Journal of African Studies* 10(3): 481–98.

Howell, Signe
1997 "Introduction." In *The Ethnography of Moralities,* ed. S. Howell, 1–22. London: Routledge.

Huber, Mary Taylor
    1988 *The Bishops' Progress*. Washington, D.C.: Smithsonian Institution Press.

Hyndman, David
    1994 *Ancestral Rain Forests and the Mountain of Gold: Indigenous Peoples and Mining in New Guinea*. Boulder: Westview Press.

Hyndman, D., and G. Morren
    1990 "The Human Ecology of the Mountain-Ok of Central New Guinea: A Regional and Inter-Regional Approach." In *Children of Afek: Tradition and Change among the Mountain-Ok of Central New Guinea,* ed. B. Craig and D. Hyndman. Oceania Monograph 40. Sydney: University of Sydney.

Ifeka-Moller, Caroline
    1974 "White Power: Social-Structural Factors in Conversion to Christianity, Eastern Nigeria, 1921–1966." *Canadian Journal of African Studies* 8(1): 55–72.

Ikenga-Metuh, Emefie
    1985 "The Shattered Microcosm: A Critical Survey of Explanations of Conversion in Africa." *Neue Zeitschrift fur Missionwissenschaft* 41: 241–54.

Jacobsen, Michael
    1995 "Vanishing Nations and the Infiltration of Nationalism: The Case of Papua New Guinea." In *Nation Making: Emergent Identities in Postcolonial Melanesia,* ed. R. J. Foster, 227–49. Ann Arbor: University of Michigan Press.

Jebens, Holger
    1995 *Wege zum Himmel. Katholicken, Siebenten-Tags-Adventisten und der Einfluß der Traditionellen Religion in Pairudu, Southern Highlands Province, Papua New Guinea*. Vol. 86. Bonn: Holos.
    1997 "Catholics, Seventh-day Adventists and the Impact of Tradition in Pairundu (Southern Highlands Province, Papua New Guinea)." In *Cultural Dynamics of Religious Change in Oceania,* ed. T. Otto and A. Borsboom, 33–43. Leiden: KITLV Press.
    2000 "Signs of the Second Coming: On Eschatological Expectation and Disappointment in Highland and Seaboard Papua New Guinea." *Ethnohistory* 47(1): 171–204.

Joas, Hans
    2000 *The Genesis of Values*. Trans. Gregory Moore. Chicago: University of Chicago Press.

Jolly, Margaret
    1994 *Women of the Place: Kastom, Colonialism and Gender in Vanuatu*. Chur, Switzerland: Harwood Academic Publishers.

Jolly, Margaret, and Martha Macintyre, eds.
    1989 *Family and Gender in the Pacific: Domestic Contradictions and the Colonial Impact*. Cambridge: Cambridge University Press.

Jones, Barbara Ann
 1980 "Consuming Society: Food and Illness among the Faiwol." Ph.D. dissertation, University of Virginia.

Jorgensen, Dan
 1981a "Life on the Fringe: History and Society in Telefomin." In *The Plight of Peripheral People in Papua New Guinea*. Vol. 1: *The Inland Situation*, ed. R. Gordon, 59–79. Cambridge: Cultural Survival.
 1981b "Taro and Arrows: Order, Entropy, and Religion among the Telefolmin." Ph.D. dissertation, University of British Columbia.
 1983 "Mirroring Nature? Men's and Women's Models of Conception in Telefomin." *Mankind* 14(1): 57–65.
 1990a "Placing the Past and Moving the Present: Myth and Contemporary History in Telefomin." *Culture* 10(2): 47–56.
 1990b "Secrecy's Turns." *Canberra Anthropology* 13(1): 40–47.
 1990c "The Telefolip and the Architecture of Ethnic Identity in the Sepik Headwaters." In *Children of Afek: Tradition and Change among the Mountain-Ok of Central New Guinea,* ed. B. Craig and D. Hyndman, 151–60. Oceania Monograph 40. Sydney: University of Sydney.
 1991 "Big Men, Great Men and Women: Alternative Logics of Gender Difference." In *Big Men and Great Men: Personifications of Power in Melanesia,* ed. M. Godelier and M. Strathern, 256–71. Cambridge: Cambridge University Press.
 1993 "Money and Marriage in Telefomin: From Sister Exchange to Daughter as Trade Store." In *The Business of Marriage: Transformations in Oceanic Matrimony,* ed. R. A. Marksbury, 57–82. Pittsburgh: University of Pittsburgh Press.
 1996 "Regional History and Ethnic Identity in the Hub of New Guinea: The Emergence of the Min." *Oceania* 66(3): 189–210.

Keane, Webb
 2002 "Sincerity, 'Modernity,' and the Protestants." *Cultural Anthropology* 17(1): 65–92.

Keesing, Roger M.
 1992 *Custom and Confrontation: The Kwaio Struggle for Cultural Autonomy.* Chicago: University of Chicago Press.

Kelly, John D.
 1995 "The Privileges of Citizenship: Nations, States, Markets, and Narratives." In *Nation Making: Emergent Identities in Postcolonial Melanesia,* ed. R. J. Foster, 253–73. Ann Arbor: University of Michigan Press.

Kermode, Frank
 1966 *The Sense of an Ending: Studies in the Theory of Fiction.* New York: Oxford University Press.

Kienzle, Wallace, and Stuart Campbell
 1938 "Notes on the Natives of the Fly and Sepik River Headwaters, New Guinea." *Oceania* 8: 463–81.

Kiernan, J. P.

1976 "The Work of Zion: An Analysis of an African Zionist Ritual." *Africa* 46(4): 340–56.

1994 "Variation on a Christian Theme: The Healing Synthesis of Zulu Zionism." In *Syncretism/Anti-Syncretism: The Politics of Religious Synthesis,* ed. C. Stewart and R. Shaw, 69–84. London: Routledge.

1997 "Images of Rejection in the Construction of Morality: Satan and Sorcerer as Moral Signposts in the Social Landscape of Urban Zionists." *Social Anthropology* 5(3): 243–54.

Kipp, Rita Smith

1995 "Conversion by Affiliation: The History of the Karo Batak Protestant Church." *American Ethnologist* 22(4): 868–82.

Knauft, Bruce M.

2002 *Exchanging the Past: A Rainforest World of Before and After.* Chicago: University of Chicago Press.

Kocher Schmid, Christin, ed.

1999 *Expecting the Day of Wrath: Versions of the Millennium in Papua New Guinea.* Boroko: National Research Institute.

Kraniauskas, John

2000 "Hybridity in a Transnational Frame: Latin-Americanist and Post-Colonial Perspectives on Cultural Studies." In *Hybridity and Its Discontents: Politics, Science, Culture,* ed. A. Brah and A. E. Coombes, 235–56. London: Routledge.

Kristeva, Julia

1982 *Powers of Horror: An Essay on Abjection.* Trans. Leon S. Roudiez. New York: Columbia University Press.

Kulick, Don

1992 *Language Shift and Cultural Reproduction: Socialization, Self, and Syncretism in a Papua New Guinea Village.* New York: Cambridge University Press.

Laidlaw, James

2002 "For an Anthropology of Ethics and Freedom." *Journal of the Royal Anthropological Institute* 8(2): 311–32.

Laitin, David D.

1986 *Hegemony and Culture: Politics and Religious Change among the Yoruba.* Chicago: University of Chicago Press.

Lambek, Michael

1992 "Taboo as Cultural Practice among Malagasy Speakers." *Man,* n.s., 27(2): 245–66.

2000 "The Anthropology of Religion and the Quarrel between Poetry and Philosophy." *Current Anthropology* 41(3): 309–20.

Lambert, Frank

1999 *Inventing the "Great Awakening."* Princeton: Princeton University Press.

Landau, Paul S.
2000 "Hegemony and History in Jean and John L. Comaroff's *Of Revelation and Revolution* (Review Article). *Africa* 70(3): 501–19.

Langmore, Diane
1989 *Missionary Lives: Papua 1874–1914.* Honolulu: University of Hawaii Press.

Larkin, Clarence
1920 *Dispensational Truth or God's Plan and Purpose in the Ages.* Enl. and rev. ed. Glenside, Pa.: Rev. Clarence Larkin Est.

Lattas, Andrew
1992 "Skin, Personhood and Redemption: The Double Self in West New Britain Cargo Cults." *Oceania* 63(3): 27–54.
1993 "Sorcery and Colonialism: Illness, Dreams and Death as Political Languages in West New Britain." *Man*, n.s., 28: 51–77.
1998 *Cultures of Secrecy: Reinventing Race in Bush Kaliai Cargo Cults.* Madison: University of Wisconsin Press.

Latukefu, Sione, ed.
1989 *Papua New Guinea: A Century of Colonial Impact, 1884–1984.* Port Moresby: National Research Institute and University of Papua New Guinea.

Lawrence, Peter
[1964] 1971 *Road Belong Cargo: A Study of the Cargo Movement in the Southern Madang District New Guinea.* Atlantic Highlands, N.J.: Humanities Press.

Leavitt, Stephen C.
1989 "Cargo, Christ, and Nostalgia for the Dead: Themes of Intimacy and Abandonment in Bumbita Arapesh Social Experience." Ph.D. dissertation, University of California, San Diego.

LeRoy, John
1979 "The Ceremonial Pig Kill of the South Kewa." *Oceania* 49: 179–209.

Lindstrom, Lamont
1984 "Doctor, Lawyer, Wise Man, Priest: Big-Men and Knowledge in Melanesia." *Man*, n.s., 19: 291–309.
1990 *Knowledge and Power in a South Pacific Society.* Washington, D.C.: Smithsonian Institution Press.

LiPuma, Edward
1988 *The Gift of Kinship: Structure and Practice in Maring Social Organization.* Cambridge: Cambridge University Press.
2000 *Encompassing Others: The Magic of Modernity in Melanesia.* Ann Arbor: University of Michigan Press.

Lohmann, Roger
2000 "The Role of Dreams in Religious Enculturation among the Asabano of Papua New Guinea." *Ethos* 28(1): 75–102.

MacIntyre, Alasdair
  1984 *After Virtue: A Study in Moral Theory.* Notre Dame: University of Notre Dame Press.

Mahmood, Saba, and Nancy Reynolds
  1995 "Introduction." *Stanford Humanities Review* 5(1): iii–ix.

Mair, L. P.
  1970 *Australia in New Guinea.* Melbourne: Melbourne University Press.

Malkki, Liisa H.
  1995 "Refugees and Exile: From 'Refugee Studies' to the National Order of Things." *Annual Review of Anthropology* 24: 495–523.

Martin, David
  1990 *Tongues of Fire: The Explosion of Protestantism in Latin America.* Oxford: Basil Blackwell.
  2002 *Pentecostalism: The World Their Parish.* Oxford: Blackwell.

Mason, Alistair
  2000 "Arminianism." In *The Oxford Companion to Christian Thought: Intellectual, Spiritual, and Moral Horizons of Christianity,* ed. A. Hastings, A. Mason, and H. Pyper, 41. Oxford: Oxford University Press.

Maxwell, David
  1999 *Christians and Chiefs in Zimbabwe: A Social History of the Hwesa People.* Westport, Conn.: Praeger.

McDowell, Nancy
  1980 "It's Not Who You Are But How You Give That Counts: The Role of Exchange in a Melanesian Society." *American Ethnologist* 7(1): 58–70.
  1985 "Past and Future: The Nature of Episodic Time in Bun." In *History and Ethnohistory in Papua New Guinea,* ed. D. Gewertz and E. Schieffelin, 26–39. Oceania Monograph 28. Sydney: University of Sydney.
  1988 "A Note on Cargo Cults and Cultural Constructions of Change." *Pacific Studies* 11(2): 121–34.

McGuire, Meredith B.
  1982 *Pentecostal Catholics: Power, Charisma, and Order in a Religious Movement.* Philadelphia: Temple University Press.

Merlan, Francesca, and Jeffrey Heath
  1982 "Dyadic Kinship Terms." In *Languages of Kinship in Aboriginal Australia,* ed. J. Heath, F. Merlan, and A. Rumsey, 107–24. Sydney: Oceania Linguistic Monographs.

Merlan, Francesca, and Alan Rumsey
  1991 *Ku Waru: Language and Segmentary Politics in the Western Nebilyer Valley, Papua New Guinea.* Cambridge: Cambridge University Press.

Meyer, Birgit
  1999 *Translating the Devil: Religion and Modernity among the Ewe in Ghana.* Trenton, N.J.: Africa World Press.

2001 " 'You Devil Go Away From Me!' Pentecostalism, African Christianity, and the Powers of Good and Evil." In *Powers of Good and Evil: Social Transformation and Popular Belief,* ed. P. Clough and J. P. Mitchell, 104–34. New York: Berghahn Books.

Mihalic, F.
1986 *The Jacaranda Dictionary and Grammar of Melanesian Pidgin.* Milton: Jacaranda Dictionary.

Moore-Gilbert, Bart
1997 *Postcolonial Theory: Contexts, Practices, Politics.* London: Verso.

Morren, George E. B.
1981 "A Small Footnote to the 'Big Walk': Environment and Change among the Miyanmin of Papua New Guinea." *Oceania* 52(1): 39–65.
1986 *The Miyanmin: Human Ecology of a Papua New Guinea Society.* Ann Arbor: UMI Research Press.

Morris, Colin
1972 *The Discovery of the Individual: 1050–1200.* New York: Harper and Row.

Munn, Nancy
1986 *The Fame of Gawa: A Symbolic Study of Value Transformation in a Massim (Papua New Guinea) Society.* New York: Cambridge University Press.
1990 "Constructing Regional Worlds in Experience: Kula Exchange, Witchcraft, and Gawan Local Events." *Man,* n.s., 25(1): 1–17.

Murphree, Marshall W.
1969 *Christianity and the Shona.* London: Athlone Press.

Murphy, W. T.
1997 *The Oldest Social Science: Configurations of Law and Modernity.* Oxford: Clarendon Press.

Myhre, Knut Christian
1998 "The Anthropological Concept of Action and Its Problems: A 'New' Approach Based on Marcel Mauss and Aristotle." *Journal of the Anthropological Society of Oxford* 29(2): 121–34.

Naficy, Hamid
1993 *The Making of Exile Cultures: Iranian Television in Los Angeles.* Minneapolis: University of Minnesota Press.

Nederveen Pieterse, Jan
1995 "Globalization as Hybridization." In *Global Modernities,* ed. M. Featherstone, S. Lash, and R. Robertson, 45–68. London: Sage.

Needham, Rodney
1983 *Against the Tranquility of Axioms.* Berkeley: University of California Press.

O'Hanlon, Michael
1993 *Paradise: Portraying the New Guinea Highlands.* London: British Museum Press.

Oates, W., and L. Oates
  1968 *Kapau Pedagogical Grammar.* Vol. 10. Canberra: Australian National University.
Obeyesekere, Gananath
  1992 *The Apotheosis of Captain Cook: European Mythmaking in the Pacific.* Princeton: Princeton University Press.
Ortner, Sherry B.
  [1984] 1994 "Theory in Anthropology since the Sixties." In *Culture/Power/History: A Reader in Contemporary Social Theory,* ed. N. B. Dirks, G. Eley, and S. B. Ortner, 372–411. Princeton: Princeton UniversityPress.
Papastergiadis, Nikos
  2000 *The Turbulence of Migration: Globalization, Deterritorialization and Hybridity.* Cambridge: Polity Press.
Parish, Steven M.
  1994 *Moral Knowing in a Hindu Sacred City: An Exploration of Mind, Emotion, and Self.* New York: Columbia University Press.
Parsons, Talcott
  1991 "The Place of Ultimate Values in Sociological Theory." In *Talcott Parsons: The Early Essays,* ed. C. Camic, 231–57. Chicago: University of Chicago Press.
Peel, J. D. Y.
  1968 *Aladura: A Religious Movement among the Yoruba.* London: Oxford University Press.
  1977 "Conversion and Tradition in Two African Societies: Ijebu and Buganda." *Past and Present* 77: 108–41.
  1995 "For Who Hath Despised the Day of Small Things? Missionary Narratives and Historical Anthropology." *Comparative Studies in Society and History* 37(3): 581–607.
Pigg, Stacy Leigh
  1992 "Inventing Social Categories through Place: Social Representations and Development in Nepal." *Comparative Studies in Society and History* 34(3): 491–513.
Piot, Charles
  1999 *Remotely Global: Village Modernity in West Africa.* Chicago: University of Chicago Press.
Pitt-Rivers, Julian
  1971 *The People of the Sierra.* Chicago: University of Chicago Press.
Polier, Nicole
  1995 " 'When Australia Was the Big Name for Papua New Guinea' ": The Colonial Constitution of Faiwolmin Subjects." *Journal of Historical Sociology* 8(3): 257–77.
Poole, Fitz John Porter
  1976 "The Ais Am: An Introduction to Male Initiation Ritual among the Bimin-Kuskusmin of the West Sepik District, Papua New Guinea." Ph.D. dissertation, Cornell University.

1982 "The Ritual Forging of Identity: Aspects of Person and Self in Bimin-Kuskusmin Male Initiation." In *Rituals of Manhood*, ed. G. H. Herdt, 99–154. Berkeley: University of California Press.

1985 "Coming into Social Being: Cultural Images of Infants in Bimin-Kuskusmin Folk Psychology." In *Person, Self, and Experience: Exploring Pacific Ethnopsychologies*, ed. G. M. White and J. Kirkpatrick, 183–242. Berkeley: University of California Press.

Rambo, Lewis R.
1993 *Understanding Religious Conversion*. New Haven: Yale University Press.

Read, K. E.
1959 "Leadership and Consensus in a New Guinea Society." *American Anthropologist* 61(3): 425–36.

Renck, Gunther
1990 *Contextualization of Christianity and Christianization of Language: A Case Study from the Highlands of Papua New Guinea*. Erlangen: Verlag der Ev.Luth. Mission.

Ricoeur, Paul
1981 "Narrative Time." In *On Narrative*, ed. W. J. T. Mitchell, 165–86. Chicago: University of Chicago Press.

1984 *Time and Narrative*. Vol 1. Trans. Kathleen McLaughlin and David Pellauer. Chicago: University of Chicago Press.

Robbins, Joel
1994 "Equality as a Value: Ideology in Dumont, Melanesia and the West." *Social Analysis* 36: 21–70.

1995 "Dispossessing the Spirits: Christian Transformations of Desire and Ecology among the Urapmin of Papua New Guinea." *Ethnology* 34(3): 211–24.

1997a "666, or Why Is the Millennium on the Skin? Morality, the State and the Epistemology of Apocalypticism among the Urapmin of Papua New Guinea." In *Millennial Markers*, ed. P. Stewart and A. Strathern, 35–58. Townsville: Centre for Pacific Studies, James Cook University.

1997b "When Do You Think the World Will End? Globalization, Apocalypticism, and the Moral Perils of Fieldwork in 'Last New Guinea.'" *Anthropology and Humanism* 22(1): 6–30.

1998a "Becoming Sinners: Christian Transformations of Morality and Culture in a Papua New Guinea Society." Ph.D. dissertation, University of Virginia.

1998b "Becoming Sinners: Christianity and Desire among the Urapmin of Papua New Guinea." *Ethnology* 37(4): 299–316.

1998c "On Reading 'World News': Apocalyptic Narrative, Negative Nationalism, and Transnational Christianity in a Papua New Guinea Society." *Social Analysis* 42(2): 103–30.

1999 "'This Is Our Money': Modernism, Regionalism, and Dual Currencies in Urapmin." In *Money and Modernity: State and Local Currencies in Contemporary Melanesia,* ed. J. Robbins and D. Akin, 82–102. Pittsburgh: University of Pittsburgh Press.

2001a "God Is Nothing but Talk: Modernity, Language and Prayer in a Papua New Guinea Society." *American Anthropologist* 103(4): 901–12.

2001b "Introduction: Global Religions, Pacific Island Transformations." *Journal of Ritual Studies* 15(2): 7–12.

2001c "Secrecy and the Sense of an Ending: Narrative, Time and Everyday Millenarianism in Papua New Guinea and in Christian Fundamentalism." *Comparative Studies in Society and History* 43(3): 525–51.

2001d "Whatever Became of Revival: From Charismatic Movement to Charismatic Church in a Papua New Guinea Society." *Journal of Ritual Studies* 15(2): 79 90.

2002 "On the Critical Uses of Difference: The Uninvited Guest and *The Invention of Culture.*" *Social Analysis* 46(1): 4–11.

2003 "Properties of Nature, Properties of Culture: Possession, Recognition, and the Substance of Politics in a Papua New Guinea Society." *Suomen Antropologi* 28(1): 9–28.

Forthcoming "Dreaming and the Defeat of Charisma: Disconnecting Dreams from Leadership among the Urapmin of Papua New Guinea." In *Dream Travelers: Sleep Experiences and Culture in the Western Pacific,* ed. R. Lohmann. New York: Palgrave Macmillan.

n.d. "The Humiliations of Sin: Christianity and the Modernization of the Subject among the Urapmin." Unpublished manuscript.

Robbins, Joel, and David Akin

1999 "An Introduction to Melanesian Currencies: Agency, Identity, and Social Reproduction." In *Money and Modernity: State and Local Currencies in Melanesia,* ed. D. Akin and J. Robbins, 1–40. Pittsburgh: University of Pittsburgh Press.

Robbins, Joel, Pamela J. Stewart, and Andrew Strathern, eds.

2001 *Charismatic and Pentecostal Christianity in Oceania.* Special Issue. *Journal of Ritual Studies* 15(2).

Robin, Robert W.

1981 "Revival Movement Hysteria in the Southern Highlands Province, Papua New Guinea." *Journal for the Scientific Study of Religion* 20(2): 150–63.

1982 "Revival Movements in the Southern Highlands Province of Papua New Guinea." *Oceania* 52(4): 320–43.

Rowley, C. D.

1965 *The New Guinea Villager.* Melbourne: F. W. Cheshire.

Rumsey, Alan

1998 "The Personification of Social Totalities in the Pacific." *Journal of Pacific Studies* 23(1): 48–70.

2000 "Agency, Personhood and the 'I' of Discourse in the Pacific and Beyond." *Journal of the Royal Anthropological Institute* 6(1): 101–15.

Sack, Peter
    1985 " 'Bobotoi' and 'Pulu': Melanesian Law: Normative Order or Way of
    Life?" *Journal de la Société des Oceanistes* 41(80): 15–23.

Sahlins, Marshall
    1976 *Culture and Practical Reason.* Chicago: University of Chicago Press.
    1981 *Historical Metaphors and Mythical Realities: Structure in the Early
    History of the Sandwich Islands Kingdom.* Ann Arbor: University of
    Michigan Press.
    1985 *Islands of History.* Chicago: University of Chicago Press.
    1990 "China Reconstructing or Vice Versa: Humiliation as a Stage of Eco-
    nomic 'Development,' with Comments on Cultural Diversity in the Mod-
    ern World System." In *Toward One World Beyond All Barriers,* 78–96.
    Seoul: Seoul Olympic Sports Promotion Foundation.
    1992 "The Economics of Develop-Man in the Pacific." *Res* 21: 13–25.
    1995 *How "Natives" Think: About Captain Cook, for Example.* Chicago:
    University of Chicago Press.

Scaglion, Richard
    1985 "Kiaps as Kings: Abelam Legal Change in Historical Perspective."
    In *History and Ethnohistory in Papua New Guinea,* ed. D. Gewertz and
    E. Schieffelin, 77–99. Oceania Monograph 28. Sydney: University of
    Sydney.
    1990 "Legal Adaptation in a Papua New Guinea Village Court." *Ethnology*
    29(1): 17–33.

Schapera, I.
    1938 "Contact between European and Native in South Africa (cont.): 2. In
    Bechuanaland." In *Methods of Study of Culture Contact in Africa,* ed.
    B. Malinowski, 25–37. London: Oxford University Press.

Schieffelin, Bambi
    1996 "Creating Evidence: Making Sense of Written Words in Bosavi." In *In-
    teraction and Grammar,* ed. E. Ochs, E. Schegloff, and S. Thomson, 435–
    60. Cambridge: Cambridge University Press.
    2000 "Introducing Kaluli Literacy: A Chronology of Influences." In *Regimes
    of Language: Ideologies, Polities, and Identities,* ed. P. V. Kroskrity, 293–
    327. Santa Fe, New Mex.: School of American Research Press.

Schieffelin, Edward L.
    1995 "Early Contact as Drama and Manipulation in the Southern Highlands
    of Papua New Guinea: Pacification as the Structure of the Conjuncture."
    Comparative Studies in Society and History 37(3): 555–80.

Schluchter, Wolfgang
    1996 *Paradoxes of Modernity: Culture and Conduct in the Theory of Max
    Weber.* Trans. Neil Solomon. Stanford: Stanford University Press.

Schmidt, Leigh E.
    1997 "Practices of Exchange: From Market Culture to Gift Economy in the
    Interpretation of American Religion." In *Lived Religion in America: To-
    ward a History of Practice,* ed. D. D. Hall, 69–91. Princeton: Princeton
    University Press.

Schwartz, Theodore
  1962 *The Paliau Movement in the Admiralty Islands 1946–1954.* Anthropological Papers 49, pt. 2. New York: American Museum of Natural History.

Shanahan, Daniel
  1992 *Toward a Genealogy of Individualism.* Amherst: University of Massachusetts Press.

Simpson, Colin
  1953 *Adam with Arrows.* Sydney: Angus and Robertson.

Smith, Barry R.
  1980 *Warning.* New Zealand: Smith Family Evangelism.
  1985 *Second Warning.* New Zealand: Smith Family Evangelism.
  n.d.a *Final Notice.* New Zealand: Barry Smith Family Evangelism.
  n.d.b *Postscript.* New Zealand: Barry Smith Family Evangelism.

Smith, Michael French
  1994 *Hard Times on Kairiru Island: Poverty, Development, and Morality in a Papua New Guinea Village.* Honolulu: University of Hawai'i Press.

Smith, Timothy L.
  1957 *Revivalism and Social Reform in Mid-Nineteenth-Century America.* New York: Abingdon.

Soeffner, Hans-Georg
  1997 *The Order of Rituals: the Interpretation of Everyday Life.* Trans. Mara Luckmann. New Brunswick, N.J.: Transaction Publishers.

Stasch, Rupert
  2002 "Joking Avoidance: A Korowai Pragmatics of Being Two." *American Ethnologist* 29(2): 335–65.

Stewart, Pamela J., and Andrew Strathern
  2001 *Humors and Substances: Ideas of the Body in New Guinea.* Westport, Conn.: Bergin and Garvey.

Stewart, Pamela J., and Andrew Strathern, eds.
  1997 *Millennial Markers.* Townsville: Centre for Pacific Studies, James Cook University.
  2000 *Millennial Countdown in New Guinea.* Special Issue. *Ethnohistory* 47(1).

Stoler, Ann Laura
  1995 *Race and the Education of Desire: Foucault's "History of Sexuality" and the Colonial Order of Things.* Durham: Duke University Press.

Strathern, Andrew
  1972 *One Father, One Blood: Descent and Group Structure among the Melpa People.* London: Tavistock.
  1973 "Kinship, Descent and Locality: Some New Guinea Examples." In *The Character of Kinship,* ed. J. Goody, 21–34. Cambridge: Cambridge University Press.
  1977 "Melpa Food-Names as an Expression of Ideas on Identity and Substance." *Journal of the Polynesian Society* 86(4): 503–11.

Strathern, Andrew, and Pamela J. Stewart

    1998 "The Embodiment of Responsibility: 'Confession' and 'Compensation' in Mount Hagen, Papua New Guinea." *Pacific Studies* 21(1–2): 43–64.

    2000 *Arrow Talk: Transaction, Transition, and Contradiction in New Guinea Highlands History*. Kent: Kent State University Press.

Strathern, Marilyn

    1987 "Conclusion." In *Dealing with Inequality: Analysing Gender Relations in Melanesia and Beyond*, ed. M. Strathern, 278–302. Cambridge: Cambridge University Press.

    1988 *The Gender of the Gift: Problems with Women and Problems with Society in Melanesia*. Berkeley: University of California Press.

    1997 "Double Standards." In *The Ethnography of Moralities*, ed. S. Howell, 127–51. London: Routledge.

Stringer, Martin D.

    1999 *On the Perception of Worship: The Ethnography of Worship in Four Christian Congregations in Manchester*. Birmingham: University of Birmingham Press.

Synan, Vinson

    1997 *The Holiness-Pentecostal Tradition: Charismatic Movements in the Twentieth Century*. Grand Rapids: Eerdmans.

Taussig, Michael

    1993 *Mimesis and Alterity: A Particular History of the Senses*. New York: Routledge.

Thielman, Frank

    1994 *Paul and the Law: A Contextual Approach*. Downers Grove, Ill.: InterVarsity Press.

Thomas, Nicholas

    1991 *Entangled Objects: Exchange, Material Culture, and Colonialism in the Pacific*. Cambridge, Mass.: Harvard University Press.

    1994 *Colonialism's Culture: Anthropology, Travel and Government*. Princeton: Princeton University Press.

Trompf, G. W.

    1994 *Payback: The Logic of Retribution in Melanesian Religions*. Cambridge: Cambridge University Press.

Tsing, Anna

    2000 "The Global Situation." *Cultural Anthropology* 15(3): 327–60.

Turner, Charles

    1992 *Modernity and Politics in the Work of Max Weber*. London: Routledge.

Tuzin, Donald

    1982 "Ritual Violence among the Ilahita Arapesh: The Dynamics of Moral and Religious Uncertainty." In *Rituals of Manhood: Male Initiation in Papua New Guinea*, ed. G. H. Herdt, 321–55. Berkeley: University of California Press.

    1989 "Visions, Prophecies, and the Rise of Christian Consciousness." In *The*

Religious Imagination in New Guinea, ed. G. Herdt and M. Stephen, 187–208. New Brunswick: Rutgers University Press.

1997 *The Cassowary's Revenge: The Life and Death of Masculinity in a New Guinea Society.* Chicago: University of Chicago Press.

Valeri, Valerio
2000 *The Forest of Taboos: Morality, Hunting, and Identity among the Huaulu of the Moluccas.* Madison: University of Wisconsin Press.

van der Veer, Peter
2000 " 'The Enigma of Arrival': Hybridity and Authenticity in the Global Space." In *Debating Cultural Hybridity: Multi-Cultural Identities and the Politics of Anti-Racism,* ed. P. Werbner and T. Modood, 90–105. London: Zed.

Verhey, Allen D.
1993 "Ethical Lists." In *The Oxford Companion to the Bible,* ed. B. M. Metzger and M. D. Coogan, 201–2. New York: Oxford University Press.

Wagner, Roy
1967 *The Curse of Souw: Principles of Daribi Clan Definition and Alliance.* Chicago: University of Chicago Press.

1974 "Are There Social Groups in the New Guinea Highlands?" In *Frontiers of Anthropology,* ed. M. Leaf, 95–122. New York: Van Nostrand.

1977 "Analogic Kinship: A Daribi Example." *American Ethnologist* 4(4): 623–42.

[1975] 1981 *The Invention of Culture.* Chicago: University of Chicago Press.

1986 *Asiwinarong: Ethos, Image, and Social Power among the Usen Barok of New Ireland.* Princeton: Princeton University Press.

Weber, Max
1946 *From Max Weber: Essays in Sociology.* Trans. H. H. Gerth and C. Wright Mills. New York: Oxford University Press.

Weber, Timothy P.
1987 *Living in the Shadow of the Second Coming: American Premillennialism, 1875–1982.* Chicago: University of Chicago Press.

Westerholm, Stephen
1988 *Israel's Law and the Church's Faith.* Grand Rapids: Eerdmans.

Westermark, George D.
1986 "Court Is an Arrow: Legal Pluralism in Papua New Guinea." *Ethnology* 25(2): 131–49.

Wheatcroft, Wilson G.
1976 "The Legacy of Afekan: Cultural Symbolic Interpretations of Religion among the Tifalmin of New Guinea." Ph.D. dissertation, University of Chicago.

White, Geoffrey M.
1980 "Social Images and Social Change in a Melanesian Society." *American Ethnologist* 7(2): 352–70.

1991 *Identity through History: Living Stories in a Solomon Islands Society.* Cambridge: Cambridge University Press.

White, Hayden
1987 *The Content of the Form: Narrative Discourse and Historical Representation.* Baltimore: Johns Hopkins University Press.

Whitehead, Harriet
2000 *Food Rules: Hunting, Sharing, and Tabooing Game in Papua New Guinea.* Ann Arbor: University of Michigan Press.

Whitehouse, Harvey
1995 *Inside the Cult: Religious Innovation and Transmission in Papua New Guinea.* Oxford: Clarendon Press.

Wicker, Hans-Rudolf
2000 "From Complex Culture to Cultural Complexity." In *Debating Cultural Hybridity: Multi-Cultural Identities and the Politics of Anti-Racism,* ed. P. Werbner and T. Modood, 29–45. London: Zed.

Wood, Mike
1995 " 'White Skins,' 'Real People,' and 'Chinese' in Some Spatial Transformations of the Western Province, PNG." *Oceania* 66(1): 23–50.

Worsley, Peter
1968 *The Trumpet Shall Sound: A Study of "Cargo" Cults in Melanesia.* New York: Schocken.
1996 Foreword. In *The State and Its Enemies in Papua New Guinea,* ed. A. Wanek, vii–xi. Richmond: Curzon Press.

Young, Michael W.
1971 *Fighting with Food: Leadership, Values and Social Control in a Massim Society.* Cambridge: Cambridge University Press.
1983 *Magicians of Manumanua: Living Myth in Kalauna.* Berkeley: University of California Press.

Index

Compositor:	G&S Typesetters, Inc.
Text:	10/13 Sabon
Display:	Sabon
Cartographer:	Bill Nelson
Index:	Andrew Christenson